TRANSFORMING INFANT WELLBEING

Transforming Infant Wellbeing brings together science and policy to highlight the critical importance of the first 1001 days of infancy: the period from conception to the second birthday. Introduced and edited by Penelope Leach, who uniquely combines academic knowledge of infant development with the ability to write about it for wide audiences, the book has at its heart 25 original articles by acknowledged experts in different aspects of infant health and development. Brought together, they showcase innovative science and best practices to a wide range of readers: to scientific colleagues in different disciplines; to politicians and policy makers; to local authority commissioners and specialist advisors; statutory and voluntary organisations and parents.

This book has a two-fold purpose in science and in social policy. First, to collect new papers by leading scientists in a single volume, which ensures they reach a broad audience. Second, by introducing and commenting on the significance of these new findings, the book highlights both the benefits that accrue to society when it acts accordingly, and the costs, financial and social, of our failure to do so.

In the last 50 years, interest in infant development and especially maternal and infant mental health has burgeoned. A large number of issues at the forefront of child development research mirror those of yesterday, but the research brought to bear upon them has transformed. Thanks largely to technological and statistical advances, we now know a great deal that researchers of earlier generations could only surmise. However, increasing knowledge of infancy has not been matched by an increasing impact on parents and professionals, politicians and policy makers. Bringing contemporary studies involving pregnancy, birth, infancy and toddlerhood together, along with the undisputed evidential findings that flow from them, large gaps between what is known and what is done become apparent. By focusing on what can be done to fill those gaps, *Transforming Infant Wellbeing* renders inescapable the need to rethink current priorities. It represents essential reading for researchers, parents and policy makers of infancy.

Penelope Leach is a research psychologist specalising in infant development. She is a fellow of the British Psychological Society and a Senior Research Fellow of the Institute for the Study of Children, Families and Social Issues, Birkbeck, University of London and of the Tavistock and Portman NHS Trust. She is a Visiting Professor at the Faculty of Education, University of Winchester.

Penelope was vice President of the then Health Visitors' Association (1988–1999) and President of the National Childminding Association (1999–2006). She has also worked with organisations concerned with early years education and with children's rights, including the Children's Rights Development Unit, the NSPCC and its sister organisations in Ireland, the US and Canada. In 1998, she was a founder member of AIMH (Association for Infant Mental Health – UK) of which she is now a director. Between 1997–2005 she co-directed the largest-ever English study of childcare: (www.familieschildrenchildcare.org). Penelope's recent research focus is on infant neuroscience (See 'Infant Rearing in the Context of Contemporary Neuroscience' in the *Handbook of Child Wellbeing* eds Korbin and Asher, Springer. 2013) which is increasingly producing evidence of the crucial and long-lasting importance of infants' earliest relationships and experiences.

TRANSFORMING INFANT WELLBEING

Research, Policy and Practice for the First 1001 Critical Days

Edited by
Penelope Leach

Routledge
Taylor & Francis Group

LONDON AND NEW YORK

First published 2018
by Routledge
2 Park Square, Milton Park, Abingdon, Oxon OX14 4RN

and by Routledge
711 Third Avenue, New York, NY 10017

Routledge is an imprint of the Taylor & Francis Group, an informa business

British Library Cataloguing-in-Publication Data
A catalogue record for this book is available from the British Library

Library of Congress Cataloging-in-Publication Data
Names: Leach, Penelope, editor.
Title: Transforming infant wellbeing : research, policy and practice for the first 1001 critical days / edited by Penelope Leach.
Description: Abingdon, Oxon ; New York, NY : Routledge, 2017.
Identifiers: LCCN 2017013026 (print) | LCCN 2017032250 (ebook) |
ISBN 9781315452890 (Master eBook) | ISBN 9781138689534 (hardback)
| ISBN 9781138689541 (pbk.)
Subjects: LCSH: Maternal and infant welfare. | Infants—Development. |
Infants—Care.
Classification: LCC HV697 (ebook) | LCC HV697.T675 2017 (print) |
DDC 362.7—dc23
LC record available at https://lccn.loc.gov/2017013026

ISBN: 978-1-138-68953-4 (hbk)
ISBN: 978-1-138-68954-1 (pbk)
ISBN: 978-1-315-45289-0 (ebk)

Typeset in Bembo
by Florence Production Ltd, Stoodleigh, Devon, UK

CONTENTS

NOTES ON CONTRIBUTORS

Stella Acquarone (PhD) is the founder and Director of the Parent Infant Centre (offering the first accredited training in Parent Infant Psychotherapy in the UK), Child Focus Consultancy and ipAn, an affiliated charity International pre-Autistic Network (www.infantmentalhealth.com). She is a practicing adult, adolescent, child and infant–parent psychoanalytic psychotherapist and has worked in the NHS for 32 years. Recognised world-wide as an authority on how to assess, diagnose and treat at-risk babies, she has pioneered studies in early infant clinical research and development and has developed many clinical innovations, she is a member of the United Kingdom Council for Psychotherapy, the British Psychological Society. the Association of Child Psychotherapists and the British Psychoanalytic Council. and lectures internationally on all aspects of infant–parent development and psycho-therapy.

Kirsten Asmussen is a developmental psychologist with expertise in the parent/child relationship and author of the Evidence-Based Parenting Practitioner's Handbook (Routledge, 2011). Kirsten previously worked at the National Academy for Parenting Research at King's College London, where she managed the Commissioning Toolkit — a DfE funded project that assessed the quality of parenting interventions against standards of evidence and best practice.

Al Aynsley-Green is Professor Emeritus of Child Health at the University of London, Visiting Professor in Advocacy for Children and Childhood, Nottingham Trent University, and former first Children's Commissioner for England.

Robin Balbernie is clinical director of PIP UK, a charity dedicated to help establish infant mental health teams across the country. Previously he was a consultant child psychotherapist in Gloucestershire. He also worked with children's centres as clinical lead of the team providing an infant mental health service, known locally and nationally as 'Secure Start'. He is an advisor to the Association of Infant Mental

Health and the WAVE Trust and was a member of the Young Minds' Policy and Strategy Advisory Group.

Jane Barlow (DPhil, FFPH Hon) is Professor of Evidence-Based Intervention and Policy Evaluation at the Department of Social Policy and Intervention, University of Oxford. Jane's main research interest is the role of early parenting in the aetiology of mental health problems, and the evaluation of early interventions aimed at improving parenting practices during pregnancy and the postnatal period.

Haroon Chowdry joined the EIF with a background in research and analysis, having previously worked at the Institute for Fiscal Studies as a Senior Research Economist. There he carried out quantitative research into various issues around education and skills, including: socio-economic inequalities in children's education and behaviour, participation rates in further and higher education, the implications of school and higher education funding, and welfare-to-work policy. He has taught courses on evaluation and cost-benefit analysis at the Institute of Education.

Peter Cooper is Research Professor in Psychopathology at the University of Reading, and is honorary Professor at the Universities of Stellenbosch and Cape Town, South Africa. Together with Lynne Murray, he has conducted work on postnatal depression, its epidemiology, effects on parenting and child development, and its treatment, in both the UK and in South Africa. In addition to his academic papers, he is Series Editor for Constable & Robinson's 'Overcoming' series of self-help manuals for a range of psychological disorders, and author of the series title on bulimia nervosa.

Chris Cuthbert is Director of Development for A Better Start at the Big Lottery Fund. He was previously Deputy Director of the Social Exclusion Task Force in the Cabinet Office and Head of Strategy and Development at the National Society for Prevention of Cruelty to Children. Chris is writing in a personal capacity. He is grateful to numerous colleagues for sharing their specialist subject expertise. Particular thanks are due to Helen Duncan, Jenny Kurinczuk, Nicola Heslehurst and Jennifer Hollowell for their generous advice and contributions.

Jill Domoney (PhD) is a clinical psychologist and researcher based at the Section of Women's Mental Health in the Institute of Psychiatry, Psychology and Neuroscience, King's College London. She specialises in perinatal and infant mental health in both clinical work and research activities. Her research to date has included exploring the links between paternal mental health and child outcomes, developing interventions for antenatal depression, and evaluating perinatal interventions for couples where there is domestic violence.

Angela Donkin (PhD) is a Deputy Director at the UCL Institute of Health Equity and has been leading research for over 25 years. She leads work on children, indicators, employment and income. She has written articles and managed work on optimal children's outcomes and measurement, improving children's mental health, the social determinants of children's outcomes and parenting programmes. Before joining IHE in 2012, Angela was responsible for overseeing the independent reviews on Early Intervention for Graham Allen MP at the Cabinet Office.

Pasco Fearon is a developmental and clinical psychologist, and is joint Director of the Doctoral Training Programme in Clinical Psychology at University College London. He did his degree in Experimental Psychology at Cambridge University and completed his PhD and clinical doctorate at University College London and University of Wales, Bangor, respectively. His research focuses on understanding the roots of social and emotional adjustment and of mental health difficulties, and particularly the role of parent–child interactions, attachment security and parenting in these outcomes. In addition to his scientific research he is involved in a range of clinical studies developing and testing interventions for parents, infants and young children and in policy work related to children's mental health.

Leon Feinstein is the Director of Evidence for the Children's Commissioner. From 2013 to 2016 Leon was the Director of Evidence at the Early Intervention Foundation (EIF) and Visiting Professor at the LSE's Centre for the Analysis of Social Exclusion. From 2003 to 2008 Leon was Professor of Education and Social Policy at the Institute of Education, undertaking interdisciplinary quantitative and qualitative research on education and social policy. Between 2008 and 2013 Leon worked in the Treasury and the Cabinet Office on policy implementation and performance policy.

Peter Fonagy (OBE, FMedSci, FBA, PhD) is Freud Memorial Professor of Psycho-analysis and Head of the Research Department of Clinical, Educational and Health Psychology at University College London; Chief Executive of the Anna Freud Centre, London; Consultant to the Child and Family Program at the Menninger Department of Psychiatry and Behavioural Sciences at Baylor College of Medicine; and holds visiting professorships at Yale and Harvard Medical Schools.

Ruth Gardner (PhD FRSA) is Honorary Senior Research Fellow at the Centre for Child and Family Studies, University of East Anglia. From 2010 to 2013 she was Head of Strategy and Development for child neglect at the National Society for the Prevention of Cruelty to Children.

Vivette Glover is Professor of Perinatal Psychobiology at Imperial College London. Her research has shown the effects of the emotional state of the mother during pregnancy, both on the developing fetus and longer term on the child, and the biological mechanisms that may underlie such fetal programming. She has published over 400 papers. She has been an advisor to the Department of Health, the Early Intervention Foundation, the NSPCC, Best Beginnings and the biometric lead for A Better Start. Her work is contributing to changes in policy, with a growing awareness that better emotional care for women in pregnancy can improve the outcome for the next generation.

Alain Gregoire is Consultant Perinatal Psychiatrist and Honorary Senior Lecturer at the University of Southampton, UK. He initially began his postgraduate training in obstetrics, but on seeing that women with perinatal mental illness were the most ill, yet least well cared for of all his patients, he switched to train in Psychiatry at the Institute of Psychiatry and Maudsley Hospital. He set up and leads the national award winning Hampshire Perinatal Service, which provides comprehensive integrated community and inpatient care to women with severe mental health problems in pregnancy and postnatally. He was the founder and is Chair of the UK Maternal Mental Health Alliance, a coalition of over 80 national organisations committed to improving maternal mental health care and outcomes for mothers and their infants. He is a major contributor to the development of policy, guidance and clinical services in parental and infant mental health in the UK and abroad.

Angie S. Guinn (MPH) was a graduate research assistant at the Mark Chaffin Center for Healthy Development in the School of Public Health at Georgia State University. She completed her Master's degree in Public Health with a focus in Epidemiology in May 2016, completing her thesis on SafeCare. She is currently completing a fellowship sponsored by the Oak Ridge Institute for Science and Education (ORISE) research participation programme hosted at the Centers for Disease Control within the Division of Violence Prevention.

Jane Iles (PhD) is a Clinical and Research Psychologist working at the Centre for Psychiatry at Imperial College London. Jane's research has focused on maternal and paternal mental health during the perinatal period, links to child outcomes, and early attachment-based intervention programmes. Jane also has a background working clinically to support children and families.

Hilary Kennedy is an educational psychologist, an Honorary Research Associate at UCL and a leading developer of Video Interaction Guidance (VIG) in the United Kingdom. She has coedited two books on VIG with Miriam Landor and Liz Todd. Video Interaction Guidance: A Relationship-Based Intervention to Promote Attunement, Empathy and Wellbeing in 2011 and Video Enhanced Reflective Practice (VERP: Professional Development through attuned interaction) in 2015. She is currently a freelance VIG trainer working with many perinatal projects around the United Kingdom and is involved in international VIG developments in the Czech Republic, Finland, Greece, Italy, Turkey, Ecuador and Mexico.

Penelope Leach is a research psychologist and one of the world's leading experts in child development. She is a director of Association for Infant Mental Health – UK and the author of many books for parents, including *Your Baby and Child, The Essential First Year* and *Child Care Today*. She is Visiting Professor, Faculty of Education, University of Winchester, and Hon. Snr Research Fellow, Institute for the Study of Children, Families and Social Issues, Birkbeck, University of London, and at the Tavistock and Portman NHS Trust.

Tim Loughton became the MP for East Worthing and Shoreham in 1997, after a career in the City of London. He was a high profile Shadow Minister for Health and Children from 2003 during the Conservative Party's time in opposition before being appointed Parliamentary Under-Secretary for Children and Families following the 2010 General Election. Until 2012 he led on several areas of successful reform in child protection, children in care, child sexual exploitation and adoption in particular. From the backbenches Tim continues to work vigorously in support of improving support for vulnerable children and speaking up for young people and has also been a member of the influential Home Affairs Select Committee. He became Chairman of the Parent Infant Partnership (PIP UK) charity in 2013 committed to promoting attachment science and also chairs the All Party Group for Children and the APPG for Conception to Age 2 (first 1001 days) which is undertaking important work to improve government's work in perinatal mental health and early nurturing for young children.

John R. Lutzker (PhD) is a Distinguished University Professor of Public Health and Director of the Mark Chaffin Center for Healthy Development at Georgia State University. He has published over 170 professional articles and seven books. Among his awards, Outstanding Research Career Award from the American Professional Society on the Abuse of Children. He is on the editorial boards of six professional journals.

Sir Michael Marmot has led research groups on health inequalities for over 35 years. He was Chair of the Commission on Social Determinants of Health (CSDH), which was set up by the World Health Organization in 2005. He served as President of the British Medical Association (BMA) in 2010-2011, and is the new President of the British Lung Foundation and President of the World Medical Association.

Jack Martin has a BA degree in Philosophy from King's College London and an MSc in Public Policy from University College London. He joined EIF in April 2014. He works primarily on reviews of evidence, and has contributed to a number of EIF What Works reviews including the EIF Inter-Parental Relationships review.

Alina Morawska A/Prof Alina Morawska is the Deputy Director (Research) at the Parenting and Family Support Centre, The University of Queensland. Her research focuses on behavioural family intervention as a means for promoting positive family relationships, and the prevention and early intervention for young children at risk of developing behavioural and emotional problems. She completed her PhD in Clinical Psychology at the University of Queensland in 2004, for which she received the Australian Psychological Society's Excellent PhD Thesis in Psychology Award.

Lynne Murray is Research Professor in Developmental Psychology at the University of Reading, and honorary Professor at the Universities of Strellenbosch and Cape Town, South Africa. Together with Peter Cooper, she has conducted work on postnatal depression, its epidemiology, effects on parenting and child development, and its treatment, in both the United Kingdom and in South Africa.

Margaret O'Brien is Professor of Child and Family Policy, University College London and Director of the Thomas Coram Research Unit, United Kingdom. For over 30 years she has conducted extensive research on fathers and family life with a focus on work-family policies, parenting and family support. Since 2015 she has become one of the coordinators of the International Network on Leave Policies and Research, which consists of over 60 members, all of whom are experts on leave issues and who come from 40 countries across the world.

Carmine M. Pariante is Professor of Biological Psychiatry and a Consultant Perinatal Psychiatrist in the South London and Mausdley NHS Trust. He is Head of the Sections of Stress, Psychiatry and Immunology and Perinatal Psychiatry at King's College London. He is particularly well known for his work on stress, neuro-inflanunation and mental health, and proposes that pregnancy and the in-utero environment is where the intergenerational transmission of childhood exposure to stress and maltreatment occurs.

Susan Pawlby is a Clinical Child Psychologist and Lecturer in the Section of Perinatal Psychiatry at King's College London, the Institute of Psychiatry, Psychology and Neuroscience and a member of the Multidisciplinary Team on the Channi Kumar Mother and Baby Unit at the Bethlem Royal Hospital, South London and Maudsley NHS Trust. Dr Pawlby has worked in clinical and research contexts and has demonstrated the importance of mental health in pregnancy in securing the wellbeing and mental health of the offspring through infancy, childhood, adolescence and young adulthood.

Dominic Plant carried out his PhD with Dr Pawlby and Professor Pariante at King's College London. His work on the South London Child Development Study demonstrated that exposure to prenatal depression and childhood maltreatment results in persistent psychological and biological changes in the adult offspring. Dr Plant has now completed his Doctorate in Clinical Psychology and has a special interest in working with trauma patients.

Richard Pratt has been working as a Clinical Psychologist in Norfolk since 2008. His main focus has been attachment and the parent-infant relationship. He currently is one of the clinical leads for the Norfolk Parent Infant Mental Health Attachment Team.

Christine Puckering is one of the authors of the Mellow Parenting programmes. She is a clinical, forensic and neuropsychologist by trade with a strong interest in early infancy and early parent-child relationships. She was awarded a Winston Churchill Travelling Fellowship in 2015 to study how other countries with good child wellbeing indicators support good parent-infant relationships. She was runner up in the Andrea Leadsom Award for Outstanding Contributions to Infant Mental Health in 2016.

Paul Ramchandani (PhD) is Professor of Child and Adolescent Mental Health at Imperial College, London. He also works clinically as a Consultant Child and

Adolescent Psychiatrist in a busy NHS service. Paul leads a research group studying perinatal mental illness and the prevention of mental health problems in infancy and childhood. Details of the current work of the team can be found at the pPOD website (www.ppod.org.uk).

Camilla Rosan (DCIin Psych, CPsychol) is a perinatal clinical psychologist and couple therapist by background and works at the Mental Health Foundation where she leads a national portfolio of policy, research and programme development work relating to families, infants, children and young people. She combines this role with leading the International Training School of Infancy and Early Years (ITSIEY), which is an international training collaboration between UCL, Kings College, Yale University, the Anna Freud Centre and the Tavistock and Portman NHS Trust.

Matthew R. Sanders Professor Matthew Sanders is considered a world leader in the development, implementation, evaluation and dissemination of population-based approaches to parenting and family interventions. Founder of the Triple P-Positive Parenting Program, he is a Professor of Clinical Psychology and the Director of the Parenting and Family Support Centre at the University of Queensland, Australia. He is also also an Honorary Professor at Manchester University, University of South Carolina, Glasgow Caledonian University and the University of Auckland. Professor Sanders has built a highly regarded international reputation for conducting outstanding research and translating it into practical programs that promote stronger families and prevent and address childhood behavior problems.

Verity Smith studied for a BSc and MSc in Psychology at University of Warwick. She worked as the Assistant Psychologist for the PIMHAP since its inception with a particular emphasis on the evaluation of PIMHAP's first year of operation.

Diane S. Speier (PhD) acquired her qualifications in psychology in New York, with a specialty in The Psychology of Parenthood, a clinical training in hypnosis and another clinical training in Integral Regression Therapy, completed in 1997. Meanwhile Diane became a certified childbirth educator in 1978, attending births as a doula and teaching classes to pregnant and postnatal women for 20 years. She was the founder and director of The Family Tree Centre for Parents in New York before immigrating to the UK where in 2002 she received her PhD in Women's Studies at The University of Manchester. Diane practices psychotherapy and hypnotherapy specializing in perinatal psychology, the psychology of parenthood, the psychophysiology of birth, postnatal depression and recovery from birth trauma.

Danny Taggart is a lecturer in Clinical Psychology at the University of Essex. Previously he worked for several years at the Priory Children's Centre in Great Yarmouth with disadvantaged families, both in a specialist clinical service and a community psychology initiative, The Great Yarmouth Father's Project.

Catherine Thomas is a community child and adolescent psychiatrist working in East Anglia. She is joint Clinical Lead for the Norfolk Perinatal Infant Mental Health Attachment Service. She has extensive training and experience in the assessment and treatment of children and families with complex attachment difficulties, including developmental trauma.

Angela Underdown has a background in children's public health and was an Associate Professor at Warwick University Medical School and Deputy Director of Warwick Infant and Family Wellbeing Unit. Angela is a Video Interaction Guidance (VIG) supervisor and recently delivered a research project working with families whose babies were born at or before 32 weeks' gestation. She supervises social work staff using VIG at the Family Drug and Alcohol Court (FDAC) in London. Angela led the writing and production of the 'Getting to Know Your Baby' videos www.your-baby.org.uk. She authored the NSPCC's Baby Steps Perinatal Programme which has been developed and evaluated by the NSPCC. Angela is Infant Mental Health (IMH) Advisor to the Institute of Health Visiting and has recently trained 300 IMH champions nationally. She has written and published widely on infant mental health topics.

Mary E. Young (MD, DrPH) is a pediatrician specialising in global health and child development. For the past three decades, she worked at the World Bank leading global efforts to inform world leaders and policymakers about Early Childhood Development (ECD) and guiding efforts in international public health and child health and development. Currently, she is Director of Center for Child Development at the China Development Research Foundation, Senior Advisor to Harvard University's Center on the Developing Child, and Adjunct Professor of Pediatrics at University of Hawaii Medical Center.

PREFACE

Interest in infant development and especially parental and infant mental health has burgeoned in the last 50 years. Studies of the '50s, '60s and '70s by individuals who are now recognised as the greatest names in the study of infancy – such as John Bowlby, Renee Spitz, Mary Main, Donald Winnicott, Robert Hinde and Mary Ainsworth – remain the foundations of contemporary thinking. But while those studies directed attention and interest to infancy as a research area, and led speculation about possible links between early experiences and later development, few could move beyond clinical observations and developing theory to outcome studies and scientific evidence.

John Bowlby, prescient as he so often was, wrote an article in Nursery World in 1953 which was called 'The Study of the Heart's Affections' and launched attachment theory to the general public. The article was reprinted in 2015 on the occasion of Nursery World's 90th anniversary and its comments on research are as relevant today as they were 70 years ago:

> A major difficulty in this sort of research is that, unless you follow up children over the years, you cannot learn how they develop as a result of their early experiences. To do this would be a very ambitious and expensive undertaking. Although ultimately we must hope that such long-term follow ups will be done, we think it is none the less well worthwhile to do short-term studies to begin with. There are many things to be done. For instance, we can study a number of children from birth onwards and see what happens to them, or alternatively, we can study children's responses to a situation known to be upsetting, such as separation. The Tavistock Research Unit is doing the latter. And for the present we have decided to do nothing but current studies. These will be carried on over, perhaps, 2 or 3 years and will certainly be extended if money is available. Many of the things which are being discovered by research workers in this field have long been known intuitively to mothers. They know

how responsive their babies are to their own moods, and the closeness of the bond which links them together. And they realise how necessary their presence is to a small child when he is afraid or ill, or in strange surroundings, or when danger threatens. These things are being rediscovered in a scientific way, and as time goes on, this knowledge, which experienced mothers already have, is being broadened and deepened. And only by putting it on a scientific basis can it be made available to the multitude of professional workers who now deal with children and set themselves up to advise parents. Perhaps, indeed, if this research goes favourably, the experts may one day really know more than the experienced mother, who has for long been the victim of much mistaken advice.

Bowlby, J.

The research has gone favourably. An extraordinarily large number of the issues that are at the forefront of child development studies today – including attachment – mirror those of yesterday but the research brought to bear upon them has transformed our understanding of them. Thanks very largely to technological and statistical advances we now know a great deal that researchers of earlier generations could only surmise. Pressure for change in attitudes to children and in perceptions of their needs and the importance not only to them but to society as a whole, of those needs being met, is increasingly supported by scientific evidence; by information from neuroscience, and especially from infant brain development.

Knowledge and interest concerning infancy has not only deepened but also spread far beyond involved professionals. Parents and future-parents, grandparents and carers have become increasingly self-conscious and concerned about their roles. But today's debates about children's wellbeing and happiness and about parents' priorities and possibilities still reflect those of the past while some of the issues that needed to be addressed half a century ago have been exacerbated rather than resolved. Most notable perhaps is the conflict for parents between paid work and child care; between earning enough money to spend on a child and having enough time to spend with her. If you are a parent in the 21st century it may be literally true that 'time is money'.

Opinions and beliefs are always – rightly – open to argument but sound science, by definition, is not. Bowlby and many others expected that once those longstanding arguments and issues were subject to good science that is widely known and believed, their power to influence both personal and public policy would be greatly increased. So far that is not generally the case. Despite outcome studies whose findings have unquestioning peer acceptance and are the best possible guides to priorities in policy making and resource distribution, the increase in available knowledge and understanding of perinatal, infant and early childhood development, has not yet been matched by an increase in action by adult society; by parents and professionals, politicians and policy makers. We do not do what we know should be done.

The 1001 Critical Days Campaign launched by Andrea Leadsom in 2013, and its lecture series organised by Clair Rees and held in parliament in 2014–2015 brought together some of the outstanding contemporary research concerning pre-conception and perinatal mental health. It enabled professionals from different specialities to communicate not only with politicians, policy makers and service providers but also with each other. The knowledge and the sharing were the inspiration for this book and I thank them both.

Widely shared knowledge is valuable in itself but the more closely it is matched to policy and political action the more valuable it becomes. This book project has a two-fold purpose, in science and in social policy. First the publication of 25 new papers by leading scientists, will draw attention to areas of preconception, perinatal and infant development in which, thanks to contemporary outcome studies, much of what used to be clinical opinion is now scientific fact. Second, introducing and commenting on the significance of these findings will highlight the benefits to society of acting accordingly. Neglecting action that nobody has considered, or that only some people consider likely to be beneficial, is often unfortunate but always forgivable, but neglecting action whose benefits are proven and widely recognised is surely inexcusable.

'Transforming Infant Wellbeing: Research, policy and practice in the first 1001 Critical Days' brings together contemporary research involving pregnancy, birth, infancy and toddlerhood and focusing on outcome studies. The undisputed evidential findings that flow from these studies show up large, sometimes shocking, gaps between information and action, between what is known and what is done. All of us who have contributed to this book hope that focusing on those gaps, on what could be done to fill them and the positive differences such actions would make to the lives of individuals, families, groups and society as a whole, from one generation to the next, will render inescapable the need to rethink current priorities.

Bowlby, J. (1953). *The Study of the Heart's Affections*. London: Nursery World.

ACKNOWLEDGEMENTS

The idea for this book was inspired by the 1001 Critical Days Campaign which was launched by Andrea Leadsom MP in September 2013. A cross-party initiative, it was presented at each political party conference in October 2013; by Andrea Leadsom for the Conservatives, the Rt Hon Frank Field for Labour, Paul Burstow for the Liberal Democrats and Caroline Lucas for the Green Party.

As part of the 1001 Critical Days agenda in Parliament, a seven-part lecture series, sponsored by Andrea Leadsom MP, Frank Field MP and Tim Loughton MP was organised in 2014–2015 by Clair Rees, now Executive Director of the charity PIP-UK and a parliamentary early years adviser. The lecture series brought together science and policy, highlighting the importance of the period from conception to the second birthday from socio/moral, scientific and economic perspectives. The presentations were outstanding, showcasing both innovative science and best practice, and facilitating internationally and nationally published experts in their fields in presenting to a wider audience: to colleagues in other disciplines, to politicians, think tanks, specialist advisors, commissioners and local authorities and to an interdisciplinary representation of front line professions who form a coalition of statutory and voluntary organisations throughout the United Kingdom.

This book began as a spin-off from that impressive body of work. The idea was generously supported by Clair Rees and welcomed by Andrea Leadsom and Tim Loughton. I thank them all for facilitating this exciting project. The book is designed to build on and expand the 1001 Critical Days agenda and ensure that it has widespread and lasting influence. If it succeeds in this it will be due to 40 leading scientists who have contributed the 26 original papers around which it is built. I am as grateful for their hard work as I am excited by their research.

Meanwhile the first 1001 Critical Days Campaign is now represented in Parliament by Tim Loughton (Conservative), who chairs the APPG 'Conception to Age 2', Frank Field (Labour), Norman Lamb (Liberal Democrat) Caroline Lucas

(Green party), Mark Durken (SDLP), Philippa Whitford (SNP) and Liz Savile-Roberts (Plaid Cymru). It is supported by almost every charity concerned with the early years and especially by the Wave Trust, the NSPCC and PIP-UK. Everyone concerned shares a determination to illuminate the importance to children, their families and society, now and in generations to come, of understanding and prioritising contemporary research findings concerning these first days of life. I hope that 'Transforming Infant Wellbeing: Research, policy and practice for the first 1001 Critical Days' will help.

Penelope Leach 2017

PART I

Issues in infant wellbeing

1

FIFTY YEARS OF CHILDHOOD

Penelope Leach

Starting at the beginning: Why the first 1001 days are critical

This millennium has seen the 'early years' attracting a great deal of interest among parents and professionals, policy makers and politicians, and therefore, of course, from media. Until recently, though, 'the early years' were usually taken to refer to ages 3–5; post-infancy and pre-school with most of the research work focusing on cognitive development, school readiness and nonparental child care. Children's earliest years, the ones that matter most, do not start with birthdays or even births but with conception. The first 1001 days are critical because they take a person from potential to actual, from conception to the second birthday; and it is during that period of fetal development, infancy and toddlerhood that the brain is growing and developing with maximum (and astonishing) speed (Sheridan & Nelson, 2009) that renders it more open to and dependent on outside influence than it will ever be again. Optimal brain development throughout those days not only gives a new child the best possible start in life but also enables him or her to make the most of the lifetime which is to follow. The reverse is also true.

It has been and often still is assumed that how babies' brains grow in size and complexity, forming the connections and interconnections that make them 'work', depends on infants' physical maturation and the genetic inheritance passed on to them by their parents. But recent international research findings – counter-intuitive and therefore not widely recognised – have established that brain development depends principally on interactions between a baby's genes and his environment (Szyf, 2009).

An infant's first environment is the uterus. A developing fetus receives complex biochemical signals from the mother via the placenta; signals which can be affected not only by her diet and lifestyle, including her nutrition and consumption of alcohol and other drugs, but also by her emotional state. Extreme maternal stress, for example, can affect the function of the placenta in such a way that it allows more of the stress hormone, cortisol, to reach and affect the fetus' brain and influence the way that brain is developing and which genes are turned on or off, when and by how much (p. 98 Glover) Talge et al., (2007). Such an infant is likely to have a lifelong increased risk of any of a range of problems from being anxious or depressed in his turn (p. 47 Pawlby), to being a slow learner, suffering conditions such as ADHD and even having some physical problems such as asthma (O'Connor et al., 2005).

Neurology meets attachment science: Why mothers matter

When a baby is born his environment is no longer the womb but is still almost entirely his mother (or whoever stands in for her as his 'primary caregiver') and the interactions that make up his relationship with her. The newborn's brain is still an unfinished project (Tau, 2010) that can only be optimally completed by the social and emotional relationships within which attachment grows. Parents or people who stand in for parents actually build babies' brains (Balbernie, 2001).

Nurture by caring adults is hard wired into children's brains even before they are born. After birth, if a baby doesn't have a loving special adult – being cared for perhaps by several different and changing people in an institution, or receiving minimal, inconsistent or inappropriate adult attention – the structure and chemistry of his brain will probably adapt defensively (Nelson, 2014). He may develop extra strong fear and anger reactions, or intense attack and defense impulses. He may become hyper-vigilant, his brain suffused with cortisol which floods his body until or unless someone turns it off by comforting him. Repeated episodes of acute stress, when nobody regulates his feelings, can damage his capacity to learn, possibly forever, and permanently affect his response system so that it becomes hyper-sensitive. Such an individual over-reacts to minor stress with major fear and anxiety, not only as a baby but as a child, an adolescent and an adult too. We all know such hypersensitive people although we seldom recognise that the source is in their earliest infancy.

People who lack nurture from one or more caring adults in these first critical days of their lives achieve less in education and in the world of work, are more likely to behave antisocially and are less healthy, physically as well as mentally, than individuals who were given a better start. Furthermore the harm done to them is likely to be perpetuated in an intergenerational cycle if they have children of their own (Glover, Champagne, 2015).

Social influences on brain development

It takes most of the first year for a human infant to reach the level of development most mammals have achieved at birth. At least three quarters of the upper brain – the cerebral cortex whose eventual great size and complexity comprises everything that makes him human – grows and develops its interconnections only after birth.

The hippocampus, temporal cortex, prefrontal and anterior cingulate are all immature at birth but grow so rapidly during the first year that by his first birthday a baby's brain has more than doubled its weight. It is because this vital human brain-building happens outside the womb that it is so open to social influence. The longest period of complete dependency experienced by any species permits and even requires an intense social bond to develop between parent (or other caregiver) and child. The baby's genetic inheritance is there from the beginning, of course, but the extent to which some or all of those genes will be expressed and the baby's genetic potential fulfilled, depends on social input from his environment. It is this intense bond that generates the biochemicals that facilitate brain growth and rich neural connections (p. 28 Fearon).

A healthy newborn baby's brain has all the neurons she needs (p. 171 Balbernie). She does not need to make any more now or in the future. What she needs is not more neurons but more connections to link them up and make them work for her; complex connections between different areas of the brain and a growing ability to use particular areas of it. A dramatic burst of these 'synaptic connections' in the prefrontal cortex takes place in the second half of the first year so that they achieve their highest density just when the attachment relationship between the baby and her parents (or other primary attachment figures) is building towards peak intensity.

An infant brain requires a balance between different biochemicals for optimal growth and development and it is positive, enjoyable interactions with the mother or a nurturing person which secure that balance. For example, early positive experiences increase glucose metabolism, and higher levels of glucose washing through the growing brain increase the richness of its network of neuronal connections. The capacity for pleasure – and the anticipation of pleasure throughout life that we summarise as optimism – depends on the numbers of dopamine receptors and opiate receptors that develop in the baby's brain, especially in the prefrontal cortex. Dopamine, a neurotransmitter which is released from the brainstem and makes its way to the prefrontal cortex, enhances the uptake of glucose, helping new tissue to grow in the prefrontal brain. It also produces an energising and stimulating effect that has earned it the nickname 'the feel good hormone'. A baby who experiences high levels of warm, rewarding contact with the mother or other primary attachment figure (and/or is particularly successful in the genetic lottery) may develop a brain with high numbers of dopamine synapses. In contrast, a baby who is deprived of affectionate contact with his mother or mothering person or lives with high levels of stress, may have a permanent scarcity of dopaminergic neurons because stress hormones, such as cortisol, effectively 'turn them off'.

More and more research is demonstrating the long-term importance of social and emotional experiences in the environment to building baby brains (Belsky & de Haan, 2011). In these first 2 years the mother, the father or whoever is the child's primary attachment figure *is* an infant's environment and any interruption of the contact and the attunement between them is stressful. Only repairing the attunement ('making up with mum' as a 5-year-old might call it) turns the stress-reactions off again. When researchers compare children of any age on any aspect of development – language, say, or persistence in learning, resilience when things go wrong, or sociable play with other children – the tuned-in-ness and responsiveness of their mothers or principal attachment figures in these first years explains more of the difference between high- and low-achieving children than anything else, more even than differences in socio-economic circumstances (p. 119 Young).

Attachment: Starting at the beginning, staying influential forever

It is extraordinary that the overwhelming importance of that first relationship is still not universally recognised. It was 75 years ago, in 1940 and a year after his death that Freud's unfinished work 'An outline of psychoanalysis' was published. In it he described mothers' close and loving bonds with their infants as 'unique, without parallel, established unalterably for a whole lifetime as the first and strongest love-object and the prototype of all love relations'.

This was an important part of the extraordinarily broad swathe of ideas from which John Bowlby derived his formulation of attachment theory (Bowlby, 1969; 1973; 1980). As well as psychoanalysis Bowlby called on animal behaviour, evolutionary biology, psychology and even the dawning field of information processing. In 'Attachment' (1969/1982) Bowlby showed that the perspectives of both Freud and Darwin were relevant to his understanding of the mother-baby bond. Stepping even further ahead of his time he speculated about the brain systems involved in this evolutionary mechanism.

Attachment theory has gone through a number of reformations and continues to develop. From the beginning Bowlby said that the attachment between mother and infant was an emotional bond not just a sharing of information, but as long as psychological research was focused on *behavioural* models, it was attachment behaviours rather than attachment feelings that attracted interest. By the 1980s, psychology's focus had shifted away from behavioural towards cognitive models so cognitive representations of attachment, especially Bowlby's 'internal working models', life-long templates for the reliability of relationships, dominated attachment research. By the 1990s however, theoretical and clinical science moved towards a deeper study of *emotion*, the central core of attachment theory. Alan Schore described the shift like this:

> I integrated the current studies of brain development and developmental psychology of the first 2 years of life to create a theory of social-emotional development. Over the last two decades we have seen an explosion of studies on emotion and with them a paradigm shift. Beginning in 'the decade of the brain,' neuroscience, especially affective and social neuroscience, began to explore the brain system involved in not just behaviour, language, and cognition, but the processing of bodily-based emotion.

(Schore, 1994)

Now, a generation on, attachment theory, through its close links with neuroscience and especially infant brain development, has become a coherent interdisciplinary theory of infants' emotional and social development that has dramatically changed our understanding of human infancy (p. 28 Fearon).

Attachment is a survival mechanism. All human beings have an inbuilt genetic predisposition to seek refuge with an attachment figure when they are alarmed or distressed. People go on forming attachments throughout life, to non-familial adults, to childhood and adolescent peers and to adult sexual partners, but the first attachment to the primary caregiver forged in the first year of life is the crucial foundation for all that follow. Secure attachment relationships are the base and motivating force a child needs in order to have the self confidence and courage to explore, to learn and to relate to other people. A child who has a secure attachment can explore and experiment freely provided the person who is his 'secure base' is available, or trusted to become available if he needs her. Her readiness to give any help he needs increases his sense of security and the assistance she gives models for him solutions to his current problem.

While all children must attach themselves to a primary caregiver – who will usually be the mother – the nature of the attachment varies according to their early experience of the relationship, especially whether it is valuable, reliable and safe. Attachment is a two–way, mutually reinforcing process depending on both mother and infant playing their part. Secure attachment develops through the mother's attunement and responsiveness to the baby's signals and his resulting confidence that she will be there for him when he needs her. By reflecting back the baby's feelings she lends them meaning, and by balancing and moderating them she provides him with emotional regulation before he can self-regulate. In insecure attachment, of any of several types, the infant lacks a mental representation of his primary caregiver (mother) as reliably there for him and responsive to his feelings. Attachment is a genetic imperative. Such infants must still attach themselves to their primary caregiver but will develop different strategies for getting close to her and gaining her attention, the strategy adopted depending on the infant's experience of the mother's behaviour.

Mary Ainsworth's pioneering work (Ainsworth, 1973) assessed the nature of toddlers' attachment by means of the 'strange situation test', which observes children's responses to brief separation from their mothers, contact with a stranger and reunification with their mothers. The attachment classifications Ainsworth described remain the cornerstone of infant attachment research although in recent years they have been refined and expanded, especially in what is known as the Dynamic Maturational Model of attachment (Crittenden, 2000 a&b). In Ainsworth's classification there are four groups, each of which is further subdivided in clinical work. Group B, secure attachment; Group C anxious–resistant insecure attachment; Group A, anxious–avoidant insecure attachment and Group D, disorganised attachment.

Parenting

In the last 50 years the frontiers of medical science and associated technology have been pushed forward without a matching commitment to social science and human relations. We know much more about the reproductive biology of parenthood than we know about the social, emotional and psychological impacts of parenting and we devote far greater research resources to producing physically healthy babies than to rearing emotionally stable children. Indeed, while contraception, formula milks, disposable nappies and a host of other childcare aids have dramatically reduced the burdens of traditional mothering, that role itself has been partially invalidated and not replaced with a workable restructuring of gender roles and relationships. What is needed now is a reappraisal of the importance of parenthood and fresh approaches to supporting parents.

If children are to grow up fulfilling their genetic potential, intensive, personalised and long-lasting care is not a theoretical ideal but an essential. It is obvious that babies have to be fed, warmed and protected, but it is less obvious that if physical care is all they are given, many fail to meet their full potential (and we shall never know what that was), some fail to thrive and a few die (Nelson et al., 2014).

At the beginning of an infant's life outside the womb, the mother – if she is available – or the father, grandmother or whoever serves as his primary caregiver, is in charge of his emotional as well as his physical care: his feelings as well as his body. Somebody needs to be there, tuned in to the baby's shifting states and always ready to adjust his environment and experiences to keep him comfortable. With the left hand 'cognitive' part of his brain still in the future, a baby does not think or learn: he reacts with his right brain (and his newly separated body) experiencing deep primitive feelings of hunger, fear, anger, excitement and joy. The baby himself does not have the brain capacity to 'regulate' the intensity of those feelings. The mother (or 'primary attachment figure') must lend her brain to preventing them overwhelming his: feeding or reassuring him before hunger or fear reach panic levels; noticing his feelings and intervening to calm and balance him. A mother or primary caregiver who is tuned-in to the baby has him always somewhere in her mind whatever else she is doing. When people talk of a mother responding to a baby 'right brain to right brain' (Schore, 2013) they mean that she responds to him without conscious thought. When he cries she does not need to use her developed adult left brain to think about what she has heard; decide what it means and plan what she is going to do about it. She simply responds, finding herself away from the TV and halfway to the cot before she becomes aware of having heard a cry.

Caring adults need to be feeling teachers also. The baby must gradually learn to self-regulate; to adjust her own states, keep herself comfortable when she can and cope with discomfort when she must. In interaction with parents, basic states for which the baby has no words but we might describe as 'feeling happy' or 'feeling unhappy' become differentiated. Happiness may arise from the sensual pleasures of sucking or cuddling; from amusement, affection or interest. Unhappy feelings

may range from anger or fear to annoyance or frustration. As well as being qu
to notice and respond to their baby's feelings, parents also have to help the baby
to become aware of them; identifying her feelings and labelling them clearly so
that over time the baby will come to recognise and moderate them. Usually this
kind of teaching happens quite unselfconsciously but not always. Adults who are
particularly uncomfortable with their own feelings may find it impossible to deal
effectively with the baby's (p. 47 Pawlby; p. 107 Speier). The caregiver who cannot
bear anger in herself is likely to feel very distressed and uncomfortable when her
1-year-old screams with rage.

For almost three generations the relationships between infants and parents,
fathers as well as mothers, and the nature of attachment, its real significance, even
its existence, have been debated. Now there remains no scope for argument. It is
a fact that the emotional environment of infancy, consisting almost entirely of
relationships with the parents or their surrogates, shapes the individual emotionally,
psychologically and neurologically, for good or for ill, forever (p. 171 Balbernie.
p. 28 Fearon). This information is not universally welcome. Nobody wants to think
about babies' vulnerability to suffering, whether caused by abuse or trauma,
separation or neglect, constant stress or lack of opportunity. Nobody wants to think
about it so many people who have no direct contact with babies don't think about
them at all and have scant empathy with friends and colleagues who have babies.
Parents think about children all the time, of course, but many are not comfortable
facing the responsibility of their own and each others overwhelming importance
to their child, finding the idea that relationships in infancy (or the lack of them)
are likely to leave lifelong results (p. 163 Sanders) excruciating. And while policy
makers and politicians (whether or not they are parents themselves) may pay lip-
service to understanding what lifelong impacts on infant individuals mean for the
society those babies will grow into and eventually control, few act accordingly,
giving the earliest months of life the greatest priority.

The failure of Western societies to do their best for infants and young children
has only become apparent as research knowledge of what is and is not desirable
has accumulated. That process has been so gradual and specialised that it is still
difficult to see the wood of societal disaster for its separate trees. Millions of adults
are troubled about individual children, groups of children and particular aspects of
childhood: parents struggling to bring up their own, while balancing time at home
and in the workplace; health professionals and educators whose job descriptions
emphasise the positive enhancement of children's development but whose working
weeks are dominated by attempts to compensate them for earlier disadvantage; child
protection agencies reeling under revelations of institutionalised child abuse;
economists and policy makers watching more and more programs, public money
and philanthropy draining through social problems like water through a beach on
a falling tide. But most families, professionals and institutions look no further than
their own particular spinneys. The overall development of society in the last 50
years has been inimical to the nurturance of children and we have all allowed it
to be so.

Is there ever going to be acknowledgment of a priority for the first 1001 critical days which is both moral and practical and not just for today's children but for everybody's future? Are we ever going to find the political will to insist on public action?

References

Ainsworth, M.D.S. (1973). The Development of Infant-Mother Attachment. In B.M. Campbell and H.N. Ricciuti (Eds.), *Review of Child Development Research*. Vol 3. 1–94. Chicago: University of Chicago Press.

Belsky, J., & de Haan, M. (2011). Annual Research Review: Parenting and children's brain development: The end of the beginning. *J. Child Psychology and Psychiatry, 52*(4), 409–428.

Bowlby, J. (1982). *Attachment*. 2nd ed. New York: Basic Books.

Champagne, F.A. (2015). Epigenetics of the developing brain. *Zero to Three, 35*(3), 2–8.

Freud, S. (1940). An outline of psychoanalysis. *International Journal of Psycho-Analysis, 21*, 27–84.

Leach P., (2014). Infant rearing in the context of contemporary neuroscience 2281–2318. In Asher Ben-Arieh et al. (Ed.), *Handbook of Child Wellbeing*. Springer Reference.

Nelson, C.A., Fox, N.A. & Zeanah, C.H. (2014). *Romania's Abandoned Children*. Cambridge, MA: Harvard University Press.

O'Connor, R.E., Harty K.R. & Fulmer, D. (2005). Tiers of intervention in Kindergarten through third grade. *Journal of Learning Disabilities, 38*, 532–538.

Schore, A.N. (1994). *Affect Regulation and the Origin of the Self: The Neurobiology of Emotional Development*. Hillsdale, NJ: Lawrence Erlbaum.

Schore, A.N. (2013). *The Science of the Art of Psychotherapy*. New York: W.W. Norton and co.

Sheridan, M. & Nelson C.A. (2009). Neurobiology of fetal and infant development: Implications for infant mental health. In C.H. Zeanah (Ed.), *Handbook of Infant Mental Health*. 3rd ed. New York: The Guilford Press.

Szyf, M. (2009) The Early Environment and the Epigenome. *Biochimics et Biophysica Acta, 1790*(9), 877–885.

Talge, N.M., Neal, C. & Glover, V. Early Stress, Translational Research and Prevention Science Network: Fetal and Neonatal Experience, effects on child and adolescent mental health. (2007) Antenatal maternal stress and long-term effects on child neurodevelopment: how and why? *Journal of Child Psychology and Psychiatry, 48*, 245–261.

2

CHANGING SOCIETY'S ATTITUDES TO CHILDREN AND FAMILIES

Al Aynsley-Green

The British Medical Association in its hard–hitting analysis in *'Growing up in the UK'* concluded that 'politicians have been failing children on a grand scale' by not giving them the priority they deserve in political ideology, policy and resources (bma.org). This is relevant in the light of the Chief Medical Officer's report on the state of the nation's children's health, concluding that 'We should be ashamed of the state of our children's health' (gov.uk).

I know from my work over the last 40 or more years that we have amazing youngsters and supportive families in the UK today. The majority of children are law abiding and loved by their families and work hard to achieve success. Many children are courageously overcoming difficulties that are not of their making with countless numbers of hard-working staff trying their best to support them and their families.

Children, generally, are healthy and few die compared to 50 years ago. Science has transformed the treatment and prevention of diseases with immunisation diminishing the toll of infectious illnesses.

The culture of some services has also been transformed. For example parents have unlimited access to their sick children in hospital, and increasing importance is given to the voice of children and young people based on Article 12 of the United Nations Convention on the Rights of the Child. Facilities have also improved including new children's hospitals and schools. The dedication of staff needs to be celebrated too.

Despite all this, however, reports from authoritative organisations have repeatedly documented that for too many children, outcomes for health, education, social care, youth justice and poverty are some of the worst in the developed world, with the UK falling, to the bottom of, for example, the UNICEF international league table on the well being of children (unicef.org).

Services to support children and young people with emotional and mental ill health are a prime example of the enormity of failure of political will for the best interests of children. Such illnesses affect 1 in 10 children, but less than 25 per cent of those are able to access the services they need (NHS England). These deficiencies have been addressed, with promises of new funding proclaimed, yet to date there is little evidence of impact on the real lives of children so afflicted. Practitioners in mental health services cannot escape responsibility for allowing this situation to have developed unchallenged for so many years.

One issue which went unchallenged is exposure of the fetal brain to alcohol, which has long been known to be the single most important preventable cause of brain damage today, its effects ranging from severe physical and mental disability to subtle effects predisposing exposed individuals to anti-social behaviour and criminality (FASD Resources, 2015). Until last year there has been a state of denial here in England of the importance of the subject. However, a flurry of parliamentary activity led by a small number of motivated MPs and voluntary organisations has at last generated traction, with the UK Chief Medical Officers now recommending that women should not drink alcohol during pregnancy (Alcohol Guidelines Review, 2016). Even here, though, much still remains to be done, including providing adequate diagnostic and support services, educating young people on the risks of alcohol in pregnancy and the compulsory labelling of alcohol products for their risk to unborn children.

International scrutiny supports the view that our poor performance in realising children's best interests is a result of the lack of political will to give children the focus they deserve. The most recent periodic review by the United Nations Committee on the Rights of the Child in the UK concluded that while progress has been made, the UK must improve its performance in several key domains of activity (crae.org).

It is not only officialdom that needs to change. Public attitudes to children and especially young people, as reported in media, are far from satisfactory. An outstanding example is the lack of controls over the installation in public places of the 'Mosquito' ultrasonic device, designed to make it impossibly uncomfortable for children and young people, whose hearing is more acute than ours, to gather or to stay within its perimeter. Similarly the presence of crying babies on aircraft and in restaurants generates heated demands for 'child-free premises', reinforcing the Victorian ideal of children 'being seen but not heard'. Moreover, it is only 8 years ago that the report from the Barnardo's charity *'Breaking the cycle, believe in children'* (Barnado's, 2008) on attitudes to children and young people reported that 54 per cent of adults believed children behave like animals; 45 per cent agreed they are feral; 49 per cent believed they are a danger to each other and to adults; 43 per cent agreed something has to be done to protect us from children; and most adults believed that 50 per cent of crime is committed by children.

What does this all mean for infants and for their mental health and development? There can be no doubt of the importance of the early years in setting children on their life-long trajectories of resilience and physical and emotional health. But it is against the backdrop above that we need to ask whether infant mental health in the UK is likely to be given the priority and importance it deserves.

Being positive, the 1001 Critical Days Manifesto explicitly addresses the crucial importance of the 1001 days from conception to the age of two (The 1001 Critical Days Manifesto, 2015). For the first time, senior politicians across the political spectrum are supporting a key manifesto, with its justification based on hard economic assessment of the consequences of not promoting the secure attachment of the infant to its carers and not giving them effective support.

This manifesto follows other recent initiatives including the Early Intervention Foundation (eif.org), the development of Family Nurse Practitioners (fnp.nhs), and the Troubled Families programme (gov.uk), all designed to address challenges in families and children early, and with targeted interventions. Rigorous evaluation of the success of such programmes in improving outcomes is urgently needed, preliminary evidence from the Troubled Families initiative being far from reassuring (The Guardian, 2015).

However, while early intervention programmes such as these are welcome, they are not part of an overall political strategy of priority for children and families as was the case with the Every Child Matters policy programme of the previous government (Every Child Matters, 2003). Indeed the economic policies of the last 6 years have led to austerity and that austerity has seriously and selectively disadvantaged young children and families. This is confirmed in the BMA's recent report on the effects of austerity (BMA, 2016) and exemplified by the closure of children's Sure Start Centres and the loss and demotivation of childcare staff. Many speak of feeling like 'rabbits in the headlights' as local government, charities and statutory agencies struggle to survive. There is a sense of hopelessness in many localities that does not bode well for a fresh focus on infant mental health.

So what needs to be done?

Infant mental health and wellbeing must be seen in the overall context of children and childhood in the UK today. I propose that thinking, and designing services, around the *needs* of children and their families could deliver a vital paradigm shift, but delivering this change in attitude is a major challenge against the reality of competition for influence, power and money. I further propose – and many of the following papers support this – that, the *nurture* of children must become everybody's business: parents and families; communities; schools; faith groups; voluntary organisations and professional staff as well as national and local government (Aynsley-Green, 2010).

What is needed from government to deliver this is:

1   A political ideology that treats children as a priority and as citizens in their own right.
2   An explicit commitment from the very top and an intellectual framework for an overall policy, with defined objectives and desired outcomes.

3   Integrated responsibility across government for all aspects of policy affecting children.
4   Ensuring the best possible resources are made available.
5   A delivery framework that focuses on the multidisciplinary training of staff.

What is needed locally is:

1   An understanding of the local context for children, young people and families and defining the 'patch'.
2   'Mapping' from routine data collections
    a. The population and its demography.
    b. Who's who? What's where? Who's doing what?
3   A vision for what services should look like, developing a strategy to promote the best interests of children, young people and families, coupled with defined objectives and metrics.
4   Listening to children, young people and families.
5   Explicit definitions of responsibility and accountability.
6   Partnerships and working with the media.

The responsibility of researchers and practitioners is to ensure that data, evidence and the results of research are translated into effective advocacy to change policy and practice (Aynsley-Green).

Children conceived, born or growing up today will be adults whose productivity has to support an ever-ageing population. We don't only want healthy, educated, creative and resilient children, we need them. This should drive a 'holistic' approach to children's policies and practices. We know what has to be done! No more reports are needed!

We must encourage a change in attitude to the importance of children, young people and families by politicians, professional staff, media and the public. My challenge to each and every reader of every paper in this book is this: here is the evidence. What are you going to do about it? It is action and not further navel gazing that is needed.

References

The 1001 Critical Days Manifesto. (2015). Available online at www.1001criticaldays.co.uk. (accessed 9 September 2016)

Aynsley-Green, A. (2010). Should the nurture of children be everybody's business. Available online at www.thersa.org/discover/videos/event-videos/2010/06/should-the-nurture-of-children-be-everybodys-business (accessed 22 November 2016)

Aynsley-Green, A. (2014). Translating research into political advocacy to improve infant and child health. *Early Human Development* 90; 761–764. Available online at www.earlyhumandevelopment.com/article/S0378–3782(14)00208-4/fulltext. (accessed 22 November 2016)

Barnardo's report (2008). 'The shame of Britain's intolerance of children'. Available online at https://barnardos.org.uk/news_and_events/media_centre/press_releases.htm?ref=42088. (accessed 22 November 2016)

British Medical Association. (2016). Cutting away at our children's futures. Available online at www.bma.org.uk/collective-voice/policy-and-research/public-and-population-health/child-health/cutting-away-at-our-childrens-future. (accessed 22 November 2016)

Early Intervention Foundation. Available online at www.eif.org.uk. (accessed 9 September 2016)

Every Child Matters (2003). Available online at www.education.gov.uk/consultations/downloadableDocs/EveryChildMatters.pdf. (accessed 9 September 2016)

The Family Nurse Partnership. Available online at http://fnp.nhs.uk. (accessed 9 September 2016)

FASD Resources, Province of Manitoba. (2015). Available online at https://gov.mb.ca/healthychild/fasd/fasdresources_en.pdf. (accessed 9 September 2016)

Future in mind: Promoting, protecting and improving our children and young people's mental health and wellbeing. NHS England (2015) Available online at https://gov.uk/government/uploads/system/uploads/attachment_data/file/414024/Childrens_Mental_Health.pdf (accessed 22 November 2016)

Growing up in the UK. Available online at www.bma.org.uk (accessed 9 September 2016)

Is the success of the government's troubled families scheme too good to be true? The Guardian (2015). Available online at www.theguardian.com/society/2015/nov/11/troubled-family-programme-government-success-council-figures. (accessed 9 September 2016)

Prevention pays – our children deserve better. (2013). Available online at https://gov.uk/. . ./chief-medical-officer-prevention-pays-our-children-deserve-better. (accessed 9 September 2016)

The Troubled Families Programme. Available online at https://www.gov.uk/government/uploads/system/uploads/attachment. . .

The wellbeing of children: How does the UK score? (2008). Available online at https://unicef.org.uk/Images/Campaigns/ReportCard11_CYP.pdf. (accessed 9 September 2016)

UK Chief Medical Officers' Alcohol Guidelines Review. (2016). Available online at https://gov.uk/government/uploads/system/uploads/attachment. . ./summary.pdf. (accessed 9 September 2016)

United Nations Convention on the Rights of the Child: Concluding observations on the fifth periodic report of the United Kingdom of Great Britain and Northern Ireland. July (2016). Available online at http://crae.org.uk/media/93148/UK-concluding-observations2016.pdf. (accessed 22 November 2016)

PART II

Evidence

A: Early experiences and later outcomes

3

CIRCUITS AND CIRCUMSTANCES

Importance of earliest relationships and their context

Robin Balbernie

Any system is most flexible while being built. Human brains under construction are designed to rapidly adapt to the family setting. Babies have no comparisons, and the quality of relationships is the prime component of their world. For the first years of life parents lend their brains to their child, sliding their unconscious into this growing mind. 'From a basic biological perspective, the child's neuronal system – the structure and functioning of the developing brain – is shaped by the parent's more mature brain. This occurs within emotional communication' (Siegel, 1999: 278).

Early brain development

As human brains and groups grew larger in the course of evolution each had more tasks to perform and so became more complex. With increasing neuroplasticity the ratio between nature and nurture also changed as the environment being adapted to became more social than physical. 'Most of human knowledge cannot be anticipated in a species-typical genome . . . and thus brain development depends on genetically based avenues for incorporating experiences into the developing brain' (Shonkoff & Phillips, 2000: 53).

Building on foetal developments the brain rapidly expands at term as neural networks burgeon; and it starts with a scramble for survival as the outgoing message-carrying fibres from each neuron (axons) seek appropriate connections with the input connections to other neurons (dendrites).

> Owing to the uncertainty in the number of neurons that will reach their appropriate destination and the appropriateness of the connections they form, the brain overproduces both neurons and connections during development, with the peak of synapse formation being between one and two years, depending upon the region of the cortex.
>
> (Kolb and Gibb, 2011: 266)

Overproduction necessitates a subsequent reduction, and this pruning to match demands quickly fits structure to environment.

Strictly speaking the synapse is the minute gap between the axon of one neuron and a dendrite of another, and at this synaptic cleft electrical signals convert to chemical messengers (neurotransmitters) in order to cross the space and then bind to receptors on the dendrite side to be reconverted to electrical signals. Synaptic transmission configures the way in which neurones respond to experience. The pattern of synaptogenesis is largely under the control of genes that are expressed, or not, by individual experiences, a process that cannot be separated from early experience as 'there is abundant evidence that many genes require experience in order to be activated, and that one of the effects of experience on a developing organism is often to modify the activity of a gene' (Johnston, 2008: 22). A gene has no effect if not expressed and it cannot be expressed unless the DNA is accessible.

Epigenetic mechanisms alter a gene's function without affecting its inherited sequence, instituting a secondary level of information within the genome; and these have the capacity to change gene expression in response to environmental pressures by adding a chemical signature above the gene that determine whether or not it is expressed. Collectively these markers are known as the epigenome, and its task is to programme the genome. This process lies behind the diversity of cells, each bearing the same DNA sequence, within an organism and the 'sensitivity of the epigenetic machinery to the environment offers a conduit through which the environment can sculpt the genome and have a long-term impact on health' (Szyf, 2009: 879). Within the developing mind neurobiological signalling sets off the production of gene regulatory proteins, which then attract or repel the enzymes that in turn add or remove epigenetic markers to alter the form and structure of DNA. 'For the growing brain of a young child, the social world supplies the most important experiences influencing the expression and regulation of genes' (Siegel, 2012: 32). These first relationships write our cellular software.

> 'Because the experience of high versus low levels of maternal care leads to changes in the transcription of hundreds of genes within the brain, it is likely that early rearing experiences lead to significant shifts in the epigenetic profile of the entire genome – the epigenome'
>
> (Champagne, 2015: 6)

Although epigenetic markings are long lasting they are also potentially capable of being reversed (Syf, 2009) by both psychotherapeutic and pharmacological treatments. Animal studies demonstrate that 'abundant maternal care sets in motion a series of epigenetic changes in gene-expression patterns that make "well-loved" animals more resilient with robust, life-long resistance against various stressors' (Panksepp and Biven, 2012: 308). On the other hand, epigenetic transmission might be why some babies adopted at birth have later emotional struggles – they carry survival traits appropriate to the abusive childhood of a parent (Raine, 2013); although this is inseparable from foetal programming since 'the epigenome of a prenatally developing infant is sensitive to the mother's experiences, the prenatal environment, and even the experience of birth' (Roth & Sweatt, 2011: 404).

Early experiences between caregiver and child, those that shape the preverbal foundations for subsequent development, impose a neurobiological bias that will affect whether or not any future modification is built on rock or sand. 'Emotionally stimulating interactions generate brain growth, whereas dysregulated affect and prolonged stress result in neuron loss throughout cortical-limbic circuits' (Cozolino, 2014: 83). Environmental demands tailor the neural networks designed to deal with them in a variety of interlinking ways from epigenetic changes to the sculpting of neuronal networks and the programming of the stress response. In this way neural plasticity builds adaptive sensory, cognitive, emotional and reactive structures with minimal fixed genetic guidance. The potential number of connections in the human brain is unimaginable, and these must become refined down to create an efficient match with their individual environment. An Inuit child may differentiate sea colours invisible to an urban dweller; an infant exposed to domestic violence has a much speedier danger-detecting and response mechanism than a child raised in a happier family.

Those neuronal networks that carry the most signals are reinforced; and with sufficient passage of electrical and chemical signals the glial cells create an insulating myelin sheath around the axon-dendrite fibre that prevents elimination, speeds up transmission and stops the short circuits that cause a synaesthesia-like transitional period in the neonate. These have now formed a permanent circuit. These stabilised myelinated, synapses will tend to endure; while those that were not used frequently enough in early childhood will disappear. They have to disappear in order to make room and avoid the metabolic cost of excess neurons. By eliminating seldom-used pathways the brain leaves space for sturdier neural networks. This process of synaptic pruning is an extremely efficient method for adapting the baby's neural circuits to the exact demands of the family habitat.

> 'The strength and vulnerability of the human brain lie in its ability to shape itself to enable a particular human being to survive its environment. Our experiences, especially our earliest experiences, become biologically rooted in our brain structure and chemistry from the time of our gestation and most profoundly in the first months of life'
>
> (Karr-Morse & Wiley, 1997: 277)

Phases of fortune

The central nervous system requires environmental directives in order to develop efficiently. Experience-expectant brain growth takes place when synaptic proliferation has primed the brain to use external information in order to build basic skills in the most appropriate way. 'Experience during a sensitive period customizes a developing neural circuit to the needs of the individual. Experience provides precise information about the individual or about the environment that often cannot be predicted and, therefore, cannot be genetically coded' (Knudsen, 2004: 1415). Such sensitive periods allow events to instruct neural circuits to process or represent information in a way that creates adaptive abilities for the individual in that particular environment. As the brain prunes away the unused circuits, those that are regularly used will become established and increasingly difficult to alter over time. Declining plasticity means that it is easier to influence the configuration of a baby's developing brain than it is to rewire parts of its circuitry in later years. Pruning in areas involved with higher cognitive functions continues through adolescence.

The different areas within the brain are formed in a hierarchical fashion, starting with the life support, autonomic nervous system circuits and then moving up to the more complex sensory pathways (vision and hearing). The conduits that connect the baby to the world of people are the first to develop after birth, followed by early language skills, emotional regulation and higher cognitive functions. Connections proliferate and prune in a functional order. The timing is determined genetically but the biological imperative to adapt affects whether the eventual neural networks are strong or weak. This process ensures that specialised circuits emerge and are set in place automatically. These waves of synaptic proliferation provide fuzzy-edged stages for growth and adaptation. A brain cannot develop in isolation and context provides serial opportunities – or threats. There are two overlapping mechanisms that form and consolidate axonal connections: 'experience-expectant brain development is a time-limited function that depends on experience occurring during a sensitive or critical period of development. By contrast, experience-dependent development can occur at any time in the life cycle' (Sheridan and Nelson, 2009: 47). Although there is an initial discrete period for visual acuity, when practice is essential, it appears that other areas of brain functioning have sensitive periods that allow for development outside of the first time window. 'But once a given brain region has passed the refinement stage, its critical period has ended, and the opportunity to rewire it is significantly limited' (Eliot, 2001: 38). Attachment is an example of a developmental progression that is particularly sensitive to the environment since 'the *formation* of an attachment may reflect an experience-expectant process but the *quality* of the attachment may reflect an experience-dependent process' (Nelson et al., 2014: 302). And results from the Bucharest Project demonstrate sensitive periods for general intelligence (although continuing support is necessary for optimal results), level of brain activity and the formation of secure attachments (Fox et al., 2014).

The prefrontal cortex is the most complex area of the brain and is the site of self-awareness, abstract thought, decision making, self-regulation, imagination and theory of mind. The prefrontal cortex does not completely mature until the end of adolescence with the full development of executive functioning. This part of the brain was the latest to evolve and allows humans to internalise self-control from the quality of caregiving and create mental time travel, integrating the past with the present and possible future. The ability to fine-tune emotional responses begins with the wiring up of the right orbitofrontal cortex at about 9 months. This regulates both branches of the autonomic nervous system, integrating the internal state of the body with its environment.

> 'The orbitofrontal regions are not functional at birth. Over the course of the first year, limbic circuitries emerge in a sequential progression, from amygdala to anterior cingulate to insula and finally to orbitofrontal. And so as a result of attachment experiences, this system enters a critical period of maturation in the last quarter of the first year'
>
> (Schore, 2003a: 42)

Prior to this phase the limbic system, the launch pad of emotions, has come on line at about age 5 months onwards. This rather loosely defined area of the brain assigns value, or emotional significance, to sensation and perception and through this instils a sense of motivation. Family context programmes emotional hardware and software.

However, the limbic system is not solely concerned with emotion; a central structure, the hippocampus, has a cognitive function with the laying down and retrieval of long-term episodic memory and generating a sense of context. The hippocampus contains cortisol receptors and can be disrupted when flooded by this steroid hormone, part of the stress response, which then weakens the ability of the temporal lobe memory system to form explicit memories. But roughly speaking, the bodily manifestations of emotion originate in the lower limbic system, while the upper tier (including the orbitofrontal cortex in the early maturing right hemisphere) governs a conscious awareness of what we are feeling. In post-traumatic stress disorder the individual may be overwhelmed by out of context feelings that have been stored in the amygdala, which never forgets, but remain unaware of their origin.

Once the first birthday has passed most of the windows of brain development are open. Many of the neural networks that lie behind a lifetime of skills, responses and potential are beginning to take shape. From about 18 months toddlers are gaining more control of their bodies, their motor skills are developing and with the myelination of the corticospinal fibres innervating the legs, walking has taken off. They are becoming more aware of other people's feelings and beginning to learn to share. This is the time of the child's love affair with the whole world – unless we spoil it with teaching. Play, not instruction, is vital for an infant's future; for who can tell what might be turned up by a mind that is not as limited in conceiving possibilities as an adult's? It takes a dreary grown up to deny the significance of play. From an evolutionary perspective children's 'uninhibited useless pretence turns out to be among the most deeply functional human activities' (Gopnik, 2009: 73). There is a strong likelihood that 'the dynamic brain changes evoked by play facilitate brain growth and maturation, perhaps by epigenetically creating prosocial circuits of the brain, perhaps partly by refining frontal-lobe executive functions' (Panksepp & Biven, 2012: 380). Whatever is being done by or done to infants, within the span of 2 years much of a child's brain growth and density is complete. Between the ages of three and five, most of the remaining windows of opportunity in a child's brain development begin to close, but not slam shut.

Maltreatment

Neurological plasticity is the basis of adaptation and survival within the family. But, 'Plasticity is a double-edged sword that leads to both adaptation and vulnerability' (Shonkoff & Phillips, 2000: 94). The brain will modify itself to fit the environment; if this is hostile or depriving rather than loving it makes no difference to the mechanism. It is now accepted that early childhood abuse specifically alters limbic system maturation, producing neurobiological alterations that act as a biological substrate for a variety of psychiatric consequences. These include affective instability, inefficient stress tolerance, memory impairment, psychosomatic disorders, and dissociative disturbances' (Schore, 2012: 81). It might not change the process, but it does make a difference to the final product. 'These early imprints can be remarkably long lasting because very early stressful life experiences have left emotional systems sensitized or desensitized, with permanent, epigenetically induced high-stress reactivity and excessive primary-process negativistic feeling' (Panksepp & Biven, 2012: 434).

When babies and toddlers are exposed to traumatising family relationships they have experienced scaregivers who were out of touch, frightening or frightened, and so could not terminate the infant's attachment anxieties. They needed protection from their protectors; and the chronic stress such a paradox creates is toxic to tender brains.

> 'Early traumatic attachments induce significantly increased rates of apoptosis and circuit overpruning in the developing limbic system and represent the origins of the enduring structural impairments of both borderline and antisocial (sociopathic) personality disorders. This would lead to a deficit of the higher right brain regulation of lower right subcortically driven aggressive states'

> (Schore, 2003: 299)

Such overwhelming stress directly impacts the key structural developmental processes in a nascent brain. A meta-analysis of 12 whole-brain imaging studies concluded that 'childhood maltreatment is associated with abnormalities in the right orbitofrontal-temporo-limbic regions that form the paralimbic system, which is known to be implicated in affect and motivational processing and the self-regulation of social and emotional behaviors' (Lim et al., 2014). These deficits would bias individuals towards the negative end of the spectrum for making, valuing and sustaining relationships. 'Repeated experiences of terror and fear can be engrained within the circuits of the brain as states of mind. With chronic occurrence, these states can become more readily activated (retrieved) in the future, so that they become characteristic traits of the individual' (Siegel, 2012: 55).

Neglect is as harmful as abuse. All forms of deprivation will have an adverse influence on the early growing brain. This includes poverty; as 'low SES environments influence the rate of human infant brain development . . . The differences seen were localised to the frontal and parietal volumes, with children from lower income families having smaller volumes in these brain areas' (Hanson et al., 2013: 5). This would compromise executive functions, sensory integration and visual attention. These results show the same process of deprivation, although many orders less, as found in a sample of Romanian institutionalised infants who, in relation to comparable groups, showed a reduction in both grey and white matter resulting in a smaller head circumference, a reduction in the corpus callosum and overall 'smaller brains and . . . dramatic reductions in the brain's electrical activity compared to never-institutionalised children' (Nelson et al., 2014: 209).

In situations of maltreatment within the family survival takes precedence and the social brain becomes specialised for offensive and defensive purposes, with the subsequent physiological toll of being on permanent high alert. A child growing up surrounded by fear and unpredictability will only be able to develop neural systems and functional capabilities that reflect this disorganisation.

> 'In the developing brain, stress and elevated levels of stress chemicals may lead to adverse brain development through the mechanisms of accelerated loss (or metabolism) of neurons, delays in myelination, abnormalities in developmentally appropriate pruning, inhibition of neurogenesis, or a stress-induced decrease in brain growth factors'
>
> (De Bellis, 2005: 158)

The swathe of neurological reactions to the experience of threat and stress in foetus and infant has the potential to compromise all areas of pro-social development, casting a long shadow of unhappiness on both the individual and society (Teicher & Samson, 2016).

Care and repair

The older the child then the harder and more costly it becomes to rewire certain areas of the brain. Thus, without intervention a child who has experienced maltreatment as an infant will unwittingly continue with patterns of responses that are engraved in the neural networks and biochemistry of the mind, even if conditions change. The early prevention of maltreatment is a priority for adult mental health provision since the 'Structural and functional abnormalities initially attributed to psychiatric illness may be a more direct consequence of abuse' (Teicher & Samson, 2016: 241) than a cause. Relationship-based interventions have the capacity to take advantage of the continuing neural plasticity of the brain. '(R)ecent research in brain imaging, molecular biology, and neurogenetics has shown that psychotherapy

... affects regional cerebral blood flow, neurotransmitter metabolism, gene expression, and persistent modifications in synaptic plasticity' (Glass, 2008: 1589). Instruction alone is inadequate.

> 'If we want to change posttraumatic reactions, we have to access the emotional brain and do 'limbic system' therapy: repairing faulty alarm systems and restoring the emotional brain to its ordinary job of being a quiet background presence that takes care of the housekeeping of the body'
>
> (Van der Kolk, 2014: 205)

Any intervention for a traumatized child or an adult who cannot shake off responses that once were means of survival must begin with creating safety within a relationship.

Conclusion

The quality of children's early relationships will be reflected in the architecture of their brains. Most children have reasonable parenting within loving and appropriately responsive relationships, and grow up able to contribute to society. But a significant percentage has no alternative to the ordeal of inescapable unhappiness within the family, so that their brains are programmed 'to develop along an alternative pathway adapting itself to survive and reproduce in a malevolent stress-filled world' (Teicher et al., 2003: 34). We can offer help to stressed and vulnerable families before something goes wrong; but this help needs to be on all levels from political to personal if it is to be effective in changing today's threatened emerging minds to a resource for the future. To create a more responsible, caring and encouraging society a generation ahead we need to consider how the brains of babies today are being sculpted by influences outside of their control. And then do something about it.

- Early relationships have a significant effect on the preverbal neurochemical foundations of the mind.
- Positive or negative experiences will programme the brain's future biases accordingly.
- A mind set on survival and the anticipation of threat will become a danger to others and a drain on society.
- Both policy and resources allocation needs to think a generation ahead.

References

Champagne, F.A. (2015). Epigenetics of the developing brain. *Zero to Three*, *35*(3), 2–8.
Cozolino, L. (2014). *The Neuroscience of Human Relationships: Attachment and the Developing Brain*. Second Edition. New York: W. W. Norton and Company.
De Bellis, M.D. (2005). The psychobiology of neglect. *Child Maltreatment*, *10*(2), 150–172.
Eliot, L. (2001). *Early Intelligence: How the Brain and Mind Develop in the First Five Years of Life*. London: Penguin Books.

Fox, N.A., Zeanah, C.H. & Nelson, C.A. (2014). A matter of timing: Enhancing positive change for the developing brain. *Zero to Three*, *34*(3), 4–9.

Glass, R.M. (2008). Psychodynamic psychotherapy and research evidence. Bambi survives Godzilla? *The Journal of the American Medical Association*, *300*, 1587–1589.

Gopnik, A. (2009). *The Philosophical Baby*. London: The Bodley Head.

Hanson, J.L., Hair, N., Shen, D.G., Shi, F., Gilmore, J.H., Wolfe, B.l. & Pollak, S.D. (2013). Family poverty affects the rate of human brain growth. *Plos One*. *8*(12), 1–9. Accessed 22/12/2013 from: www.plosone.org

Johnston, T.D. (2008). *Genes, experience, and behavior*. pp. 18–24 In: Fogel, A., King, B.J. and Shanker, S.G. (Eds.), *Human Development in the Twenty-First Century*. Cambridge: Cambridge University Press.

Karr-Morse, R. & Wiley, M.S. (1997). *Ghosts from the Nursery: Tracing the Roots of Violence*. New York: The Atlantic Monthly Press.

Knudson, E.I. (2004). Sensitive periods in the development of the brain and behavior. *Journal of Cognitive Neuroscience*, *16*(8), 1412–1425.

Kolb, B. & Gibb, R. (2011). Brain plasticity and behaviour in the developing brain. *Journal of the Canadian Academy of Child and Adolescent Psychiatry*, *20*(4), 265–276.

Lim, L., Radua, J. & Rubia, K. (2014). Gray matter abnormalities in childhood maltreatment: A voxel-wise meta-analysis. *American Journal of Psychiatry*, *171*(8), 854–863.

Nelson, C.A., Fox, N.A. & Zeanah, C.H. (2014). *Romania's Abandoned Children*. Cambridge, MA: Harvard University Press.

Panksepp, J. & Biven, L. (2012). *The Archaeology of Mind: Neuroevolutionary Origins of Human Emotions*. New York: W. W. Norton and Company.

Raine, A. (2013). *The Anatomy of Violence: The Biological Roots of Crime*. London: Allen Lane, Penguin.

Roth, T.L. & Sweatt, J.D. (2011). Annual Research review: Epigenetic mechanisms and environmental shaping of the brain during sensitive periods of development. *The Journal of Child Psychology and Psychiatry*, *52*(4), 398–408.

Schore, A.N. (2003). *Affect Regulation and Disorders of the Self*. New York: W.W. Norton and Co.

Sheridan, M. and Nelson, C.A. (2009). *Neurobiology of fetal and infant development: Implications for infant mental health*. pp. 40–58 In: Zeanah, C. H. (Ed.), *Handbook of Infant Mental Health*. Third Edition. New York: The Guilford Press.

Shonkoff, J.P., and Phillips, D.A. (Eds.) (2000). *From Neurons to Neighbourhoods: The Science of Early Childhood Development*. Washington D.C.: National Academy Press.

Siegel, D.J. (1999). *The Developing Mind: Towards a Neurobiology of Interpersonal Experience*. New York: The Guilford Press.

Siegel, D.J. (2012). *The Developing Mind (Second Edition)*. New York: The Guilford Press.

Szyf, M. (2009). The early environment and the epigenome. *Biochimica et Biophysica Acta*, *1790*(9), 877–885.

Teicher, M.H., Andersen, S.L., Polcari, A., Anderson, C.M., Navalta, C.P. & Kim, D.M. (2003). The neurobiological consequences of early stress and childhood maltreatment. *Neuroscience and Biobehavioral Reviews*, 27, 33–44.

Teicher, M.H. & Samson, J.A. (2016). Annual Research Review: Enduring neurobiological effects of childhood abuse and neglect. *Journal of Child Psychology and Psychiatry*, *57*(3), 241–266.

Van der Kolk, B.A. (2014). *The Body Keeps The Score*. New York: Viking.

4

ATTACHMENT THEORY

Research and application to practice and policy

Pasco Fearon

Attachment is a key aspect of early human development. It refers to the close bond a child has to his/her parents or carers, which serves the purpose of helping a child feel safe, and comforted when worried or anxious. A great deal of research has been undertaken to understand how attachment develops, what factors influence the extent to which a child forms a secure or insecure attachment relationship to a caregiver, what this might mean for later outcomes and how attachment difficulties might be treated or prevented. This chapter provides an overview of research in this field and discusses the implications of this work for clinical practice and policy.

Attachment refers to the tendency of infants and young children to turn to parent figures for comfort and support when frightened, stressed or ill. It is thought to have been shaped by natural selection to ensure that young children survive in the face of a range of threats, such as predation, injury or illness. The field grew out of ground-breaking integrative theoretical work by John Bowlby (Bowlby, 1969) and by the work of Mary Ainsworth (Ainsworth, 1978) who put the topic on a sound empirical footing by developing several key tools for studying attachment in humans, most notably the Strange Situation Procedure (Ainsworth, 1978).

When we think about the term attachment, it is important to distinguish between attachment *behaviour* and an attachment *bond*. An attachment bond is not immediately apparent, but we infer it when we observe, over a period time, a consistent tendency that a child has to discriminate certain key individuals, to whom they direct their attachment *behaviour*. Attachment behaviour is an immediate and directly observable series of actions that children (and indeed adults in different forms) display when they are anxious or uncertain, whose purpose appears to be organised around bringing about contact with a caregiver for comfort or support (Cassidy, 2008).

The kinds of behaviours that children may display when they seek to make contact with their carer in this way are very diverse, but broadly speaking they fall into three main types: 1) signalling or communication (e.g. calling, crying), 2) proximity seeking (e.g. crawling, walking, reaching) and contact maintenance (e.g. clinging). Children also keep track of their attachment figures, and, especially as they get older, will monitor how available their parent is from moment to moment (physically or psychologically available). The ways in which children manifest their attachment behaviours changes enormously with age, but what remains quite consistent is the purpose they serve – feeling safe through making contact. In older children language – often at a distance – is a very important way in which children may achieve contact and feel comforted, whereas young children rely much more heavily on physical contact (see Marvin & Britner, 2008).

Bowlby argued that throughout the course of routine experiences with carers, children develop expectations about how they will be responded to by carers, and these expectations form a kind of working model that guides how and when they should deploy their attachment behaviour. These working models are thought to be quite stable over time, and shape how children behave both within their primary attachment relationships and in other important relationship later in life. Crucially, Bowlby argued that these models also form the basis of a child's developing sense of themselves and of the world – whether they are worthy of care from others, and whether others are caring and benign, or rejecting and hostile. This is a central concept that attachment researchers have used to understand how attachment may influence children's functioning in relationships in later life and how attachment in early life might affect children's chances of experiencing social and emotional difficulties or disorders.

It is important to note that the processes that lead to the establishment of a long-term attachment bond (i.e. forming an attachment) are quite different to those that trigger attachment behaviour (Ainsworth, 1991). This is an important issue because some forms of difficulty in relation to attachment seem to be linked to formation of attachment bonds (or the breaking of them), while others are linked to the way in which attachment behaviour is expressed within an already formed and continuous bond. Attachment disorders, for example, which are described further, are most likely examples of the former, whereas insecure attachment is better understood as the latter. The levels of clinical concern associated with these two domains of attachment problem are quite different, and strategies to prevent or treat them will also be different.

Measurement

Normative patterns

The Strange Situation Procedure is the most commonly used tool for studying infant attachment (Ainsworth, 1978). It involves an encounter with a stranger and two brief separations from a parent in an unfamiliar setting. The procedure is valid for infants aged approximately 11–18 months. In a now classic and well-established manner, infants vary in striking ways in how they respond to this procedure, particularly the way their attachment behaviour is organised when they are reunited with their parent. These divide into two broad classifications – 'secure' and three types of 'insecure' attachment: avoidant, resistant and disorganised. These classifications have become a major focus of research, with findings indicating that the majority of infants in low-risk circumstances (approximately 65 percent) are described as 'secure'; approximately 15 percent as avoidant; 10 percent as resistant and 15 percent as disorganised. It is this latter category that has attracted the most attention clinically, as it appears most closely related to more severe forms of adverse parental care, and to raised risk of psychopathology (Rutter, Kreppner & Sonuga-Barke, 2009). The prevalence of the different insecure subtypes varies considerably across culture (see Van Ijzendoorn & Kroonenberg, 1988). A host of similar measures have been developed for assessing attachment in older children (Solomon & George. 2008).

Causes of attachment security and insecurity

Based on many hours of intensive home-based observation of young infants and their mothers, Mary Ainsworth originally proposed that the extent to which the parent was sensitive and responsive to the infant's attachment cues was the key factor in influencing whether a child developed a secure or insecure attachment (Ainsworth, 1978). Since then, this theory has been supported by an impressive collection of cross-sectional and longitudinal studies (De Wolff & van Ijzendoorn, 1997). However, although this association has been replicated many times the size of the association is not large, which suggests that there is more that we need to understand about the factors that influence attachment security and insecurity, either in the way it is measured, or in the kinds of behaviours involved, or both (Belsky, 2008). Notably, randomised controlled trials of clinical interventions designed to improve sensitive parenting have been shown to increase the likelihood of secure attachment, suggesting the association is more than correlation – it reflects a causal process (Belsky, 2008). But while sensitivity of parenting may be thought of as the most important immediate determinant of attachment security, a host of broader contextual factors also appear to be consistently associated with security and insecurity, including parental depression, social support, marital quality and poverty (Bokhorst et al., 2003). Importantly, evidence indicates that genetic factors play a quite limited role in the development of attachment in infants and pre-schoolers (eg Fearon et al., 2014), though it may be more important in adolescence (Van Ijzendoorn et al., 1999).

Disorganised attachment appears to be related to rather different features of parenting than the other insecure attachment categories. The starkest example of this concerns maltreatment, which has been found to be related to markedly raised rates of disorganised attachment (Van Ijzendoorn et al., 1999). Furthermore, in populations where rates of maltreatment are likely to be low, insensitive parenting appears not to be closely related to disorganisation (Van Ijzendoorn et al., 1999). Instead, a quite different set of parenting features has been implicated, representing behaviour that has been described as frightened/frightening or extremely insensitive (Main & Hesse, 1990).

Attachment disorders

Although insecure attachment, and particularly disorganised attachment, is associated with a raised risk of later poor adjustment, the risk is relatively weak and probabilistic (Fearon et al., 2010). Insecure attachment patterns should therefore not be considered intrinsically problematic, and are not considered disorders. More severe problems in the area of attachment that could be described as disorders have been identified however, and these are almost exclusively observed in conditions of highly adverse care, such as abuse, neglect or institutional care. There are two types of disorder relevant to attachment. The first is known as Reactive Attachment Disorder (RAD) in the DSM-5,[1] (previously called RAD-inhibited-sub-type in DSM-IV). RAD is marked by a striking absence of attachment behaviour towards carers, extreme withdrawal, unexplained emotional volatility (e.g. fearfulness, anger) even during nonthreatening interactions, a pervasive tendency not to seek comfort from carers when distressed, and a lack of social responsiveness or reciprocity. The second disorder is known as Disinhibited Social Engagement Disorder (DSED), which was previously referred to as RAD-disinhibited subtype. DSED is marked by indiscriminate social approach behaviour, lack of sensitivity to social/personal boundaries (e.g. non-normative physical contact or intimacy with strangers), over-friendliness and a lack of wariness of strangers (e.g. wandering off with strangers). DSED is no longer considered an attachment disorder within DSM-5, because evidence indicates that disinhibited behaviour can co-occur with otherwise seemingly normal attachment behaviour (sometimes even of the secure type) towards caregivers (Zeanah & Gleason, 2015). Nevertheless, there is probably a close connection between attachment and the lack of selectivity of approach towards adults observed in DSED, and this is a topic that continues to be debated among scholars and clinicians (Lyons-Ruth, 2015).

It is important to note that RAD and DSED are quite distinct from the normative patterns of attachment described in the previous section, both in terms of the behaviours that define them and the circumstances that appear to give rise to them. Existing evidence suggests that normative attachment patterns represent variations in the organisation of attachment related to the style or quality of parenting among children who have formed one or more selective attachment bonds. In contrast, RAD and DSED most likely represent the consequences of severe disruption in the continuity of an attachment bond, or the failure to establish a selective attachment bond in the first place (Rutter, Kreppner & Sonuga-Barke, 2009).

Later outcomes linked to early attachment

The question of whether and how early attachment insecurity is associated with, or might cause, later difficulties with social and emotional adjustment has been a very significant area of research with obvious potential policy implications (Fearon et al., 2010; Schneider, Atkinson & Tardiff, 2001; Groh et al., 2014; Groh et al., 2012) When considered together, and synthesised using meta-analysis, the findings of these studies provide some important indications regarding the scope and limits of the impact of attachment on socio-emotional development. The evidence indicates, for example, that attachment security is more strongly correlated with childhood social competence and externalising behaviour problems (e.g. aggression) than with internalising problems (like anxiety) (Fearon et al., 2010; Schneider, Atkinson & Tardiff, 2001; Groh et al., 2014). This evidence appears broadly consistent with the idea that early attachment is linked most closely to children's functioning in social relationships (given that many externalising problems in childhood reflect difficulties with peer relationships). Another remarkable finding from this work is that the effects of attachment do not appear to decline over time – associations remained the same in all these outcomes regardless of the age at which they were measured or the length of the gap between the assessment of attachment and outcome (which varied widely). Thus, the evidence broadly supports the idea that secure attachment is associated with better socio-emotional outcomes, at least in childhood, but also highlights the fact that the effects of attachment are not large and deterministic, and that there is specificity in the insecure subtypes associated with different outcomes.

Intervention

A host of studies has attempted to promote desirable early childhood outcomes by supporting parents or carers to increase their sensitivity and responsiveness to a child's attachment cues and thereby, in principle at least, improve security of attachment. In the majority of these studies, the focus has been on prevention, and promoting attachment security as a way enhancing children's resilience and reducing the risk for later emotional or behavioural problems. Other intervention studies have targeted groups where attachment problems are clinically identified or are likely to be significantly in need of intervention – for instance, children who have experienced maltreatment and may be in foster care, or late-placed national or international adoptees.

Preventive interventions

One very strong example of a successful preventive intervention was developed by Van Den Boom (Van Den Boom, 1995). Van Den Boom, on the basis of observational studies, noted a range of insensitive parenting behaviours that often arise when infants are highly irritable and difficult to care for. These behaviours (e.g. overly intrusive, or disengaging when the infant becomes irritable) then formed the targets of her intervention. One hundred highly irritable neonates were allocated at random to the intervention or a control group. Home visits to mothers and infants in the treatment group focused on maternal interaction skills, helping mothers to follow the infant's lead, respond appropriately to their cues, encouraging soothing when the infant was distressed, and increasing playful interactions. Large positive effects on maternal sensitivity, and infant attachment security, were found and these were maintained at a 3.5-year follow-up. Another very popular and effective approach is to use video-feedback to help parents and carers to tune into their infants' or young children's attachment cues and communications (Juffer, Bakermans-Kranenburg & van IJzendoorn, 2008). A meta-analysis of a wide range of attachment-focused interventions (Bakermans-Kranenburg, van IJzendoorn & Juffer, 2003) showed that these were most effective when they were short (less than 16 sessions in length), focused clearly on sensitivity as defined by Ainsworth, and begun after age 6 months. Two very important further points emerged from this analysis. First, interventions tended to be successful in relation to attachment outcomes if they had been successful in improving parental sensitivity – so getting that first step right, so to speak, is crucial. Second, interventions were also more successful when the population that was offered support had a large percentage of insecure infants. In other words, the impact is greater when the 'room to move' — from insecurity to security — is large; the implication is that targeted, rather than universal, prevention may be the most effective and cost-effective approach. Sensitivity-based interventions have also been shown to be at least partially effective in reducing disorganisation (Bakermans-Kranenburg, van IJzendoorn & Juffer, 2005).

Interventions with fostered, adopted and maltreated children

Several intervention packages have been developed that are specially designed to support attachment in the context of foster care, adoption and maltreatment. The Attachment and Biobehavioural Catch-Up (ABC) programme is a 10-session intervention, which includes video-feedback techniques, and addresses mutual processes between parent and child that may interfere, directly or indirectly, with the child's self-regulatory capacities and attachment. These include parental interaction skills; parental attributions; and how the carer's own childhood history may contribute to current parenting attitudes and behaviour. This approach has been found to improve attachment behaviour and normalise stress patterns as indicated by the hormone cortisol (see NICE, 2015). Similar programmes have been developed to reduce disorganised attachment among children who have been maltreated (Bernard et al., 2012 and Moss et al., 2011), and these appear to be quite effective. For example, Moss and colleagues (Moss et al., 2011) developed an eight-session video-feedback programme for preschool children who had experienced maltreatment or neglect (but remained with their parents). The intervenors, who had been trained in attachment theory and research, visited families in their home and supported families in enhancing the quality of their interactions with the child (i.e. promoting sensitivity), as well as supporting families in managing day-to-day challenges and stressors. The intervenors made extensive use of video-feedback to highlight positive interactions and explore parents' thoughts and feelings about those interactions, as well as set goals with parents for between-session activities and plan future sessions. Post-treatment, the authors found substantial benefits for the treated group compared to the control group (to which participating families were allocated at random). More than 40 per cent of the treatment group changed from insecure to secure, compared to only 15 per cent in the control group. A recent NICE guideline (NICE, 2015) specifically recommended video-feedback programmes and sensitivity training as evidence-based interventions for promoting attachment security among children in care or on the edge of care (having experienced, or being at high risk of experiencing, maltreatment). This guideline is likely to have a substantial impact on practice over the coming years.

Conclusion

Attachment theory, and the research it has given rise to, has been extremely important in promoting understanding of the developmental significance of early caregiving experiences for children's emotional and social adjustment. This body of theory and research has been used to considerable positive effect to develop focused and effective interventions to increase resilience and to support children with attachment difficulties.

More research and clinical innovation is still needed, however, to:

- test whether and how attachment interventions can have sustained effects on children's long-term adjustment
- identify which children benefit most from such interventions
- refine and improve interventions to maximise benefits
- address a wider range of family circumstances and difficulties
- develop interventions that are specifically designed to tackle disorganisation
- develop and test interventions to treat reactive attachment disorder
- through research and policy initiatives, make such interventions widely available to families within routine health and social care systems.

Note

1   DSM = Diagnostic and Statistical Manual of Mental Disorders

References

Ainsworth, M.S., Blehar, M.C., Waters, E., and Wall, S. (1978). *Patterns of Attachment: A Psychological Study of the Strange Situation*. Hillsdale, NJ: Lawrence Erlbaum.

Ainsworth, M.S. (1991). Attachments and other affectional bonds across the life cycle. In: Parkes, C.M, Stevenson Hinde, J. (Eds.), *Attachment Across the Life cycle, iii*. London, England UK: Tavistock/Routledge; 1991. p. 33–51.

Bakermans-Kranenburg, M.J., van IJzendoorn, M.H., and Juffer, F. (2003). Less is more: meta-analyses of sensitivity and attachment interventions in early childhood. *Psychol Bull, 129*, 195–215.

Bakermans-Kranenburg, M.J., van IJzendoorn, M.H., and Juffer, F. (2005). Disorganized attachment and preventive interventions: a review and meta-analysis. *Infant Mental Health Journal, 26*, 191–216.

Belsky, J., Fearon, R.P. (2008). Precursors of attachment security. In: Cassidy, J. Shaver, P.R., (Eds.), *The Handbook of Attachment: Theory, Research and Clincal Applications*. 2nd ed. New York: The Guildford Press. pp. 295–316.

Bernard, K., Dozier, M., Bick, J., Lewis-Morrarty, E., Lindhiem, O., and Carlson, E. (2012). Enhancing attachment organization among maltreated children: results of a randomized clinical trial. *Child Development, 83*, 623–636.

Bokhorst, C.L., Bakermans-Kranenburg, M.J., Fearon, R.M., van IMH., Fonagy, P., and Schuengel, C. (2003). The importance of shared environment in mother-infant attachment security: a behavioral genetic study. *Child Development, 74*, 1769–1782.

van den Boom, DC. (1995). Do first-year intervention effects endure? Follow-up during toddlerhood of a sample of Dutch irritable infants. *Child Development. 66*, 1798–1816.

Bowlby, J. (1969). *Attachment and Loss, Vol. 1: Attachment*. London: Hogarth Press and the Institute of Psycho-Analysis.

Cassidy, J. (2008). The nature of the child's ties. In: Cassidy, J., Shaver P.R., (Ed.) *The Handbook of Attachment: Theory, Research and Clincal Applications*. 2nd ed. pp. 3–22. New York: The Guildford Press.

De Wolff, M., and van Ijzendoorn, M.H. (1997). Sensitivity and attachment: A meta-analysis on parental antecedents of infant attachment. *Child Development, 68*, 571–591.

Fearon, R., Bakermans-Kranenburg, M.J, van IJzendoorn, M.H, Lapsley, A.M, and Roisman, G.I. (2010). The significance of insecure attachment and disorganization in the development of children s externalizing behavior: a meta-analytic study. *Child Development, 81*, 435–456.

Fearon, P., Shmueli-Goetz, Y., Viding, E., Fonagy, P., and Plomin, R. (2014). Genetic and environmental influences on adolescent attachment. *Journal of child psychology and psychiatry, and allied disciplines, 55*, 1033–1041.

Groh, A.M., Roisman, G.I., van IJzendoorn, M.H., Bakermans-Kranenburg, M.J., and Fearon, R. (2012). The significance of insecure and disorganized attachment for children's internalizing symptoms: a meta-analytic study. *Child Development, 83*, 591–610.

Groh, A.M., Fearon, R.P., Bakermans-Kranenburg, M.J., van Ijzendoorn, M.H., Steele, R.D, and Roisman, G.I. (2014). The significance of attachment security for children's social competence with peers: a meta-analytic study. *Attach Hum Dev, 16*, 103–136.

Juffer, F., Bakermans-Kranenburg, M.J, and van IJzendoorn, M.H. (2008). Promoting positive parenting: an attachment-based intervention, 19, 238. New York, NY: Taylor & Francis Group/Lawrence Erlbaum Associates. Monographs in parenting series.

Lyons-Ruth, K. (2015). Commentary: should we move away from an attachment framework for understanding disinhibited social engagement disorder (DSED)? A commentary on Zeanah and Gleason. *Journal of child psychology and psychiatry, and allied disciplines, 56*, 223–227.

Lyons-Ruth, K., Bronfman, E., and Parsons, E. (1999). Atypical attachment in infancy and early childhood among children at developmental risk. IV. Maternal frightened, frightening, or atypical behavior and disorganized infant attachment patterns. *Monographs of the Society for Research in Child Development, 64*, 67–96; discussion 213–220.

Main, M., and Hesse, E. (1990). Parents' unresolved traumatic experiences are related to infant disorganized attachment status: is frightened and/or frightening parental behavior the linking mechanism? In: Greenberg, M.T., Cicchetti, D., (Eds.), *Attachment in the Preschool Years: Theory, Research, and Intervention The John D and Catherine T MacArthur Foundation series on mental health and development*. xix. Chicago, IL: University of Chicago Press. pp. 161–182

Marvin, R.S., and Britner, P.A. (2008). Normative development: the ontogeny of attachment. In: Cassidy, J., Shaver, P.R., (Eds.), *The Handbook of Attachment: Theory, Research and Clincal Applications*. 2nd ed. New York: The Guildford Press. pp. 269–294

Moss, E., Dubois-Comtois, K., Cyr, C., Tarabulsy, G.M., St-Laurent, D., and Bernier, A. (2011). Efficacy of a home-visiting intervention aimed at improving maternal sensitivity, child attachment, and behavioral outcomes for maltreated children: a randomized control trial. *Development and Psychopathology, 23*, 195–210.

NICE. (2015). Children's attachment: attachment in children and young people who are adopted from care, in care or at high risk of going into care. London: National Institute for Health and Care Excellence.

Rutter, M., Kreppner, J., and Sonuga-Barke, E. (2009). Emanuel Miller Lecture: Attachment insecurity, disinhibited attachment, and attachment disorders: where do research findings leave the concepts? *J Child Psychol Psychiatry, 50*, 529–543.

Schneider, B.H., Atkinson, L., and Tardif, C. (2001). Child-parent attachment and children's peer relations: A quantitative review. *Dev Psychol, 37*, 86–100.

Solomon, J., and George, C. (2008). The measurement of attachment security and related constructs in infancy and early childhood. In: Cassidy, J., Shaver, P.R. (Eds.), *The Handbook of Attachment: Theory, Research and Clincal Applications*. 2nd ed. New York: The Guildford Press. pp. 383–416

Van-Ijzendoorn, M.H, Kroonenberg, P.M. (1988). Cross-cultural patterns of attachment: a meta-analysis of the strange situation. *Child Development, 59*, 147–156.

Van-Ijzendoorn, M.H., Schuengel, C., and Bakermans-Kranenburg, M.J. (1999). Disorganized attachment in early childhood: meta-analysis of precursors, concomitants and sequelae. *Dev Psychopathol, 11*, 225–249.

Zeanah, C.H., and Gleason, M.M. (2015). Annual research review: attachment disorders in early childhood–clinical presentation, causes, correlates, and treatment. *Journal of child psychology and psychiatry, and allied disciplines, 56*, 207–222.

5

MATERNAL REPRESENTATIONS IN PREGNANCY

Importance of the mothers' relationship with their unborn babies

Jane Barlow

During the past two decades, there has been increasing recognition of the importance of the developing relationship with the unborn baby in terms of its association with parenting in the postnatal period. Pregnancy is recognised to be a unique period in the sense that the parent's representations of self and others (i.e. their conscious and unconscious mental images) are reactivated and reorganised in response to the developing relationship with the unborn baby (Stern 1995), and research has focused on three areas in particular: a) representations of the mother's own attachment experiences (e.g. Internal Working Models – Bowlby 1973; 1982); b) representations of her baby, herself as a mother; and her relationship with her own mother; and finally c) a variation of the latter that involves representations of the baby as a person with a mind of their own (otherwise known as 'reflective functioning – RF' or 'mind-mindedness – MM').

This interest in the parent's relationship with the baby during pregnancy is based on research showing that this relationship predicts both the quality of the parent-infant interaction in the postnatal period (e.g. Benoit et al., 1997), and the infant's attachment at 1 year (e.g. Theran et al., 2005). These outcomes are important because parent-infant interaction has been shown to be an important predictor of infant attachment security (De Woolf, 1997), and attachment security has been found to be significantly associated with better outcomes in childhood across all developmental domains (Sroufe, 2005), while an insecure or disorganised attachment is associated with later developmental problems (Fearon et al., 2010) and psychopathology (Steele & Siever, 2010).

This chapter summarises what the research now tells us about the relationship between representations about the baby in pregnancy, and later outcomes postnatally, specifically parent-infant interaction, and infant attachment security at 12 months. The paper begins by summarising some of the key tools by which such prenatal representations are measured, and goes on to examine what the research tells us about the relationship between such representations about the baby in pregnancy, and later outcomes. The chapter concludes by examining the implications for practice by key groups of practitioners working with pregnant women.

Assessment of prenatal attachment and representations of the unborn child

A range of both interview (e.g. Working Model of the Child Interview – Zeanah 1986) and parent-report (e.g. Child Concept Questionnaire – Gloger-Tippelt 1992) tools have been developed to examine the mother's mental representations of her unborn baby, and this section examines two of the most commonly used interview measures.

The Working Model of the Child Interview (WMCI) (Zeanah et al., 1986), which is the most frequently used measure of representations, is a semi-structured interview comprising 28 initial probes, to examine the parent's representations or working model of their relationship to a particular child either pre- or postbirth. It identifies three categories of relationship – 'Balanced'; 'Disengaged' or 'Distorted'. Women who are described as 'Balanced', for example, can provide rich and detailed information about their experiences of their pregnancies, and these narratives are on the whole highly coherent. These pregnant women talk fluently not only about their positive thoughts and feelings about their unborn baby but also their negative feelings. Women who are 'Disengaged', however, appear to be uninterested in the unborn baby or their relationship with him or her. They also show little interest in what their babies' future traits and behaviours might look like, or in themselves as mothers. Women described as 'Distorted' tend to express intrusive or tangential thoughts about their own experiences as children, and these women also often view their unborn baby primarily as an extension of themselves or their partner (Levendosky, 2011: 11).

The Pregnancy Interview (PI) (Slade, Grunebaum, Huganir, & Reeves, 1987; Slade, 2007) is a semi-structured clinical interview with 39 questions and probes, developed to assess the mothers reflective functioning (RF) about her baby. The interview, which is administered during the third trimester, assesses a variety of aspects of the mother's view of her emotional experience with pregnancy and her expectations and fantasies regarding her future relationship with her child. Mothers are asked to describe their current relationship to the fetus as well as what they imagine the baby will be like. In addition, the interview aims to capture the mother's prenatal representations of herself as a caregiver, focusing in particular on the mother's capacity to identify with, respond to, and anticipate the needs of her fetus at present and her newborn in the near future. In contrast to the WMCI (with classifications as balanced, disengaged or distorted), the parent development interview (PDI) produces an overall RF score ranging from 1 to 9 with scores of less than 5 suggesting low RF.

Maternal representations in pregnancy

The next section examines findings from longitudinal studies that have examined the association between a) maternal representations of the baby in pregnancy or

b) maternal RF/MM in pregnancy, and parent-infant interaction and/or infant attachment security.

a) Maternal representations in pregnancy and later outcomes

A number of studies have examined the concordance (i.e. association) between maternal representations in pregnancy and infant attachment security at 12–14 months postnatal as measured by the Strange Situation Procedure (SSP) (Ainsworth, Bell, & Stayton, 1971). Most of these studies used the WMCI to classify maternal prenatal representations with one study (Crawford & Benoit, 2009) adding a further 'Disrupted' category and another an 'Irrational Fear' category (Atkinson et al., 2009), to the existing 'Balanced', 'Disengaged' and 'Distorted' categories. These additional categories are aimed at capturing the type of representations that are associated with caregiver behaviours that are atypical or anomalous and have been found to be associated with a 'Disorganised' attachment (Madigan et al., 2006).

A number of studies that have used the standard three WMCI classifications (Benoit, Parker, & Zeanah, 1997; Huth-Bocks, 2004; 2011; Atkinson et al., 2009; Madigan et al. 2015) showed strong associations between a 'Balanced' WMCI and 'secure' attachment classification postnatal, although one study showed a borderline significant association between the overall WMCI and statistically significant (SS) classifications (Atkinson et al., 2009) and one study showed concordance only when the two insecure categories (i.e. Avoidant and Anxious/Ambivalent) were combined, due to a range of contextual risk factors, including maternal depression and infant behaviours (Hugh-Bocks et al., 2011) and domestic violence (Huth-Bocks et al., 2004). The two studies that used the additional 'Disrupted' or 'Irrational Fear' categories as part of the WMCI showed that they both predicted a 'Disorganised' attachment classification in the infant at 12–14 months (Atkinson et al., 2009; Crawford & Benoit, 2009).

A number of studies have examined the association between maternal representations in pregnancy and parent-infant interaction postnatal. Representations in pregnancy were assessed using a range of interviews (e.g. WMCI; WMCI-Disrupted; PI; Interview of Maternal Representations During Pregnancy – IRMAG; IRMAG-Revised) and self-report (e.g. Child Concept Questionnaire) tools, and parent-infant interaction was assessed using a range of standardised measures to assess the quality of such interaction postnatal (e.g. Emotional Availability Scale – EAS; Atypical Maternal Behaviour Instrument for Assessment and Classification – AMBIANCE; Munich Communication Diagnostic Scale, Still Face). Some of the samples included in these studies were high-risk in terms of involving women who had, for example, been exposed to intimate partner violence (Theran et al., 2005), who were drug-using (Flykt et al., 2012), or at depressive, psychosocial or cumulative risk (Tambelli Odorisio, & Lucarelli, 2014).

The results of this diverse set of studies suggest that there is a consistent association between representations in pregnancy and parent-infant interaction postnatal, irrespective of how such representations are measured (i.e. parent report or interview technique). For example, the findings of the two studies that used the WMCI (Theran et al., 2005) or WMCI-D (Crawford et al., 2009) suggest that while 'Balanced' representations are associated with more optimal interaction; affective or emotional deactivation in pregnancy as indicated by a 'Disengaged' classification is on the whole associated with more controlling interactions; while affective or emotional over-activation as indicated by a 'Distorted' classification is associated with more hostile interactions; and unresolved trauma as indicated by a 'Disrupted' classification is associated with 'frightened' and 'frightening' interactions with the infant.

Most studies that have examined this area have found an association between such representations and parent-infant interaction, suggesting that as with attachment, such representations are, once again, a significant predictor of outcome in the postnatal period.

b) Maternal RF/MM in pregnancy and later outcomes

As suggested above, maternal RF and mind-mindedness (MM) represent slightly different forms of representation about the baby from those that are assessed using the WMCI. Specifically, RF and MM focus more explicitly on the mother's views about the baby in terms of the baby's personhood or mind, and in the case of the Parent Interview, produces an RF score ranging from 0 to 14 as opposed to the categories that are used with the WMCI. A number of studies have shown that maternal RF (Slade 2005) and MM (Meins, Fernyhough, Fradley & Tuckey, 2001) are associated with parent-infant interaction (Slade et al., 2005; Grienenberger, Kelly and Slade, 2005) or attachment postnatal (Meins et al., 2001; 2012). But what is the relationship between such functioning in pregnancy and parenting postnatal? A small number of studies have measured the association between RF (e.g. Graf, 2000; Ueng-McHale, 2009; Perry et al., 2015) or MM (e.g. Arnott and Meins, 2005) in pregnancy and parent-infant interaction postnatal, but there are currently no studies of its impact prenatal on infant attachment security.

One study showed no significant associations between RF in pregnancy and AMBIANCE scores at 4–6 months postpartum (p = 0.46) for a sample of women half of whom were in receipt of an intervention, but analysis with only a small number of control group women (n = 18) found that RF in pregnancy was significantly associated with the quality of affective communication between control mothers and babies at 4 months of age, although 59 per cent were still rated as having interaction characterised as being 'disrupted'. This suggests that the degree of disruption may be predicted by this measure antenatal, but not the proportion of women classified as Disrupted (Ueng-McHale, 2009).

One further study also coded maternal affect in the PI based on one domain of the PI only (i.e. developing representations of the baby), and found an association that was borderline significant between negative maternal affect prenatally and insecure attachment. Thus mothers preoccupied by feelings of fear, anxiety or anger in pregnancy, as opposed to those whose feelings were characterised primarily by joy and hope, were less likely to have a securely attached child at 14 months (Graf, 2000).

One study that used a measure of MM in pregnancy found that predictions about the child's characteristics in pregnancy were associated with more appropriate comments about internal states in interaction postnatal. These findings were for mothers only. The results for fathers showed somewhat counter intuitively that antenatal predictions about the unborn child's characteristics were positively associated with misinterpretations of the infant's thoughts and feelings postnatal (see next section for further discussion).

A study that included women on an opiate substitution programme found no relationship between the PI and emotional availability at 3 and 6 months (Perry et al., 2015).

Pathways – the intergenerational transmission of attachment

The above research suggests that the mother's relationship with the baby in pregnancy is associated with both parent–infant interaction and with infant attachment postnatally, with more optimal ratings of the relationship in pregnancy being associated with better interaction and more secure attachment.

This is consistent with research that shows a high level of stability for such representations across the perinatal period. For example, a recent systematic review of the WMCI (Vreeswijk et al. 2015) found a significant association between prenatal and postnatal representations. However, this review also found some significant differences in the distributions of mothers' prenatal and postnatal classifications, with mothers having more balanced representations and less disengaged representations in the postnatal period than they did in the prenatal period (Vreeswijk et al., 2015). This suggests that some women change classification over this period, possibly as a consequence of life events such as a traumatic birth, or the joy of the relationship with the baby postbirth. Theran et al. (2005) found that women who were classified as 'Balanced' prenatally and 'Unbalanced' postnatally had better interactions with their baby than those who were classified as 'Unbalanced' at both timepoints, suggesting a buffering impact for such representations in pregnancy even if they are not maintained.

Although the evidence is somewhat mixed, representations of the baby have been found to be influenced by a range of factors (e.g. presence of two to three children under 7 years in the household and planning of the current pregnancy; childhood maltreatment; domestic violence; prenatal health behaviours; maternal education, social support and substance use). Recently Vreeswijk et al. (2015) also found that mothers having more risk factors during pregnancy were more likely to have distorted than balanced or disengaged prenatal representations.

However, possibly one of the most significant factors affecting the mother's relationship with the baby in pregnancy is the mother's own attachment status. A number of studies have measured maternal representations of the mother's own attachment (i.e. her internal working models) using the Adult Attachment Inventory (AAI) and her baby's attachment in the postnatal period (e.g. Fonagy, Steele &

Steele, 1991; Shah et al., 2010; Madigan et al., 2015). The results show a strong association between maternal representations of the mother's own attachment and her infant's attachment at 12 months (ibid.). For example, one study showed that 75 per cent of the time the mother's representations of attachment predicted infant attachment at 1 year (Fonagy, Steele & Steele, 1991).[1] This phenomenon is known as the 'intergenerational transmission of attachment', and the research presented suggests that maternal representations in pregnancy may play a significant role in this intergenerational transmission process. This has in fact been confirmed by a recent study (Madigan et al., 2015) that examined whether mothers' representations of their own attachment history as measured by the Adult Attachment Interview (AAI) exert an impact on infant attachment via the child-specific representations of that relationship as measured by the WMCI. This study showed that consistent with this 'prototype' hypothesis, there was a high level of correspondence between mothers' AAI and infant attachment using the SSP, and that these were fully accounted for by scores on the WMCI prenatal but not postnatal. Another recent study also showed an association between maternal attachment as measured by the AAI and maternal-fetal attachment (MFA) (Alhusen et al., 2013).

There is also evidence from the included studies that representations in pregnancy related to trauma history play a role in the transmission of trauma from one generation to the next through its impact on the interaction. For example, Ahifs-Dunn (2015) found that women classified as disrupted in terms of their prenatal representations using the WMCI-D, had more severe histories of childhood maltreatment and intimate partner violence in pregnancy; however, only severity of childhood interpersonal trauma was associated with disruption in maternal prenatal representations of the child, which in turn was associated with less secure infant attachment.

Implications for practice

This research has a number of important implications for practice. First, it points to the potential importance of assessing maternal representations in pregnancy, to identify and intervene with those women whose representations or reflective functioning are of concern in the third trimester of pregnancy. This could involve the use of simple screening questionnaires such as the Prenatal Parental Reflective Functioning Questionnaire (P-RFQ: Pajulo et al., 2015), which is a brief instrument (i.e. 14 items) that can be implemented by universal healthcare practitioners such as midwives, health visitors, and public health nurses, or the Antenatal Promotional Interview at 28 weeks, which also has probes aimed at assessing this relationship.

It also points to the need to develop and evaluate brief methods of supporting women who present with such classifications. These could range from the use of simple public health type approaches that involve sharing information with pregnant women about the importance of the developing relationship with the unborn baby (see for example the website – Getting to Know Your Baby – www.your-baby.org.uk) and simple techniques to promote the relationship (e.g. talking to baby; stroking the bump etc.), to the use of more intensive methods of working with women who have a 'Disrupted' classification, and may be presenting with mental health problems and/or substance dependency/history of trauma. In these circumstances, mentalisation-based programmes such as Minding the Baby (Sadler et al., 2013), that begin in pregnancy and continue into the postnatal period, may be needed.

Conclusion

The research summarised in this chapter suggests that prenatal representations of the baby are associated with parent–infant interaction and infant attachment security, and that reflective functioning/mind-mindedness are also associated with parent–infant interaction.

These findings have important implications for practice because they suggest that developments in pregnancy in terms of the mother's relationship with the unborn baby have a strong influence on her later parenting, and thereby on the infant's attachment security, the latter being strongly associated with the long-term development of the child. Perhaps mostly importantly, they suggest the need for practitioners to work during pregnancy to explore the woman's thoughts and feelings about the fetus/unborn baby, and to work to support those women about whom there are concerns. The 28-week Promotional Interview conducted as part of the Healthy Child Programme, provides a prime opportunity to do this.

Key messages

- Pregnancy is an important period in terms of the developing relationship between the parent and unborn baby, although most of the research to date focuses only on the mother-baby relationship.
- There is a significant association between the relationship that is developed in pregnancy and both mother-infant interaction and infant attachment postnatally.
- The relationship with the developing baby should be assessed in pregnancy to identify women in need of additional support.

References

Ainsworth, M.D.S., Bell, S.M., & Stayton, D.J. (1971). Individual differences in strange situation behavior of one-year-olds. In H. R. Schaffer (Ed.), *The Origins of Human Social Relations*. New York: Academic Press.

Ahlfs-Dunn, S. (2015). The Impact of Maternal Interpersonal Trauma on Infant Social-Emotional Development: The Critical Role of Disrupted Maternal Representations of the Child. Eastern Michigan University, ProQuest Dissertations Publishing, 3726183.

Arnott, B., & Meins, E. (2008). Continuity in mind-mindedness from pregnancy to the first year of life. *Infant Behavior and Development, 31,* 647–654.

Atkinson, L., Leung, E., Goldberg, S., Benoit, D., Poulton, L., Myhal, N., & Blokland, K. (2009). Attachment and selective attention: Disorganization and emotional Stroop reaction time. *Development and Psychopathology, 21,* 99–126.

Barlow, J., & van Bakel H.J.A. (forthcoming). Maternal representations in pregnancy and concordance with parent-infant interaction and attachment postnatal: Findings of a systematic review.

Benoit, D., Parker, K.C.H., & Zeanah, C.H. (1997). Mothers' representations of their infants assessed prentally: Stability and association with infants' attachment classifications. *Journal of Child Psychology and Psychiatry, 38*(3), 307–313.

Bowlby, J. (1973). *Separation.* New York: Basic Books.

Bowlby, J. (1982). *Attachment.* 2nd ed. New York: Basic Books.

Bronfman, E., Madigan, S., & Lyons-Ruth, K. (1992–2009). *Atypical Maternal Behavior Instrument for Assessment and Classification (AMBIANCE). Manual for Coding Disrupted Affective Communication.* Cambridge, MA: Department of Psychiatry, Harvard Medical School; Unpublished manual.

Crawford, A., & Benoit, D. (2009). Caregivers' disrupted representations of the unborn child preict later infant-caregiver disorganized attachment and disrupted interactions. *Infant Mental Health Journal, 30*(2), 124–144.

De Wolff, M.S., & van Ijzendoorn, M.H. (1997). Sensitivity and attachment: A meta-analysis on parental antecedents of infant attachment security. *Child Development,* 68, 604–609.

Department of Health. (2009). Healthy Child Programme: Pregnancy and the First 5 Years of Life. https://www.gov.uk/government/publications/healthy-child-programme-pregnancy-and-the-first-5-years-of-life: accessed June 16th 2016.

Fearon, R.P., Bakermans-Kranenburg, M.J., Van IJzendoorn, M.H, Lapsley, A.M., & Roisman, G.I. (2010). The significance of insecure attachment and disorganization in the development of children's externalizing behavior: A meta-analytic study. *Child Development, 81,* 435–456.

Flykt, M., Punamaki, R.L., Belt, R., Biringen, Z., Salo, S., Posa, T., & Pajulo, M. (2012). Maternal representations and emotional availability among drug-abusing and nonusing mothers and their infants. *Infant Mental Health Journal, 33*(2), 123–138.

Fonagy, P., Steel, H., & Steele, M. (1991). Maternal representations of attachment during pregnancy predict the organization of infant-mother attachment at one year of age. *Child Development, 62,* 891–905.

Gloger-Tippelt, G. (1992). Die Entwicklung eines Personenschemas vom ersten Kind. Thesis, University of Heidelberg.

Graf, F.G. (1999). *Affect in maternal representations and infant-mother attachment.* A dissertation submitted to the Graduate Faculty in Psychology in partial fulfillment of the requirements for the degree of Doctor of Philosophy, The City University of New York.

Huth-Bocks, A.C., Theran, S.A., Levendosky, A.A., & Bogat, G.A. (2011). A social-contextual understanding of concordance and discordance between maternal prenatal representations of the infant and infant-mother attachment. *Infant Mental Health Journal, 34*(4), 405–426.

Levendosky, A.A., Bogat, G.A., & Huth-Bocks, A.C. (2011).The influence of domestic violence on the development of the attachment relationship between mother and young child. *Psychoanalytic Psychology, 28*(4), 512–527.

Lyons-Ruth K, Bronfman E, & Parsons, E. (1999). Maternal frightened, frightening, or atypical behavior and disorganized infant attachment patterns. In J.I. Vondra, D. Barnett, (Eds.), *Monographs of the Society for Research in Child Development.* 3, Serial No. 258. Vol. 64. pp. 67–96. Atypical patterns of infant attachment: Theory, research, and current directions.

Madigan, S., Bakermans-Kranenburg, M.J., van Ijzendoorn, M.H., Moran, G., Pederson, D.R., & Benoit, D. (2006). Unresolved states of mind, anomalous parenting behaviour, and disorganized attachment: A review and meta-analysis of a transmission gap. *Attachment and Human Development, 8,* 89–111.

Madigan, S., Hawkins, E., Plamondon, A., Moran, G., & Benoit, D. (2015). Maternal representations and infant attachment: an examination of the prototype hypothesis. *Infant Mental Health Journal, 36*, 459–468.

Mayes, L.C, & Leckman, J.F. (2007). Parental representations and subclinical changes in postpartum mood. *Infant Mental Health Journal, 28*, 281–295.

Meins, E., Fernyhough, C., deRosnay, M., Arnott, B., Leekam, S.R., & Turner, M. (2012). Mind-mindedness as a multidimensional construct: Appropriate and nonattuned mind-related comments independently predict infant–mother attachment in a socially diverse sample. *Infancy, 17*(4), 393–415.

Meins, E., Fernyhough, C., Fradley E., & Tuckey, M. (2001). Rethinking maternal sensitivity: Mothers' comments on infants' mental processes predict security of attachment at 12 months. *Journal of Child Psychology and Psychiatry, 42*, 637–648.

Mercer, R.T., Ferketich, S.L., May, K., Rolizzotto, R., Mazloom, E., & Merkatz, I. (1991). The effect of fetal movement counting on maternal attachment to the fetus. *American Journal of Obstetrics and Gynecology, 165*, 988–991.

Muller, M.E, & Mercer, R.T. (1993). Development of the prenatal attachment inventory. *Western Journal of Nursing Research, 15*, 199–215.

Pajulo, M., Tolvanen, M., Karlsson, L., Halme-Chowdhury, E., Öst, C., Luyten, P., Mayes, L., & Karlsson, H. (2015). The Prenatal Parental Reflective Functioning Questionnaire: Exploring factor structure and construct validity of a new measure in the Finn brain birth cohort pilot study. *Infant Mental Health Journal, 36*(4):399–414.

Perry N., Newman L.K., Hunter, M., & Dunlop, A. (2015). Improving antenatal risk assessment in women exposed to high risks. *Clinical Child Psychology and Psychiatry, 20*(1), 84–105.

Sadler, L.S., Slade, A., Close, N., Webb, D.L., Simpson, T., Fennie, K., & Mayes, L.C. (2013). Minding the baby: Enhancing reflectiveness to improve early health and relationship outcomes in an interdisciplinary home-visiting program. *Infant Mental Health Journal, 34*, 391–405.

Shah, P.E., Fonagy, P., & Strathearn, L. (2010). Is attachment transmitted across generations? The plot thickens. *Clinical child psychology and psychiatry, 15*(3), 329–345.

Slade, A., Grunebaum, L., Huganir, L., & Reeves, M. (1987, 2002, 2011). *The Pregnancy Interview, revised*. The Psychological Center, City College of New York.

Slade, A. (2007). *The Pregnancy Interview, Revised*. Manuscript.

Sroufe, L.A. (2005). Attachment and development: A prospective, longitudinal study from birth to adulthood. *Attachment & Human Development, 7*(4), 349–367.

Steele, H., & Siever, L. (2010). An attachment perspective on borderline personality disorder: Advances in gene–environment considerations. *Current Psychiatry Reports, 12*(1), 61–67.

Stern, D. (1995). *The Motherhood Constellation: A Unified View of Parent–Infant Psychotherapy*. New York, NY: Basic Books.

Tambelli, R., Odorisio, F., & Lucarelli, L. (2014). Prenatal and postnatal maternal representations in nonrisk and at-risk parenting: Exploring the influence on mother-infant feeding interactions. *Infant Mental Health Journal, 35*(4), 376–388.

Theran, S.A., Levendosky, A.A, Bogat, G.A, & Huth-Bocks, A.C. (2005). Stability and change in mothers' internal representations of their infants over time. *Attachment & Human Development, 7*(3), 253–268.

Thun-Hohenstein, L., Wienerroither, C., Schreuer, M., Seim, G., & Wienerroither, H. (2008). Antenatal mental representations about the child and mother-infant interaction at three months post partum. *European Child and Adolescent Psychiatry, 17*, 9–19.

Ueng-McHale, J.Y. (2009). Parental Reflective Functioning and Maternal Representations of the Child in Pregnancy: Their Influence on Affective Communication between Mothers and their Young Infants in Families At Risk. A dissertation submitted to the Graduate Faculty in Psychology in partial fulfillment of the requirements for the degree of Doctor of Philosophy. The City University of New York.

Vreeswijk, C.M.J.M., Maas, J.B.M, & Van Bakel, H.J.A. (2012). Parental representations: A systematic review of the Working Model of the Child Interview. *Infant Mental Health Journal, 33*(3), 314–328.

Zeanah, C.H., Keener, M.A., & Anders, T.F. (1986). Adolescent mothers' perceptions of their infants before and after birth. *American Journal of Orthopsychiatry, 57*, 351–360.

6

KEEPING THE BABY IN MIND

New insights into the link between maternal childhood trauma, mental health problems in pregnancy and outcomes for the child

Susan Pawlby, Dominic Plant, Carmine M. Pariante

Our clinical work on the Channi Kumar Mother and Baby Unit (MBU) at the South London and Maudsley NHS Trust, and our research conducted in the Section of Perinatal Psychiatry at the Institute of Psychiatry, Psychology and Neuroscience at King's College London, have provided evidence for the link between maternal childhood trauma, perinatal psychiatric disorders and outcomes for the offspring, revealing the true emotional costs of trauma and mental health problems in the perinatal period – and in pregnancy in particular. Indeed, using prospective data from the South London Child Development Study (SLCDS) (1986–2015) we have demonstrated how the offspring of women who were maltreated in their childhoods and became depressed in pregnancy, are at risk of maltreatment and psychopathology themselves. The antenatal period provides a window of opportunity for women to discuss their own childhood experiences, as they themselves become mothers.

Child maltreatment constitutes a major public health issue (World Health Organization, 2015). It is defined as acts of commission or omission towards children (commonly defined as up to 18 years of age) that cause significant harm or the potential or threat of harm to children's development and health. The most widely acknowledged forms of child maltreatment include i) physical abuse, ii) sexual abuse, iii) emotional or psychological abuse and iv) neglect (Cicchetti & Toth, 2005; Gilbert et al., 2009; Norman et al., 2012). In England over 49,000 children were subjects of a child protection plan as recorded in 2015: over 22,000 for being exposed to neglect, over 18,000 for being exposed to emotional abuse, over 3,000 for being exposed to physical abuse and over 2,000 for being exposed to sexual abuse (Department for Education, 2015). It is estimated that up to 80 per cent of acts of child maltreatment are perpetrated by parents and guardians, and multiple abuse types and neglect are often found to co-occur (Gilbert et al., 2009).

Child maltreatment and adult psychopathology

Recent research has investigated the long-term psychological sequelae of child maltreatment. An established link between child maltreatment and adult mental health problems has been documented in the literature. Study findings have indicated that child maltreatment is associated with adult occurrence of major depressive disorder (MDD), post-traumatic stress disorder (PTSD), substance use disorders, antisocial personality disorder, borderline personality disorder and suicide attempts (Bierer et al., 2003; Bifulco et al., 2002; Collishaw, et al., 2007; Green et al., 2010; Norman et al., 2012). The effects of child maltreatment appear to be persistent. For example a recent meta-analysis revealed that it is associated with an elevated risk for developing recurrent and chronic MDD through adulthood (Nanni et al., 2012). Moreover, child maltreatment has been identified as a key risk factor for mood disorders at vulnerable life stages such as the perinatal period in women.

As well as effects on aspects of adult mental health, child maltreatment has also been shown to predict poorer adult functioning, further highlighting its long-term debilitating potential (McLaughlin et al., 2010).

Childhood maltreatment and psychopathology in the perinatal period: Generation 1

Evidence from our clinical work with mothers with severe mental illness (SMI) on the Channi Kumar MBU at the Bethlem Royal Hospital, South London and Maudsley NHS Foundation Trust and King's Health Partners in London supports and extends these findings. The MBU is a 13-bedded in-patient unit where mothers with schizophrenia, bipolar disorder, psychosis, severe depression and anxiety disorders who either relapse or become ill for the first time in pregnancy or following the birth can be admitted with their unborn or new baby.

Of a representative group of 50 mothers with SMI admitted to the unit between January 2013 and December 2014, 78 per cent had suffered one or more forms of abuse as derived from the Childhood Experience of Care and Abuse Questionnaire (CECA-Q, Bifulco et al., 2005). Of these women 39 per cent had experienced physical, 35 per cent sexual and 63 per cent emotional abuse (Table 6.1). In contrast, data from a group of 45 mothers with no past or current psychiatric disorder from the same catchment area, recruited in pregnancy and taking part in a prospective longitudinal study in Psychiatric Research and Motherhood (PRAM), showed that 24 per cent had experienced some form of abuse: 2 per cent physical, 11 per cent sexual and 13 per cent emotional. MBU mothers were therefore nine times more likely to have experienced some form of abuse (physical, sexual or emotional) than the comparison mothers (Vaillancourt, 2015). Moreover, compared with the comparison group, the MBU mothers' mean scores on scales of maternal and paternal neglect and maternal and paternal antipathy were significantly higher (Table 6.1).

TABLE 6.1 Group differences in experience of childhood abuse

	MBU N = 50	Comparison N = 45	Group effect
Physical Abuse, %	39	2	$\chi^2_{(1)}$ p<.001, OR 28.39, CI 3.62–222.79
Sexual Abuse, %	35	11	$\chi^2_{(1)}$ p = .008, OR 4.26 CI 1.43–12.70
Emotional Abuse, %	63	13	$\chi^2_{(1)}$ p < .001, OR 9.83, CI 3.49–27.67
Any Abuse, %	78	24	$\chi^2_{(1)}$ p < .001, OR 9.35, CI 3.56–24.51
	MBU N = 50	Comparison N = 41	Group effect
	Mean (SD)	Mean (SD)	
Maternal Neglect[a]	21.70 (11.89)	11.27 (4.79)	$t_{(67)} = -5.67$, p < .001
Paternal Neglect[b]	24.20 (11.17)	13.28 (6.28)	$t_{(80)} = -5.86$, p < .001
Maternal Antipathy[c]	23.98 (10.69)	14.63 (6.90)	$t_{(83)} = -5.00$, p < .001
Paternal Antipathy[d]	24.36 (12.15)	12.25 (4.56)	$t_{(65)} = -6.50$, p < .001

[a] N = 91 (MBU: 50, Comparison: 41); [b] N = 90 (49, 41); [c] N = 90 (50, 40); [d] N = 90 (50, 40)

Completion of the CECA-Q while on the mother and baby unit enabled women who had suffered childhood abuse to disclose details of these difficult experiences, sometimes for the very first time, in a safe environment, and work through some of the psychological issues that had surfaced, as they themselves became mothers.

We have also demonstrated the increased risk of depression in pregnancy among women who have experienced childhood abuse in the South London Child Development Study (SLCDS), a prospective, longitudinal community study begun in 1986 when the women were pregnant (Plant et al., 2013). Of 125 women seen when the offspring were 16 year old, 22 (17.6 per cent) reported having experienced abuse in their childhoods, and 26 (20.8 per cent) mothers overall met criteria for a clinical diagnosis of depression at 36 weeks of pregnancy. Of the 103 nonmaltreated mothers, 12.6 per cent were depressed during pregnancy. By contrast, of the mothers who experienced childhood maltreatment, a significantly greater proportion (59.1 per cent) was depressed antenatally [$\chi^2_{(1)}$ = 23.76, p < 0.001, odds ratio (OR) 10.00, 95 per cent confidence interval (CI) 3.57–28.01]. Logistic regressions revealed that mothers' experiences of childhood maltreatment significantly predicted their antenatal depression (b = 2.30, Wald statistic = 19.21, $df_{(1)}$, p < 0.001). This finding remained unchanged when controlling for other risk factors such as the mothers' own juvenile antisocial symptoms, their history of psychiatric problems and their relationship status during pregnancy, none of which contributed significantly to the explained variance when in the presence of maternal childhood maltreatment. Maternal experience of maltreatment in childhood was the single most powerful predictor of the later occurrence of clinical depression during pregnancy. Women who had experienced maltreatment as children were 10 times more likely than nonmaltreated women to become depressed in pregnancy. A recent systematic review (Biaggi et al., 2016) confirmed that a history of childhood abuse was one of the most relevant factors associated with depression in pregnancy, along with lack of a partner or of social support, domestic violence, a personal history of psychiatric illness, an unplanned or unwanted pregnancy, adverse life events and high-perceived stress, present or past pregnancy complications and pregnancy loss.

Antenatal depression and offspring psychopathology: Generations 1 to 2

Over the last decade, a handful of longitudinal studies have demonstrated an association between maternal depression in pregnancy and the development of depressive psychopathology in exposed offspring from 13 through to 18 years of age (Pawlby et al., 2009; Pearson et al., 2013; O'Donnell et al., 2014). In the SLCDS we have now been able to show that this association extends into young adulthood. Offspring exposed to maternal depression in pregnancy were 3.4 times [95 per cent CI (1.5, 8.1), $\chi^2_{(1)}$ = 8.4, p = 0.004] more likely than those not so exposed to be depressed at the age of 25 years. Of the 35 offspring exposed to maternal depression in utero, 20 (57.1 per cent) met DSM-IV criteria for a clinical diagnosis of depression; in contrast, of the 68 nonexposed offspring, only 19 (27.9 per cent) met criteria for a depression diagnosis. The mean number of depressive symptoms was also significantly higher among prenatally exposed offspring (M = 3.4, s.d. = 3.0) compared to nonprenatally exposed offspring (M = 1.7, s.d. = 2.8, z = 72.8, p = 0.004). Notably, we did not find that exposure to maternal depression after birth contributed to this association. Although there was a high degree of association between maternal depression in pregnancy and depression in the first postnatal year [$\chi^2_{(1)}$ = 11.5, p = 0.001, OR = 4.3, 95 per cent CI (1.8, 10.4)], we did not find a significant association between maternal depression in the postnatal period and offspring depression in adulthood [$\chi^2_{(1)}$ = 2.1, p = 0.15, OR = 1.8, 95 per cent CI (0.8, 4.2)].

However, offspring exposure to maternal depression during childhood (1–16 years) was associated significantly with offspring adulthood depression [OR = 4.2, 95 per cent CI (1.8, 10.2), $\chi^2_{(1)}$ = 11.1, p = 0.001]. Analysis suggested a 'chronicity' effect, whereby offspring exposed to maternal depression over a greater number of developmental periods during childhood experienced more severe depression in adulthood (n = 100, rs = 0.31, p < 0.01). The mean number of depressive symptoms among offspring exposed to maternal depression across one developmental period was 3.0 (s.d. = 3.1), among those exposed across two developmental periods (M = 3.3, s.d. = 3.5) and among offspring exposed across all three developmental periods (M = 3.6, s.d. = 3.4). Mothers depressed during the offspring's childhood were significantly more likely to have been depressed during pregnancy, 77.1 per cent, compared to mothers not depressed during the offspring's childhood years, 22.9 per cent [OR = 4.8, 95 per cent CI (1.9, 12.2), $\chi^2_{(1)}$ = 12.0, p < 0.001].

The biological priming that leads from exposure to depression in utero to depression in offspring

Our finding that offspring exposure to maternal depression during pregnancy and not in the first postnatal year is associated with depression in adulthood suggests that exposure to maternal depression specifically during pregnancy represents a unique setting for the intergenerational transmission of risk for depression, which is independent from further exposure to maternal depression after birth.

This account is in line with the theoretical premise of foetal programming, whereby exposure of offspring to an adverse intrauterine environment, can result in changes in foetal brain development in regions relevant to stress reactivity, such as the hypothalamic-pituitary-adrenal (HPA) axis and inflammatory response system. Indeed, HPA axis dysregulation and inflammation are routinely observed in depressed individuals and studies have shown that pregnancy per se is associated with increased maternal HPA axis activity and inflammation, which can be further exacerbated by the experience of depression during this time. Furthermore we have recently shown, in this same cohort, that exposure to maternal prenatal depression predicts significantly elevated offspring inflammation at age 25 (OR = 11.8, p = 0.04), independently of child maltreatment and adulthood depression (Plant et al., 2016). Our findings are exceptional: fetal exposure to maternal depression during pregnancy has effects on immune function that persist for up to a quarter of a century after birth, and potentially explain not only the risk of depression in the offspring of these mothers, but even the risk of physical ill health.

Antenatal depression and offspring maltreatment: Generation 1 to 2

Evidence has also shown that maternal affective disorders in pregnancy are associated with offspring vulnerability to adverse childhood experiences. Lereya and Wolke (2013) found that prenatal maternal depression and anxiety predicted offspring peer victimisation at age 8. In tests for indirect effects, prenatal maternal depression and anxiety were found to lead indirectly to peer victimisation through maladaptive parenting styles and conflict. In the 25-year-old phase of the SLCDS the prevalence of childhood maltreatment among the adult offspring was more than twice as high among those exposed to maternal depression in utero (48.6 per cent), compared to nonexposed offspring, 27.9 per cent, $\chi^2_{(1)}$ = 4.3, p = .038 OR = 2.4, 95 per cent CI (1.0, 5.7). The link between maternal affective disorders in pregnancy and offspring maltreatment is likely attributable to changes in the mothers' caregiving and attachment behaviours and her ability to protect her child, the impact of multiple family adverse factors, such as financial, housing and relationship difficulties, as well as potential foetal programming of a more difficult offspring temperament, all of which could increase vulnerability to being maltreated.

Child maltreatment and psychopathology: Generation 2

The 25-year-old data from the SLCDS showed that offspring exposure to child maltreatment was associated significantly with offspring diagnosis of depression in adulthood [OR = 2.6, 95 per cent CI (1.1, 6.1), $\chi^2_{(1)}$ = 5.2, p = 0.022]. Furthermore there was a positive correlation between the severity of child maltreatment and severity of adulthood depression rated by the number of symptoms (r^s = 0.30, p < 0.01). Analysis revealed that offspring exposed to one form of maltreatment had the lowest number of depressive symptoms (M = 2.6, s.d. = 3.3), while offspring exposed to three forms experienced the greatest number of depressive symptoms (M = 5.5, s.d. = 3.2), indicative of a 'dose-response' relationship.

Pathway from exposure to maternal depression in pregnancy to offspring depression in young adulthood

The prospective, longitudinal nature of the SLCDS has allowed us to examine the pathways from exposure to maternal depression in pregnancy to offspring depression in young adulthood. As we have already shown, further offspring exposure to maternal depression in childhood and exposure to child-maltreatment were both found to be associated with exposure to maternal depression in pregnancy and with depression in young adulthood. Path analyses have shown that exposure to child maltreatment, and not exposure to further episodes of maternal depression during childhood, was a mediating mechanism linking offspring exposure to maternal depression in pregnancy and depression in young adulthood (Plant et al., 2015).

Conclusions and recommendations for interventions

We have come a long way in translating into clinical practice our findings showing that a woman's mental state in pregnancy does have an effect on the next generation. Now women are asked about their mental state in pregnancy (NICE, 2009), perinatal psychiatric services have been vastly improved, and both women and health professionals are more aware of the importance of good mental health and the reduction of stress during pregnancy. However, we still do not appreciate the true costs of depression in pregnancy. These go well beyond the wellbeing of the mother or the short-term health of the baby and project into the offspring adult life – with a long-lasting impact of mother's childhood experiences of trauma onto offspring mental health that spans two generations and up to 30 years of life.

Understanding the true costs of depression in pregnancy is essential for prioritising treatment strategies. Every day, women and their clinicians face the difficult process of weighing up the advantages and disadvantages of starting antidepressant treatment during pregnancy. Emphasis is always on the evidence of potential adverse effects of antidepressants on offspring outcomes (which remains far from conclusive), neglecting the evidence that untreated depression can have negative consequences on offspring outcomes. Moreover depressed pregnant women are more likely to smoke, to drink alcohol and to have less regular antenatal care, and one very recent study that has attempted to adjust for such variables has found no substantial increase in the risk of malformations attributable to antidepressants (Huybrechts et al., 2014).

Where do these studies leave the patients and the professionals? While starting an antidepressant in pregnancy may be perceived as 'an action', carrying moral responsibility (and liability), the alternative 'no action' of leaving a depressed woman untreated may harm the offspring through exposure to toxic life styles and an abnormal *in utero* biology. While nonpharmacological treatments may work in these women (for example, interpersonal psychotherapy, exercise or omega-3 fatty acids), antidepressants will likely remain the mainstream option for moderate to severe depression in pregnancy. 'Not to treat' is no longer the safest choice.

In the next decade we feel sure that we will see a greater appreciation of the value in pregnancy of asking a woman about her mood and about her own childhood experiences, as she herself becomes a mother. Parenthood is perhaps one of the most important demands that we face as adults and yet we have little or no preparation or education in the skills needed, relying largely on what we experienced as children ourselves.

Pregnancy is a time when we can support women who have suffered trauma in their own childhood so that the intergenerational transmission of maltreatment and subsequent mental health difficulties can be prevented.

Recommendations

- Discuss pregnant women's own experiences of childhood care and abuse to help identify women who may need extra antenatal support.
- Train midwives to listen and respond appropriately to any disclosures.
- Ensure that therapeutic resources are available and train specialists to make appropriate referrals for talking therapies for women who disclose traumatic childhood events and have compromised mood.

References

Biaggi, A., Conroy, S., Pawlby, S., & Pariante, C. M. (2016). Identifying the women at risk of antenatal anxiety and depression: a systematic review. *Journal of Affective Disorders, 191*, 62–77.

Bierer, L.M., Yehuda, R., Schmeidler, J., Mitropoulou, V., New, A.S., Silverman, J.M., & Siever, L.J. (2003). Abuse and neglect in childhood: relationship to personality disorder diagnoses. *CNS Spectrums, 8*, 737–754.

Bifulco, A., Moran, P.M., Baines, R., Bunn, A., & Stanford, K. (2002). Exploring psychological abuse in childhood: II. Association with other abuse and adult clinical depression. *Bulletin of the Menninger Clinic, 66*, 241–258.

Bifulco, A., Bernazzani O., Moran P.M., & Jacobs, C. (2005). The childhood experience of care and abuse questionnaire (CECA.Q): validation in a community series. *British Journal of Clinical Psychology, 44*, 563–581.

Choi, K.W., & Sikkema, K.J. (2015). Childhood maltreatment and perinatal mood and anxiety disorders: a systematic review. *Trauma, Violence, & Abuse,* 17. pii: 1524838015584369.

Cicchetti, D., & Toth, S.L. (2005). Child maltreatment. *Annual Review of Clinical Psychology, 1*, 409–438.

Collishaw, S., Pickles, A., Messer, J., Rutter, M., Shearer, C., & Maughan, B. (2007). Resilience to adult psychopathology following childhood maltreatment: evidence from a community sample. *Child Abuse & Neglect, 31*, 211–229.

Department for Education. (2015). *SFR 41/2015: Characteristics of children in need: 2014–15.* Retrieved from https://www.gov.uk/government/statistics/characteristics-of-children-in-need-2014-to-2015

Gilbert, R., Widom, C. S., Browne, K., Fergusson, D., Webb, E., & Janson, S. (2009). Burden and consequences of child maltreatment in high-income countries. *Lancet,* 373, 68–81.

Green, J.G., McLaughlin, K.A., Berglund, P.A., Gruber, M.J., Sampson, N.A., Zaslavsky, A.M., & Kessler, R.C. (2010). Childhood adversities and adult psychiatric disorders in the national comorbidity survey replication I: associations with first onset of DSM-IV disorders. *Archives of General Psychiatry, 67*, 113–123.

Huybrechts, K.F., Palmsten, K., Avorn, J., Cohen, L.S., Holmes, L.B., Franklin, J.M., . . . Hernandez-Diaz, S. (2014). Antidepressant use in pregnancy and the risk of cardiac defects. *The New England Journal of Medicine,* 370, 2397–2407.

Lereya, S.T., & Wolke, D. (2013). Prenatal family adversity and maternal mental health and vulnerability to peer victimisation at school. *Journal of Child Psychology and Psychiatry, 54*, 644–652.

McLaughlin, K.A., Green, J.G., Gruber, M.J., Sampson, N.A., Zaslavsky, A.M., & Kessler, R.C. (2010). Childhood adversities and adult psychopathology in the National Comorbidity Survey Replication (NCS-R) III: associations with functional impairment related to DSM-IV disorders. *Psychological Medicine, 40*, 847–859.

Nanni, V., Uher, R., & Danese, A. (2012). Childhood maltreatment predicts unfavorable course of illness and treatment outcome in depression: a meta-analysis. *American Journal of Psychiatry, 169*, 141–151.

National Collaborating Centre for Mental Health. (2007). Antenatal and Postnatal Mental Health: Clinical Management and Service Guidance. NICE Clinical Guidelines, No. 45. *The British Psychological Society.*

Nemeroff, C.B. (2004). Neurobiological consequences of childhood trauma. *Journal of Clinical Psychiatry, 65*, 18–28.

Norman, R.E., Byambaa, M., De, R., Butchart, A., Scott, J., & Vos, T. (2012). The long-term health consequences of child physical abuse, emotional abuse, and neglect: a systematic review and meta-analysis. *PLoS Medicine,* 9, e1001349.

O'Donnell, K.J., Glover, V., Barker, E.D., & O'Connor, T.G. (2014). The persisting effect of maternal mood in pregnancy on childhood psychopathology. *Development and Psychopathology, 26*, 393–403.

Pawlby, S., Hay, D.F., Sharp, D., Waters, C.S., & O'Keane, V. (2009). Antenatal depression predicts depression in adolescent offspring: prospective longitudinal community-based study. *Journal of Affective Disorders, 113*, 236–243.

Pearson, R.M., Evans J., Kounali D., Lewis G., Heron J., Ramchandani, P.G.,. . . . Stein, A. (2013). Maternal depression during pregnancy and the postnatal period: risks and possible mechanisms for offspring depression at age 18 years. *JAMA Psychiatry, 70*, 1312–1319.

Plant, D.T., Barker, E.D., Waters, C.S., Pawlby, S., & Pariante, C.M. (2013). Intergenerational transmission of maltreatment and psychopathology: the role of antenatal depression. *Psychological Medicine, 43*, 519–528.

Plant, D.T., Pariante, C.M., Sharp, D., & Pawlby, S. (2015). Maternal depression during pregnancy and offspring depression in adulthood: role of child maltreatment. *British Journal of Psychiatry, 207*(3), 213–220.

Plant, D.T., Pawlby, S., Sharp, D., & Pariante, C.M. (2016). Prenatal maternal depression is associated with offspring inflammation at 25 years: a prospective longitudinal cohort study. *Translational Psychiatry* 6(11): e936.

Vaillancourt, K. (2015). Maternal history of abuse and maternal 'mind-mindedness' in a sample of mothers with severe mental illness treated in a Mother-Baby Inpatient Unit. (Thesis submitted as part requirement for the Doctorate of Clinical Psychology, King's College London, IoPPN).

World Health Organization. (2015). *Preventing youth violence: an overview of the evidence.*

7

POSTNATAL DEPRESSION AND THE UNDER-TWOS

Lynne Murray and Peter Cooper

Postnatal depression (PND) is a common disorder that can have a negative impact on the mother–child relationship and on child development in the longer term. This is particularly likely when the depression is severe and persistent. There is no good evidence that PND can be prevented, and therefore it is important to understand the strengths and limitations of available treatments, and their implications for the child. Although relatively brief treatments seem to be moderately successful in helping mothers to recover from depression in the early postnatal months, there is little evidence for their long-term benefits to maternal depression and child development. It is important, therefore, that rigorous effective treatments be developed, of sufficient intensity and duration to prevent the child's exposure to maternal disorder and associated parenting difficulties through at least their first 2 years.

Postnatal depression

PND is similar to depression at other times. That is, it includes a prolonged period of low mood, and profound loss of interest and enjoyment. Other symptoms are mood-related disturbances in sleep, irritability, concentration impairment, retardation, agitation, feelings of guilt and hopelessness, and suicidal thoughts or impulses. PND is, therefore, a distressing disorder that significantly affects daily functioning. Estimates of its prevalence have generally been around 13 per cent, although they vary depending on the population, with higher rates in conditions of adversity (see review of O'Hara & McCabe, 2013). While depression in the early months following delivery appears to be more common than at the end of the first postnatal year, there is no compelling evidence for a raised prevalence over the whole postnatal year relative to an equivalent nonpuerperal period.

The course of PND is variable. For about half the women with PND, the onset predates the birth. Further, while the majority steadily improve over the postnatal year, for around a third the depression persists, and these chronic cases tend to be more severe. These episodes pose most risk for adverse child outcomes, and therefore their identification and treatment is of particular importance.

Risk factors for PND are largely the same as for depression at other times, and include a history of depression, stressful life events, personality factors (i.e. neuroticism and low self-esteem), a poor marital relationship and poor social support. However, none of these factors individually confers substantial risk, and even collectively, their predictive power is limited (Cooper, Murray, Hooper & West, 1996), meaning that reliable antenatal identification of those at risk for PND is currently not possible. This is partly because early postnatal factors can increase risk, such as severe maternity blues and difficult infant temperament.

Effects of PND on mother-child relationships

The symptoms of PND are likely to affect a mother's interpersonal relationships, including that with her infant (see review of Murray, Halligan & Cooper, 2017).

Difficulties in bonding with the infant have been found when mothers are depressed, as well as problems with general caretaking, including reduced breast feeding, inappropriate accessing of medical services, poor sleep management, and, in one US study, poorer safety practices (Field, 2010).

Depressed mothers are often caught up in their own experience, and studies of mother-infant face-to-face engagements in the postnatal months show they find it difficult to focus on their infant and notice their signals and interests, and respond appropriately. These difficulties are particularly likely if the mother experiences additional problems, such as living in conditions of poverty or low social support. Rather than the intuitive adjustments normally shown during face-to-face engagements (e.g. imitating infant expressions, adjusting responses to support the infant's positive engagement) (Murray, De Pascalis, Bozicevic, Hawkins, Sclafani & Ferrari, 2016), depressed mothers tend to show one of two kinds of interaction difficulty. Thus, they may withdraw from their infant, and become unresponsive and self-absorbed, or they may behave in an intrusive, sometimes even hostile, manner, overriding their infant's signals and behaviour. Both these interaction patterns cause clear signs of infant distress and disengagement from the interaction.

In low-risk samples, interaction disturbances are generally less marked, although subtle effects of depression have still been found. These mainly involve reduced maternal sensitivity to infant signals, as well as less affectionate touching. Mothers' speech to their infants is also affected by depression, being slower and less responsive, and lacking the 'exaggerated', modulated intonation contours normally seen in 'baby talk'. The disturbances in maternal responsiveness in low-risk samples are most evident when the depression is severe and persists, or during interactions taking place under challenging conditions, as is any accompanying infant disengagement and distress.

Studies of older infants of postnatally depressed mothers have often examined the quality of attachment to the mother, and have generally found increased likelihood of insecurity. Just as with earlier interactions, however, background adversity and the chronicity of depression are important, and increase the risk for infant insecurity. By contrast, risk is reduced if, despite being depressed, mothers can remain sensitive or are securely attached themselves.

Aside from insecure attachment, continuing difficulties in mother-child interactions have been found when the mother has experienced PND, including reductions in child responsive engagement with their mother in the preschool years, even though maternal depression has remitted. Nevertheless, such problems are more likely in the context of PND that becomes chronic, even in low-risk populations.

Although difficulties in mother-child relationships in the context of PND have been highlighted, it should be stressed that this does not always apply, and some depressed mothers are highly sensitive to their infants and young children and have good relationships with them. It is also the case that parenting difficulties, and even depression itself, can arise as a function of *infant* characteristics, such as irritable behaviour or inconsolable crying, reflecting the complex, bi-directional nature of early relationship processes.

Neural and physiological aspects of effects of PND on mother-infant relationships

PND and related interaction disturbances are associated not only with changes in infant behaviour, but also in brain activity, and particularly greater electro-encephalogram (EEG) frontal asymmetry due to relatively more right versus left activation. This is more likely if the mother's depression persists and is accompanied by noncontingent or withdrawn interactions, and is important because it is associated with more negative infant behaviour and behaviour problems in early childhood.

Studies of maternal PND have also examined child HPA axis functioning, and have generally found elevated basal cortisol and/or reactivity in offspring of affected mothers (see review of Halligan, 2014). These effects have been found to be related to the interaction difficulties associated with PND in infancy, early childhood and the longer term, when, as for EEG asymmetry, early withdrawn maternal behaviour appears to be particularly important.

Psychological development of children of postnatally depressed mothers

Given the influence of early relationships on child development, there has been concern about the longer-term development of children of PND mothers, with studies examining child and adolescent functioning in a range of areas (see review of Murray, Halligan & Cooper, 2017).

Cognitive development

Several longitudinal studies have found children of PND mothers to show cognitive difficulties, including difficulties with language, IQ, learning ability and academic achievements. Nevertheless, effects are not uniform and, in the main, poorer functioning has been found to be confined to boys, and/or to those also exposed to other risks (e.g. low maternal education or SES, neonatal problems), or subsequent episodes of maternal depression.

It is well established that responsive, or contingent, interactions are important for child cognitive development, and several studies have found that depressed mothers' reduced responsiveness accounts for the poorer cognitive functioning of their infants and preschool children. Notably, long-term effects of impaired interactions have also been found. Thus, in one study, depressed mothers' reduced responsiveness at 2 months accounted for their boys' poor cognitive performance at 18 months, and this effect was still evident at 16 years in these boys' substantially poorer results in public exams, even when subsequent exposure to maternal depression and the quality of later mother–child interactions was taken into account (Murray, Arteche, Fearon, Halligan, Croudace & Cooper, 2010).

Aside from contingency, the *quality* of parental responsiveness is important for child cognition. This includes the ability to capture and support infant attention, and typically involves vocal modulations which are often reduced in the context of depression, and which are associated with less efficient infant learning. More generally, depressed parents are less likely to engage in practices that scaffold and enrich their child's experience of the environment, such as book-sharing, a technique that benefits child language development and attention. Finally, emotion-regulation processes during parent–infant interactions may be important, with infant distress, often arising when maternal contacts are intrusive, being likely to impair attention and information retrieval.

Emotional and behavioural problems

Maternal reports have often shown associations between PND and child emotional and behavioural problems from late infancy through the preschool and school years. However, for externalising problems, these associations are generally better accounted for by chronic (and particularly severe) or concurrent maternal depression, and by associated risk factors, rather than by the postnatal episode itself. For internalising problems, by contrast, there is more evidence for raised rates of difficulties in children of PND mothers, even when controlling for subsequent maternal depression and background risk.

This general pattern of findings is also reflected in independent assessments of child problems. Studies that have taken subsequent maternal depression and other risk factors into account generally show that raised rates of child externalising problems are better explained by the combination of PND and ongoing difficulties, rather than PND alone, with boys possibly being more vulnerable. With regard to internalising problems, and again consistent with maternal reports, there is more evidence for a specific association with PND. Thus, independent of subsequent maternal depression and other risk factors, teacher reports have shown increased rates of withdrawn and anxious behaviour, low ego-resilience and poor social competence. Evidence of internalising problems has emerged from other kinds of assessment, too. These include observations of free play at school, where reduced social responsiveness has been observed in children of PND mothers, as well as child cognitions reflecting vulnerability (e.g. self-denigration and low self-competence).

Three aspects of lowered maternal sensitivity may be particularly relevant to the child emotional and behavioural difficulties described above. First, Field (1995) suggested a 'contagion effect', whereby infants show increased sad affect and distress either by modelling their mothers' depressed behaviour, or by being directly affected by the mother's sad affect. This suggestion is reflected in the matching of negative emotional expressions in depressed mother-infant interactions, and the effects of maternal sad voice quality at 2 months on later child affective disorder. Second, maternal 'failures of interactive repair' have been highlighted. Normally, mothers support their infant's immature capacities to regulate their behaviour and affect by repairing disruptions to infant engagement (e.g. infant distress, or avoidance) (Tronick & Gianino, 1986), and providing 'emotional scaffolding', but depressed mothers find this more difficult to do, particularly with boy infants. Finally, the hostility and coercive behaviour of some depressed mothers (especially those experiencing adversity) may directly provoke infant distress and behavioural dysregulation. This difficult infant behaviour can become a stable pattern, precipitating further maternal negativity and intrusiveness, with ensuing vicious cycles of negative interaction, culminating, in one study, in raised rates of conduct problems and ADHD symptoms by age 5-to-8 years (Morrell & Murray, 2003).

Psychiatric disorder in adolescence

Children of depressed parents are at raised risk for depression and anxiety themselves, and this has also been found to apply to children of PND mothers in some, although not all, studies (see review of Murray, Halligan and Cooper, 2016): Hammen and Brennan (2003) found depression in 15-year-olds was affected by the occurrence of maternal depression at any time in the first 10 years, including during infancy, particularly if it was severe or became chronic. In a UK study, over 40 per cent of children of PND mothers experienced an episode by age 16 years, more than four times the rate among offspring of women without PND (Murray, Arteche, Fearon, Halligan, Goodyer & Cooper, 2011). In this study, chronic maternal depression and marital conflict were also influential, although neither accounted for the impact of PND on adolescent mental state. Pearson et al. (2013) similarly found PND to predict offspring depression in adolescence (18 years), controlling for earlier (although not concurrent) maternal depression, particularly when mothers had a low level of education. Finally, by contrast, Naicker and colleagues (2012) found no effects of PND on 12–15-year-olds' 'emotional disorder', although maternal depression occurring between 2 and 5 years did raise risk, even controlling for current maternal depression.

A number of potential pathways might contribute to increased risk of psychiatric disorder in offspring of PND mothers. Aside from possible biological processes involving EEG activity or HPA axis functioning, particular cognitions concerning close relationships and the self increase risk for depression. These pathways may develop in early childhood. In one longitudinal study, for example, the raised rate of depressive disorder in offspring of PND mothers at 16 years was accounted for by a process starting with insecure infant attachment, and progressed through low cognitive resilience in children at 5 and 8 years (Murray et al., 2011).

Prevention and treatment of PND

Ideally, PND should be prevented. However, studies to date have been disappointing (see review of Murray, Halligan & Cooper, 2017). Thus, there is little evidence concerning possible preventive effects of pharmacological treatment (Howard, Hoffbrans, Henshaw, Boath & Bradley, 2005), and indeed there have been concerns about the impact of antidepressants on fetal and infant development (Grigoriadis et al., 2014). Furthermore, although recent reviews (Dennis & Dowswell, 2013; Sockol, Epperson & Barber, 2013) concluded that psychological and psychosocial preventive interventions do reduce depressive symptoms and the rate of PND, important caveats are required: first, many of the studies included women who were already depressed, either antenatally or in the immediate postnatal period; and any evidence of reduced subsequent depression therefore confounds preventive with treatment effects. Second, the impact of these interventions, while statistically significant, was generally only modest (e.g. Sockol et al. (2013) report a mean effect size across studies of 0.18). More recently, a preventive trial that targeted high-risk women antenatally, and provided counselling and support aimed at enhancing maternal sensitivity, found no benefit to mothers' mood, mother-infant interactions, or infant outcome (Cooper, De Pascalis, Woolgar, Romaniuk & Murray, 2015); and a systematic review of 86 quantitative trials concluded that there was no clear evidence for a preventive effect (Morell et al., 2016). It is, therefore, questionable whether preventive interventions are effective in relation to PND.

A number of approaches to treating PND have been examined (see Murray, Halligan & Cooper, 2017). Two studies of pharmacological medication compared a selective serotonin reuptake inhibitor with a psychological treatment (counselling (Appleby, Warner, Whitton & Faragher, 1997) or CBT (Misri, Reebye, Corral, & Milis 2004)), or their combination; both found the two modes of treatments to be similarly beneficial, and neither found additive effects. Nevertheless, sample sizes were small, and follow-up limited. Further, the possibility of drug transmission to the infant requires investigation, as elevations in breast milk have been reported, and, despite some claims to the contrary (e.g. Goodman, Broth, Hall & Stowe,

2008), there is no good evidence that treating PND pharmacologically improves the mother–child relationship. In sum, the efficacy of antidepressant medication for PND requires further evaluation.

Two reviews of randomised controlled trials concluded that a variety of psychological interventions (including cognitive behaviour therapy (CBT), interpersonal therapy (IPT), psychoanalytic therapy, counselling, social support) were moderately effective and similarly beneficial in terms of speeding up recovery from depressive symptomatology (Dennis & Hodnett, 2007). Notably, however, treatments were generally brief, and typically focussed on the moderate depressions occurring in the early postpartum months, and there is little evidence for their sustained benefit to maternal mood or the mother–infant relationship and infant development.

A related approach has been to focus on improving *parenting,* rather than depression, with meta-analytic studies of treatments such as interactive coaching, relationship facilitation based on the Neonatal Behavioural Assessment Scale (NBAS), and infant massage, showing overall short-term benefits (Tsivos, Calam, Sanders & Wittkowski, 2015). Nevertheless, these interventions, like those for PND itself, have also tended to be rather brief, and often delivered early in the postnatal year, and short-term gains have similarly been only modest (Kersten-Alvarez, Hosman, Riksen-Walraven, Van Doesum & Hoefnagels, 2011), with the few longer-term follow-ups failing to show positive benefits (e.g. Murray, Cooper, West & Romaniuk, 2003; Kersten-Alvarez, Hosman, Riksen-Walraven, Van Doesum & Hoefnagels, 2010). It is notable that these disappointing findings contrast with those of research by Cicchetti and colleagues (Cicchetti, Rogosh & Toth, 2000; Toth, Rogosch Many & Cichhetti, 2006), in which children of PND mothers who received toddler-parent psychotherapy over a full year (starting on average at 20 months postpartum) showed significant benefits in terms of cognition and attachment relative to a nontreated control group. These results, particularly when considered in the light of the fact that child outcome is particularly likely to be adverse in the context of chronic and more severe PND, suggest that it is important that treatment be mounted that is of sufficient intensity and duration to bring about substantial and lasting changes in maternal functioning and the mother–infant relationship.

Conclusions

- PND is common, and has negative effects on the mother–infant relationship and child development, particularly when it is severe and chronic.
- Effective interventions are required to prevent the child's exposure to the more serious maternal depressions and their associated parenting difficulties through the first 2 years, in order to prevent adverse child outcome.
- Effective treatments for persistent and severe depressions probably need to be intensive and relatively long-lasting.
- Monitoring of maternal mood should continue beyond initial postnatal screens, particularly for women who experience early PND, so that further support can be provided if required.

References

Appleby, L., Warner, R., Whitton, A., and Faragher, B. (1997). A controlled study of fluoxetine and cognitive-behavioural counselling in the treatment of postnatal depression. *British Medical Journal, 314*, 932–936.

Cicchetti, D., Rogocsh, F.A., and Toth, S.L. (2000). The efficacy of toddler-parent psychotherapy for fostering cognitive development in offspring of depressed mothers. *Journal of Abnormal Child Psychology, 28*, 135–148.

Cooper, P.J., De Pascalis, L., Woolgar, M., Romaniuk, H., and Murray, L. (2015). Attempting to prevent postnatal depression by targeting the mother–infant relationship: a randomised controlled trial. *Primary Health Care Research & Development, 16*(4), 383–397.

Cooper, P.J., Murray, L., Hooper, R., and West, A. (1996). The development and validation of a predictive index for postpartum depression. *Psychological Medicine, 26*, 627–634.

Cuijpers, P., Brannmark, J.G., van Straten, A. Warmeerdam, L., and Andersson, G. (2008). Psychological treatment of postpartum depression: a meta-analysis. *Journal of Clinical Psychology, 64*, 103–118.

Dennis, C.L., and Dowswell, T. (2013). Psychosocial and psychological interventions for preventing postpartum depression. *Cochrane Database of Systematic Reviews, 28*(2), CD001134. doi: 10.1002/14651858.CD001134.pub3.

Dennis, C.L., and Hodnett, E. (2007). Psychosocial and psychological interventions for treating postpartum depression. *Cochrane Database of Systematic Reviews*, CD006116.

Field, T.M. (1995). Infants of depressed mothers. *Infant Behaviour and Development, 18*, 1–3.

Field, T. (2010). Postpartum depression effects on early interactions, parenting, and safety practices: a review. *Infant Behavior and Development, 33*, 1–6.

Forman, D.R., O'Hara, M.W., Stuart, S., Gorman, L.L., Larsen, K.E., and Coy, K.C. (2007). Effective treatment for postpartum depression is not sufficient to improve the developing mother–child relationship. *Development and Psychopathology, 19*, 585–602.

Goodman, S.H., Broth, M.R., Hall, C.M., and Stowe, Z.N. (2008) Treatment of postpartum depression in mothers: secondary benefits to the infants. *Infant Mental Health Journal, 29*, 492–513.

Grigoriadis, S., VonderPorten, E.H., Mamisashvili, L., Tomlinson, G., Dennis, C.L., Koren, G., Steiner, M., Mousmanis, P., Cheung, A., and Ross, L.E. (2014). Prenatal exposure to antidepressants and persistent pulmonary hypertension of the newborn: systematic review and meta-analysis. *British Medical Journal, 348*, f6932.

Halligan, S. L. (2014). Neurobiological outcomes in the offspring of postnatally depressed mothers: causes and consequences. In C.M. Pariante, S. Conroy, P. Dazzan, L. Howard, S. Pawlby, and T. Senevirante (Eds.), *Perinatal Psychiatry: The Legacy of Channi Kumar*, pp. 160–174. Oxford: OUP.

Hammen, C., and Brennan, P.A. (2003). Severity, chronicity, and timing of maternal depression and risk for adolescent offspring diagnoses in a community sample. *Archives of General Psychiatry, 60*, 253–258.

Howard, L.M., Hoffbrand, S., Henshaw, C., Boath, L., and Bradley, E. (2005). Antidepressant prevention of postnatal depression. *Cochrane Database of Systematic Reviews* CD004363.

Kersten-Alvarez, L., Clemens, M.H., Hosman, J., Riksen-Walraven, M., Van Doesum, K., and Hoefnagels, C. (2011). Which preventive interventions effectively enhance depressed mothers' sensitivity? A meta-analysis. *Infant Mental Health Journal, 32*, 362–376.

Kersten-Alvarez, L.E., Hosman, C.M., Riksen-Walraven, J.M., Van Doesum, K., and Hoefnagels, C., (2010). Long-term effects of a home-visiting intervention for depressed mothers and their infants. *Journal of Child Psychology and Psychiatry, 51*(10), 1160–1170.

Kersten-Alvarez, L.E., Hosman, C. M., Riksen-Walraven, J., van Doesum, K. T., Smeekens, S., and Hoefnagels, C. (2012). Early school outcomes for children of postpartum depressed mothers: comparison with a community sample. *Child Psychiatry and Human Development*, *43*, 201–218

Misri, S., Reebye, P., Corral, M., and Milis, L. (2004) The use of paroxetine and cognitive-behavioral therapy in postpartum depression and anxiety: a randomized controlled trial. *Journal of Clinical Psychiatry*, *65*, 1236–1241.

Morrell, J., & Murray, L. (2003) Parenting and the development of conduct disorder and hyperactive symptoms in childhood: a prospective longitudinal study from 2 months to 8 years. *Journal of Child Psychology and Psychiatry*, *44*(4), 489–508.

Morrell, J., Sutcliffe, P., Booth, A., Stevens, J., Scope, A., Stevenson, M., Harvey, R., Bessey, A., Cantrell, A., Dennis, C.L., & Stewart-Brown, S. (2016) A systematic review, evidence synthesis and meta-analysis of quantitative and qualitative studies evaluating the clinical effectiveness, the cost-effectiveness, safety and acceptability of interventions to prevent postnatal depression. *Health Technology Assessment*, *20*(37), ISSN 1366–5278.

Murray, L., Arteche, A., Fearon, P., Halligan, S., Croudace, T., and Cooper, P. (2010). The effects of maternal postnatal depression and child sex on academic performance at age 16 years: a developmental approach. *Journal of Child Psychology and Psychiatry*, *51*, 1150–1159.

Murray, L., Arteche, A., Fearon, P., Halligan, S., Goodyer, I., and Cooper, P. (2011). Maternal postnatal depression and the development of depression in offspring up to 16 years of age. *Journal of the American Academy of Child and Adolescent Psychiatry*, *50*, 460–470.

Murray, L., De Pascalis, L., Bozicevic, L., Hawkins, L, Sclafani, V., and Ferrari, P.F. (2016). The functional architecture of mother-infant communication, and the development of infant social expressiveness in the first two months. *Scientific Reports* 6:39019. DOI: 10.1038/srep39019

Murray, L., Halligan, S.L., and Cooper, P.J. (2017). Postnatal depression and child development. In C. Zeanah (Ed.), *Handbook of Infant Mental Health 4th Edition* (in press).

Naicker, K., Wickham, M., and Colman, I. (2012). Timing of first exposure to maternal depression and adolescent emotional disorder in a national Canadian cohort. *PLoS One*, *7*(3), e33422. doi:10.1371

O'Hara, M.W., and McCabe, J.E. (2013). Postpartum depression: current status and future directions. *Annual Review Clinical Psychology*, *9*, 379–407.

Pearson, R., Bornstein, M. Cordero, M., Scerif, G., Mahedy, L., Evans, J., Abioye, A., and Stein, A. (2016). Maternal perinatal mental health and offspring academic achievement at age 16: the mediating role of childhood executive function. *Journal of Child Psychology and Psychiatry*, *57*(4), 491–501.

Pearson, R., Evans, J., Kounali, D., Lewis, G., Heron, J., Ramchandani, P., O'Connor, T., and Stein, A. (2013). Maternal depression during pregnancy and the postnatal period risks and possible mechanisms for offspring depression at age 18 years. *JAMAPsychiatry*, *70*(12), 1312–1319.

Sockol, L.E., Epperson, C.N., and Barber, J.P. (2013). Preventing postpartum depression: a meta-analytic review. *Clinical Psychology Review*, *33*, 1205–1217.

Toth, S.L., Rogosch, F.A., Manly, J., and Cicchetti, D. (2006). The efficacy of toddler-parent psychotherapy to reorganize attachment in the young offspring of mothers with major depressive disorder: a randomized preventive trial. *Journal of Consulting and Clinical Psychology*, *74*, 1006–1016.

Tronick, E.Z., and Gianino, A.F. (1986). The transmission of maternal disturbance to the infant. *New Directions for Child and Adolescent Development*, *34*, 5–11.

Tsivos, Z.-l., Calam, R., Sanders, M. R., and Wittkowski, A. (2015). Interventions for postnatal depression assessing the mother–infant relationship and child developmental outcomes: a systematic review. *International Journal of Women's Health, 7,* 429–447.

Van Doesum, K., Riksen-Walraven, J.M., Hosman, C.M., and Hoefnagels, C. (2008). A randomized controlled trial of a home-visiting intervention aimed at preventing relationship problems in depressed mothers and their infants. *Child Development, 79*(3), 547–561.

B: Perinatal risk factors with demonstrable long-term ill-effects

8

HEALTH INEQUALITIES AND THE IMPORTANCE OF ACTION ON PERINATAL RISK FACTORS

Angela Donkin and Michael Marmot

Prof. Sir. Michael Marmot lists three key ways in which the perinatal period can impact upon longer-term health inequalities: through low birth weight, through not breast feeding and through suboptimal bonding and attachment. He stresses that socioeconomic adversity increases the risk of all three. Actions to reduce the risk, stress and impacts of socio-economic adversity in households expecting children is therefore critical.

Socio-economic adversity during the prenatal period is associated with an increased risk of having a low birth weight baby (Dibben, Sigala & Macfarlane, 2006). Teenage pregnancy can also have a negative impact on birth weight because of competition between the mother's and the baby's growth needs (Baker et al., 2009), and also because teenage diets tend to be poor (Bates et al., 2012). Teenage pregnancies remain approximately twice as high for women living in England's most deprived areas compared with least deprived (NHS Maternity Statistics, 2012–13). For each kilogram increase in birth weight, improvements can be seen in cognitive tasks and educational achievement (Jefferis, Power & Hertzman, 1958). These in themselves can decrease subsequent inequalities.

Breast feeding, relative to formula feeding, is associated with a decreased risk of later obesity (Arenz et al., 2004; Owen et al., 2005; McAndrew et al., 2012), and women in lower socioeconomic status (SES) groups are less likely to breast-feed (McAndrew et al., 2012). Furthermore, maternal depression, which is more prevalent in low-income households, can have a negative impact on the ability of mothers to breastfeed successfully (Gutman, Brown & Akerman, 2009; Jennings, Stagg & Connors, 1991).

Poor mental health, housing and money worries, together with alcohol and substance abuse can place considerable stress on families, and prevent parents from being able to provide the practical and emotional support that their children need (NSPCC, 2015). These issues are all more prevalent in lower socio-economic groups and can lead to children having insecure forms of attachment. Insecure attachment is associated with poorer language and behaviour before school, and with significantly elevated levels of aggression, defiance and hyperactivity (Moullin, Waldfogel & Washbrook, 2014). Negative effects continue into life, with insecure children more likely to leave school without further education, employment or training ahead of them, be more likely to perpetuate domestic violence (Dutton & Corvo, 2006), and have higher levels of alcohol and substance abuse than secure children (Brennan & Shaver, 1995; Walsh, 1992). In addition, insecure attachment is linked to a higher risk for a number of health conditions, including strokes, heart attacks and high blood pressure, and suffering pain, for example from headaches and arthritis (McWilliams & Bailey, 2010).

Actions to reduce the risk, stress and impacts of socio-economic adversity in households with, or expecting children is crucial.

References

Arenz, S., Ruckerl, R., Koletzko, B., and von Kries, R. (2004). Breast-feeding and childhood obesity – a systematic review. *International Journal of Obesity and Related Metabolic Disorders, 28*, 1247–1256.

Baker, P., Wheeler, S., Sanders, T., Thomas, J., Hutchinson, C., Clarke, K., Berry, J., Jones, R., Seed, P., and Poston, L. (2009). A prospective study of micronutrient status in adolescent pregnancy. *The American Journal of Clinical Nutrition, 89*, 1114–1124.

Bates, B., Lennox, A., Prentice, A., Bates, C., and Swan, G. (2012). The National Diet and Nutrition Survey, headlines results from years 1, 2 and 3 (combined) of the Rolling Programme (2008/9 and 2010/11), www.gov.uk.

Brennan, K.A., and Shaver, P.R. (1995). Dimensions of adult attachment, affect regulation, and romantic relationship functioning. *Personality and Social Psychology Bulletin, 21*(3), 267–283.

Dibben, C., Sigala, M., and Macfarlane, A. (2006). Area deprivation, individual factors and low birth weight in England: Is there evidence of an 'area effect'? *Journal of Epidemiol Community Health, D60*(12), 1053–1059.

Dutton, D.G., and Corvo, K. (2006). Transforming a flawed policy: A call to revive psychology and science in domestic violence research and practice. *Aggression and Violent Behavior, 11*(5), 457–483.

Gutman, L., Brown, J., and Akerman, R. (2009). *Nurturing parenting capability: the early years.* Research report 30, Centre for research on the wider benefits of learning.

Health & Social Care Information Centre (2013). *NHS Maternity Statistics – England, 2012–13.*

Jefferis, B.J., Power, C., and Hertzman, C. (2002). Birth weight, childhood socioeconomic environment, and cognitive development in the 1958 British birth cohort study. *British Medical Journal, 325*(7359), 305–308.

Jennings, K.D., Stagg, V., and Connors, R.E. (1991). Social networks and mothers' interactions with their preschool children. *Child Development, 62*, 966–978.

McAndrew, F., Thompson, J., Fellows, L., Large, A., Speed, M., and Renfrew, M.J. (2012). *Infant Feeding Survey 2010.* Health & Social Care Information Centre.

McWilliams, L.A., and Bailey, S.J. (2010). Associations between adult attachment ratings and health conditions: Evidence from the national comorbidity survey replication. *Health Psychology, 29*(4), 446–453.

Moullin, S., Waldfogel, J., Washbrook, E. (2014). *Baby Bonds. Parenting, Attachment and a Secure Base for Children*. London: The Sutton Trust.

NSPCC (2015). Neglect. Signs, symptoms and effects. Available at: www.nspcc.org.uk/preventing-abuse/child-abuse-and-neglect/neglect/signs-symptoms-effects-neglect/ (accessed 24 October 2016).

Owen, C.G., Martin, R.M., Whincup, P.H., Smith, G.D., and Cook, D.G. (2005). Effect of infant feeding on the risk of obesity across the life course: A quantitative review of published evidence. *Pediatrics, 115*, 1367–1377.

Walsh, A. (1992). Drug-use and sexual-behavior – users, experimenters, and abstainers. *Journal of Social Psychology, 132*(5), 691–693.

9

STACKED ODDS

How social background can stifle early child potential

Chris Cuthbert

Inequalities emerge early in the life course. Indeed, with striking evidence of a social gradient in maternal health and wellbeing even before birth, some might argue the dice are already loaded in the womb. Later in this volume Young sets out the compelling economic case for investment in the first 1001 days. This chapter brings together evidence about the social patterning of outcomes during pregnancy and the first years of life, adding a social justice dimension to the case for investment in prevention in early childhood.

Over recent years, evidence from multiple disciplines has accumulated, helping shape our understanding of the factors that are important for early childhood development (ECD). In this chapter, data on inequalities are described under the rubric of four essential conditions for a successful start in life.

1. *A healthy pregnancy and birth:* Physical *and mental* health in pregnancy are crucial to babies' development.
2. *Healthy early relationships:* Babies need their caregivers to provide sensitive, responsive and consistent care.
3. *Effective support for parents:* Parents under pressure need to help themselves if they are to have the emotional resources to care effectively for their baby.
4. *A safe and stimulating environment:* To play, to learn and to explore.

The reported studies use a range of different definitions of social background including measures of income, education, occupational status and area deprivation. This chapter aims to span a range of individual indicators of ECD, highlighting the striking social gradient that runs across many of the outcomes considered. While it is recognised that adverse outcomes often cluster, and that risks can accumulate over time (Kuh and Ben-Shlomo, 2014), it is beyond the remit of this chapter to cover research on multiple adversities in any depth. Where possible, data on ethnic disparities are also reported.

Healthy pregnancy and birth

It is now several decades since epidemiologists pioneered studies into the impacts of *physical health* in pregnancy on children's long-term development. These scientists demonstrated the adverse consequences of poor maternal nutrition in pregnancy and of exposure to teratogens such as alcohol, tobacco and illicit drugs. More recently, the lens has widened to examine the impacts of *mental ill-health* in pregnancy, with research charting how exposure to high levels of stress during pregnancy can affect child development (Glover, 2014).

Maternal obesity in pregnancy (Kuh and Ben-Sclomo, 2014)[1]

The health risks of obesity in pregnancy include: increased risks of miscarriage, gestational diabetes, stillbirth, metabolic and developmental abnormalities; and risks of later obesity, diabetes and hypertension for the child (Molyneaux, 2014). A recent systematic review (NHS Digital, 2016) has also provided evidence that women who are obese when they become pregnant are more likely to experience elevated depression symptoms in pregnancy and after birth. Yet, despite knowledge of these risks, only recently have data on maternal obesity in pregnancy been reported as experimental statistics (Heslehurst et al., 2010).

Heslehurst et al. investigated maternal obesity in pregnancy in England by constructing a retrospective representative sample of 619,323 live births between 1989 and 2007. Over this period, the incidence of first trimester obesity increased markedly, from 7.6 to 15.6 per cent. A more recent snapshot of data from 77 maternity units in England in 2015[2] found 21 per cent of women with a recorded BMI were obese at the time of booking, suggesting maternal obesity may be continuing to increase.

Heslehurst found the odds of obesity (BMI > 30) increased with area deprivation (Figure 9.1), even after controlling for employment status, age, parity and ethnicity. In more detailed analyses, she found evidence that with higher classes of obesity ('severely', 'morbidly' and 'super-morbidly' obese) the association with deprivation increased.

In a separate study (Heslehurst, 2012), Heslehurst investigated maternal obesity and ethnicity, using a sample of 502,474 births in England (1995–2007). This used WHO's obesity criteria for Asian women (BMI > 27.5) and the general BMI criteria for all other women (≥30.0). After adjusting for confounders, Pakistani women had 2.19x the odds of obesity in pregnancy compared to White women. Black (OR 1.7), Indian (OR 1.49) and Bangladeshi (OR 1.15) women all had higher odds of obesity than White women; whereas Mixed (OR 0.79) and Chinese/Other (OR 0.63) faced lower odds.

Smoking

The adverse effects of smoking in pregnancy are well established and include increased risks of low birth weight, stillbirth and sudden infant death syndrome

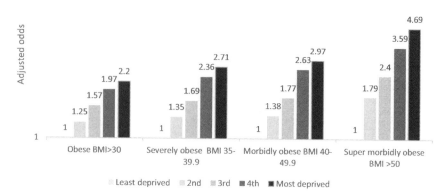

FIGURE 9.1 Adjusted odds of maternal obesity in pregnancy, by Index of Multiple Deprivation in England (1989–2007)

(US Department of Health & Human services, 2004). UK studies find a clear social gradient to smoking during pregnancy. The Growing Up in Scotland (GUS) study 2010 (The Scottish Government, 2015) found 49 per cent of mothers from the lowest income quintile smoked in pregnancy, compared to 8 per cent of mothers from the highest quintile. Data from the UK Infant Feeding Survey (IFS) (McAndrew et al., 2012) show that women from routine and manual groups and women who have never worked have much higher rates of smoking in pregnancy than women in managerial, professional or intermediate groups (Figure 9.2).

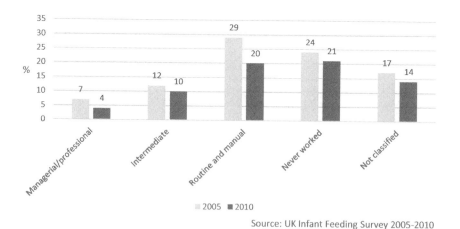

Source: UK Infant Feeding Survey 2005-2010

FIGURE 9.2 Smoking throughout pregnancy in the UK by NS-SEC (mother's occupation)

Encouragingly, all social classes saw reductions between 2005 and 2010, with particularly striking improvements among the routine and manual groups.

In her analysis of 2010 IFS data, Fitzpatrick (Fitzpatrick, 2016) discerned five distinct patterns of smoking across the pre-conception, pregnancy and postnatal periods (Box 9.1). Fitzpatrick compared the odds of being a 'persistent smoker' rather than a 'pregnancy inspired quitter' between different occupational groups. After adjusting for a range of socio-demographic and pregnancy related factors, she found women in routine occupations had 1.91x the odds of persisting to smoke (rather than quitting during pregnancy) compared to managerial or professional women (p < 0.01). Women who had never worked had 7.58x the odds (p < 0.001), suggesting this is a priority group for health promotion.

BOX 9.1 Women's smoking patterns during the preconception, pregnancy and postnatal period

74.1%	'Non-smokers'	Low probability of smoking at all time points
10.1%	'Persistent smokers'	High probability of smoking throughout
10.2%	'Pregnancy inspired quitters'	High probability of smoking before pregnancy, but low probability during and after
4.4%	'Temporary quitters'	Reduced probability of smoking in pregnancy, followed by relapse after baby is born
1.1%	'Postnatal quitters'	Quit after baby is born

Alcohol in pregnancy

Exposure to high levels of alcohol in pregnancy can cause significant lifelong harms to the developing fetus, including through fetal alcohol spectrum disorders (Department of Health, 2016). While definitive evidence of the harms of low levels of exposure to alcohol in pregnancy remains illusive, the Chief Medical Officer for England has recently adopted a 'precautionary' approach, advising women that: 'If you are pregnant or planning a pregnancy, the safest approach is not to drink alcohol at all, to keep risks to your baby to a minimum.'

The picture for alcohol consumption in pregnancy bucks the social trend we observe for many other outcomes. It is actually women from more *advantaged* backgrounds who are most likely to drink alcohol in pregnancy. IFS 2010 data (McAndrew et al., 2012) show a clear social gradient to women's drinking both *before* and *during* pregnancy.

Similarly, in the 2010 GUS study (The Scottish Government, 2015), 34 per cent of mothers from the highest income quintile drank alcohol in pregnancy, compared to 11 per cent from the lowest quintile. Compared to the previous wave of the GUS study in 2005, the gap between these income groups had widened and was driven by a larger increase in abstinence among mothers from the lowest

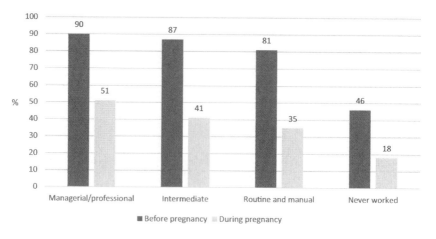

Source: UK Infant Feeding Survey (2010)

FIGURE 9.3 Alcohol consumption before and during pregnancy, by NS-SEC

income quintile (8 per cent increase in abstinence) compared to the highest group (3 per cent increase).

Mental ill health

Perinatal mental illness comprises a range of conditions of differing severity. Depression is the most common condition, affecting around 10–14 per cent of mothers at some stage in pregnancy or after the birth of their child (Joint Commissioning Panel for Mental Health, 2012). Without effective management, maternal mental illnesses can have a range of adverse effects on children's physical health and development including risks of prematurity, low birth weight, irritability and sleep problems in infancy, and later behavioural and academic difficulties (Hogg, 2012). Failure to effectively address perinatal depression, anxiety and psychosis has been estimated to cost £8.1 billion for each one year cohort of births in the UK (Bauer et al., 2014) – 72 per cent of this sum relates to costs for dependent children.

In an analysis of the General Practice records of 116,457 UK women with at least one live birth (Ban et al., 2012), Ban examined mothers' mental health status across three time periods: 9 months before pregnancy; during pregnancy; and 9 months after birth.

Figure 9.4 shows the absolute risks of maternal depression in pregnancy by deprivation quintile. The data are stratified by age and show significant differences by deprivation. Among 25–34 year olds, the most deprived quintile face 2.39x the odds of depression in pregnancy, compared to the least deprived quintile (p < 0.001). Among 35–45 year olds, the most deprived quintile face 2.63x the odds of depression compared to the least deprived quintile (p < 0.001). Among mothers aged 15–24, the gradient is less pronounced, but differences are still significant overall (p < 0.001).

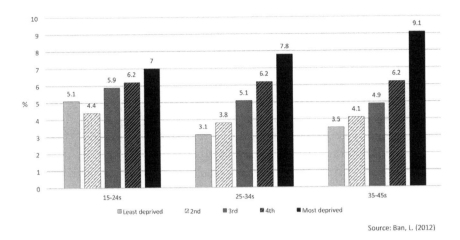

Source: Ban, L. (2012)

FIGURE 9.4 Absolute risk of maternal depression in pregnancy by deprivation quintile

Ban found deprivation status was associated with higher risks of each of the mental health conditions (anxiety, depression, serious mental illnesses) considered both during pregnancy and in the first 9 months after birth. Interestingly, the association was consistently more pronounced among the oldest group of mothers.

Infant mortality

There is strong evidence from UK meta-analyses (Weightman, 2012), of the relationship between social class and infant mortality (pooled odds ratio of 1.52) and of the relationship between area deprivation and infant mortality (pooled OR 1.72). Furthermore, the relationship between infant mortality and area deprivation in the UK has persisted over time (Norman et al., 2008). And across Organisation for Economic Co-operation and Development (OECD) countries, Wickham (Wickham et al., 2016) has demonstrated an association between countries such as the United Kingdom with higher proportions of children living in relative poverty (< 60 per cent median income) and higher infant mortality.

New analysis from the Policy Research Unit in Maternal Health and Care at the National Perinatal Epidemiology Unit shows a clear gradient in infant mortality by quintile of the Index of Multiple Deprivation (Figure 9.5).

Official UK data (ONS Statistical bulletin, 2015) on child deaths highlight ethnic disparities in infant mortality, with particularly high rates among babies from Caribbean, Pakistani and African families (Figure 9.6). Ethnic disparities in infant mortality are not simply due to the socio-economic backgrounds of these groups since, for example Bangladeshi and Pakistani families with infants share a similar socio-economic profile but have very different rates of infant mortality (Hollowell et al., 2011) Explanations for variations by ethnicity are 'complex, involving the

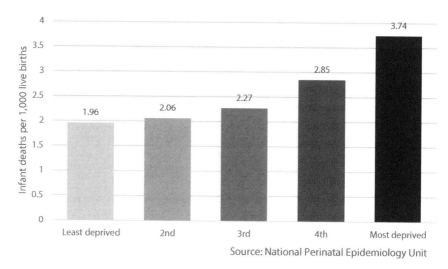

FIGURE 9.5 Infant mortality by index of multiple deprivation, England 2012

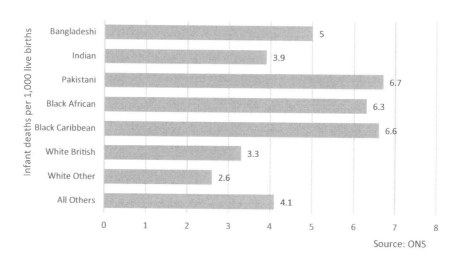

FIGURE 9.6 Infant mortality rate by ethnicity, England and Wales 2013

interplay of deprivation, physiological, behavioural and cultural factors' (Gray et al., 2009).

Low birth weight is an important risk factor for infant mortality and it too is strongly patterned by social background. Weightman's meta-analysis of UK studies (Weightman, 2012) provides evidence of the relationship between low birth weight and area deprivation (pooled odds ratio of 1.81) and between birth weight and social class (pooled odds ratio of 1.79).

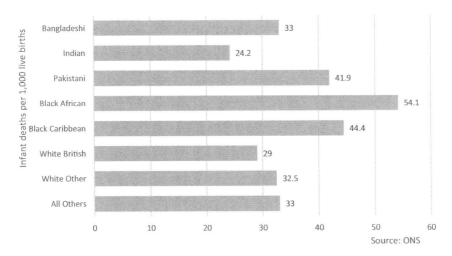

Source: ONS

FIGURE 9.7 Infant mortality for low birthweight births by ethnicity, England and Wales 2013

Figure 9.7 shows clear disparities between different ethnic groups in terms of mortality rates for low birth weight babies. Low birth weight babies from Black African, Black Caribbean and Pakistani families have especially high rates of mortality compared to the other groups.

Healthy early relationships

Breast feeding

Beyond the well charted benefits to physical health of both mother and baby (Victoria et al., 2016), breast feeding can also be beneficial in supporting early bonding and emotional health.

Figure 9.8 shows the incidence of breast feeding by mother's occupational status, using IFS data for 2005 and 2010. In both waves of the survey there is evidence of a relationship between breast feeding and occupation. Encouragingly, the data show increases in breast feeding between the two waves of research, with the largest increases in the lower groups.

The GUS study (The Scottish Government, 2015) measured the disparity in breast feeding by income in 2010, with 55 per cent of Scottish women from the lowest income quintile not breast feeding, compared to 19 per cent among women from the highest income quintile. However, the size of the gap between the two groups had reduced by 7 per cent compared to the 2005 wave of GUS, demonstrating it is possible to reduce the gap. There was also an increase in duration of breast feeding between the two waves of research which was driven by improvements among mothers from more deprived backgrounds.

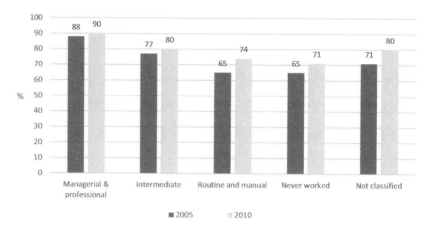

Source: UK Infant Feeding Survey (2005-10)

FIGURE 9.8 Incidence of breastfeeding in the UK, by NS-SEC (mother's occupation)

In the 2010 IFS (McAndrew et al., 2012) data on ethnic background were collected from mothers in Scotland, England and Wales (but not in Northern Ireland). The survey found large ethnic differences in terms of breast feeding initiation, with rates of over 9 in 10 among Asian (95 per cent), Black (96 per cent), Chinese or other ethnic origin mothers (97 per cent) compared with just under 9 in 10 (89 per cent) for mixed race mothers and only four fifths of White mothers (79 per cent). Analysis of data from the Born in Bradford cohort study (Santorelli et al., 2013) found that Pakistani and other South Asian mothers were significantly more likely than White mothers to initiate breast feeding and to still be breast feeding at 4 months. However, rates of exclusive breast feeding at 4 months were not significantly different once socio-economic, life style and birth factors were accounted for.

Attachment and parental sensitivity

Although established in meta-analyses (Fearon et al., 2010) as important to child development, measures of attachment security and parental sensitivity are not routinely captured at a population level. Therefore, it is difficult to find social epidemiological research on this issue. This is an important gap and there is a case for investment in developing and testing a tool for routine collection of data on the quality of the parent-infant relationship.

Social and emotional development

The GUS study 2010 (The Scottish Government, 2010) measured children's social and emotional development at 4 years old using the Strengths and Difficulties Questionnaire (SDQ), which covers the following domains: 'child conduct', 'hyper-

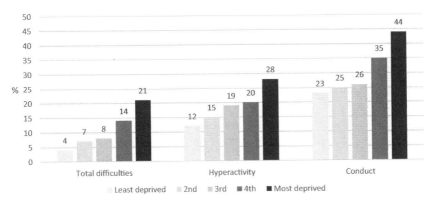

Source: Scottish Government (2010) Growing Up In Scotland

FIGURE 9.9 Strengths and Difficulties scores by equivalised household income quintiles in Scotland (2010)

activity', 'peer problems', 'prosocial behaviour' and 'emotions'. The researchers found a very clear relationship between all of the SDQ domains and the Scottish Index of Multiple Deprivation. They also found a clear association between SDQ scores and household income (Figure 9.9).

Effective support for parents

When families are struggling to cope with the pressures in their lives, it can be hard for parents to provide babies with the sensitive care and support they need. This section first describes a recent study looking at patterns of general 'parenting stress' according to mothers' level of education; it then highlights how some families are exposed to situations of more acute adversity and social exclusion, which can impact upon parenting capacity and child wellbeing.

Parenting stress

Parkes used data from the 2010 GUS study (Parkes et al., 2015) to examine patterns of parenting stress among mothers of 10-month old children, according to level of maternal education. GUS used a short version of the Parental Stress Scale (Berry, 1995), which taps into mothers' perceptions of their levels of: choice and control over their life; ability to balance different responsibilities; and time and flexibility, since having a child. The data showed a 'U' shaped distribution, with evidence of higher stress among both higher *and* lower educated mothers compared to mothers with 'intermediate' levels of education. Parkes was interested to find out whether these patterns might be related to variations in access to support for the mother.

She found access to social support accounted for around a half of the excess stress reported by women from both lower and higher education backgrounds.

In both cases, less frequent contact with grandparents (compared to the intermediate education group) helped explain their higher levels of parenting stress. However, apart from support from grandparents, the support deficits that were important in explaining stress among high-education mothers were distinct from those that were important for low-education mothers. Among higher educated mothers, reliance on formal childcare and the infrequency of contact with friends were important factors explaining parenting stress. These findings are in line with theories that emphasise the stress and intrusion of higher status employment roles (Schieman, 2009). Among lower educated mothers, smaller and less effective networks, as well as barriers (low awareness and poor perceptions) to professional parent support were significant factors. This analysis is valuable for policy and practice because it differentiates the particular forms of support most likely to be beneficial in mitigating stress depending on mothers' education.

Invisible babies

Research for the NSPCC's *All Babies Count* report series (Cuthbert, 2011; Rayns et al., 2013; Hogg, 2015; Galloway, 2014) estimated the numbers of children in the United Kingdom living in families facing complex problems such as parental imprisonment, alcohol and drug misuse, homelessness and domestic abuse.

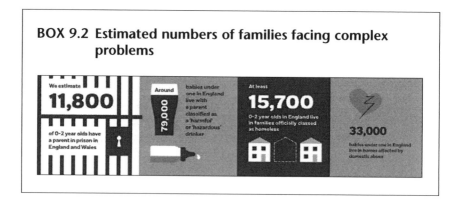

BOX 9.2 Estimated numbers of families facing complex problems

We estimate **11,800** of 0-2 year olds have a parent in prison in England and Wales

Around **79,000** babies under one in England live with a parent classified as a 'harmful' or 'hazardous' drinker

At least **15,700** 0-2 year olds in England live in families officially classed as homeless

33,000 babies under one in England live in homes affected by domestic abuse

Routine data collection on these groups remains extremely poor, meaning children's needs frequently go-undetected and opportunities for preventative services and support are missed. Where such data are collected, there is still a need for improved mechanisms for linking and sharing data between agencies.

A safe and stimulating environment

The Millennium Cohort Study (MCS) has shown how children from poorer backgrounds are less likely to have access to gardens and parks, with obvious implications for their opportunities for play, physical exercise and social interaction.

MCS data show that perceptions of community safety are lower in more deprived areas. Further, mothers' perceptions of neighbourhood have been shown to influence children's behavioural development, even after controlling for individual socio-economic factors (Sheiwe, 2011).

As well as the importance of access to safe outdoor and public spaces, researchers have increasingly come to recognise the important influence on child development of the 'home learning environment'.

Language

The classic US study by Hart and Risley looking at acquisition of vocabulary, famously found a 30 million word gap by age 3 between children from 'professional' and 'welfare' families (Hart & Risley, 1995). In South West England, Roulstone (Roulstone et al., 2010) found a strong association between social disadvantage and language at 24 months. And in turn, that language skills at 24 months are strongly associated with children's performance at the start of primary school.

In the earliest days, weeks and months of life, parental responsiveness to the baby's initiatives plays a critical role in the development of language and communication skills. Roulstone's analysis showed that the number of words a child was able to say at 24 months, the number of words they were able to understand at 24 months and use of word combinations at 24 months were all significant predictors of performance at school entry. Furthermore, the following measures of the 'communication environment' were also significant: book ownership at 6 months; frequency of trips to the library; attendance at crèche or preschool; 'Home' score at 18 months; and amount of TV on in the home at 18 months.

These findings are important, particularly because there are obvious opportunities for promoting parent–child interaction and improving the home learning environment. For example, the 2010 GUS study found the only 62 per cent of parents from the lowest income quintile looked at books or read stories to their child at 10 months of age, compared to 81 per cent of parents from the highest quintile.

Experience in Scotland demonstrates the potential to reduce inequalities over time. In the GUS study (The Scottish Government, 2015) the gap in age 3 vocabulary scores between children from the lowest and highest income quintiles reduced between 2005 and 2010. The gap also narrowed in relation to problem solving scores at age 3.

In a US study (Rowe, 2008), Rowe found parents from more advantaged backgrounds talked to their two-and-a-half-year-old children more, used more diverse and complex language and made less use of directive utterances. This in turn was associated with larger vocabulary among their children. Rowe was interested to understand what factors might explain this relationship and her modelling showed that parents' knowledge of child development was an important mediating factor, suggesting that beliefs about child development influence day-to-day communication patterns with their children. This finding has important implications for policy and practice, suggesting that if knowledge and beliefs about child development can be altered, then this might support language promoting behaviours and ultimately children's language development.

The widening gap

In this chapter we have seen how the social gradient emerges early in life, even in pregnancy. Evidence from the MCS suggests that by the age of 3 this gap is already substantial; and that between 3 and 5 it continues to grow. Dearden (Dearden et al., 2011) found that children from poorer backgrounds had lower language scores at ages 3 and 5. Figure 9.10 shows her analysis of how children's position on the tests changed between ages 3 and 5. She found that 'not only do children from lower SEP quintiles have lower average outcomes at age 3, but they are also more likely to stay in the bottom 40 per cent of achievers and more likely to drop out of the top 40 per cent'.

So what explains this socio economic gap? Dearden found that parental education and family background factors (particularly mother's age at birth) were important. But she also found that factors such as the 'home learning environment', 'mother-child closeness' and breast feeding played a role, suggesting opportunities for intervention.

Conclusions

In this chapter we have seen how the social gradient emerges early in the life course – even before birth – and is consistently found across many outcomes important for ECD. The presence of a social gradient demonstrates the need for a progressive, population-based response and dispels the myth of a marginalised 'underclass'.

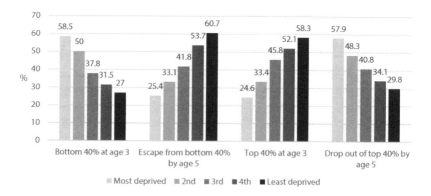

Source: Adapted from Dearden (2010)

FIGURE 9.10 British Ability Scale (BAS) scores by SEP quintile, dynamics between ages 3 and 5

None of these disparities is inevitable. The evidence we have seen of improvements over time shows it is possible to overcome the burdens of early disadvantage.

There are both direct and indirect means of tackling inequalities (Donkin et al., 2014). Money matters and poverty reduction is clearly a direct and important policy lever. But income is only one of the factors explaining inequalities in ECD. Other important influences on ECD, such as the home learning environment, parenting skills and maternal health behaviours in pregnancy are modifiable, suggesting important opportunities for prevention.

Many of the outcomes reviewed in this chapter are interrelated and an understanding of 'chains of risk' may be helpful in pinpointing opportunities for prevention of adverse outcomes later on.

A survey of 24,319 women in England (Henderson et al., 2013), found women in all minority ethnic groups tended to have less access to maternity care – with fewer antenatal checks, fewer scans, less screening and fewer home visits postnatally – than White women. Women from minority groups were 'less likely to feel spoken to so they could understand, to be treated with kindness, to be sufficiently involved in decisions and to have confidence and trust in the staff'. Until these stark disparities are addressed, it is unlikely we will see substantial improvements in outcomes for their children.

The first 1001 days offer an extraordinary opportunity to break the link between social background and children's life chances. Because parents exert such a crucial influence on their children's development, it will be essential to 'think family'. This will mean both efforts to reduce the stressors parents face; and also to build parental capabilities so they are in the best possible position to give their babies the care they need.

Policy recommendations

1. Early identification: Local areas should ensure that data on family vulnerabilities is routinely captured during pregnancy and early childhood, and that this information is used to enable more appropriate and timely access to services.

2. Population needs analysis: Data sharing protocols and systems should be put in place to ensure that anonymised data on vulnerabilities during pregnancy and early childhood can be aggregated and factored into the local Joint Strategic Needs Assessment (JSNA) and service planning.

3. Guidance: Public Health England's National Child and Maternal Health Intelligence Network and NHS Digital should provide guidance and support to local areas to enhance pregnancy and ECD data collection processes, including capture of data on family vulnerabilities, inequalities and ethnicity.

4. Attachment measure: Research should be carried out to develop and test an instrument for the measurement of parental sensitivity and the parent-infant relationship, ensuring it is both scientifically robust, yet practical enough for administration in routine practice.

5. Accountability: Local areas should be required to monitor and report on inequalities in key outcomes during pregnancy and early childhood, by ethnicity and appropriate measure(s) of family background. In England, this could be published via the Public Health Outcomes Framework. Governments should produce a biannual report to Parliament showing progress in improving pregnancy and ECD outcomes, including in reducing inequalities.

Note

1 This is defined in terms of pre-pregnancy or early pregnancy obesity, rather than BMI incorporating gestational weight gain. www.gov.uk/government/statistics/maternity-services-monthly-statistics-july-and-august-2015.

References

Ban, L., Gibson, J.E., West, J., Fiaschi, L., Oates, M.R., & Tata, L.J. (2012). Impact of socio-economic deprivation on maternal perinatal mental illnesses presenting to UK general practice. *British Journal of General Practice*, 62(603), e671–e678.

Bauer, A., Parsonage, M., Knapp, M., Iemmi, V., & Adelaja, B. (2014). The costs of perinatal mental health problems. London: Centre for Mental Health & London School of Economics: Personal Social Services Research Unit.

Berry, J.O. (1995). The Parental Stress Scale: initial psychometric evidence. *Journal of Social & Personal Relationships*, 12, 463–472.

Bromley, C. and Cunningham-Burley, S. (2010). *Growing Up in Scotland: health inequalities in the early years*. Edinburgh: Scottish Government.

Cuthbert, C. (2011). *All babies count: Prevention and protection for vulnerable babies*. London: NSPCC.

Davies, S.C. (2015). *Annual report of the Chief Medical Officer, 2014, the health of the 51%: women*. London: Department of Health.

Dearden, L., Sibieta, L., & Sylva, K. (2011). The socio-economic gradient in early child outcomes: evidence from the MCS. *Longitudinal & Life Course Studies*, 2(1), 19–40.

Department of Health. (2016). *Alcohol guidelines review—report from the guidelines development group to the UK Chief Medical Officers*. London: Department of Health.

Donkin, A., Roberts, J., Tedstone, A., & Marmot, M. (2014). Family socio-economic status and young children's outcomes. *Journal of Children's Services*, 9(2), 83–95.

Fearon, R.P., Bakermans-Kranenburg, M.J., Van IJzendoorn, M.H., Lapsley, A.M., & Roisman, G.I. (2010). The significance of insecure attachment and disorganization in the development of children's externalizing behavior: a meta-analytic study. *Child Development*, 81(2), 435–456.

Fitzpatrick, K.E., Gray, R., & Quigley, M.A. (2016). Women's longitudinal patterns of smoking during the pre-conception, pregnancy and postnatal period: evidence from the UK Infant Feeding Survey. *PLoS One*, 11(4), e0153447.

Galloway, S. (2014). *An unfair sentence: All babies count: spotlight on the criminal justice system*. London: NSPCC

Glover, V. (2014). Maternal depression, anxiety and stress during pregnancy and child outcome: what needs to be done. *Best Practice & Research Clinical Obstetrics & Gynaecology*, 28(1), 25–35.

Graya, R., Headleyb, J., Oakleya, L., Kurinczuka, J.J., Brocklehursta, P., & Hollowella, J. (2009). Towards an understanding of variations in infant mortality rates between different ethnic groups in England and Wales. Inequalities in infant mortality project briefing paper 3. Oxford: National Perinatal Epidemiology Unit.

Hart B., & Risley, T. (1995). *Meaningful differences in the everyday experiences of young American children*. Baltimore: Paul Brookes.

Henderson, J., Gao, H., & Redshaw, M. (2013). Experiencing maternity care: the care received and perceptions of women from different ethnic groups. *BMC Pregnancy and Childbirth*, 13(1), 196.

Heslehurst, N., Rankin, J., Wilkinson, J.R., & Summerbell, C.D. (2010). A nationally representative study of maternal obesity in England, UK: trends in incidence and demographic inequalities in 619,323 births, 1989–2007. *International Journal of Obesity*, 34, 420–428.

Heslehurst, N., Sattar, N., Rajasingam, D., Wilkinson, J., Summerbell, C. D., & Rankin, J. (2012). Existing maternal obesity guidelines may increase inequalities between ethnic groups: a national epidemiological study of 502,474 births in England. *BMC Pregnancy and Childbirth*, 12(1), 156.

Hogg, S. (2012). *Prevention in mind*. London: NSPCC.

Hogg, S. (2015). *An unstable start. All babies count: spotlight on homelessness*. London: NSPCC.

Hollowell, J., Kurinczuk, J.J., Brocklehurst, P., & Gray, R. (2011). Social and ethnic inequalities in infant mortality: a perspective from the United Kingdom. *Seminars in Perinatology*, 35(4), 240–244.

Joint Commissioning Panel for Mental Health. (2012). *Guidance for commissioners of perinatal mental health services*. London: Joint Commissioning Panel for Mental Health.

Kuh, D., & Ben-Shlomo, Y. (2004). *A lifecourse approach to chronic disease epidemiology*. Oxford: OUP.

McAndrew, F., et al. (2012). *Infant Feeding Survey 2010*. London: NHS Digital.

Molyneaux, E., Poston, L., Ashurst-Williams, S., & Howard, L.M. (2014). Obesity and mental disorders during pregnancy and postpartum: a systematic review and meta-analaysis. *Obstet Gynecol*, 123(4), 857–867.

NHS Digital Maternity services monthly statistics, England, April 2016, experimental statistics. Available from: http://digital.nhs.uk/catalogue/PUB21506 (Accessed 25th September 2016).

Norman, P.P., Gregory, I., Dorling, D., & Baker, A. (2008). Geographical trends in infant mortality: England and Wales, 1970–2006. *Health Statistics Q*, 40, 18–29.

ONS Statistical bulletin (2015). Pregnancy and ethnic factors influencing births and infant mortality: 2013. London: ONS.

Parkes, A., Sweeting, H., & Wight, D. (2015). Parenting stress and parent support among mothers with high and low education. *Journal of Family Psychology*, 29(6), 907–918.

Rayns, G., Dawe, S., & Cuthbert, C. (2013). *All babies count: spotlight on drugs and alcohol*. London: NSPCC,

Roulstone, S., Law, J., Rush, R., Clegg, J., & Peters, T. (2010). *Investigating the role of language in children's early educational outcomes*. London: Department for Education RR134.

Rowe, M. (2008). Child directed speech: relation to socioeconomic status, knowledge of child development and child vocabulary skill. *Journal of Child Language*, 35(1), 185–205.

Santorelli, G., Petherick, E., Waiblinger, D., Cabieses, B., & Fairley, L. (2013). Ethnic differences in the initiation and duration of breast feeding – results from the Born In Bradford Birth Cohort Study. *Paediatric & Perinatal Epidemiology*, 27(4), 388–392.

The Scottish Government. (2015). *Tackling inequalities in the early years. Key messages from 10 years of the Growing Up in Scotland study*. Edinburgh: The Scottish Government.

Schieman, S. (2009). When work interferes with life: work-non-work interference and the influence of work related demands and resources. *American Sociological Review*, 74, 966–988.

Sheiwe, A. (2011). A good place for bringing up children? Mother's neighbourhood perceptions and children's behavioural development in the Millennium Cohort Study. *Journal of Epidemiology & Public Health*, 65, A6-A7.

US Department of Health & Human Services. (2004). *The health consequences of smoking: A report of the Surgeon General*. Atlanta, GA: US Department of Health & Human Services, Centers for Disease Control and Prevention.

Victora, C.G., Bahl, R., Barros, A.J., França, G.V., Horton, S., Krasevec, J., Murch, S., Sankar, M.J., Walker, N., Rollins, N.C., & Group, T.L.B.S. (2016). Breastfeeding in the 21st century: epidemiology, mechanisms, and lifelong effect. *The Lancet*, 387, 475–490.

Weightman, A.L. (2012). Social inequality and infant health in the UK. Systematic review and meta-analyses. *BMJ Open*.

Wickham, S., Anwar, E., Barr, B., Law, C., & Taylor-Robinson, D. (2016). Poverty and child health in the UK: using evidence for action. *Archives of Disease in Childhood*, 1–8.

10

ANTENATAL AND POSTNATAL MENTAL HEALTH PROBLEMS

Prevention and treatment

Alain Gregoire

In the past 20 years there has been a steady increase in interest and activity in the field commonly referred to as perinatal mental health, which is concerned with the mental health of women in pregnancy and postnatally and the impact of poor health at this time on them and their children. In the UK these developments have included research, clinical practice and policy, but they have not been accompanied by a significant increase in the availability of good quality care, or improved outcomes for women and their families. This lack of progress has been due to a widespread lack of appreciation of the importance of this area of health to the current generation and the next, leading to an absence of the sustained and coordinated effort required from multiple agencies to address the complexity of needs involved. A national campaign in the UK to address these two issues has led to a considerable shift in both attitudes and action, but if we are to improve the future health and wellbeing of populations throughout the world greater priority needs to be given to maternal mental health.

Antenatal and postnatal mental health: Impact on women's lives

The impact of mental health problems on women's lives in the reproductive years is dramatic. Depression, for example, is the most important cause of life-years lost through disability or premature death in women at this time (WHO, 2004). The prevalence of depression at any time throughout the perinatal period emerges consistently from most studies at around 10 to 15 per cent (e.g. Evans et al., 2001). Calculations of total period prevalence in pregnancy produced rates of nearly 13 per cent in pregnancy and 22 per cent in the first year postnatal (Gavin et al., 2005). As such, the prevalence of this severely disabling condition exceeds that of most major physical health complications that occur during pregnancy and postnatally.

Yet specialist maternity services, provided universally in high-income countries and in some low- and middle-income countries, focus almost exclusively on physical health, sometimes to the complete exclusion of this common and disabling condition. The long-term course of depression is no less alarming. As is true of depression at other times, depression in the perinatal period is often a chronic and recurrent condition: 30 per cent of women will continue to experience this beyond the first year after birth (Wisner et al., 2004), with over 40 per cent experiencing subsequent episodes (Cooper & Murray, 1995).

The perinatal period does not appear to offer protection from any form of mental health problem: the full range of conditions, including depression, obsessive compulsive disorder and PTSD occur at this time, generally at similarly high, or slightly increased, rates to those found at other times in women's lives. An important exception is postpartum psychosis, which in the first few weeks after birth represents the highest risk period for psychosis described in human lives (e.g. Kendell et al., 1987), affecting about one in 500 women. The majority of these present with major disturbance of mood and are probably episodes of bipolar disorder. Women with pre-existing diagnoses of bipolar disorder are at substantially increased risk in the immediate postnatal period (Munk-Olsen et al., 2009). When compared to non-postnatal women, those with a postpartum psychosis are more rapidly and severely symptomatic (Wisner & Wheeler, 1994). The highest period of risk appears to be in the first few days but continues for about 3 months postpartum (Valdimarsdóttir et al., 2009). The risk of recurrence in subsequent pregnancies exceeds 50 per cent (Robertson et al., 2005)

Although most nonpsychotic conditions may not be substantially increased in prevalence during the perinatal period, they are often a source of greatly increased distress and disability at this time. Obsessive-compulsive disorder is about twice as common in the perinatal period (Russell et al., 2013; Fairbrother et al., 2016) but more importantly is very commonly associated with extremely distressing obsessional thoughts of harming the baby, and one study of women suffering from postnatal OCD found that they were affected by their symptoms for an average of 9.6 hours a day (Challacombe, 2016).

In addition to causing substantial suffering and disability, mental disorders are an important cause of maternal death. The UK Confidential Enquiry into Maternal Deaths found that nearly 10 per cent of women who died in the UK during pregnancy or in the first 6 weeks postnatally had died from mental health related causes (MBRRACE, 2015). From 6 weeks to 1 year postnatally, almost a quarter of all maternal deaths were related to mental health problems. The enquiry report emphasises that these mental health problems can develop very rapidly and effective action is often not taken quickly enough.

Antenatal and postnatal mental health: Impact on children's lives

It is now established from the consistent findings of research over the past 20 years or so that perinatal mental health problems can have lasting effects on the emotional, behavioural, intellectual and social development of children exposed as foetuses or infants. These findings are described in more detail by Balbernie (00–01).

The high prevalence of mental health problems during pregnancy and postnatally and the potentially long-term long-lasting effects on the offspring make this a substantial public health issue. In addition to the human suffering and disability involved, the economic implications are considerable. Bauer et al. (2014) conducted an economic analysis of data relating to outcomes for mother and child for just three conditions, postpartum psychosis and depression and antenatal anxiety, in relation to the UK. They found that the costs attributable to these conditions was £8.1billion, of which approximately three quarters related to the economic burden of the adverse outcomes for children over the subsequent 10 years only (whereas evidence now indicates that these outcomes persist at least into their twenties).

Interventions for improving mental health

Nurturing children, and young children in particular, is probably the most important activity we undertake for the future of our species. Since being a good enough parent is probably also one of the most difficult things we do, it is not unreasonable to suggest that all parents should have support from others.

NICE (2014) systematically reviewed evidence for the full range of interventions in prevention and treatment of perinatal mental health problems, using a systematic approach and multiple meta-analyses. The evidence for the effect of any interventions, from peer support to formal therapies, on the whole population without identified risk factors was too weak to make any recommendations. However, studies of samples of women with previous anxiety or depression, and 'sub-threshold' symptoms, showed more consistently positive benefit from both guided self-help and formal psychological therapies. Thus, prediction of risk based on past history and current low-level symptoms can lead to effective prevention. There was little evidence, however, that using other known environmental risk factors for prediction and targeted prevention can produce significant benefit across a range of outcomes for mother or child.

Evidence is emerging that the mother's own past history of childhood maltreatment may be the most important predictor of poor mental health in the perinatal period (Plant, et al., 2013). The strong link between childhood trauma in mothers and outcomes for their children seem to be mediated in part by their mental health in the perinatal period. Studies of benefits from interventions targeted at women with the risk factor of maltreatment in their own childhoods, have not so far been reported, but the complex psychological, physiological and epigenetic processes involved in this intergenerational transmission of mental health vulnerabilities are the subject of much current research (Pawlby et al., 00–04).

It has long been known that traumatic experiences in adults are associated with the well-described syndrome of post-traumatic stress disorder (PTSD) and that childhood maltreatment increases vulnerability to mental disorders. Surprisingly, the link between childhood traumatic experiences and the symptoms of PTSD appears to have been largely ignored, possibly because we have been distracted by the somewhat enigmatic and rather unstable concept of 'borderline personality disorder'. Various studies have shown that in excess of 80 per cent of people with a diagnosis of 'borderline personality disorder' describe maltreatment in childhood (e.g. Perry & Herman, 1993). This is almost certainly an under estimate given methodological difficulties. Hobson et al. (2005) found that about 80 per cent of infants of mothers with 'borderline personality disorder' were disorganised in their attachments at 13 months. To complete this tragic intergenerational story, over 50 per cent of maltreated children develop personality disorder in adulthood (Johnson et al., 1999). Given these findings and the difficulty in distinguishing between the features of borderline personality disorder and complex PTSD it could be postulated that these are at least overlapping or indeed possibly the same conditions. Although this may appear to be an issue of semantics, the diagnosis of personality disorder elicits damaging pejorative assumptions, attitudes and behaviours, whereas the term PTSD is a more sympathetic concept, which acknowledges some of the roots of individual suffering. It also opens up the opportunity for more productive research and clinical practice to help this generation and the next. This is a crucially important issue in research and clinical practice as the prevalence among women of child-bearing age is high and they have high levels of contact with health services. Furthermore, the emotional instability associated with this condition leads to high scores on depression and anxiety questionnaires and a risk of misdiagnosis and poorly tailored care. Finally, the research on intergenerational effects of parental mental health problems has consistently pointed to personality disorders as the diagnosis most predictive of poor child outcomes (e.g. Howard et al., 2003).

The evidence for the benefits of psychological and pharmacological treatments on maternal outcomes in women with perinatal mental health problems was consistent and robust enough on systematic review and meta-analysis to lead to several treatment recommendations by NICE (2014). These recommended interventions include:

- low intensity psychological intervention for mild anxiety and depression
- high intensity psychological intervention for anxiety, including PTSD, and depression
- antidepressants for moderate to severe depression, with or without combining with high intensity psychological intervention
- antidepressants for women with a past history of severe depression and current mild-to-moderate symptoms
- psychological interventions and antipsychotic medications for women with bipolar disorder.

Most of the research demonstrating the effectiveness of these interventions has been carried out in high-income countries. Far fewer intervention studies have been done in low- and middle-income countries. In general, though, these few demonstrate positive effects from low intensity psychological interventions delivered by primary care workers with minimal training (Rahman et al., 2013).

Although these maternal mental health conditions are known to have potential for adverse effects on the child, there is little consistent evidence that treatment of the maternal conditions, even if effective, has a significant impact on child outcomes. This suggests that specific interventions aimed at improving outcomes for these children, possibly through interventions targeting the parent infant relationship, may be necessary. However, in this area too, consistent evidence of improved outcomes for children of women with mental health problems is scant (NICE, 2014). This is an important area of current research. In the meantime, given the importance and scale of this issue, there is a strong clinical consensus in support of delivering interventions that have been shown in other contexts to improve parent infant attachment and short-term child outcomes. These include video feedback programmes and parent-infant psychotherapy (NICE NG26, 2016).

Services: Society's investment in human infrastructure

The variety of treatment approaches required to meet the diverse needs of women and their families, demands a range of services coordinated across a pathway of care. Furthermore, interventions, for prevention or treatment, rely on identification of those women who need them. Rates of detection by professionals of women with past histories of mental health problems, as well as women who are currently unwell, is poor even in high-income countries with well developed universal services (Gavin et al, in press). Thus, services must implement processes for routine identification within pathways that lead to appropriate interventions. This requires the collaboration of all services and professionals involved, including maternity and primary care services. In the UK for example, pathways involve midwives, obstetricians, general practitioners, health visitors and mental health professionals in primary care and specialist services (NICE, 2014a). The particular perinatal needs of women and their families has led to the gradual development of subspecialists among most of these professional groups, for example specialist mental health midwives and health visitors who support the development and implementation of pathways and provide training and supervision to their colleagues (NSPCC, 2014).

Some level of training is required by all professionals involved. All midwives and health visitors need an understanding of normal psychological experiences, and to be able to distinguish them from symptoms of disabling problems that benefit from treatment. For example, thoughts of accidentally harming the baby are universal among new mothers and thoughts that they might deliberately harm the baby occur in about 50 per cent (Fairbrother & Woody, 2008), whereas frequent and repeated thoughts, amounting to obsessive-compulsive disorder are experienced by about 2 per cent of women (Fairbrother et al., 2016). Professionals working with women at this time need to be able to confidently reassure and support women with these normal but at times alarming thoughts and not over react to them, but equally they must recognise and know how to get the right help for women with more significant difficulties. It is essential that services define such activities as part of their role, give them the time to fulfill this role, and establish pathways of care that give them the support they need and the opportunity for onward referral.

The services most adapted to these needs are specialist perinatal mental health services operating both community and inpatient (mother and baby unit) services for women with severe mental health problems. They provide multidisciplinary care for prevention and treatment as well as support to other professionals and services across the rest of the pathway. There is evidence that by focussing on the mother–infant relationship as well as the mother's illness, infant outcomes can be improved by such services (Kenny et al., 2013).

These specialist services have developed in the UK as part of a stratified model of care. This is best described as a pathway showing the elements of care that patients with different types and levels of need should access and the interrelationships between those elements. In general women with more severe and complex conditions (defined by diagnosis, duration and disability) require the more complex and specialised levels of care. Women with milder conditions, who constitute the vast majority, need generalised support or less specialised forms of mental health intervention from universal (maternity or health visiting) or primary-care-based services. However, there are close connections between all elements. For example, Jane, suffering with a moderate level of depression receives care from her midwife and a therapist in primary care, but also needs specialist information to help her make a decision about whether to continue antidepressant medication; Shona, who has bipolar disorder receives care from a nurse and doctor in the perinatal mental health team and needs the support and care of her midwife, GP, health visitor, and local mothers and babies support group.

Despite the enormous human and economic burden caused by poor maternal mental health and the clear evidence for effective, and indeed cheap, health interventions, most women, whether in high-, middle- or low-income countries, do not have access to the healthcare they need (Bauer, 2013; WHO, 2008). The stories of unrecognised and untreated suffering told by so many women (e.g. see MMHA, Everyone's Business Real Life Stories) and examples of inadequate care leading to maternal deaths in the UK (MBRRACE, 2015), demonstrate that even in a high-income country like the UK, women are suffering as a result of inhumane, discriminatory and dangerous service provision.

In the UK, severe inequity of access to mental health services across the country and gross lack of parity with access to maternity physical healthcare, has led to the formation of the Maternal Mental Health Alliance (see MMHA website) and its campaign for better maternal mental healthcare.

The campaign, with a primary message embodied in the title 'Everyone's Business', initially targeted national UK politicians and national management of the health service, with considerable success (MMHA, Everyone's Business Evaluation). The united voice of the MMHA representing over 80 national patient and professional organisations provided the influence needed to open doors at every level, giving powerful opportunities to demonstrate the importance of this area, the urgent need for action, and the value to individuals and society of providing good quality care. The three most influential tools produced by the campaign have been an economic report commissioned from the London School of Economics (Bauer et al., 2014), a National Map of current services and the stories of individual women and families (MMHA Everyone's Business: Real Life Stories). This is a potent visual image of areas with complete absence of specialist perinatal services, coloured red, in most parts of the UK.

The MMHA and the campaign appear to be effecting significant change. There has been a dramatic shift in perceptions and policy: from being perceived as a minor issue, often not worthy of any mention, perinatal mental health is now an accepted and declared priority in mental healthcare and indeed across the whole of healthcare and social policy. Government, up to the most senior level including the prime minister, have committed themselves to improved services through both public declaration, and allocation of new and substantial financial resources: £365 million of extra money has been provided to the NHS to fund the development of comprehensive new services across England over the next 5 years, with equivalent sums available for Wales. The NHS in England has been given a mandate by the government to ensure that these services are delivered, and has engaged in a programme of change to ensure this happens.

Future directions

There are many questions in the field of maternal and infant mental health that remain unanswered and require further research. In particular, the immeasurable potential benefit of better understanding and interventions that could effect positive intergenerational changes must be explored. However, countless women and their families throughout the world are failed every day and suffer unnecessarily because so much of what research has already revealed is not leading to change in social policy, clinical practice or service delivery. We all have a responsibility, and indeed an investment, in changing this unacceptable situation personally, locally, nationally and globally.

Three key actions for a better future:

- All countries should have policies on maternal mental health including in particular public health, maternity care and mental healthcare.
- All professionals working with women in pregnancy and postnatally should consider what role they can play in improving maternal mental health, ensure they have the skills and knowledge to fulfil that role and work with others to fulfil that role.
- All organisations involved in the health or wellbeing of parents or children or of populations should consider what role they can play in improving maternal mental health and work with others to fulfil that role.

References

Bauer, A., Parsonage, M., Knapp, M., Iemmi, V., & Adelaja, B. (2014). *The Costs of Perinatal Mental Health Problems.* London: London School of Economics and Centre for Mental Health. http://eprints.lse.ac.uk/59885/1/__lse.ac.uk_storage_LIBRARY_Secondary_libfile_shared_repository_Content_Bauer,%20M_Bauer_Costs_perinatal_%20mental_2014_Bauer_Costs_perinatal_mental_2014_author.pdf

Challacombe, F.L., Salkovskis, P.M., Woolgar, M., Wilkinson, E.L., Read, J., & Acheson, R. (2016). Parenting and mother-infant interactions in the context of maternal postpartum obsessive-compulsive disorder. *Effects of obsessional symptoms and mood, 44,* 11–20. doi:10.1016/j.infbeh.2016.04.003. Epub 2016 May 31.

Cooper, P.J., & Murray, L. (1995). Course and recurrence of postnatal depression. *The British Journal of Psychiatry, 166,* 191–195.

Evans, J., Heron, J., Francomb, H., Oke, S., & Golding, J. (2001). Cohort study of depressed mood during pregnancy and after childbirth. *British Medical Journal, 323,* 257–260.

Fairbrother, N., & Woody, S.R. (2008). New mothers' thoughts of harm related to the newborn. *Archives of Womens Mental Health,* 11(3), 221–229. doi:10.1007/s00737-008-0016-7

Fairbrother, N., Janssen, P., Antony, M., Tucker, E., & Young, A. (2016). Perinatal anxiety disorder prevalence and incidence. *Journal of Affective Disorders, 200,* 148–155.

Gavin, N.I., Gaynes, B.N., Lohr, K.N., Meltzer-Brody, S., Gartlehner, G., & Swinson, T. (2005). Perinatal depression: A systematic review of prevalence and incidence. *Obstetrics and Gynecology,* 106(5 Pt 1), 1071–1083.

Gavin, N.I., Meltzer-Brody, S., Glover, & Gaynes, B.N. (in Press). Perinatal depression: Screening accuracy and outcomes.

Hobson, R.P., Patrick, M., Crandell, L., García-Pérez, R., & Lee, A. (2005). Personal relatedness and attachment in infants of mothers with borderline personality disorder. *Developmental Psychopathology Spring,* 17(2), 329–347.

Howard, L., Shah, N., Salmon, M., & Appleby, L. (2003). Predictors of social services supervision of babies of mothers with mental illness after admission to a psychiatric mother and baby unit. *Social Psychiatry and Psychiatric Epidemiology,* 38(8), 450–455.

Johnson, J.G., Cohen, P., Brown, J., Smailes, E.M., & Bernstein, D.P. (1999). Childhood maltreatment increases risk for personality disorders during early adulthood. *Archives of General Psychiatry,* 56(7), 600–606. doi:10.1001/archpsyc.56.7.600

Kendell, R.E., Chalmers, J.C., & Platz, C. (1987). Epidemiology of puerperal psychoses. *The British Journal of Psychiatry,* 150(5), 662–673. doi:10.1192/bjp.150.5

Kenny, M., Conroy, S., Pariate, C., Seneveratne, G., Pawlby, S. (2013). Mother infant interaction in mother and baby unit patients: Before and after treatment. *Journal of Psychiatric Research,* 47(9), 1192–1198. http://dx.doi.org/10.1016/j.jpsychires.2013.05.012

MBRRACE (2015). Saving Lives. The Confidential Enquiry into Maternal Deaths. https://npeu.ox.ac.uk/downloads/files/mbrrace-uk/reports/MBRRACE-UK%20Maternal%20Report%202015.pdf

MMHA. The Maternal Mental Health Alliance. http://maternalmentalhealthalliance.org

MMHA. Everyone's Business Evaluation Paper. http://everyonesbusiness.org.uk/wp-content/uploads/2016/07/Everyones-Business-Campaign-Evaluation-Briefing-Paper.pdf

MMHA. Everyone's Business: Real Life Stories. http://everyonesbusiness.org.uk/?page_id=144

Munk-Olsen, T., Laursen, T.M., Mendelson, T., Pedersen, C.B., Mors, O., Mortensen, P.B. (2009). Risks and predictors of readmission for a mental disorder during the postpartum period. *Archives of General Psychiatry,* 66(2), 189–195. doi:10.1001/archgenpsychiatry.2008.528

NICE (National Institute for Health and Care Excellence) (2014). Antenatal and Postnatal Mental Health, Clinical Guideline 192 https://www.nice.org.uk/guidance/cg192

NICE (National Institute for Health and Care Excellence). (2014a). Pathways: Antenatal and Postnatal Mental Health. http://pathways.nice.org.uk/pathways/antenatal-and-postnatal-mental-health

NSPCC (2014). Prevention in Mind. http://everyonesbusiness.org.uk/wp-content/uploads/2014/06/NSPCC-Spotlight-report-on-Perinatal-Mental-Health.pdf

Perry, J.C., & Herman, J.L. (1993). Trauma and defence in the etiology of borderline personality disorder. In Borderline Personality Disorder: Etiology and Treatment, J. Paris (ed.). Washington, DC: American Psychiatric Press.

Plant, D., Barker, E.D., Waters, C.S., Pawlby, S., Pariante, C. (2013). Intergenerational transmission of maltreatment and psychopathology: The role of antenatal depression. *Psychological Medicine, 43*(3), 519–528. doi:10.1017/S0033291712001298. Epub 2012 Jun 14.

Rahman, A., Fisher, J., Bower, P., Luchters, S., Tran, T., Yasamy, M.T., Saxena, S., Waheed, W. (2013). Interventions for common perinatal mental disorders in women in low- and middle-income countries: A systematic review and meta-analysis. *Bulletin of the World Health Organization,* 91(8), 593–601I. doi:http://dx.doi.org/10.2471/BLT.12.109819 [PDF]

Robertson, E., Jones, I., Haque, S., Holder, R., Craddock, N. (2005). Risk of puerperal and non- puerperal recurrence of illness following bipolar affective puerperal (post-partum) psychosis. *British Journal of Psychiatry, 186,* 258–259.

Russell, E.J., Fawcett, J.M., & Mazmanian, D. (2013). Risk of obsessive-compulsive disorder in pregnant and postpartum women: A meta-analysis. *Journal of Clinical Psychiatry, 74*(4), 377–385.

Valdimarsdóttir, U., Hultman, C.M., Harlow, B., Cnattingius, S., Sparén, P. (2009). Psychotic illness in first-time mothers with no previous psychiatric hospitalizations: A population-based study. *PLoS Medicine,* 6, e13.

WHO (World Health Organization). (2004). Global Burden of Disease, Part 4. http://who.int/healthinfo/global_burden_disease/GBD_report_2004update_part4.pdf

WHO (World Health Organization). (2008). Maternal mental health and child health and development in low and middle income countries: Report of the meeting held in Geneva, Switzerland, 30 January–1 February. ISBN 978 92 4 159714 2.

Wisner, K.L., Wheeler, S.B. (1994). Prevention of recurrent postpartum major depression. *Hospital and Community Psychiatry, 45,* 1191–1196.

Wisner, K.L, Perel, J.M., Peindl, K.S., Hanusa, B.H. (2004). Timing of depression recurrence in the first year after birth. *Journal of Affective Disorders, 78,* 249–252.

11

STRESS IN PREGNANCY CAN CHANGE FETAL AND CHILD DEVELOPMENT

Vivette Glover

Stress during pregnancy can change fetal and child development in harmful ways (Glover, 2014). If we want to improve infant and child wellbeing, we need to do more to support mothers during pregnancy. The environment in the womb can alter the development of the fetus, with a long-lasting effect on the child (Barker, 2003). This process is called 'fetal programming', but the term programming does not imply that this trajectory cannot be changed later. Sensitive mothering, for example, can reverse at least some of the effects of antenatal stress (Bergman et al., 2010). Brains can be changed to some extent, for better or worse, throughout life, but for many influences it is more plastic, or more easy to alter, early on.

Types of outcome affected

Many types of infant and child outcome can be altered by antenatal stress, both neurodevelopmental and physical (Glover, 2015; Monk, 2001). Different children are affected in different ways, or not at all. The neurodevelopmental problems for the child include an increased risk of emotional and behavioural problems, including anxiety and depression, ADHD, conduct disorder (O'Connor et al., 2002), autism spectrum disorder (Hecht et al., 2016) and cognitive difficulties (Laplante et al., 2008). These problems can last at least until late adolescence (Pearson et al., 2013).

If the mother is stressed while she is pregnant she is more likely to smoke or drink, and to be stressed, anxious or depressed postnatally, which may affect her parenting. All these can have independent effects on the development of the fetus, infant or child. But even when all these factors are taken into account, the independent effects of antenatal maternal mood remain clear. We found that if the mother was in the top 15 per cent for symptoms of antenatal anxiety or depression, this doubled the risk (from about 6 to 12 per cent) of her child having a mental disorder at age 13, even after allowing for a wide range of confounding factors (O'Donnell et al., 2014a).

The physical effects of antenatal stress on the fetus and infant include increased risk of premature birth and being smaller for gestational age (Glover, 2014). Antenatal stress is also associated with increased risk of asthma (Khashan et al., 2012). Other studies have shown associations with the telomere length in the infant (Entringer et al., 2012), and also with the pattern of the intestinal microbiome (Zijlmans et al., 2015). The telomere is the structure at the end of each chromosome, which protects it from damage. A reduced telomere length might be associated with living less long. The microbiome is the pattern of different bacteria that are present, especially in the intestine. Disruption of the microbiome in early life has the potential to influence neurodevelopment and long-term mental health outcomes (O'Mahony et al., 2015).

Different types of stress

Child outcomes have been found to be altered in association with many different types of antenatal stress. These include increased antenatal symptoms of anxiety and depression, increased pregnancy-related anxiety (concerns about the outcome of the pregnancy) and a bad relationship with the partner (Glover, 2014). Pregnancy-specific anxiety, in particular, has been found to be associated with adverse outcomes for the child (Nolvi et al., 2016). Stress in pregnancy can also be caused by exposure to a natural disaster, such as an ice storm in Canada (King & Laplante, 2005), or to man-made acute disasters such as 9/11 (Yehuda et al., 2005). Clearly it is not just a diagnosed mental illness in the mother that can affect fetal and child development, but a much wider range of types of stress. Furthermore it is also not only extreme or 'toxic' stress that can have an effect. Studies have shown that mothers who say they were exposed to more 'daily hassles' had children with more problems (Huizink et al., 2002).

A history of trauma or abuse in the mother's childhood is an important factor. This can amplify the effects of antenatal depression on child behavioural problems (Pawlby et al., 2011), and the effects of antenatal anxiety on babies being small for gestational age (Blackmore et al., 2016). A maternal history of trauma is thus relevant to infant outcomes too.

We still do not know whether different types of stress have different effects on child outcomes. Most forms of stress, anxiety and depression are associated with raised levels of the stress hormone cortisol, but others, such as post-traumatic stress disorder (PTSD) which can be present in mothers exposed to early abuse or trauma, are associated with lower cortisol levels (Daskalakis et al., 2013), and may have different effects through different mechanisms.

The evidence is still not clear either about which gestational ages are the most sensitive. The risk of schizophrenia is increased by maternal exposure to very severe stress such as the death of an older child, but only in the first trimester (Khashan et al., 2008). But for most outcomes it is not only the first trimester that is important.

The brain continues to develop throughout gestation and indeed long after birth, and the way it develops can continue to be changed by the environment.

Biological mechanisms

Genetics

Not all children are affected by antenatal stress, and those that are can be affected in different ways. This is in part due to the nature of the postnatal care. Sensitive mothering can buffer some, although not all, of the effects of the mother's mood in pregnancy (Bergman et al., 2010). But the effects of antenatal stress on the child's development also depend on the genetic makeup of the child him or herself. There is not one single gene type that predisposes to problems such as anxiety, depression or ADHD, but very many gene variants, all of small effect. The particular combination of gene variants (or polymorphisms) in the fetus will affect how the in utero environment changes the development of the fetal brain. We have shown, for example, that if the child has a particular variant of the gene brain-derived neurotrophic factor (BDNF, which controls neuronal growth) and the mother is anxious during pregnancy then the child is slightly, but significantly more likely, to suffer from symptoms of anxiety or depression (O'Donnell et al., 2014b) though the risk for ADHD or cognitive development is not affected. However if the child has a particular variant of the gene for COMT (the enzyme that breaks down dopamine, adrenaline and noradrenaline) and the mother is anxious during pregnancy the child is more likely to have problems with specific types of memory, and with ADHD (in preparation). Hill and colleagues (Hill et al., 2013) have shown that the infant's form of the gene that breaks down serotonin affects the association between antenatal exposure to the stress of life events, and how fussy or irritable the infant is at 5 weeks old.

The genetic make-up of the mother is important too. If the mother has one particular variant of the gene that controls the transport of serotonin into cells, and is exposed to antenatal stress, her child is more likely to have symptoms on the autism spectrum, (Hecht et al., 2016).

Biological changes in the mother and the placenta

We do not yet know what biological changes in the mother, caused by stress, anxiety or depression, are most important for fetal programming. Cortisol may be involved, but other factors are likely to be at least as, if not more important (Glover et al., 2010). An alteration in the mother's immune functioning in antenatal depression is likely to be involved (Gilman et al., 2016).

There is evidence that a change of function of the placenta is important too. The placenta protects the fetus from potentially toxic or harmful chemicals from the mother, but how it does this, and the extent to which it filters or breaks down substances, depends on the signals it receives from the mother. If the mother is anxious or stressed there is less of the enzyme which breaks down cortisol in the placenta (O'Donnell et al., 2012). If the mother has more symptoms of depression, there is also more of the receptor which responds to cortisol (Raikkonen et al., 2015). Thus the mother's mood may alter the fetal exposure to cortisol, independently of raising cortisol levels in the mother. And increased fetal exposure to cortisol can affect the development of the fetal brain (Bergman et al., 2010). Epigenetic changes (see below) in the placental gene which breaks down cortisol, have been shown to be associated with alterations in fetal behaviour (Monk et al., 2016). There are probably other important changes in the placenta too (Glover, 2015), including in the control fetal exposure to serotonin.

Epigenetics

Many of the changes observed in the infant and child due to fetal programming are probably due to epigenetic modifications, including in the brain (Meaney et al., 2007; Monk et al., 2012). Epigenetic means 'on top of genetics', and epigenetic changes are due to the addition of extra chemical groups, to the DNA. These control whether each gene is turned on or off, and if it is turned on, by how much. Every cell in the body has the same basic DNA sequence, and it is epigenetic modifications which determine whether a cell becomes that of a specific tissue, such as a liver cell or a muscle cell. And within each tissue, including the brain, the environment can cause further epigenetic changes, which may last throughout the lifetime, or which may be reversible. Such changes can help to determine how the wiring pattern in the brain develops, and which pathways are more sensitive or more or less active.

Epigenetic changes to the receptor for cortisol have been particularly studied in the context of prenatal stress. Pregnancy-specific anxiety has been found to be associated with the epigenetic pattern of the gene for this receptor in the cord blood of the newborn (Hompes et al., 2013). Interpersonal violence during the mother's pregnancy has been found to be associated with similar changes in the blood of their adolescent children (Radtke et al., 2011). Prenatal exposure to the stress of a Canadian Ice storm has been shown to be associated with a change to the epigenetic pattern of genes which control the response of the immune system in 13-year-old children (Cao-Lei et al., 2016).

Sex differences

Many studies are finding that the effects of antenatal stress are somewhat different in boys and girls (Glover & Hill, 2012). By adolescence the pattern of emotional, behavioural or cognitive problems are different in the two sexes. Girls are more likely to be anxious or depressed, whereas boys are more likely to be aggressive and break rules. Boys are also more likely to suffer from ADHD and learning difficulties. Antenatal stress can increase the risk of all these problems in a sex-specific way (O'Connor et al., 2002).

Different effects in the two sexes are also starting to be reported in infants, and even earlier, in the fetus (Doyle et al., 2015). One study showed that antenatal maternal anxiety predicted lower vagal reactivity, but only in boys. The authors conclude that their findings are consistent with 'sex differences in fetal programming, whereby prenatal risks are associated with increased stress reactivity in females but decreased reactivity in males, with distinctive advantages and penalties for each sex' (Tibu et al., 2014).

Evolution

Why does antenatal stress have all these effects on infant and child development? A plausible explanation comes from considering their possible significance in evolution (Glover, 2011). For our ancestors much stress will have come from real physical danger, either from dangerous animals such as snakes for example, or from hostile tribes. Many of the changes observed in today's children could well have been adaptive, or protective in situations of real danger. Fetal programming could help to prepare the child for his or her future environment. Greater anxiety in the child could cause more vigilance and a faster detection of danger. Some of the features of ADHD, especially readily distracted attention, could also be protective and associated with a quicker detection of a hostile presence. Rapid reaction, including aggression, may also have helped to cope with attack.

Global perspective

Almost all the research into the effects of antenatal maternal stress, anxiety and depression on fetal, infant and child development, has been carried out in higher income countries. But the effects in lower and middle income countries are likely to be even more severe (Herba, Glover, Ramchandani & Rondon, 2016 Lancet Psychiatry in press). There is often little support after major natural disasters, such as earthquakes. Levels of intimate partner violence are often high; many of the mothers suffer from iron or iodine deficiency, or from infections such as HIV. The pattern of the microbiome has been found to differ in Caucasian and non-Caucasian women. Different genetic patterns in different populations may also alter the programming effects of antenatal depression (Teh et al., 2014). Future research should not be confined to the richer countries.

Interventions

These findings have important clinical implications (Glover, 2014). If maternal depression, anxiety or stress during pregnancy can increase the risk for an adverse outcome for the child, then interventions to reduce such distress should improve the outcome. Most of the adverse effects described above are due to changes in the second and third trimesters. Therefore, although it is best to start interventions as early as possible, there is likely to be benefit from later interventions too.

We know that most anxiety, depression and stress experienced by pregnant women are currently undetected and untreated.

Although much is known about how to treat depression and anxiety, including use of antidepressants for severe depression, and talking therapies such as cognitive behavioural therapy (CBT) for the less severe, there has been little research to investigate benefit to the infant or the child. The only intervention which starts during pregnancy and has included long-term follow-up studies is the Nurse Family Partnership. This gives considerable support to women during pregnancy as well as in the first 2 years, although it was not designed specifically to improve mental health or emotional wellbeing. It has had very impressive results in the United States (Olds et al., 1998), although less so, to date in the United Kingdom. A recent study has shown that brief antenatal CBT for anxiety or depression during pregnancy had very promising effects on the development of the infant. At 9 months there were improvements in problem solving, self-regulation and stress reactivity, which were independent of maternal postnatal mood (Milgrom et al., 2015).

Other types of intervention may be of benefit also. There is interest in the potential benefits of yoga, massage or listening to music for the reduction of anxiety and depression during pregnancy.

Conclusion

Much research shows that if a mother experiences stress, anxiety or depression during pregnancy her child is at increased risk for a range of emotional, behavioural, cognitive and physical problems. To improve infant wellbeing we need to improve the emotional care of pregnant women.

Recommendations

- Health professionals should detect and help with antenatal depression, anxiety, pregnancy-related anxiety, and other types of stress, including the relationship with the partner, and a history of trauma. It is not just a diagnosed mental illness or 'toxic stress' that matters.
- We should not worry women more or make them feel guilty, but offer more support.
- Employers, partners, friends, grandparents can all be encouraged to help support the emotional wellbeing of pregnant women and improve the outcome for the next generation.

References

Barker, D.J. (2003). The developmental origins of adult disease. *Eur J Epidemiol, 18,* 733–736.

Bergman, K., Sarkar, P., Glover, V., & O'Connor, T.G. (2010). Maternal prenatal cortisol and infant cognitive development: moderation by infant-mother attachment. *Biological Psychiatry, 67,* 1026–1032.

Blackmore, E.R., Putnam, F.W., Pressman, E.K., Rubinow, D.R., Putnam, K.T., Matthieu, M.M., Gilchrist, M.A., Jones, I., & O'Connor, T.G. (2016). The effects of trauma history and prenatal affective symptoms on obstetric outcomes. *J Trauma Stress, 29*, 245–252.

Cao-Lei, L., Veru, F., Elgbeili, G., Szyf, M., Laplante, D.P., & King, S. (2016). DNA methylation mediates the effect of exposure to prenatal maternal stress on cytokine production in children at age 13(1/2) years: Project Ice Storm. *Clin Epigenetics, 8*, 54.

Daskalakis, N.P., Lehrner, A., & Yehuda, R. (2013). Endocrine aspects of post-traumatic stress disorder and implications for diagnosis and treatment. *Endocrinol Metab Clin North Am, 42*, 503–513.

Doyle, C., Werner, E., Feng, T., Lee, S., Altemus, M., Isler, J.R., & Monk, C. (2015). Pregnancy distress gets under fetal skin: maternal ambulatory assessment and sex differences in prenatal development. *Dev Psychobiol, 57*, 607–625.

Entringer, S., Buss, C., & Wadhwa, P.D. (2012). Prenatal stress, telomere biology, and fetal programming of health and disease risk. *Science signaling, 5*, pt12.

Gilman, S.E., Cherkerzian, S., Buka, S.L., Hahn, J., Hornig, M., & Goldstein, J.M. (2016). Prenatal immune programming of the sex-dependent risk for major depression. *Transl Psychiatry, 6*, e822.

Glover, V. (2011). Annual Research Review: prenatal stress and the origins of psychopathology: An evolutionary perspective. *J Child Psychol Psychiatry, 52*, 356–367.

Glover, V. (2014). Maternal depression, anxiety and stress during pregnancy and child outcome; what needs to be done. *Best Pract Res Clin Obstet Gynaecol, 28*, 25–35.

Glover, V. (2015). Prenatal stress and its effects on the fetus and the child: possible underlying biological mechanisms. *Adv Neurobiol, 10*, 269–283.

Glover, V., & Hill, J. (2012). Sex differences in the programming effects of prenatal stress on psychopathology and stress responses: an evolutionary perspective. *Physiol Behav, 106*, 736–740.

Glover, V., O'Connor, T.G. & O'Donnell, K. (2010). Prenatal stress and the programming of the HPA axis. *Neuroscience and biobehavioral reviews, 35*, 17–22.

Hecht, P.M., Hudson, M., Connors, S.L., Tilley, M.R., LIU, X., & Beversdorf, D.Q. (2016). Maternal serotonin transporter genotype affects risk for ASD with exposure to prenatal stress. *Autism Res.*

Hill, J., Breen, G., Quinn, J., Tibu, F., Sharp, H., & Pickles, A. (2013). Evidence for interplay between genes and maternal stress in utero: Monoamine Oxidase A polymorphism moderates effects of life events during pregnancy on infant negative emotionality at 5 weeks. *Genes, brain, and behavior.*

Hompes, T., Izzi, B., Gellens, E., Morreels, M., Fieuws, S., Pexsters, A., Schops, G., Dom, M., Van bree, R., Freson, K., Verhaeghe, J., Spitz, B., Demyttenaere, K., Glover, V., Van den bergh, B., Allegaert, K., & Claes, S. (2013). Investigating the influence of maternal cortisol and emotional state during pregnancy on the DNA methylation status of the glucocorticoid receptor gene (NR3C1) promoter region in cord blood. *J Psychiatr Res, 47*, 880–891.

Huizink, A.C., de Medina, P.G., Mulder, E.J., Visser, G.H., & Buitelaar, J.K. (2002). Psychological measures of prenatal stress as predictors of infant temperament. *J Am Acad Child Adolesc Psychiatry, 41*, 1078–1085.

Khashan, A.S., Abel, K.M., Mcnamee, R., Pedersen, M.G., Webb, R.T., Baker, P.N., Kenny, L.C., & Mortensen, P.B. (2008). Higher risk of offspring schizophrenia following antenatal maternal exposure to severe adverse life events. *Arch Gen Psychiatry, 65*, 146–152.

Khashan, A.S., Wicks, S., Dalman, C., Henriksen, T.B., Li, J., Mortensen, P.B., & Kenny, L.C. (2012). Prenatal stress and risk of asthma hospitalization in the offspring: a Swedish population-based study. *Psychosomatic Medicine, 74*, 635–641.

King, S., & Laplante, D.P. (2005). The effects of prenatal maternal stress on children's cognitive development: Project Ice Storm. *Stress, 8*, 35–45.

Laplante, D.P., Brunet, A., Schmitz, N., Ciampi, A., & King, S. (2008). Project Ice Storm: prenatal maternal stress affects cognitive and linguistic functioning in 5 1/2-year-old children. *Journal of the American Academy of Child and Adolescent Psychiatry, 47*, 1063–1072.

Meaney, M.J., Szyf, M., & Seckl, J.R. (2007). Epigenetic mechanisms of perinatal programming of hypothalamic-pituitary-adrenal function and health. *Trends Mol Med, 13*, 269–277.

Milgrom, J., Holt, C., Holt, C.J., Ross, J., Ericksen, J., & Gemmill, A.W. (2015). Feasibility study and pilot randomised trial of an antenatal depression treatment with infant follow-up. *Arch Womens Ment Health, 18*, 717–730.

Monk, C. (2001). Stress and mood disorders during pregnancy: implications for child development. *Psychiatr Q, 72*, 347–357.

Monk, C., Spicer, J., & Champagne, F.A. (2012). Linking prenatal maternal adversity to developmental outcomes in infants: the role of epigenetic pathways. *Development and psychopathology, 24*, 1361–1376.

Monk, C., Feng, T., Lee, S., Krupska, I., Champagne, F.A., & Tycko, B. (2016). Distress During Pregnancy: Epigenetic Regulation of Placenta Glucocorticoid-Related Genes and Fetal Neurobehavior. *Am J Psychiatry, 173*(7), 705–713.

Nolvi, S., Karlsson, L., Bridgett, D.J., Korja, R., Huizink, A.C., Kataja, E.L., & Karlsson, H. (2016). Maternal prenatal stress and infant emotional reactivity six months postpartum. *J Affect Disord, 199*, 163–170.

O'Connor, T.G., Heron, J., Golding, J., Beveridge, M., & Glover, V. (2002). Maternal antenatal anxiety and children's behavioural/emotional problems at 4 years. Report from the Avon Longitudinal Study of Parents and Children. *Br J Psychiatry, 180*, 502–508.

O'Donnell, K.J., Bugge, J.A., Freeman, L., Khalife, N., O'Connor, T.G., & Glover, V. (2012). Maternal prenatal anxiety and downregulation of placental 11beta-HSD2. *Psychoneuroendocrinology, 37*, 818–826.

O'Donnell, K.J., Glover, V., Barker, E.D., & O'Connor, T.G. (2014a). The persisting effect of maternal mood in pregnancy on childhood psychopathology. *Dev Psychopathol, 26*, 393–403.

O'Donnell, K.J., Glover, V., Holbrook, J.D., & O'Connor, T.G. (2014b). Maternal prenatal anxiety and child brain-derived neurotrophic factor (BDNF) genotype: effects on internalizing symptoms from 4 to 15 years of age. *Dev Psychopathol, 26*, 1255–1266.

O'Mahony, S.M., Clarke, G., Dinan, T.G., & Cryan, J.F. (2015). Early-life adversity and brain development: Is the microbiome a missing piece of the puzzle? *Neuroscience.*

Olds, D., Henderson Jr, C.R., Cole, R., Eckenrode, J., Kitzman, H., Luckey, D., Pettitt, L., Sidora, K., Morris, P., & Powers, J. (1998). Long-term effects of nurse home visitation on children's criminal and antisocial behavior: 15-year follow-up of a randomized controlled trial. *Jama, 280*, 1238–1244.

Pawlby, S., Hay, D., Sharp, D., Waters, C.S., & Pariante, C.M. (2011). Antenatal depression and offspring psychopathology: the influence of childhood maltreatment. *Br J Psychiatry, 199*, 106–112.

Pearson, R.M., Evans, J., Kounali, D., Lewis, G., Heron, J., Ramchandani, P.G., O'connor, T.G., & Stein, A. (2013). Maternal depression during pregnancy and the postnatal period: risks and possible mechanisms for offspring depression at age 18 years. *JAMA Psychiatry.*

Radtke, K.M., Ruf, M., Gunter, H.M., Dohrmann, K., Schauer, M., Meyer, A., & Elbert, T. (2011). Transgenerational impact of intimate partner violence on methylation in the promoter of the glucocorticoid receptor. *Transl Psychiatry, 1*, e21, 1–6.

Raikkonen, K., Pesonen, A.K., O'reilly, J.R., Tuovinen, S., Lahti, M., Kajantie, E., Villa, P., Laivuori, H., Hamalainen, E., Seckl, J.R., & Reynolds, R.M. (2015). Maternal depressive symptoms during pregnancy, placental expression of genes regulating glucocorticoid and serotonin function and infant regulatory behaviors. *Psychol Med, 45*, 3217–3226.

Teh, A.L., Pan, H., Chen, L., Ong, M.L., Dogra, S., Wong, J., Macisaac, J.L., Mah, S.M., Mcewen, L.M., Saw, S.M., Godfrey, K.M., Chong, Y.S., Kwek, K., Kwoh, C.K., Soh, S.E., Chong, M.F., Barton, S., Karnani, N., Cheong, C.Y., Buschdorf, J.P., Stunkel, W., Kobor, M.S., Meaney, M.J., Gluckman, P.D., & Holbrook, J.D. (2014). The effect of genotype and in utero environment on interindividual variation in neonate DNA methylomes. *Genome Res, 24*, 1064–1074.

Tibu, F., Hill, J., Sharp, H., Marshall, K., Glover, V. & Pickles, A. (2014). Evidence for sex differences in fetal programming of physiological stress reactivity in infancy. *Dev Psychopathol*, 1–10.

Yehuda, R., Engel, S.M., Brand, S.R., Seckl, J., Marcus, S.M., & Berkowitz, G.S. (2005). Transgenerational effects of posttraumatic stress disorder in babies of mothers exposed to the World Trade Center attacks during pregnancy. *J Clin Endocrinol Metab, 90*, 4115–4118.

Zijlmans, M.A., Korpela, K., Riksen-Walraven, J.M., de Vos, W.M., de Weerth, C. (2015). Maternal prenatal stress is associated with the infant intestinal microbiota. *Psychoneuroendocrinology, 53*, 233–245.

12

BIRTH TRAUMA

Diane S. Speier

Childbirth is a major physical, emotional and social experience in a woman's life, usually anticipated with a mixture of joyful excitement and apprehension. Since the medicalisation of childbirth that began in the twentieth century and is escalating internationally in the twenty-first century, with excessively high caesarean section and induction of labour rates, some mothers are overwhelmed by the intensely medical orientation to birth, exacerbated by care that feels unsafe and lacks compassion, kindness and dignity. Traumatic distress and post-traumatic stress disorder (PTSD) are the extreme result of medically driven and dehumanised maternity care transmuting expectations for a positive and fulfilling life event into a nightmare in which the perception of injury or threat to their integrity is the devastating psychophysiological outcome for some mothers.

PTSD following childbirth is a relative newcomer in the field of perinatal mental illness, with published studies only in the last 20 years (McKenzie-McHarg, 2004; Ayers, McKenzie-McHarg & Slade, 2015), compared to the extensive knowledge base that exists about postnatal depression (PND). Because there is significant overlap in symptoms between the two conditions, traumatised women are often misdiagnosed with postnatal depression. Measures used to detect depression do not identify PTSD, so childbirth-related PTSD disrupts the transition to parenthood, leaving untreated women (and partners) struggling to cope with life. This chapter will examine the causes, risk factors and predictors, prevalence, and impact of traumatic birth on parents and on infant attachment, development and parent-infant bonding, including a discussion on prevention, treatment for PTSD and outcomes.

Introduction to birth trauma

The causes of birth trauma are multifaceted, involving some or all of the following: a high degree of obstetric interventions and/or complications; deficient and unsympathetic care during labour and delivery that women perceive as unsafe, dehumanised, disrespectful and uncaring; a perceived lack or loss of control and feeling powerless over events; intolerable pain; a partner being absent or not supportive during the birth; and the actions or inactions of maternity staff leaving women feeling unsupported and not listened to. The symptoms of trauma include re-experiencing through recurrent, intrusive and distressing recollections of the event; avoidance of stimuli associated with the trauma and numbing of general responsiveness; and persistent symptoms of increased arousal. There is significant distress and/or impairment in functioning and physiological reactivity to cues that resemble an aspect of the traumatic event.

The fifth edition of the *Diagnostic and Statistical Manual of Mental Disorders* (DSM), released in 2013 (American Psychiatric Association), updated and redefined the criteria for diagnosing PTSD and will probably increase the prevalence rates for PTSD following childbirth (McKenzie-McHarg, et al., 2015). However, the implications of the new diagnostic criteria are as yet unknown as all published research on birth trauma has used the DSM-IV diagnostic criteria. A current definition of birth trauma was developed by Cheryl Tatano Beck, Jeanne Watson Driscoll and Sue Watson in their ground-breaking book *Traumatic Childbirth* (2013). Birth trauma is 'an event occurring during the labour and delivery process that involves actual or threatened serious injury or death to the mother or her infant. The birthing woman experiences intense fear, helplessness, loss of control and horror'. Although the loss of control element is not included in DSM-IV definition, after years of research Beck revised the definition to include 'an event occurring during labour and delivery where the woman perceives she is stripped of her dignity' (Beck, Driscoll & Watson 2013: 8). The emotional impact of PTSD may include anger and self-blame, loss of positive affect, isolation and dissociation from others, and suicidal ideation (McKenzie-McHarg et al., 2015). Childbirth is unique among stressors that lead to PTSD because birth is generally undertaken voluntarily and viewed as a positive event with culturally positive connotations. The event usually takes place in a formal care context, and there are at least two people to consider at all times – mother and baby (Poote & McKenzie-McHarg, 2015). Diagnosis is complicated by the nature of life with a newborn: stress, anxiety and fatigue are naturally elevated after childbirth, and maternal preoccupation with the newborn is a normal aspect of the postpartum, so care must be taken not to overpathologise.

Because the baby is a reminder of the traumatic event, the mother is confronted with a double bind regarding typical avoidance behaviours of traumatised individuals. She is expected to embrace her new infant and instead she is being psychophysiologically triggered by him or her (Czarnocka & Slade, 2000; Ayers, Wright & Ford, 2015). This can disturb the bonding process from the mother's perspective, and create attachment problems as the baby is seeking positive interactions with its mother that are not forthcoming during this critical period. Traumatised mothers are not able to attune to their infants, or respond to cues, and fail to comfort and reassure them, making their emotional withdrawal a profound and long-lasting effect (Van der Kolk, 2015). Another distinct aspect of birth trauma is the 'anniversary effect', common to all trauma, where every birthday of the child can be a triggering occasion instead of a celebration, with agonising levels of distress in anticipation and during the event, which must be hidden from others (Beck, 2006).

Postpartum PTSD is not postnatal depression but they often co-occur

There is substantial overlap in symptoms of depression and PTSD. A mother who presents with symptoms of perinatal mental illness is likely to be assessed using the Edinburgh Postnatal Depression Scale (EPDS) and diagnosed as having postnatal depression. Unfortunately this means that traumatised women may remain undetected and overlooked as the intrusions cluster of symptoms (flashbacks, nightmares, and uncontrollable thoughts) is not a factor in postnatal depression or its assessment. Furthermore the new cluster of symptoms for PTSD in the DSM-5, 'persistent and exaggerated negative beliefs, self-blame and persistent negative emotional state . . . would be recognised as potential symptoms of PND' (Poote & McKenzie-McHarg, 2015: 95), and increases the tendency to conflate the two illnesses. There is a high degree of comorbidity (concordance) between partners in a relationship, and symptoms of post-traumatic stress and postnatal depression are positively related within couples (Ayers, Eagle & Waring, 2006; Iles, Slade & Spiby, 2011). Yet, fathers'/partners' mental health needs are often overlooked by healthcare professionals, and they suffer in silence, avoiding full disclosure to protect their symptomatic partners. Robust measures that are specific to postnatal PTSD are required to ensure women and their partners are properly identified and treated.

Prevalence

When researchers began to investigate postnatal PTSD, the initial focus was on prevalence. Findings indicated that up to 3 per cent of women met the full diagnostic criteria for clinical PTSD, but there were significantly more women who did not meet all the criteria suffering from sub-clinical levels of post-traumatic distress (Czarnocka & Slade, 2000; White et al., 2006). Prevalence increases to 15.7 per cent for women in high-risk groups (Ayers, Wright & Ford, 2015; McKenzie-McHarg et al., 2015; Poote & McKenzie-McHarg, 2015). Risk factors during the antenatal period include a history of psychiatric problems, prenatal anxiety and/or depression, emotional abuse, prior trauma including sexual abuse, previous traumatic birth, and stillbirth. Perinatal risks are elevated in women who develop pre-clampsia (11 per cent experience PTSD), HELLP syndrome (hemolysis, elevated liver enzyme, low platelet) – a severe form of pre-clampsia, pregnancy loss and in mothers whose preterm infants require a stay in the neonatal intensive care unit (NICU) (Beck, Driscoll & Watson, 2013).

The perception of trauma following birth is highly subjective (Beck, 2004), and between 33 and 45 per cent of women feel traumatised by childbirth (Slade, 2006; White et al., 2006; Beck, Driscoll & Watson, 2013). Subthreshold symptomatology may still impact negatively on women's ability to function; several researchers suggest the phenomenon could be conceptualised as a continuum of post-traumatic stress (White et al., 2006; Poote & McKenzie-McHarg, 2015; Mckenzie-McHarg et al., 2015). A birth that might be objectively routine to staff can be experienced as subjectively traumatic by a mother who has encountered numerous interventions, unmanageable pain, poor communication and feelings of being disrespected, abandoned and unheard. When a birth is objectively traumatic it is understood as being so by maternity staff and they, and perhaps birth partners, can experience secondary traumatic stress from witnessing the event (Beck, Driscoll & Watson, 2013; McKenzie-McHarg et al., 2015). Unfortunately, maternity professionals may use distancing strategies that reduce empathy as self-protection, and good psychological supervision for healthcare professionals' physical and mental health is crucial (Poote & McKenzie-McHarg, 2015).

Predictors of trauma

Not everyone who experiences a traumatic birth will develop PTSD, and understanding what factors will traumatise some women and not others is essential. Pauline Slade (2006) developed a conceptual framework for predicting women likely to be traumatised that includes: i) *predisposing* factors: the personal vulnerability factors existing before or during pregnancy (mentioned above) and history, socio-economic status, nulliparity (no previous births), personality, trait anxiety, insecure attachment style and tocophobia (fear of childbirth); ii) *precipitating* factors, relating to the childbirth event: the type/number of obstetric interventions, the duration and mode of delivery, fear of harm to self and/or baby, perception of poor care or unsympathetic attitudes of clinicians, loss of control and feeling powerless, inadequate pain management, caesarean section, and perceived low levels of social support from partner or staff (Poote & McKenzie-McHarg, 2015); and 3) *maintaining* factors, aspects happening in the postnatal period: misdiagnosis, the absence of available postnatal support, or relationship conflict. These factors can be *internal* characteristics of the individual, such as age, emotional status and personality traits, or *external* features of the environment such as birth location and staffing levels, or the *interaction* of the two, including the subjective perception of support (Slade, 2006; Iles, Slade & Spiby, 2011; Quinn, Spiby & Slade, 2015). The core barrier to predicting women at risk of being traumatised is the lack of training in perinatal mental health (PMH) among maternity service clinicians (McKenzie-McHarg et al).

Dissatisfaction with support (for both partners) can be a predictor of post-traumatic stress. Managing responses to distressing or potentially traumatic events involves regular cognitive processing through discussion – and the relationship is the primary setting for this. When the father/partner is absent from the birth, a precipitating predictor for PTSD, this can adversely affect how a woman copes in labour, and she loses the chance to discuss and reframe the experience with someone aware of what happened (Czarnocka & Slade, 2000). Men's early distress interferes with adequate support or chances for discussion, especially for men avoiding intimacy; lack of trust in others results in active avoidance of discussion, preventing women from psychologically integrating the birth experience. Perceptions of satisfaction with support are highly associated within couples; positive perceptions of partner support promote higher self-confidence, self-esteem, increased disclosure of concerns, reappraisal of negative cognitions, and successful event processing (Iles, Slade & Spiby, 2011).

However, a woman's longstanding attachment patterns may override momentary support levels, and insecure attachment can compromise women's ability to recognise or utilise available support (Iles, Slade & Spiby, 2011). The literature is growing on the interaction between parental attachment styles and postnatal PTSD and depression (Iles, Slade & Spiby, 2011; Ayers et al., 2014; Quinn, Spiby & Slade, 2015). As a predisposing factor, insecure anxious attachment denotes fear of abandonment and the need for approval, and insecure avoidant attachment denotes fear of being dependent and the need for independence (Quinn, Spiby & Slade, 2015). In Ayers et al. (2014), avoidant attachment style, an operative birth, and poor intrapartum support were significantly correlated with postnatal PTSD. However, they found that attachment style is associated with PTSD only in women who have severe complications or interventions during birth.

Impact on the parent-infant bond, infant development and partner relationship

Childbirth-related PTSD has negative consequences for both the couple relationship and the parent-infant relationship (Nicholls & Ayers, 2007). A mother's emotional numbness and detachment challenge her ability to form a positive relationship or develop a balanced representation of her baby (Parfitt, Pike & Ayers, 2014). PTSD has a direct effect on the parent-baby bond (Ayers, Eagle & Waring, 2006; Parfitt & Ayers, 2009) and traumatised women describe their infants as more difficult, less easy to soothe, and prone to higher rates of distress. Breastfeeding can be problematic for a traumatised mother and Beck and Watson (2008) found the impact 'can lead women down two strikingly different paths. One path can propel women into persevering in breast-feeding, whereas the other path can lead to distressing impediments that curtailed women's breast-feeding attempts' (Beck & Watson, 2008: 228). The first path can be compensation for a distressing birth, a corrective for mothers helping them feel they can do something right in motherhood. The second path is taken by mothers who stop/choose not to breastfeed because they experience it as one more embodied failure or another source of inadequacy and shame (Beck, Driscoll, & Watson, 2013). Avoiding breastfeeding has long-range health implications for the infant.

Parental mental illness influences the infant's environment at a critical period of development; however, there is scarce research available on the long-term impact of PTSD on infant development. One study found maternal PTSD had a negative impact on infant cognitive development, and PTSD symptoms were associated with poor infant emotional regulation (Parfitt, Pike & Ayers, 2014). For preterm infants, maternal PTSD is associated with poor infant sleeping and eating patterns. Providing practical psychoeducation for parents after traumatic birth may support positive infant outcomes (McKenzie-McHarg et al., 2015). Future research on infant development related to postnatal PTSD is essential.

One primary impact on the marital relationship, beyond concordance, is active avoidance of sex to prevent conception and any reminder of the traumatic birth, affecting the reproductive choices that parents make: either to delay another pregnancy or to stop after one child. The transition to parenthood is associated with a decline in relationship satisfaction (Speier, 2015) and depression is significantly associated with a lower quality couple relationship, which then impacts on the parent-child relationship: 'while PTSD is the main contributor to difficulties in parent-baby bonding, these problems are exaggerated when the person also suffers from comorbid depression' (Parfitt & Ayers, 2009: 138). The negative impact on the partner relationship is well documented (Ayers, Eagle & Waring, 2006; Nicholls & Ayers, 2007; Parfitt & Ayers, 2009). Women can feel abandoned by their husbands and men comment on feeling rejected by their partner by the loss of intimacy and sexual contact (Ayers, Eagle & Waring, 2006; Nicholls & Ayers, 2007). When both partners experience PTSD, called 'dual couples', it continues to impact on individual and relationship functioning, and the dynamics within single and dual trauma couples may require different treatment approaches (Nicholls & Ayers, 2007). Health visitors working with families need to consider both partners' psychological reactions to birth and provide dyadic support to the couple relationship (Poote & McKEnzie-McHarg, 2015).

Prevention

Strategies for preventing postnatal PTSD can be antenatal, intrapartum or postnatal. A carefully taken history regarding anxieties, fears, expectations and previous deliveries, and prenatal screening for early identification of vulnerable women with a traumatic history and other predisposing factors, is vital (Czarnocka & Slade, 2000; Ayers et al., 2014; Poote & McKenzie-McHarg, 2015). There is often a reluctance to ask about psychological issues when no perinatal care pathway is available. The creation of a birth flow chart (not a birth plan) with contingencies for various processes and outcomes is one way of managing expectations realistically (McKenzie-McHarg et al., 2015). During labour and delivery, improved communication, pain management, an enhanced father's role, and maximising women's perceptions of control in labour are helpful in preventing post-traumatic stress symptoms (Czarnocka & Slade, 2000). Continuity of care along with compassionate care, which would require a change in the culture and values of maternity services, are essential for reducing the risks of trauma. Staff professional manner and skilful communication about aspects of the birth affect a woman's feelings of control and her ability to make informed decisions. When women feel well informed, are involved in decision making, and can make choices, this engagement is protective against traumatic birth, and healthcare professionals must acknowledge the role they play in meeting these needs (McKenzie-McHarg et al., 2015).

However, most 'prevention' is done after the birth, when the damage is done. Debriefing is one way to mitigate symptoms, but has generated mixed results, with heterogeneous approaches applied and different timing, methods, and measures used (Gamble et al., 2002; Lapp et al., 2010; Sheen & Slade, 2015). Originally designed to reduce trauma symptoms and prevent PTSD, debriefing is usually a structured intervention but it can be 'used loosely to describe a range of postbirth discussions and this has caused some confusion about the purpose and effectiveness of this intervention' (Gamble et al., 2002: 74). A review of studies found that a single debriefing in hospital before discharge did not reduce psychological morbidity and may be harmful when there is no follow-up support (Gamble et al., 2002). If done too soon, debriefing or nondirective counselling can interrupt the natural mechanisms for integrating the experience (McKenzie-McHarg, 2004). The efficacy of debriefing is greater when targeted on women at risk of developing post-traumatic stress due to perinatal events or a negative appraisal of the birth (McKenzie-McHarg et al., 2015; Sheen & Slade, 2015). Such women benefitted from nonstructured interactive interviews that allowed them to discuss their labour, ask questions and explore their feelings, resulting in a reduction in psychological distress. Sheen and Slade (2015) suggest an alternative term, 'childbirth review', as a better way of describing these interventions, welcomed by women who perceive them as acceptable and helpful.

Treatment interventions

The literature on the treatment of postnatal PTSD is sparse (Lapp et al., 2010; Beck, Driscoll & Watson, 2013; James, 2015), despite the fact that spontaneous recovery from PTSD following childbirth is uncommon (Sandstrom et al., 2010; Stramrood et al., 2012). Early therapeutic interventions included exposure therapy, which subjects the patient to a frightening stimulus, imagined or in vivo, repeated until anxiety levels are reduced, often embedded within a cognitive behavioural therapy (CBT) context (McKenzie-McHarg, 2004). The risk of exacerbating symptoms by exposure is high, and anxiety management techniques help to minimise this. Research remains inconclusive about the process and effectiveness of exposure for postnatal PTSD. There is a bidirectional relationship in which negative cognitions can trigger and maintain PTSD, and PTSD symptoms predict subsequent negative cognitions about self and the world (James, 2015). This explains why trauma-focused CBT can be an effective treatment for postnatal PTSD, combining psychoeducation, exposure, cognitive restructuring and anxiety management training (Lapp et al., 2010). Only one study has investigated the effect of CBT on PTSD after birth (Ayers, McKenzie-McHarg & Eagle, 2007). The CBT protocol was applied flexibly to two women's experiences using a combination of reliving, exposure and cognitive reappraisal techniques, central to CBT treatment of PTSD. The formulation, a featured process of CBT, is a detailed diagram that examines 'hot spots', or worst moments of the trauma, and highlights the key history, core beliefs, underlying assumptions and trigger events that impact on how thoughts, emotions and behaviours interrelate. Although this study demonstrated the effectiveness of CBT for postnatal PTSD, the small sample is a limitation, and more research is needed to establish an evidence base for clinical practice (Ayers, McKenzie-McHarg & Eagle, 2007).

Eye movement desensitisation and reprocessing (EMDR) is another treatment used for postnatal PTSD. EMDR is a multimodal, dual attention task in which the client focuses on traumatic memories, emotions and thoughts while receiving bilateral stimulation through eye movements, tapping or tones, with the aim of reducing distress and replacing negative perceptions with more positive cognitions (Lapp et al., 2010). In two studies EMDR reduced symptoms of PTSD and increased confidence. The effects were enduring (Sandstom et al., 2008; Stramrood et al., 2012). Sandstom et al.'s pilot research was a 'before and after' treatment study with follow up measures 1–3 years after to examine the constancy of the changes. Originally intended to treat pregnant women who had previously experienced a traumatic birth, only one pregnant woman participated along with three nonpregnant women. Pregnant women were reluctant to try a method that could provoke anxiety (Sandstom et al., 2008). Francine Shapiro, who developed EMDR, recommends caution during pregnancy due to potentially increased emotional arousal and the unknown effects on the fetus. However, all four women reported a reduction in post-traumatic stress after treatment, particularly intrusive thoughts, avoidance and numbing. Stramrood et al. (2012) studied EMDR with three women during their second pregnancy, and treatment resulted in fewer post-traumatic stress symptoms, confidence about their pregnancy and feeling positive about their births, despite all three women experiencing complications. Both studies had very small samples, and future large scale research to develop clinical practice protocols specific to postnatal PTSD is warranted. The optimal timing for treatment remains a topic of debate (McKenzie-McHarg, 2015), and these studies state the ideal time for EMDR treatment would be several months after traumatic birth and prior to any further pregnancy, requiring timely screening and identification for PTSD at the postpartum checkup to prevent years of symptomatic suffering (Sandstrom et al., 2010; Stramrood et al., 2012).

Any treatment for PTSD entails referral to PMH professionals and some regions of the UK lack care pathways. Collaboratives, such as the Maternal Mental Health Alliance, and the All Party Parliamentary Group for Conception to Age 2 – 1001 Critical Days – are raising awareness of the need for PMH services, but raising awareness must lead to provision of readily available and accessible PMH pathways for individuals/couples across the UK that provide sensitive and supportive care for healing postnatal PTSD.

Outcomes

The long-term effects of birth trauma can be summed up in the following outcomes:

- Postnatal PTSD and postnatal depression are often conflated, leaving traumatised parents misdiagnosed and untreated oftentimes for many years.
- The emotional withdrawal caused by birth trauma, combined with insecure adult attachment patterns and perceived inadequate support, can result in postnatal PTSD causing intergenerational bonding and attachment problems.
- Maternal PTSD has negative effects on infant cognitive development and infant emotional regulation, though research on infant development remains scarce.
- In addition to comorbidity within couples, PTSD has negative effects on the relationship, interfering with intimacy, and often reducing the size of the intended family.

References

American Psychiatric Association (2013). *Diagnostic and Statistical Manual of Mental Disorders.* 5th ed. Arlington, VA: American Psychiatric Association.

Ayers, S., Eagle, A., & Waring, H. (2006). The effects of childbirth-related post-traumatic stress disorder on women and their relationships: A qualitative study. *Psychology, Health & Medicine, 11*(4), 389–398. doi:10.1080/13548500600708409

Ayers, S., McKenzie-McHarg, K., & Eagle, A. (2007). Cognitive behaviour therapy for postnatal post-traumatic stress disorder: Case studies. *Journal of Psychosomatic Obstetrics & Gynecology, 28*(3), 177–184. doi:10.1080/01674820601142957

Ayers, S., McKenzie-McHarg, K., & Slade, P. (2015). Post-traumatic stress disorder after birth. *Journal of Reproductive and Infant Psychology, 33*(3), 215–218. doi:10.1080/02646 838.2015.1030250.

Ayers, S., Wright, D.B., & Ford, E. (2015). Hyperarousal symptoms after traumatic and nontraumatic births. *Journal of Reproductive and Infant Psychology, 33*(3), 282–293. doi:10.1080/02646838.2015.1004164

Ayers, S., Jessop, D., Pike, A., Parfitt, Y., & Ford, E. (2014). The role of adult attachment style, birth intervention and support in posttraumatic stress after childbirth: A prospective study. *Journal of Affective Disorders, 155*, 295–298. doi:10.1016/j.jad.2013.10.022.

Beck, C.T. (2004). Birth trauma: In the eye of the beholder. *Nursing Research, 53*(1), January/February, 28–35. Accession: 00006199–200401000–00005

Beck, C.T. (2006). The anniversary of birth trauma: Failure to rescue. *Nursing Research, 55*(6), 381–390. Accession: 00006199–200611000–00002

Beck, C.T., & Watson S. (2008). Impact of birth trauma on breast-feeding: A tale of two pathways. *Nursing Research, 57*(4), July/August, 228–236. doi:10.1097/01.NNR.0000313494.87282.90

Beck, C.T., Driscoll, J.W., & Watson, S. (2013). *Traumatic Childbirth.* London, Routledge.

Czarnocka, J., & Slade, P. (2000). Prevalence and predictors of post-traumatic stress symptoms following childbirth. *British Journal of Clinical Psychology, 39*, 35–51. doi:10.1348/014466500163095

Gamble, J.A., Creedy, D.K., Webster, J., & Moyle, W. (2002). A review of the literature on debriefing or non-directive counselling to prevent postpartum emotional distress. *Midwifery, 18*, 72–79. doi:10.1054/midw.2001.0287

Iles, J., Slade, P., & Spiby, H. (2011). Posttraumatic stress symptoms and postpartum depression in couples after childbirth: The role of partner support and attachment. *Journal of Anxiety Disorders, 25*, 520–530. doi:10.1016/j.janxdis.2010.12.006

James, S. (2015). Women's experience of symptoms of posttraumatic stress disorder (PTSD) after traumatic childbirth: A review and critical appraisal. *Archives of Women's Mental Health, 18*, 761–771. doi:10.1007/s00737-015-0560-x

Lapp, L.K., Agbokou, C., Peretti, C., & Ferreri, F. (2010). Management of post traumatic stress disorder after childbirth: A review. *Journal of Psychosomatic Obstetrics & Gynecology, 31*(3), 113–122. doi:10.3109/0167482X.2010.503330

McKenzie-McHarg, K. (2004). Traumatic birth: Understanding predictors, triggers, and counselling process is essential to treatment. *Birth, 31*(3), 219–221. doi:10.1111/j.0730-7659.2004.00308.x

McKenzie-McHarg, K., Ayers, S., Ford, E., Horsch, A., Jomeen, J., Sawyer, A., Stramrood, C., Thomson, G., & Slade, P. (2015). Post-traumatic stress disorder following childbirth: An update of current issues and recommendations for future research. *Journal of Reproductive and Infant Psychology, 33*(3), 219–237. doi:10.1080/02646838.2015.1031646

Nicholls, K., & Ayers, S. (2007). Childbirth-related post-traumatic stress disorder in couples: A qualitative study. *British Journal of Health Psychology, 12*, 491–509. doi:10.1348/135910706X120627

Parfitt, Y.M., & Ayers, S. (2009). The effect of post-natal symptoms of post-traumatic stress and depression on the couple's relationship and parent-baby bond. *Journal of Reproductive and Infant Psychology, 27*(2), 127–142. doi:10.1080/02646830802350831

Parfitt, Y., Pike, A., & Ayers, S. (2014). The impact of parents' mental health on parent–baby interaction: A prospective study. Infant Behav Dev, 36(4), 599–608. doi.org/10.1016/j.infbeh.2013.06.003

Poote, A., & McKenzie-McHarg, K. (2015). The experience of post-traumatic stress disorder following childbirth. *Journal of Health Visiting, 3*(2), 92–98. doi:10.12968/johv.2015.3.2.92

Quinn, K., Spiby, H., & Slade, P. (2015). A longitudinal study exploring the role of adult attachment in relation to perceptions of pain in labour, childbirth memory and acute traumatic stress responses. *Journal of Reproductive and Infant Psychology, 33*(3), 256–267. doi:10.1080/02646838.2015.1030733

Sandstrom, M., Wiberg, B., Wikman, M., Willman, A., & Hogberg, U. (2008). A pilot study of eye movement desensitisation and reprocessing treatment (EMDR) for post-traumatic stress after childbirth. *Midwifery, 24*, 62–73. doi:10.1016/j.midw.2006.07.008

Sheen, K., & Slade, P. (2015). The efficacy of 'debriefing' after childbirth: Is there a case for targeted intervention? *Journal of Reproductive and Infant Psychology, 33*(3), 308–320. doi:10.1080/02646838.2015.1009881

Slade, P. (2006). Towards a conceptual framework for understanding post-traumatic stress symptoms following childbirth and implications for further research. *Journal of Psychosomatic Obstetrics & Gynecology, 27*(2), 99–105. doi:10.1080/01674820600714582

Speier, D.S. (2015). Strengthening couple relationships to reduce the risk of perinatal mood and anxiety disorders for parents. *Journal of Health Visiting, 3*(3), 160–165. doi:10.12968/johv.2015.3.3.160

Stramrood, C.A.I., van der Velde, J., Doornbos, B., Paarlberg, K.M., Weijmar Schultz, W.C.M., & van Pampas, M.G. (2012). *Birth, 39*(1), March, 70–76. doi:10.1111/j.1523-536X.2011.00517.x

Van der Kolk, B. (2015). *The Body Keeps the Score: Mind, Brain and Body in the Transformation of Trauma.* London: Penguin Books.

White, T., Matthey, S., Boyd, K., & Barnett, B. (2006). Postnatal depression and post-traumatic stress after childbirth: Prevalence, course and co-occurrence. *Journal of Reproductive and Infant Psychology, 24*(2), 107–120. doi:10.1080/02646830600643874

C: Policies with potential to reduce risks and improve outcomes

13

INVESTING IN EARLY HUMAN DEVELOPMENT

Mary E. Young

Healthy brain development during the perinatal period and early childhood is essential to the overall health, well-being and competence of populations – and will determine whether we can build tolerant, stable, equitable, prosperous and sustainable societies. All societies need to understand this connection to cope well with the global changes under way. This chapter makes the case for investing in early child development (ECD) and embracing a 'pre-distributive' social policy, to improve human development.

Links between ECD and human development have been noted by the development community for more than 30 years, and social sector policies have become increasingly prominent as a core element for promoting economic growth and human development. However, as Heckman (2013) notes, the policies are remedial in nature and fragmented, focusing on only one problem at a time. He remarks,

> Too often, government officials design programs for children as if they lived their lives in silos, as if each stage of a child's life were independent of the other, unconnected to what came before or what lies ahead. It's time for policy makers now to look beyond silos, to begin recognising that consistent, cost-effective investment in children and youths can pay for itself.

Effective social sector policies and investments in early human development must be based on the current knowledge and science of ECD. The evidence is clear: from preconception through early childhood, the brain organises pathways and sets trajectories for cognitive, mental, socio-emotional and physical health that can last a lifetime and lay the foundation for healthy adulthood. This development is interactive, synergistic and holistic, and strategies to foster healthy ECD must be the same - comprehensive and integrative.

Poverty is a major impediment to healthy ECD, and children who are born and live in poverty often suffer developmental consequences that are difficult to overcome later and thwart a nation's ability to create a fair, sustainable and just society. The global agenda to overcome poverty and to give all children a fair chance at a healthy adulthood remains unfinished. Over the next 15 years, we need to encourage and apply effective, evidence-based policies and investments that will enhance early human development in all children and, especially, those who are disadvantaged by poverty or other social disrupters.

The science of brain development in early childhood

During the past two decades, findings in developmental neurobiology and psychology, population health, social science and economics have converged to advance phenomenally our understanding of the long reach of ECD. This research decisively shows that early-life events link with development of the brain's circuitry; dynamic gene–environment interactions; programming of immune, neurological, and endocrine systems; trajectories of human development; and chronic diseases in adulthood (McCain, Mustard, & McCuaig, 2011; Shonkoff & others, 2012).

Four key concepts summarise this understanding:

- The architecture and formation of skills are strongly influenced by neural circuits that develop from dynamic interactions between genes and early-life environments and experiences.
- Development of neural pathways and mastery of skills follow hierarchical rules sequentially 'from the bottom up', with later attainment building on earlier foundations.
- Cognitive, social, emotional and language competencies are interdependent and shaped by early experiences. All contribute to formation of lifelong capabilities.
- Adaptation continues throughout life. Capabilities are formed in predictable sequences during sensitive periods when development of specific neural circuits is most plastic and receptive to environmental influences.

This understanding has far-reaching implications. Clearly, 'getting things right the first time' is far less costly than trying to fix them later (Shonkoff et al., 2012).

Figure 13.1 depicts development of the brain's structure and function over time. Formation of synapses in the brain is experience-dependent – and begins prenatally.

Early adversity influences cognitive and noncognitive development

Research applying genetic, molecular biological, genomic and brain-imaging tools confirms that significant exposure to adversity, especially in early childhood and an environment of poverty and deprivation, can alter the structure and function

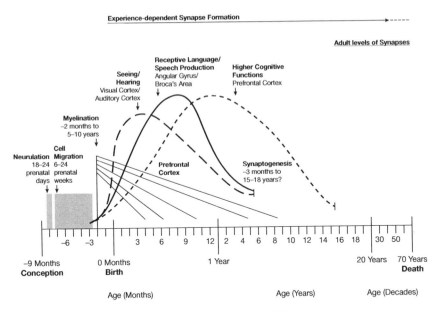

FIGURE 13.1 Development of the brain's structure and function
Source: Thompson and Nelson (2001)

of the brain's circuitry and neurological pathways to negatively affect health, learning and behaviour for life.

Low socioeconomic status (SES) in pregnant women increases the likelihood of premature birth and fetal growth retardation, and this likelihood may be explained by high stress, higher rates of infection, and poor or inadequate nutrition (Black et al., 2008, Walker et al., 2011b). These factors increase cortisol levels in mothers and fetuses, which can reduce fetal growth and trigger prematurity. Studies in rhesus monkeys show that fetal exposure to increased levels of cortisol reduces hippocampal volume, and offspring of stressed mothers have lower birth weights, impaired neuromotor development, and lifelong attention deficits and emotional dysregulation (Boivin & Hertzman, 2012).

Neuroscientists are identifying affective and cognitive systems influenced by SES (Hackman, Farah & Meaney, 2012). With a better understanding of the mechanisms of influence, researchers can design specific interventions to prevent and remediate effects of low SES in childhood. Interventions could target, for example, parents' increased depression and compromised interactions with children, which are associated with parents' low SES postnatally.

Early adversity predicts poor health outcomes

Numerous prospective, longitudinal studies in developed countries show that the severity of early life experiences predicts difficulties in adult life.

Danese and colleagues (2007) report linkages between childhood stressors (e.g. maltreatment) and immune dysregulation. The Kaiser-Permanente's Adverse Early Childhood Experience (ACE) study shows that young children exposed to traumatic or abusive childhood events are predisposed as adults to health problems, which include coronary artery disease, high blood pressure, Type 2 diabetes, obesity, cancer and depression, alcoholism, smoking and substance abuse (Hertzman & Boyce, 2010).

Violence and neglect have a severe impact. A study of children in the Gaza Strip shows a rate of emotional and behavioural problems three times higher than that of middle-class children in Canada (McCain, Mustard, & Shanker, 2007). Other extreme events such as epidemics (HIV/AIDS) and orphanhood also have negative, lasting effects (Walque, 2011).

Children reared in institutions may suffer profound deprivation, with damaging effects on brain development (Nelson et al., 2009). They tend to have lower IQs, stunted growth, and behavioural problems, and the longer their institutional deprivation is, the more pronounced the negative outcomes are.

Parenting

Longitudinal follow up of interventions (and animal studies) clearly show that positive parenting (i.e. sensitive/responsive adult–child interactions) from birth through early childhood is the essential stimulation for brain development. Positive interactions include back-and-forth communications with caregivers, vocalisation, gestures, facial expressions and body movements. They may be warm expressions by mothers or primary caregivers, physical contact and play, visual mutuality and/or vocal exchanges, and timely and appropriate responses to infants (Bornstein & others, 2008). Anand and Roope (2013) show how the frequency of children's involvement in activities with parents connects to the development of children's capabilities, notably speech and social and everyday motor skills. The results suggest connections between related activities and capabilities (e.g. visiting other families and development of social skills) and a significant role for participation in arts and crafts or singing.

Parents' communication with their children and sensitivity to their children's emotional needs mediate the effects of low SES on cognitive and socio-emotional development (NICHD, 2006). Bornstein and Putnick (2012) describe two domains of positive caregiving: cognitive (e.g. reading, telling stories, naming, counting, drawing) and socio-emotional (e.g. interpersonal playing and singing).

Poor parenting is transmitted intergenerationally. Children who experience adversities in early childhood may have lower stress tolerance and heightened stress reactivity in adulthood, and as parents, they will exhibit poor parenting skills. Interventions for at-risk children need to include services that help parents understand their own responses to parenting and the needs of their infants and young children (Mayes, 2010).

Early childhood interventions: Programs and policies

ECD programs that link health-promoting measures (e.g. good nutrition, immunisation) with nurturance, participation, care, stimulation and protection offer the best prospect for sustained, lifelong optimisation of children's development.

The lasting impact of ECD interventions for children in the first 1,000 days is well demonstrated worldwide. High-quality formal or informal ECD interventions promote competencies and skills that enable children to participate more fully and actively in society and the workforce when they become adults.

Key components of ECD programs

Key components of quality ECD programs include nutrition, health, stimulation, parent education, childcare and protection, monitoring of development, *and* strengthening of community and institutional capacity through training and awareness. When launching or scaling up large, national programs, three ingredients deserve special consideration.

Parent education and training

The aim of parenting interventions is to improve adult-child interactions by promoting parents' responsive interaction and attachment with their infants and young children. Parenting interventions may be accomplished through home visits, primary healthcare visits, group sessions with caregivers, or a combination of group sessions and home visits.

Parenting interventions have positive effects on children's cognitive and social development (Engle & others, 2011). Having a defined curriculum and messages is essential, as is systematic training for workers and opportunities for parents to practice with children and obtain feedback. All studies show that the effects of parenting interventions are larger in populations that are more disadvantaged (Nores & Barnett, 2010). Evaluations show that interventions can be successfully implemented by paraprofessionals having primary or secondary education (Engle et al., 2011) and that the frequency of visits impacts the benefits achieved (Walker, 2011).

Counselling mothers at clinics, as an alternative to home visits, has been used and evaluated in a few instances, but its effectiveness has not been established (Walker, 2011). In the WHO/UNICEF Integrated Management of Childhood Illness (IMCI) intervention, parental counselling on ECD by health professionals during parents' health visits is incorporated into the Care for Development module (Engle et al., 2011).

Income support

Studies of the timing and size of effects of income support show that an increase in parents' annual income between a child's birth and age 5 is associated with increased years of schooling (by eight-tenths of a year) and better health of the child. The effects of added income during middle childhood are smaller and not significant (Duncan, 2012).

Among mothers receiving the US Earned Income Tax Credit (EITC), those with two or more children received an increase in the size of their benefit in the 1993 EITC expansion. This increase resulted in better test scores among the children and better health among the mothers, compared with mothers who had one child and received a lower EITC benefit (Evans & Garthwaite, 2010).

Beginning in the mid-1990s, Brazil and Mexico pioneered Conditional Cash Transfer (CCT) programs, and these programs have now been implemented in all Latin American countries and in some African, Asian and European countries. Most CCT programs target disadvantaged children ages 0–6 years by transferring cash to poor families, and some condition the transfer to participation in services such as health checkups, growth monitoring, nutrition and parenting education. Evaluations are emerging and they suggest that CCT has positive effects on children's developmental outcomes (Attanasio et al., 2005).

Nutrition and stimulation

Nutrition is, of course, essential, and combining it with stimulation in ECD interventions yields synergistic, long-lasting effects on children's outcomes, as demonstrated by the Jamaica ECD intervention (Walker et al., 2011a). In Jamaica, stimulation was fostered through parenting education in weekly 1-hour home visits by trained community health workers for 2 years (Powell & Grantham-McGregor, 1989). A 20-year follow-up shows that the positive impact of stimulation on children's schooling and later productivity (i.e. higher earnings) persists, compared with children who only received nutritional supplementation (Gertler et al., 2013).

The unfinished agenda

The economic returns from investing in young children are high. The rate of return for investments in quality ECD for disadvantaged children is 7 to 10 per cent per annum, through better outcomes in education, health, sociability, economic productivity and reduced crime (Heckman, 2011). An even more compelling reason for underscoring the importance of children's early years is that early interventions help children escape the effects of poverty in this generation *and* the next generation.

Most children born into poverty are malnourished, neglected and unlikely to reach their potential – even before primary school. We are making progress in the fight against poverty, but too many families and children still live in poverty. In 2012, an estimated 12.7 per cent of the world's population lived at or below US$1.90 a day, down from 37 per cent in 1990 and 44 per cent in 1981 (World Bank 2016). East Asia had the largest reduction in extreme poverty. China alone lifted 753 million above the US$1.90-a-day threshold, out of the total reduction of 1.1 billion living in extreme poverty in the developing world between 1981 and 2011. South Asia accounted for the second largest reduction, with a decrease from 58 per cent in 1981 to 18.7 per cent in 2012, but the 2012 rate in sub-Saharan Africa stood at 42.6 per cent (World Bank 2016).

Primary school is still not an option for many, many children. In 2013, approximately 59 million primary-school-aged children worldwide were out of school (down from 100 million in 2000), and of these, 30 million lived in sub-Saharan Africa and 10 million lived in South and West Asia. Approximately 36 per cent of the out-of-school children lived in conflict-affected countries (UNESCO, 2015).

Emerging middle-income economies (e.g. China, Brazil, and India) still have deep pockets of poverty in rural or remote regions and inner cities. Socio-economic inequalities tagged to this poverty are associated with risk factors affecting children's development. The 2011 series in *The Lancet* (Engle et al., 2011, Walker et al., 2011b) illustrate a distinct gradient in preschool attendance from lowest income quintiles to richest income quintiles by region. In countries, the difference in attendance between lowest and highest quintiles can be large and in some (e.g. Nicaragua and El Salvador) as much as twofold. Differences in children's language development between the quintiles also are large.

The reach of poverty is particularly relevant where a large and growing proportion of the population is young. In 2007, the Middle East and North Africa region had a population younger than the global average, with 100 million youth ages 0–14 years. The proportion of the population under age 15 varied from 25 per cent in Tunisia to 45 per cent in West Bank/Gaza and 44 per cent in Yemen (World Bank 2008).

Disparities in children's development mirror these economic disparities, and poverty is associated with poor social indicators, especially for children born into poverty. Without the basic nutrition, healthcare and stimulation/parenting needed to promote healthy growth, many poor children enter school not ready to learn. These children do poorly in class, repeat grades and drop out at high rates. They are at a disadvantage when they look for work or enter the workplace, earning the lowest wages, and, as parents, they pass their poverty on to their children. Giving children a better chance is not only vital for attacking the worst effects of poverty today, but also may be an effective way of breaking the relentless, vicious cycle of poverty transmitted across generations.

An agenda for the next 15 years

As development agencies look forward to 2030, the framing of ECD in each country's policy and programs really matters. To move forward, countries and agencies must shift their focus from child survival to children's holistic development, nurturing and promoting each child's capabilities to the fullest, and embrace a 'pre-distributive' social policy.

Four main tasks for the next 15 years are to:

1. *Redirect social policies to focus on the early years.* Health, education, family, and social protection ministries must each assume a role and work towards the objective of linking evidence-based programs that support ('scaffold') children and families. Tasks include promoting ECD in national decision making as a first step in poverty reduction and human capital formation, building and strengthening capacity among ECD researchers and practitioners, fostering understanding of quality ECD ingredients, and targeting services to children at most risk. By adopting the concept of proportionate universality (Boivin & Hertzman, 2012), countries could reach the largest proportion of children at risk. Defined as 'programs, services and policies that are universal, but with a scale and intensity that is proportionate to the level of disadvantage' (Boivin & Hertzman, 2012), this strategy is useful for targeting ECD programs to the level of children's disadvantage.

2. *Expand public health models to incorporate the science of ECD.* Adopt broadly integrative approaches that provide an enduring continuum of care for mothers and children beginning prenatally.

3. *Assess early childhood outcomes and link these to program and policy data.* Develop a comprehensive, population-based, multinational database of children's outcomes (with and without ECD interventions).

4. *Communicate the importance of children's healthy brain development for populations' competence and wellbeing.* Increase effective demand for ECD interventions, promote a trans-disciplinary science of human development, and translate this science into ECD programs and policies that foster healthy development.

Conclusion

The first few years of a child's life have a multiplier effect for society, and healthy early development is a powerful equalizer. ECD programs are fundamentally about providing all children, who are born unknowingly into the game of life, a fair chance to succeed. Even by age 3 or 6, so many children are faced with so many obstacles. The field of play for them is not level and, for a lifetime, they will struggle uphill. As Heckman (2006) notes, investing in disadvantaged young children 'is a rare public policy initiative that promotes fairness and social justice and at the same time promotes productivity in the economy and in society at large'.

By placing children at the centre of the global agenda to reduce poverty, we can 'be the first generation to think both as nationals of our countries and as global citizens in an ever-shrinking and more connected planet' (Wolfensohn, 2001). This opportunity and challenge, set forth 15 years ago by Wolfensohn, as President of the World Bank, is even more imperative today. As he so eloquently stated, 'Our children will inherit the world we create. The issues are urgent. The future for our children will be shaped by the decisions we make and the courage and leadership we show today' (Wolfensohn, 2001).

References

Anand P., & Roope, L. (2013). Happiness and Development in Very Young Children. Discussion Paper. Economics Department, Open University, and Health Economics Research Center, Oxford University.

Attanasio, O., Battistin, E., Fitzsimons, E., & Vera-Hernandez, M. (2005). *How Effective Are Conditional Cash Transfers? Evidence from Colombia.* Open access publications. London: University College. http://discovery.ucl.ac.u

Black, R.E., Allen, L.H., Bhutta, Z.A., Caulfield, L.E., de Onis, M., Ezzati, M., Mathers, C., & Rivera, J. (2008). Maternal and child undernutrition study group. Maternal and child undernutrition: Global and regional exposures and health consequences. *The Lancet, 371*(9608), 243–60.

Boivin, M., & Hertzman, C., eds. (2012). *Early Childhood Development: Adverse Experiences and Developmental Health.* The Royal Society of Canada-Canadian Academy of Health Sciences Expert Panel (with R. Barr, T. Boyce, A. Fleming, H. MacMillan, C. Odgers, M. Sokolowski, and N. Trocmé). Ottawa.

Bornstein, M.H., Tamis-Lemonda, C.S., Hahn, C.S., & Haynes, O.M. (2008). Maternal responsiveness to young children at three ages: Longitudinal analysis of a multi-dimensional, modular, and specific parenting construct. *Developmental Psychology, 44* (May) (3), 867–874. doi:10.1037/0012–1649.44.3.867.

Bornstein, M., & Putnick, D. (2012). Cognitive and socioemotional caregiving in developing countries. *Child Development* 83 (January/February) (1), 46–61.

Danese, A., Pariante, C., Caspi, A., Taylor, A., & Poulton, R. (2007). Childhood maltreatment predicts adult inflammation in a life-course study. *Proceedings of the National Academy of Sciences of the USA, 104,* 1319–1324.

Duncan, G. (2012). Give us this day our daily breadth. *Child Development, 83* (January/February)(1), 6–15.

Engle, P.L., Fernald, L.C., Alderman, H., Behrman, J., O'Gara, C., Yousafzai, A., Cabral de Mello, M., Hidrobo, M., Ulkuer, N., Ertem, I., & Iltus, S. (2011). Global development steering group: Strategies for reducing inequalities and improving developmental outcomes for young children in low-income and middle-income countries. *The Lancet, 378,* 1339–1353.

Evans, G.W., & Garthwaite, C. (2010). *Giving Mom a Break: The Impact of Higher EITC Payments on Maternal Health.* NBER Working Paper No. 16296. Cambridge, Mass: National Bureau of Economic Research.

Gertler, P., Heckman, J., Pinto, R., Zanolini, A., Vermeer, C., Walker, S., Chang, S.M., & Grantham-McGregor, S. (2013). *Labor Market Returns to Early Childhood Stimulation: A 20-Year Followup to an Experimental Intervention in Jamaica.* NBER Working Paper No. 19185. Cambridge, MA.: National Bureau of Economic Research.

Hackman, D.A., Farah, M.J., & Meaney, M.J. (2012). Socioeconomic status and the brain: Mechanistic insights from human and animal research. *Nature Reviews Neuroscience, 11,* 651–659. www.nature.com/reviews/neuro

Heckman, J. J. (2006). Investing in Disadvantaged Young Children Is an Economically Efficient Policy. Presented at the Committee for Economic Development/The Pew Charitable Trusts/ PNC Financial Services Group Forum on Building the Economic Case for Investments in Preschool, New York, January 10.

Heckman, J.J. (2011). Letter to National Commission on Fiscal Responsibility and Budget Reform. Federal-Commision_2.10.11FINAL%20(1).pdf.

Heckman, J. (2013). The Economics of Inequality and Human Development. Keynote Presentation at the First National Congress meeting on Building a Legal Framework for Public Policies for Early Childhood, Brasilia, Brazil, April 16.

Herztman, C., & Boyce, T. (2010). How experience gets under the skin to create gradients in developmental health. *Annual Review of Public Health, 31*, 329–347.

Mayes, L. (2010). How Stress Impacts Parental Care and the Intergenerational Transmission of Parenting Abilities. Presentation at Brain and Biological Development: A Science in Society Symposium. Alberta Family Wellness Initiative. Banff, Alberta, Canada, May 31–June 4.

McCain, M., Mustard, F., & Shanker, S. (2007). *Early Years 2: Putting Science into Action*. Ontario: Council for Early Child Development.

McCain, M., Mustard, F., & McCuaig, K. (2011). *Early Years Study 3: Making Decisions, Taking Action*. Toronto: Margaret and Wallace McCain Family Foundation.

Nelson, C.A., Furtado, E.A., Fox, N.A., & Zeanah, C.H. (2009). The deprived human brain. *American Science, 97*, 222–229.

NICHD [National Institute of Child Health and Human Development] Early Child Care Research Network. (2006). Child-care effect sizes for the nichd study of early child care and youth development. *American Psychologist, 61*(2), 99–116.

Nores, M., & Barnett, W.S. (2010). Benefits of early childhood interventions across the world: (under) investing in the very young. *Economics of Education Review, 29*(2), 271–282.

Powell, C., & Grantham-McGregor, S. (1989). Home visiting of varying frequency and child development. *Pediatrics, 84*(1), 157–64.

Shonkoff, J.P., Richter, L., van der Gaag, J., & Bhutta, Z.A. (2012). The biology of adversity: Building an integrated science of child survival, early child development, and human capital formation. *Pediatrics, 129* (February) (2), 1–13. doi:10.1542/peds.2011-0366

Thompson, R.A., & Nelson, C.A. (2001). Developmental science and the media: Early brain development. *American Psychologist, 56*(1), 5–15.

UNESCO [United Nations Educational, Scientific, and Cultural Organization]. Institute for Statistics and the Education for All Global Monitoring Report. (2015). *A Growing Number of Children and Adolescents Are Out of School as Aid Fails to Meet the Mark*. Policy Paper 22/Fact Sheet 31. Paris.

Walker, S. (2011). Promoting Equity through Early Child Development Interventions for Children from Birth through Three Years of Age. In H. Alderman (ed.), *No Small Matter: The Impact of Poverty, Shocks, and Human Capital Investment in Early Childhood Development*. Human Development Perspectives. Washington, D.C: The World Bank.

Walker, S., Chang, S., Vera-Hernandez, M., & Grantham-McGregor, S. (2011a). Early Childhood Stimulation Benefits Adult Competence and Reduces Violent Behavior. *Pediatrics, 127*(5), 849–57.

Walker, S.P., Wachs, T.D., Grantham-McGregor, S., Black, M., Nelson, C., Huffman, S., Baker-Henningham, H., Chang, S.M., Hamadani, J.D., Lozoff, B., Meeks Gardner, J.M., Powell, C.A., Rahman, A., & Richter, L. (2011b). Inequality in early childhood: Risk and protective factors for early child development. *The Lancet, 378*(9799), 1325–1338. doi:10.1016/S0140-6736(11)60555-2

Walque, D. (2011). Conflicts, Epidemics and Orphanhood: The Impact of Extreme Events on the Health and Educational Achievement of Children. In H. Alderman (ed.), *No Small Matter: The Impact of Poverty, Shocks, and Human Capital Investment in Early Childhood Development*. Human Development Perspectives. Washington, D.C: The World Bank.

Wolfensohn, J.D. (2001). The Challenges of Globalization. The Role of the World Bank. Address to the Bundestag. Berlin, Germany, April 2, 2001.

World Bank (2008). *The Road Not Traveled: Education Reform in the Middle East and North Africa*. Washington, D.C: The World Bank.

World Bank. June 2016. Webpage. http://worldbank.org/en/topic/poverty/overview. Washington, D.C: The World Bank.

14

WHAT MAKES A DIFFERENCE?

Supporting families in caring for children

Peter Fonagy

This chapter will seek to address what makes a real difference in supporting families doing the work of bringing up children. I will argue that although the immediate family – the source of the primary attachment relationships – are where much of what is of significance in early development really takes place, a highly systemic approach to supporting attachment figures and providing treatment where necessary is congruent with the evidence for what works for children and young people facing mental health difficulties. It is also, as I will set out in the first section of this chapter, congruent with recent developments in our thinking in relation to mentalising and epistemic trust. And at a very human level, it is in keeping with our basic sense – although one that has perhaps been undermined by aspects of modern life – that raising children is a collective effort, that 'it takes a village to raise a child'.

The first 1000 days of life are a period of rapid and complex development, which most critically takes place in the context of the family environment. And families are doing this extraordinary work of building new minds in an ever-more complex and demanding environment. Entrenched social inequality, the cost of childcare, the cost of living, decreased social mobility, diminished access to local family and social support networks; these all form the very real backdrop against which families are operating, with very real effects. Increasing scientific knowledge – in the fields of neurobiology, developmental psychopathology and epidemiological outcome studies – all indicate that social disadvantage and adversity have a direct impact on child development (Center on the Developing Child at Harvard University, 2016; Cicchetti & Banny, 2014). The research consensus is overwhelming. And while there is no clear-cut research evidence about how to solve these wide social issues, there is a growing body of evidence on the kinds of interventions that can really make a difference to families. In the second half of this chapter I will discuss in more detail some of the interventions that the evidence shows to be effective for some of the most prevalent mental health difficulties that affect children. But I will begin by explaining how recent developments in my and colleagues' thinking on how the child's relationship with the social environment – in the first instance in the context of attachment relationships – relate to thinking about developmental psychopathology and the problem of resilience.

Creating a mentalising system around the family

We still maintain a fundamentally attachment-informed perspective of how infants need responsive caregiving from primary attachment figures as a foundation stone for their happiness and wellbeing in the here and now, and for their ongoing emotional, cognitive and social development. But in a development from the traditional emphasis on the infant-caregiver dyad, we locate these earlier relationships in a much broader context, in terms of the social support that the dyad needs, and the wider social learning and meaning conveyed to the infant by experiencing those early relationships as supported. In recent years, the theory of mentalisation has expanded to consider another important function of attachment relationships, namely their role in the development of epistemic trust – that is, trust in the authenticity and personal relevance of interpersonally transmitted knowledge (Fonagy & Allison, 2014; Fonagy et al., 2015). Epistemic trust enables social learning in a fluid and unpredictable social and cultural context, and allows individuals to adapt to and benefit from their social environment – an essential component of resilience (Fonagy, Luyten, Allison & Campbell, 2017a, 2017b).

As humans, given the social and practical complexity of our environment, much of the information we are presented with – and which we must convey – is complex and not immediately self-explanatory. Furthermore, as it can be harmful for us to accept all information indiscriminately, we often approach new ideas or facts with a self-protective scepticism – the idea that children passively accept all information they are given has not been confirmed by recent research (Chen, Corriveau & Harris, 2013; Corriveau, Meints & Harris, 2009; Fusaro, Corriveau & Harris, 2011; Harris & Corriveau, 2011). To accommodate the dilemma of needing to receive large amounts of complex social knowledge in order to function adaptively while also needing to discriminate when communicators are not reliable or well-meaning, Csibra and Gergely formulated the theory of natural pedagogy: this is the idea that humans have evolved a specialised form of social cognition which is highly sensitive to cues from the communicator, to open the channel for transmitting cultural knowledge (Csibra & Gergely, 2006, 2009, 2011). When the communicator provides the appropriate cues, the listener will respond with epistemic trust. The cues that stimulate epistemic trust in this way include eye contact, turn-taking, contingent reactivity and the use of a special tone of voice. These signals prepare the recipients of information; alerting them that the content being conveyed is relevant to them and should be incorporated as part of their general understanding of how their environment operates, that is, it should be stored as part of their procedural and semantic rather than episodic memory.

We suggest that one of the benefits of secure attachment relationships is that they generate the conditions for a general opening of epistemic trust. More generally, responding to someone contingently (a key feature of secure attachment) is an indicator of a recognition of agency. The process of mentalising that takes place in the contingent caregiving interactions of a secure attachment relationship in effect constitutes a powerful ostensive cue underpinning the relaxation of epistemic vigilance within that relationship (Fonagy et al., 2015). The child regards their caregiver as a reliable informant about the world; the social knowledge conveyed by the parent is accepted as part of their shared cultural currency that cumulatively builds up to enable the child to successfully navigate their shared social environment.

We also suggest that many forms of psychopathology may be associated with a disruption of epistemic trust and the social learning process this trust normally enables (Fonagy et al., 2015). If a caregiver is unable to mentalise their infant effectively, not only will the child's own developing capacity to mentalise be compromised but (given the importance of mentalising in providing ostensive cueing) the child's capacity for social learning will suffer. Many mental disorders have in common the feature of apparent rigidity and an incapacity to learn about the social world. Everybody seeks social knowledge, but without the reassurance and support of trusted caregivers, family or peers, the content of communication can be confusing and it may be rejected due to perceived hostile intent. In that sense, expressions of mental disorder might be considered manifestations of failings in social communication arising from epistemic mistrust, epistemic hypervigilance or outright *epistemic freezing* (petrification) (Fonagy et al., 2015). Such disruptions of epistemic trust manifest as a reluctance to update beliefs, perceptions and expectations, regardless of the social experience that might indicate that such beliefs are inappropriate or incorrect. Individuals who have experienced severe trauma and/or who are suffering from personality problems may be left with a complete inability to trust others as sources of knowledge about the world. An individual who has been traumatised in childhood, for instance, has little reason to trust others and will reject information that is inconsistent with their pre-existing beliefs. As therapists, we may consider such people 'hard to reach', yet they are simply exhibiting an adaptation to a threatening social environment in which attachment figures were not regarded as reliable.

The concept of resilience is a dominant theme in discourses on child and adolescent mental health: many factors have been associated with it – from genes to parenting style to neighbourhood – but a definitive, integrative account of what single mechanism underpins the activation of these factors has been elusive. We have recently suggested (Fonagy et al., 2017a, 2017b) that the missing link in terms of understanding the mechanism for resilience may be disrupted epistemic trust, whether through genetic propensity, environmental influence or an interaction between the two. Epistemic hypervigilance or outright epistemic freezing limits an individual's capacity to benefit from, adapt to and responsively interact with their social environment. A lack of resilience, we suggest, emerges from the absence of flexibility in relation to the social environment that is associated with epistemic mistrust.

This is a perspective on the emergence of psychological vulnerability as an outcome of disruptions in relation to social cognition. It suggests that a lack of resilience/social flexibility is a by-product of an inability to respond to cues from the social environment in order to learn how best to adapt to it. This has powerful implications for thinking about how we approach supporting families in the first 1,000 days. It strongly confirms the idea that in order to be effective, interventions to support the developing mind in infancy have to be accompanied by a social environment that reinforces flexible social learning, that is, a social environment which is supportive of mentalising and does not generate chronic, overwhelming levels of stress. We cannot expect the primary attachment figure to maintain balanced mentalising in isolation, particularly so if they are functioning in a nonmentalising social environment, and/or if their infant – either for biological or experiential reasons – has a tendency to hide their mind from their parent; that is, to be more resistant to mentalising. If a child has this tendency, the parent may appear to be 'failing' to mentalise their child, with the consequent developmental implications for the child in terms of missing out on the full experience of learning about him or herself through the feeling of being recognised and mirrored by the parent. The highly interactional and context-driven nature of mentalising certainly challenges the tendency towards parent-blaming that has traditionally coloured some aspects of the therapeutic approach

This approach, we argue, is congruent with the five key characteristics associated with positive outcomes across a range of interventions highlighted by the Harvard Centre on the Developing Child's (Center on the Developing Child at Harvard University, 2016) powerful and important new report, *From best practices to breakthrough impacts*:

1. Adults – parents, teachers, child care staff – need to strengthen their skills so they can support the healthy development of the children in their care.
2. Interventions need to be tailored to address causes of major stress for families, such as homelessness, violence, children's special needs or parental depression.
3. The health and nutrition of children and mothers must be supported before, during and after pregnancy.
4. The quality of the broader caregiving environment must be improved and access to higher-quality care for economically disadvantaged families increased.
5. Clearly defined goals must be established and a curriculum or intervention plan that is designed to achieve those goals implemented (Center on the Developing Child at Harvard University, 2016).

The report further argues compellingly that in order to make a real difference to children's lives in the early years, we have to implement shifts in the way we think about intervening to support young children. These are: i) that early experiences affect physical and mental health, not just learning; ii) that healthy brain development requires protection from excessive stress, not just a stimulating environment; and iii) achieving breakthroughs in outcomes in relation to children experiencing adversity requires us to support the adults who care for them to transform their own lives (Center on the Developing Child at Harvard University, 2016). Maltreatment and social stressors form an allostatic load that creates a cumulative burden (Rogosch, Dackis & Cicchetti, 2011). Such nonoptimal circumstances form a powerful cue, we argue, to the infant about the system in which they are functioning (one in which showing epistemic trust, for example, may not be advisable). If we are to make a real difference in the lives of children in the first 1,000 days, we have to think broadly about intervening to change what children are learning about their social world.

Targeted support for particular needs

Attachment

We now have compelling research evidence indicating that attachment is malleable, and that interventions in childhood can result in children previously showing disorganised or organised/insecure attachment patterns coming to be measured as secure (Cicchetti, Rogosch & Toth, 2006). A large meta-analysis of early preventive interventions (70 studies) aimed at parental sensitivity and infant attachment security found that such interventions did appear effective. The most effective interventions used a moderate number of sessions and a clear-cut behavioural focus in families with, as well as without, multiple problems (Bakermans-Kranenburg, van Ijzendoorn & Juffer, 2003). The interventions which focused on sensitive maternal behaviour were successful in improving insensitive parenting as well as infant attachment insecurity.

In accordance with such evidence, the NICE attachment guidelines suggest that when preschool age children have or are at risk of attachment difficulties, and are on the edge of being taken into nonparental care, intervention in the form of a video feedback programme should be provided for parents. This programme seeks to help them improve their nurturing of their infant, particularly when the infant is distressed; improve their understanding and interpretation of their child's behaviour; respond positively to cues and expressions of the child's feelings; behave in ways that are not frightening to the child; and improve self-regulation of their own feelings when nurturing the child. The NICE guidelines further recommend that this programme is delivered by a trained and experienced health or social care worker and consists of 10 sessions delivered over 3 to 4 months. Each session should include 10-20 minutes, filming of the parents interacting with the child, and then the worker should watch the video with the parents and, in this part of the process, highlight parental 'sensitivity, responsiveness and communication' as well as signs of parental strengths and improvements in behaviour (National Institute for Health and Care Excellence, 2015).

The guidelines further recommend that if the parents do not agree to take part in a video feedback programme, or if there is little improvement in parental sensitivity or child attachment, or there are other causes for concern, further interventions are indicated in the form of home-visiting programmes that take place over 18 months (National Institute for Health and Care Excellence, 2015).

Maltreatment

In cases of preschool age children who have suffered or are at risk of maltreatment, the NICE attachment guidelines recommend that, parent-child psychotherapy be considered, while addressing safeguarding concerns (National Institute for Health and Care Excellence, 2015). This psychotherapy needs to address attachment concerns and should be based on the Cicchetti and Toth model (Cicchetti et al., 2006). It is recommended that this intervention takes place weekly and lasts over a year, is delivered in the home by a trained therapist, involves directly observing child-parent interactions, and explores parental understanding of the child's behaviour and the relationship between the parents' reaction to the child's behaviour and perceptions of the child and the parents' own childhood experiences. In the randomised preventive trial conducted by Cicchetti and colleagues to compare the effectiveness of an infant-parent psychotherapy programme and psychoeducational parent intervention (PPI) for 1-year-old infants in maltreating families, substantial increases in secure attachment were found in both the treatment groups at follow-up at 26 months (whereas increases in secure attachment were not found in the community standard controls) (Cicchetti et al., 2006). However, a 12-month follow-up study found that the psychotherapy intervention had more sustained efficacy in terms of attachment security than the psychoeducational parenting intervention. The children who had received child-parent psychotherapy (CPP) had higher rates of secure attachment (55.6 per cent) and lower rates of disorganised attachment (25.9 per cent) at the 12-month follow-up assessment than children in the PPI (22.7 per cent secure and 59.1 per cent disorganised) and the community standard control (12.2 per cent secure and 49 per cent disorganised) conditions. Intriguingly, this suggests that the parenting psychoeducational interventions, although promisingly efficacious by the end of treatment, did not demonstrate a sustained efficacy (Stronach, Toth, Rogosch, & Cicchetti, 2013).

Parental mental health

Parental mental health difficulties – in particular depression and anxiety – have been shown to be a risk factor for children, especially in particular behavioural problems, insecure attachment, depression and anxiety (Halligan, Murray, Martins & Cooper, 2007; Toth, Petrnko, Gravener-Davis & Handley, 2016). There is clear evidence presented elsewhere in this book (p. 47 Pawlby; p. 37 Barlow, J.; p. 56 Murray) of the risks associated with, for example, postnatal depression. A recent systematic review and meta-analysis of interventions to prevent mental disorders in the children of parents with mental illness found that interventions to protect such children appear to be effective (Siegenthaler, Munder & Egger, 2012). A randomised preventive trial of CPP with 130 toddlers of mothers suffering with major depressive disorder found that the toddlers in the CPP treatment group had higher rates of secure attachment compared to those in the comparison intervention group and the groups of offspring of nondepressed mothers (Toth, Rogosch, Manly & Cicchetti, 2006). This study was recently extended into a randomised clinical trial (RCT) of the efficacy of interpersonal psychotherapy for economically disadvantaged mothers, which supported the efficacy of the intervention (Toth et al., 2013).

Parenting programmes

The most common reason for referring children to mental health services, and a major expenditure on health and social care and other professional resources, is conduct disorder (CD). Frequently comorbid with ADHD, and anxiety and depression, early-onset CD is associated with slightly worse outcomes than adolescent-onset CD. CD is a risk factor for later substance misuse, and a risk factor for children with CD developing antisocial personality disorder as adults is the presence of callous and unemotional traits. Adaptive parenting practices, such as warm parent–child relationship, may well act as a buffer that provides protection against the biological risk factors, for example, temperamental fearlessness – for psychopathology. Parenting programmes might be helpful for families struggling with managing their young child's behaviours in ways that are of some preventive value. Intervening at the level of the family has been shown to be particularly relevant in cases of children with conduct difficulties: we have strong evidence that changing abnormalities in families' interaction patterns through parent training has the power to alter the child's behaviour (p. 163 Sanders). There is very strong evidence (a large number of RCTs) that parent training programmes may be applied to a wide range of conduct problems and can be delivered effectively in various settings (Dretzke et al., 2005, 2009). On average, about two-thirds of conduct-disordered children under 11 years of age whose parents participate in parent training improve. When it comes to research evidence on the efficacy of parenting programmes among younger children, a review, based on eight randomised and quasi-randomised studies has shown that group-based parent training was effective in preschool children (Barlow, Smailagic, Ferriter, Bennett & Jones, 2010). The group-based interventions were brief (4–12 weeks) and were significantly effective in reducing children's problematic behavior and improving emotional and behavioural adjustments, as reported by parents (SMD = −0.25). However, the long-term benefits of group-based parent training are uncertain; three follow-up studies included in the meta-analysis showed the intervention to be effective when measured by parents but not to have a significant effect when measured by independent observations. The most well established of the parenting programmes are the Incredible Years Programme, the Triple-P Positive Parenting Program and the Oregon Social Learning Center Programs.

Conclusion

Helping children in the first 1,000 days really means helping families. In humans evolutionary past, each infant would probably have been surrounded by an extended family network of supportive adults; now, parents are increasingly isolated in their caregiving. This is at one level deeply unnatural, and also puts an unprecedented strain on parents. High-quality childcare provision, and responsive and mental-health-aware GPs, nurses and health visitors are critically important ways in which families with young children can be helped and encouraged to access services (p. 139 Lewing). Young children cannot ask for help: we need to create an environment in which their parents are able to access help on their behalf, or in which professionals are able to recognise family need and services can be accessed in a nonstigmatising way. Any parent with concerns about their child's mental health should feel able to seek help without feeling judged. This work is about supporting families, and providing interventions where needed via families. We have the research evidence to show us what works; it is now a matter of creating mentalising educational, health and social care systems that can reach out to parents, and to which parents are able to reach without shame or obstruction.

References

Bakermans-Kranenburg, M.J., van Ijzendoorn, M.H., & Juffer, F. (2003). Less is more: Meta-analyses of sensitivity and attachment interventions in early childhood. *Psychological Bulletin, 129*(2), 195–215.

Barlow, J., Smailagic, N., Ferriter, M., Bennett, C., & Jones, H. (2010). Group-based parent training programmes for improving emotional and behavioural adjustment in children from birth to three years old. Cochrane Database of Systematic Reviews, CD003680. doi:10.1002/14651858.CD003680.pub2

Center on the Developing Child at Harvard University (2016). From best practices to breakthrough impacts: A science-based approach to building a more promising future for young children and families. Cambridge, MA: Harvard University.

Chen, E.E., Corriveau, K.H., & Harris, P.L. (2013). Children trust a consensus composed of outgroup members—but do not retain that trust. *Child Development, 84*(1), 269–282. doi:10.1111/j.1467-8624.2012.01850.x

Cicchetti, D., & Banny, A. (2014). A developmental psychopathology perspective on child maltreatment. In M. Lewis & D.K. Rudolph (Eds.), *Handbook of Developmental Psychopathology*, 723–741. Boston, MA: Springer US.

Cicchetti, D., Rogosch, F.A., & Toth, S.L. (2006). Fostering secure attachment in infants in maltreating families through preventive interventions. *Development and Psychopathology, 18*(3), 623–649.

Corriveau, K. H., Meints, K., & Harris, P.L. (2009). Early tracking of informant accuracy and inaccuracy. *British Journal of Developmental Psychology, 27*(Pt 2), 331–342.

Csibra, G., & Gergely, G. (2006). Social learning and social cognition: The case for pedagogy. In M.H. Johnson & Y. Munakata (Eds.), *Processes of change in brain and cognitive development. Attention and Performance XXI*, 249–274. Oxford, UK: Oxford University Press.

Csibra, G., & Gergely, G. (2009). Natural pedagogy. *Trends in Cognitive Sciences, 13*(4), 148–153. doi:10.1016/j.tics.2009.01.005

Csibra, G., & Gergely, G. (2011). Natural pedagogy as evolutionary adaptation. *Philosophical Transactions of the Royal Society of London. Series B, Biological Sciences, 366*(1567), 1149–1157. doi:10.1098/rstb.2010.0319

Dretzke, J., Davenport, C., Frew, E., Barlow, J., Stewart-Brown, S., Bayliss, S., Taylor, R.S., Sandercock, J., & Hyde, C. (2009). The clinical effectiveness of different parenting programmes for children with conduct problems: A systematic review of randomised controlled trials. *Child and Adolescent Psychiatry and Mental Health, 3*(1), 7.

Dretzke, J., Frew, E., Davenport, C., Barlow, J., Stewart-Brown, S., Sandercock, J., Bayliss, S., Raftery, J., Hyde, C., & Taylor, R. (2005). The effectiveness and cost-effectiveness of parent training/education programmes for the treatment of conduct disorder, including oppositional defiant disorder, in children. *Health Technology Assessment, 9*(50), iii, ix–x, 1–233.

Fonagy, P., & Allison, E. (2014). The role of mentalizing and epistemic trust in the therapeutic relationship. *Psychotherapy, 51*(3), 372–380. doi:10.1037/a0036505

Fonagy, P., Luyten, P., & Allison, E. (2015). Epistemic petrification and the restoration of epistemic trust: A new conceptualization of borderline personality disorder and its psychosocial treatment. *Journal of Personality Disorders, 29*(5), 575–609. doi:10.1521/pedi.2015.29.5.575

Fonagy, P., Luyten, P., Allison, E., & Campbell, C. (2017). What we have changed our minds about: Part 1. Borderline personality disorder as a limitation of resilience. Borderline Personality Disorder and Emotion Dysregulation, 4, 11. http://doi.org/10.1186/s40479-017-0061-9

Fonagy, P., Luyten, P., Allison, E., & Campbell, C. (2017). What we have changed our minds about: Part 2. Borderline personality disorder, epistemic trust and the developmental significance of social communication. Borderline Personality Disorder and Emotion Dysregulation, 4, 9. http://doi.org/10.1186/s40479-017-0062-8

Fusaro, M., Corriveau, K.H., & Harris, P.L. (2011). The good, the strong, and the accurate: Preschoolers' evaluations of informant attributes. *Journal of Experimnetal Child Psychology, 110*(4), 561–574. doi:10.1016/j.jecp.2011.06.008

Halligan, S.L., Murray, L., Martins, C., & Cooper, P.J. (2007). Maternal depression and psychiatric outcomes in adolescent offspring: A 13-year longitudinal study. *Journal of Affective Disorders, 97*(1–3), 145–154. doi:10.1016/j.jad.2006.06.010

Harris, P.L., & Corriveau, K.H. (2011). Young children's selective trust in informants. *Philosophical Transactions of the Royal Society London. Series B, Biological Sciences, 366*(1567), 1179–1187. doi:10.1098/rstb.2010.0321

National Institute for Health and Care Excellence (2015). Children's attachment: Attachment in children and young people who are adopted from care, in care or at high risk of going into care [NG26]. London, UK: British Psychological Society and Royal College of Psychiatrists.

Rogosch, F.A., Dackis, M.N., & Cicchetti, D. (2011). Child maltreatment and allostatic load: Consequences for physical and mental health in children from low-income families. *Development and Psychopathology, 23*(4), 1107–1124. doi:10.1017/S0954579411000587

Siegenthaler, E., Munder, T., & Egger, M. (2012). Effect of preventive interventions in mentally ill parents on the mental health of the offspring: Systematic review and meta-analysis. *Journal of the American Academy of Child & Adolescent Psychiatry, 51*(1), 8–17.e18. doi:10.1016/j.jaac.2011.10.018

Stronach, E.P., Toth, S.L., Rogosch, F., & Cicchetti, D. (2013). Preventive interventions and sustained attachment security in maltreated children. *Development and Psychopathology, 25*(4 Pt 1), 919–930. doi:10.1017/S0954579413000278

Toth, S.L., Rogosch, F.A., Manly, J.T., & Cicchetti, D. (2006). The efficacy of toddler–parent psychotherapy to reorganize attachment in the young offspring of mothers with major depressive disorder: A randomized preventive trial. *Journal of Consulting and Clinical Psychology, 74*(6), 1006–1016.

Toth, S.L., Petrenko, C.L.M., Gravener-Davis, J.A., & Handley, E.D. (2016). Advances in prevention science: A developmental psychopathology perspective. In D. Cicchetti (Ed.), *Developmental Psychopathology*. New York: John Wiley & Sons, Inc.

Toth, S.L., Rogosch, F.A., Oshri, A., Gravener-Davis, J.A., Sturm, R., & Morgan-López, A.A. (2013). The efficacy of interpersonal psychotherapy for depression among economically disadvantaged mothers. *Development and Psychopathology, 25*(4 pt 1), 1065–1078. doi:10.1017/S0954579413000370

15

EVIDENCE-BASED INTERVENTION FOR THE FIRST 1001 DAYS

Kirsten Asmussen, Leon Feinstein, Haroon Chowdry, Jack Martin

The Early Intervention Foundation (EIF) which we represent was established in July 2013 to champion and support the effective use of early intervention. By 'early' we mean activities that support children's development at all ages, before problems have become entrenched. By 'intervention' we mean activities that target the needs of children and families based on early signals of longer-term risk.

The first 1001 critical days represent an ideal time to offer effective early interventions to give children the best possible start so that they can reach their full potential. Activities that benefit all families include regular health checks and flexible childcare. Families experiencing more serious difficulties also benefit from more targeted support that addresses pre-identified risks such as social disadvantage and parental mental illness.

This chapter considers the availability of evidence-based interventions that aim to support young children's early social, behavioural and cognitive development through parent-child interaction. It presents a reanalysis of the findings originally reported in the recent Foundations for Life review (FfL, Asmussen et al., 2016), which assessed the strength of evidence and costs of 75 interventions targeting parenting behaviours in families with a child under the age of 5. We observed that while the majority of programmes (35) were developed for families with a child aged 2 or younger, only four had actual evidence of improving a child outcome. In all four cases, these outcomes involved children's attachment security and/or attachment-related behaviours. By comparison, there was far greater choice of effective interventions for children between the ages of 3 and 5. For this age group, 12 out of 24 were assessed as having evidence of improving child outcomes. Ten of these programmes had good evidence of improving children's behaviour and two had evidence of supporting early learning processes.

The potential reasons for these findings are assessed here, first by describing the methods used to assess the interventions and then by summarising their characteristics in terms of their target population, strength of evidence and cost. We then consider why we found comparatively fewer effective interventions targeting the first 1001 days and suggest ways in which evaluation evidence for this age group could be improved. We argue that future programme evaluations place a greater emphasis on child outcomes and assess the extent to which programme content is age appropriate.

The early intervention foundation

The EIF was set up as a UK What Works Centre specifically to consider the extent to which interventions have evidence of supporting children's development in seven key domains: i) improved mental health and wellbeing, ii) improved school achievement and employment, iii) improved healthy lifestyle and reduced obesity, iv) reduced substance misuse, v) reduced risky sexual behaviour, vi) reduced crime and antisocial behaviour and vii) reduced child maltreatment. These domains were chosen because of their association with improved adult outcomes and their potential for reducing public spending within the mental health, employment benefit and criminal justice systems (Allen, 2011).

EIF is also interested in whether interventions have evidence of improving the contexts in which children develop. These contexts include the family, school and community. We know from research that these contexts play an important role in influencing the extent to which children will reach their full potential (Bronfenbrenner, 1979; Sameroff et al., 1993). However, we also know that positive programme impacts observed in the home or school do not always translate into benefits for children (Duncan et al., 2004; Waldfogal, 1999). This is because a variety of factors, including the programme's target age range and programme content, collectively determine the programme's effectiveness for children (Asmussen, 2011). For these reasons, we acknowledge programme impacts on the family or school to be important, but primarily consider a programme's evidence in terms of its short- and long-term impacts on child development within the seven outcome domains listed above.

The foundations for life review

The primary aim of the FfL review was to understand the efficacy of interventions for supporting parent-child interaction in three domains fundamental to children's early development:

- **Attachment** security, which allows the child to form positive expectations about him or herself and others
- **Behavioural** self-regulation, which reduces persistent aggressive and non-compliant behaviours as children development
- **Cognitive** and language process that allow children to communicate effectively and process information efficiently.

These processes are important because they lay the foundation for more sophisticated skills as children develop (Shonkoff & Phillips, 2000). These skills include the executive functions which develop most rapidly between the ages of 3 and 5 (Best & Miller, 2010; Weintraub et al., 2013). The executive functions represent more advanced cognitive and self-regulatory processes that allow children to plan, stay focused and manage their impulses and research suggests that they are highly predictive of children's success when they enter school (Best, Miller & Naglieri, 2011).

Research also increasingly suggests that the executive functions are particularly sensitive to the quality of the interaction between the parent and child during infancy and toddlerhood (e.g. Bernier, Carlson & Whipple, 2010). The quality of parent-child interaction during the early years is influenced by various factors in parents' own lives (Bronfenbrenner, 1979). While most parents successfully support their young child's nonphysical development, a significant minority struggle because of various adversities, also referred to as risk factors, that interfere with their capacity to understand and appropriately respond to their child's needs. Examples of such risk factors include inter-parental conflict, economic disadvantage and physical and mental health problems (Gordon et al., 2016; Mensah & Kiernan, 2011).

The FfL review considered the extent to which early child outcomes could be improved through universal and targeted support addressing various risk factors thought to negatively impact attachment, behavioural and cognitive processes. Specifically, this review considered:

- the strength of the evidence underpinning these interventions and the proportion that could be considered 'evidence-based' against EIF's standards of evidence
- the characteristics of these programmes in terms of their outcomes, implementation requirements (including their costs) and level of need
- the extent to which interventions were able to prevent problems from becoming established in the first place by targeting key stages in children's development,

We consider here the review's findings for interventions targeting the first 1001 days in terms of their key characteristics and the extent to which they have evidence of supporting young children's development.

Methods

Sample

The FfL review assessed 75 interventions that expressly aimed to improve nonphysical child outcomes in families with a child aged 5 or younger. These interventions were originally identified in the Best Start at Home (BSaH) 'What Works' review that made use of systematic methods to identify interventions for parents with young children that are relevant for the UK context (Axford et al., 2015). Although the BSaH review was by no means exhaustive, it identified a range of programmes that are broadly representative of the kinds of activities currently taking place in the United Kingdom.

The emphasis of the BSaH review was on early interventions developed to keep problems from becoming established in the first place. Programmes were therefore eligible for the review if they i) expressly aimed to improve at least one non-physical child outcome, ii) worked directly with parents and iii) targeted families with a child between conception and age 5. Programmes were not eligible if they represented activities that might be considered to be ongoing treatment or a form of late intervention. Examples of programmes excluded from the review included specialist interventions developed for various disabilities (e.g. autism) or families where there were child protection concerns. Further details of BSaH's search terms and eligibility criteria can be found in the full report.

The programmes identified in the BSaH review were classified in terms of their primary outcomes, children's age, families' level of need and the programme's delivery format, as described in Table 15.1. These classifications were based on the best fit for the programme's best evidence. For example, if a programme's best evidence involved an attachment-related outcome in children with a mean age of 6 months at the start of the intervention in families living in disadvantaged populations, the programme would be classified as an attachment intervention, at the Targeted-Selective level for children in infancy.

Assessment

As a UK 'What Works' centre, EIF is mandated to assess interventions with a common metric that enables them to be compared on the basis of their evidence strength. EIF has therefore developed a rigorous system that makes use of evidence standards that are consistent with other internationally recognised organisations involved in the assessment and synthesis of evaluation evidence (e.g. the Cochrane collaboration and GRADE working group). Evidence standards shared by these organisations emphasise the value of randomised controlled trials (RCTs) and similarly rigorous quasi-experimental designs (QEDs) for attributing causality to an intervention model, as described in Figure 15.1. Unlike these other organisations, however, EIF applies these standards to individual programmes rather than to bodies of practice. This is done to facilitate comparisons between interventions on the basis of evidence strength and cost. Such comparisons are useful for commissioners of children's services, who frequently need to make difficult decisions about the programmes they make available in their communities.

The EIF assessment process evaluates programmes primarily on their evidence for children, as opposed to parents or practitioners. This means that higher ratings are awarded to programmes with specific evidence of improving child outcomes. Although it is clearly more challenging to reliably assess child outcomes during

TABLE 15.1 Programme characteristics in terms of their primary outcomes, children's age, level of need and delivery format

Primary outcomes	
Attachment	Programmes that include increased attachment security as a primary outcome. Child outcomes typically include attachment security and attachment related behaviours. Parent outcomes typically include increased sensitivity and responsiveness.
Behaviour	Programmes that include improved child behaviour as a primary outcome. Child outcomes typically include reduced aggression and noncompliant behaviour. Parent outcomes typically include improved parenting practices and the increased use of non-physical discipline.
Cognitive	Programmes that aim to improve children's early learning. Child outcomes typically include improved language and cognitive milestones. Parent outcomes include improved parental teaching skills and an improved home learning environment.
Children's age	
Antenatal/Perinatal	The programmes' best evidence involves children whose parents first engaged in the programme during pregnancy.
Infancy	The programmes' best evidence involved children who began the intervention between 0 and 12 months.
Toddlerhood	The programmes' best evidence involved children who began the intervention between 12 and 36 months.
Preschool	The programmes' best evidence involved children who began the intervention between three and five years.
Level of need	
Universal	The programmes' best evidence involved families with all levels of needs, as part of universal provision.
Targeted-selective	The programmes' best evidence involved families where there was a pre-identified demographic risk (e.g. teen parenthood, economic disadvantage, etc.).
Targeted-indicated	The programmes' best evidence involved families where the parent or child had pre-identified behavioural or mental health issues.
Delivery format	
Promotion+	Promotional activities and/or short duration activities lasting six weeks or less.
Group	Programmes delivered to small groups of parents from separate families.
Home Visiting	Programmes developed specifically to be delivered in the home on a regular basis for a period longer than six weeks.
Individual	Programmes provided to families on a one-to-one basis, either in the home or other venue. Examples of individual programmes included therapeutic support and individual parent teaching.

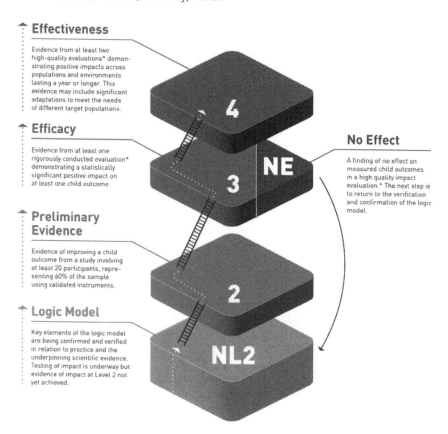

Effectiveness

Evidence from at least two high-quality evaluations* demonstrating positive impacts across populations and environments lasting a year or longer. This evidence may include significant adaptations to meet the needs of different target populations.

Efficacy

Evidence from at least one rigorously conducted evaluation* demonstrating a statistically significant positive impact on at least one child outcome.

Preliminary Evidence

Evidence of improving a child outcome from a study involving at least 20 participants, representing 60% of the sample using validated instruments.

Logic Model

Key elements of the logic model are being confirmed and verified in relation to practice and the underpinning scientific evidence. Testing of impact is underway but evidence of impact at Level 2 not yet achieved.

No Effect

A finding of no effect on measured child outcomes in a high quality impact evaluation.* The next step is to return to the verification and confirmation of the logic model.

*High quality evaluations do not need to be randomised control trials if a relevant and robust counter-factual can be provided in other ways.

FIGURE 15.1 EIF Evidence Standards

earlier periods of children's development (especially pregnancy and infancy), improvements in parenting behaviours during this time are not sufficient for assuming that benefits for children will also follow.

Programme assessment takes place through a series of checks and balances involving both internal and external experts and is overseen by the EIF Evidence Panel. Programme assessment also occurs with the full knowledge and cooperation of the programme providers, who have the opportunity to challenge their ratings if they felt the criteria had been misapplied. Further details about our assessment process are described in the FfL review.

The EIF evidence standards

The EIF evidence standards distinguish five levels of evidence that consider the degree to which a programme has been shown to have a positive, causal impact on specific child outcomes (see Table 15.2). It is worth noting that the term

TABLE 15.2 The EIF evidence standards

Level 4 (or 4+)*	Programmes with evidence from multiple rigorously conducted RCTs or QEDs. At least one of these studies must have evidence of improving a child outcome for one year or longer.
Level 3 (or 3+)	Programmes with evidence of a positive short-term child impact from at least one rigorously conducted RCT or QED.
Level 2 (or 2+)	Programmes with preliminary evidence of improving a child outcome from a pre/post study or comparison study with known biases that prohibit a causal attribution to the programme model.
NL2	Programmes whose most robust evaluation evidence does not meet the Level 2 threshold for a child outcome. These programmes may have evidence of other outcomes thought to be associated with child outcomes (e.g. parent outcomes), or their study design may not have met the Level 2 threshold because of sample or measurement issues.
No Effect (NE)	Programmes where there is evidence from a high-quality evaluation of the programme demonstrating no consistent effect on any observed parent or child outcome. This rating should not be interpreted to mean that the programme will never work, but it does suggest that the programme should likely adapt and improve its model.

*Programme may additionally be awarded a '+' if they have exceeded all of the requirements of a Level 2, 3 or 4 rating, but have not yet met the threshold of the next higher level.

'evidence based' is frequently applied to programmes with Level 3 evidence or higher, because this is the point at which there is sufficient confidence that a causal relationship between the programme model and outcomes can be assumed.

Assessing programme costs

EIF has also developed a rigorous system to compare interventions in terms of their relative input costs, that is, the overall resources required to deliver the intervention to an individual child. Resources, for the purposes of this work, are defined in terms of the activities and fees required to implement a particular intervention. These resources include the costs required to commission the programme (e.g. the programme's training fees), as well as the time required to deliver the intervention, practitioner qualifications and supervision and licensing fees. We then consider programme costs in light of the number of families reached through their delivery models, which may be group or individually based. The details of our cost scale are summarised in Table 15.3 and described in greater depth on the EIF website.

TABLE 15.3 Programme cost rating

Programme cost description	Cost rating
This programme is *high cost* to set up and deliver compared to other interventions reviewed by EIF. Programmes of this sort have an indicative unit cost range of *£2,000 or higher.*	5
This programme is *medium/high cost* to set up and deliver compared to other interventions reviewed by EIF. Programmes of this sort have an indicative unit cost range of *£1,000 to £2,000.*	4
This programme is *medium cost* to set up and deliver compared to other interventions reviewed by EIF. Programmes of this sort have an indicative unit cost range of *£500 to £999.*	3
This programme is *medium/low cost* to set up and deliver compared to other interventions reviewed by EIF. Programmes of this sort have an indicative unit cost range of *£100 to £499.*	2
This programme is *low cost* to set up and deliver compared to other interventions reviewed by EIF. Programmes of this sort have an indicative unit cost range of *£100 or lower.*	1

Findings

Table 15.4 compares the primary outcomes, level of need, delivery model, strength of evidence and relative costs of the programmes assessed through the FfL review by children's age.

Table 15.4 makes clear that less than a quarter (17 or 23 per cent) of the interventions could be considered 'evidence based'.

- Three were assessed as having Level 4 evidence of improving long-term child outcomes from two or more rigorously conducted trials.
- Fourteen were assessed as having Level 3 evidence of improving a child outcome from at least one rigorously conducted trial.
- Eighteen (24 per cent) of the programmes had preliminary evidence of improving child outcomes from a Level 2 study.
- Just under half (35 or 46 per cent) of the programmes were assessed as NL2, meaning that they had yet to undergo an evaluation study that met our Level 2 criteria for confirming a child outcome. Ten of these programmes had yet to measure a child outcome. An additional five had failed to confirm any child outcome, despite having fairly consistent evidence of improving related parent outcomes.
- Five (7 per cent) programmes were assessed as NE, with evidence from one rigorously conducted RCT observing no consistent benefits for parents or children.

TABLE 15.4 Summary of intervention characteristics in terms of primary child outcome, level of need, delivery model, children's age, evidence and cost

	First 1001 Days					
	Antenatal	Perinatal	0–24 months	2 to 3 years	3 to 5 years	Total
	(1)	(7)	(27)	(16)	(24)	(75)
Child outcome domain						
Attachment	1	7	17	2	1	28 (37.3%)
Behaviour			1	10	16	27 (36%)
Cognitive			9	4	7	20 (26.7%)
Level of need						
Universal		1	5	6	5	20 (26.7%)
Targeted-Selective	1	6	9	5	7	28 (36.3%)
Targeted- Indicated			11	5	12	27 (36%)
Delivery model						
Promotion +			7			7 (9.3%)
Group	1	2	8	10	14	35 (46.7%)
Home Visiting		4	4	1	3	12 (16%)
Individual		1	8	5	7	21 (28%)
Evidence rating						
NE		2	2	1		5 (6.7%)
NL2	1	3	17	8	6	35 (46.7%)
2			6	6	6	18 (24%)
3			2	1	11	14 (18.7%)
4		2			1	3 (4%)
Cost rating						
1 (low)		1	7	5	7	20 (33.9%)
2 (medium low)	1		9	9	7	26 (44.1%)
3 (medium)		2	1	1	5	9 (15.3%)
4 (medium high)		1	2			2 (3.4%)
5 (high)		1	1			2 (3.4%)
Missing		2	7	1	5	15 (20%)

In sum, just over one third (27) of all of the interventions assessed had evidence from least one rigorously conducted RCT. Seventeen had evidence of improving both child and parent outcomes, five had evidence of improving a parent outcome only and five had evidence of no effect. The details of these programmes are provided in Table 15.5.

We also observed that programmes targeting behavioural outcomes were more likely to be assessed as 'evidence based' (10 or 37 per cent) in comparison to

TABLE 15.5 Characteristics of the 27 interventions with evidence from a rigorously conducted evaluation by primary child outcome, strength of evidence, level of need, and delivery model

Programme name	Primary outcome	Strength of evidence	Cost	Level of need	Delivery model
Antenatal/perinatal					
Family Nurse Partnership	Attachment /cognitive	4+	5	Targeted-Selective	Home Visiting
Family Foundations	Attachment /behaviour	4	1	Universal	Group
Social Baby	Attachment /cognitive	NE	NA	Targeted-Selective	Home Visiting
MECSH	Attachment /cognitive	NE	4	Targeted-Selective	Home Visiting
Infancy					
Infant-parent psychotherapy	Attachment	3+	NA	Targeted-Indicated	Individual
Child First	Attachment /cognitive	3+	5	Targeted-Indicated	Home
Circle of Security Home Visiting	Attachment/ cognitive	NL2	2	Targeted-Indicated	Home Visiting
Parent-Infant Project	Attachment/ cognitive	NL2	4	Targeted- Indicated	Individual
VIPP	Attachment/ cognitive	NL2	2	Targeted- Indicated	Individual
Toddlers without Tears	Behaviour	NE	NA	Universal	Group
Toddlerhood					
Family Check-up	Behaviour	3+	2	Targeted-Selective	Individual
Parents as Partners	Behaviour	NL2	3	Targeted- Selective	
IndividualVIPP-SD	Behaviour	NL2	2	Targeted- Indicated	Individual
Family Links	Behaviour	NE	1	Universal	Group
Let's Learn Language	Cognitive	NE	1	Targeted- Indicated	Group
Preschool					
Child-Parent Psychotherapy	Attachment	3+	NA	Targeted-Indicated	Individual
Incredible Years Preschool BASIC	Behaviour	4+	2	Targeted- Indicated	Group
The New Forest Parenting Programme	Behaviour	3+	3	Targeted-Indicated	Individual
Triple P Group	Behaviour	3+	1	Targeted-Indicated	Group
Discussion Group Triple P	Behaviour	3+	1	Targeted-Indicated	Group
Triple P Standard	Behaviour	3	2	Targeted-Indicated	Group
Parent Corps	Behaviour	3	2	Targeted-Selective	Group
Hitkashrut	Behaviour	3	2	Targeted-Indicated	Group
Helping the Noncompliant Child	Behaviour	3	3	Targeted-Indicated	Group
Empowering Parents/ Empowering Communities	Behaviour	3	1	Targeted-Indicated	Group
REAL (Rasing Early Achievement in Literature)	Cognitive	3	3	Targeted-Selective	Home Visiting
Let's Play in Tandem	Cognitive	3	3	Targeted-Selective	Home Visiting

programmes targeting children's attachment security (5 or 16 per cent) or children's early learning (2 or 10 per cent), as illustrated in Figure 15.2.

This finding may be linked to the age at which behavioural interventions are typically offered. Figure 15.3 makes clear that behavioural interventions are more likely to target families with a toddler or preschool child in comparison to attachment programmes, which are more likely to target families the first 1001 days.

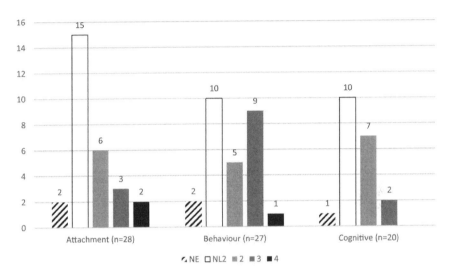

FIGURE 15.2 Distribution of strength of evidence ratings by primary child outcome

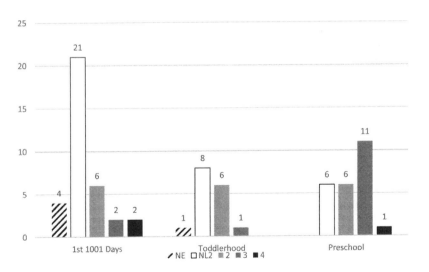

FIGURE 15.3 Distribution of strength of evidence ratings by children's age

The first 1001 days

The relationship between children's age, programme outcomes and strength of evidence are summarised in greater detail in Figure 15.4. Figure 15.4 shows that only 13 of the 35 programmes targeting pregnancy and infancy had evidence from a rigorously conducted evaluation. It is worth noting that 10 out of the remaining 22 had yet to identify or measure their impact on any specific child outcome.

Of the 13 programmes with evidence from a rigorously conducted evaluation, 11 measured their impact on attachment related outcomes. Four had evidence of improving a child outcome, five had evidence of improving parenting behaviours only and two were assessed as having 'no effect' on a parent or child outcome.

Three of the four interventions with evidence of improving child outcomes provided comprehensive support to vulnerable families for a period of a year or longer. This support aimed to improve a variety of child outcomes, although all three specifically supported the attachment relationship. The fourth programme, Family Foundations, was much shorter intervention providing support to the interparental relationship during the last trimester of the mother's first pregnancy. Family Foundations was assessed at Level 4 with observational evidence from two studies of improving children's attachment-related behaviours at year 1 and self-report evidence from parents and teachers suggesting reductions in children's noncompliant behaviour at ages 3 and 7.

Two further programmes targeting outcomes other than the attachment relationship were also assessed as having no effect. One aimed to prevent behavioural problems in later childhood through advice provided to parents at eight, 12 and 18 months. The second aimed to prevent language delay in children scoring assessed as being at risk when they were 18 months.

Ages 24 to 36 months

Just over a fifth (16 or 21 per cent) of the assessed programmes were developed for families with a child between 24 and 36 months. While two-thirds (10 or 63 per cent) aimed to improve children's behaviour, only four had evidence from a rigorously conducted evaluation. All four were developed to prevent or improve child behavioural problems, but only one had evidence of doing this. The other three could not confirm any consistent improvements in children's behaviour, although two had evidence of improving parenting practices.

Ages 3 to 5

Approximately one third (24 or 32 per cent) of the programmes were developed for families with a child between the ages of 3 and 5. Two thirds of these programmes (16 or 66 per cent) targeted children's noncompliant behaviour. Half (12 or 50 per cent) had evidence from a rigorously conducted evaluation demonstrating improvements in child outcomes. Nine of these programmes targeted children's behaviour, two targeted cognitive/language outcomes and one had evidence of

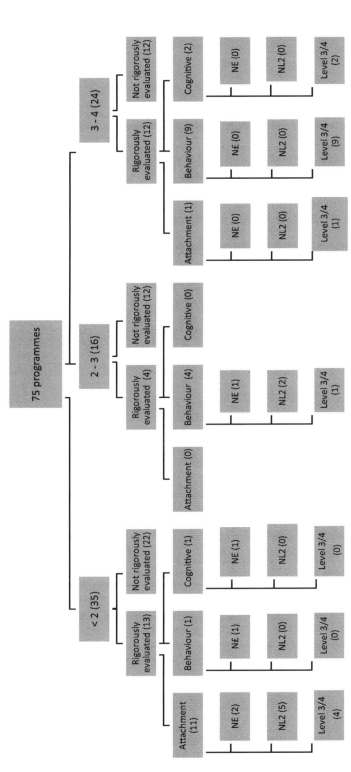

FIGURE 15.4 Distribution of interventions by children's age, primary child outcome and strength of evidence rating

increasing children's attachment security. All nine behavioural interventions had short-term evidence of reducing noncompliant child behaviour immediately upon programme completion. The majority of these programmes were group-based, lasting between 12 and 22 weeks. One of these programmes, the Incredible Years Preschool, was assessed as having Level 4 evidence with positive benefits being observed in children 10 years or longer.

Discussion

The EIF assessed the strength of evidence underpinning a range of 75 interventions developed to support the nonphysical development of children aged 5 or younger through parent–child interaction. The study observed that less than a quarter (17) had rigorous evidence of impacting child outcomes and this evidence was disproportionately skewed in favour of children between the ages of 3 and 5. By comparison, programmes targeting the first 1001 days were less likely to have undergone a rigorous evaluation and less likely to confirm a positive child outcome. Ultimately, only four interventions targeting the first 1001 days had evidence of improving a child outcome.

The relatively low number of evidence-based programmes is disappointing, but not surprising given the challenges involved in developing and evaluating interventions for families with young children (Barlow et al., 2007). The relative lack of evidence-based programmes involving the first 1001 days is surprising, however, especially when the majority of the programmes were developed for children during this period of development. We have identified two possible reasons for this.

First, the interventions targeting the first 1001 critical days were less likely to specifically consider their impact on children's development. In this respect, approximately one-third of the interventions targeting the first 1001 days failed to identify or measure any specific child outcome, targeting evaluation efforts on parenting behaviours instead. This may be because child outcomes during the early years are more difficult to reliably measure (Bedford, Walton & Ahn, 2013), but also because programme developers often assumed that parent benefits were sufficient proxies for child benefits.

We believe that this assumption could result in an over confidence in the value of many programmes targeting the first 1001 days, since their benefits for children remain ultimately unknown. While measuring programme impacts on children's development during the early years is challenging, it is nevertheless feasible, as four of the programmes assessed in this review were able to demonstrate. Methods for reliably assessing a programme's impact on young children's development include coded observations of parent and child behaviours and longitudinal follow-up studies that make use of validated pen and paper measures.

Second, we need to consider whether many of the programmes targeting the first 1001 days are necessary or sufficient for preventing problems from occurring as children grow older. We raise this question in light of the findings involving programmes developed to reduce noncompliant behaviours in very young children. Of the 13 behavioural programmes with evidence from a rigorous evaluation, one was offered during the first 2 years, three were offered during toddlerhood and nine were offered to families with a child between the ages of 3 and 5. All nine of the programmes offered during later childhood had evidence of improving child outcomes in comparison to one (out of four) behavioural interventions offered before that time.

Hence, we question whether the content of behavioural interventions offered during infancy or toddlerhood is sufficient for preventing problems from occurring in later development. We base this speculation on findings from the evaluation of the Toddlers without Tears (TwT) programme, which aimed to prevent child behavioural problems through preventative advice provided when the children were 8, 12 and 15 months old. The evaluation observed no improvements in children's behaviour, despite some initial improvements in parents' attitudes towards harsh discipline (Bayer et al., 2010; Hiscock et al., 2008). Given that noncompliant behaviours peak between 17 and 36 months (Tremblay et al., 2004) the TwT's evaluators speculated that general advice provided at early points in children's development may not have been sufficient for reducing children's behavioural problems when they actually occurred. Evidence involving parenting interventions more generally suggests that programmes may be more effective when parents have opportunities to practice key time they are participating in the intervention (Kaminski et al., 2008).

Summary and recommendations

Our findings suggest that interventions targeting the first 1001 days are not sufficiently evaluated, especially when it comes to measuring their impact on children's early development. In addition, our assessment observed that some programmes targeting the first 1001 days may not be sufficient for preventing problems as children develop. We therefore recommend that:

- Innovative research in infant wellbeing should include evaluation studies that measure the impact of parenting interventions on specific child outcomes. Methods for measuring child outcomes during early periods of development include coded observations of child behaviours and longitudinal follow-up studies.
- Innovative research in children's wellbeing should also consider the extent to which interventions offered during the first 1001 days are developmentally specific, as well as the extent to which they improve children's development over time.

References

Allen, G. (2011). *Early intervention: The next steps*. HM Government. An Independent Report to her majesty's government. London: Cabinet Office

Asmussen, K. (2011). *The Evidence-Based Parenting Practitioner's Handbook*. London: Routledge.

Asmussen, K., Feinstein, L., Martin, J., & Chowdry, H. (2016). *Foundations for Life: What Works to Support Parent Child Interaction in the Early Years*. London: The Early Intervention Foundation.

Axford, N., Sonthalia, S., Wrigley, Z., Goodwin, A., Ohlson, C., Bjornstad, G., Barlow, J., Schrader-McMillan, A., Coad, J., & Toft, A. (2015). *The Best Start at Home*. London: The Early Intervention Foundation.

Barlow, J., Kirkpatrick, S., Wood, D., Ball, M., & Stewart-Brown, S. (2007). *Family and Parenting Support in Sure Start Local Programmes*. NESS: London.

Bayer, J.K., Hiscock, H., Ukourmunne, O.C., Scalzo, K., & Wake, M. (2010). Three-year-old outcomes of a brief universal parenting intervention to prevent behaviour problems: Randomized controlled trial. *Archives of Disease in Childhood, 95*, 187–192.

Bernier, A., Carlson, S.M., & Whipple, N. (2010). From external regulation to self-regulation: Early parenting precursors of young children's executive functioning. *Child Development, 81*, 326–339.

Best, J.R., & Miller, P.H. (2010). A developmental perspective on executive function. *Child Development, 81*, 1641–1660.

Bronfenbrenner, U. (1979). Contexts of child rearing: Problems and prospects. *American Psychologist, 34*, 844.

Duncan, G.J., Magnuson, K.A., & Ludwig, J. (2004). The endogeneity problem in developmental studies. *Research in Human Development, 1*, 59–80.

Harold, G., Acquah, D., Sellers, R., Chowdry, H., & Feinstein, L. (2016). *What Works to Enhance Inter-Parental Relationships and Improve Outcomes for Children*. London: The Early Intervention Foundation.

Hiscock, H., Bayer, J.K., Price, A., & Ukoumunne, O. (2008). Universal parenting programme to prevent early childhood behavioural problems: Cluster randomized trial. *British Medical Journal, 336*, 318–321.

Kaminski, J.W., Valle, L.A., Filene, J.H., & Boyle, C.L. (2008). A meta-analytic review of components associated with parent training program effectiveness. *Journal of Abnormal Child Psychology, 36*(4), 567–589.

Mensah, F.K., & Kiernan, K.E. (2011). Maternal general health and children's cognitive development and behaviour in the early years: Findings from the Millennium Cohort Study. *Child: Care, Health and Development, 37*, 44–54.

Miyake, A., Friedman, N.P., Emerson, M.J., Witzki, A.H., Howerter, A., & Wager, T.D. (2000). The unity and diversity of executive functions and their contributions to complex 'frontal lobe' tasks: A latent variable analysis. *Cognitive Psychology, 41*, 49–100.

Sameroff, A.J., Seifer, R., Baldwin, A., & Baldwin, C. (1993). Stability of intelligence from preschool to adolescence: The influence of social and family risk factors. *Child Development, 64*(1), 80–97.

Shonkoff, J.P., & Phillips, D.A. (Eds.). (2000). *From Neurons to Neighborhoods: The Science of Early Childhood Development*. National Academies Press.

Tremblay, R.E., Nagin, D.S., Seguin, J.R., Zoccolillo, M., Zelazo, P.D., Boivin, M., Perusse, D., & Japel, C. (2004). Physical aggression during early childhood: Trajectories and predictors. *Pediatrics, 114*, 43–50.

Waldfogel, J. (1999). Early childhood interventions and outcomes. http://eprints.lse.ac.uk/6497/1/Early_Childhood_Interventions_and_Outcomes.pdf

Weintraub, S., Bauer, P.J., Zelazo, P.D., Wallner-Allen, K., Dikmen, S.S., Heaton, R.K., Tulsky, D.S., Slotkin, J., Blitz, D.L., Carlozzi, N.E., & Havlik, R.J. (2013). I. NIH toolbox cognition battery (CB): Introduction and pediatric data. *Monographs of the Society for Research in Child Development, 78*, 1–15.

16

TRANSFORMING INFANCY THROUGH PATERNITY AND PARENTAL LEAVE

Margaret O'Brien

Infant care is no longer purely a private family matter. More employed parents have to accommodate 24/7 infant care within a 24/7 globalised working life involving a trade-off between care, time and money. As more mothers return to paid employment in their child's first year, governments and employers are developing policies and provisions to support working parents with very young children. One of these measures is paternity leave, or parental leave also open to fathers. This chapter reviews what is known about fathers taking leave. Although studies are limited, there is growing evidence that taking leave has the potential to boost fathers' emotional investment in and connection with infants, with the potential to transform infant life. At a macro level, a country's parental leave regime can be an important facilitating context for achieving an optimal infant quality of life.

What is paternity and parental leave?

Paternity leave (taken around the time of a child's birth) and father-targeted parental leave schemes are expanding rapidly across the world. Although Sweden was the first country in 1974 to introduce parental leave open to fathers as well as mothers, Norway was the first country in 1993 to reserve 4 weeks of well-paid parental leave exclusively for fathers – the nontransferable 'daddy month' (Eydal et al., 2015).

By 2014 the International Labour Organisation (ILO) had found a statutory right to paternity leave in 79 of 167 countries, paid in 71 of the cases (ILO, 2014). While a global minimum ILO standard on duration of maternity leave exists (14 weeks, met by 53 per cent of countries) no such standard exists for paternity leave which globally ranges from 1 day to periods over 2 weeks. Company or government payment ranges from strong compensation, as found in Finland with 9 days at

70 per cent of earnings, to a minimal flat rate coverage as in the United Kingdom (Moss, 2016).

Parental leave is a period of longer leave available to either parent, usually after maternity or paternity leave finishes, ranging from months to 3 years, and typically unpaid. Its provision has been found in 66 countries surveyed by ILO, mostly in developed economies, Eastern Europe and Asia but only paid in 36, most generously in the Nordic countries.

Since the late 1990s strategies to enhance the visibility of fathers' entitlements to parental leave have accelerated particularly in Europe. There has been experimentation with a range of policy instruments, based on incentive, penalty and even compulsion. Part of the policy innovation has involved a form of rebranding where periods of leave time within individual or family entitlements have become reserved for fathers or father-targeted (sometimes referred to as a 'father's quota'). Through the reconfiguration, fathers' access to a period of parental leave, previously implicit, within an individual gender neutral entitlement, becomes explicit. The group includes the well-established father-sensitive regimes embedded in the majority, but not all, of the Nordic countries, and the enhanced schemes that come from countries as diverse as Germany, Portugal, Spain and Slovenia.

Within Nordic countries, one of the most innovative 'father-targeted' leave entitlements so far developed, in terms of combined time (3 months) and economic compensation (80 per cent of prior salary) is to be found in Iceland (Gislason, 2007). In 2000 the Icelandic government introduced a total of 9 months paid postbirth leave (to be taken in the first 18 months) organised into three parts: 3 months for mothers (nontransferable), 3 months for fathers (nontransferable) and 3 months which can be transferred between parents as they choose. In addition there is 13 weeks unpaid parental leave available each year for each parent. The radical nature of this national measure created intense public debate, in a country known globally for its long maternal and paternal working hours (Gíslason, 2016). The Maternity, Paternity and Parental Leave Bill was passed by the Icelandic government in 2000, following several years' deliberation about men's societal role and gender equality, including a government committee on the Gender Role of Men.

The Iceland 3+3+3 month model has significantly shifted male behaviour in a relatively short period of time. By 2006 over 90 per cent of Icelandic fathers took parental leave. Gíslason (2007: 15) notes: 'Probably, there have never been more Icelandic fathers active in caring for their children than there are today.' Kolbeinn, Eydal and Gíslason (2008: 153) describe how the normative pattern is for Icelandic men to take most of their dedicated days but typically not to utilise the shared component: 'You may well be regarded as weird if you don't use the paternity leave, but the same does not hold for using the shared entitlement.'

In the same decade a radical break in family policy to create an incentive for fathers to take leave was introduced in Germany against a leave policy background which supported mothers to stay out of the labour market for 3 years after the birth of a child (Geisler & Kreyenfield, 2011). A new highly paid 2 months, 'Elterngeld', was added to a shorter 12-month parental leave period. The reform concentrated high payment onto a shorter 12-month parental leave period, with an extra 2 months of high payment if fathers take 2 months of leave. The proportion of fathers taking leave more than tripled from 3.5 per cent in the last quarter of 2006 to 13.7 per cent in the second quarter of 2008 and has risen incrementally since (Moss, 2016).

Men's behaviour is very receptive to public policies developed to extend their engagement with infants. Key ingredients which enhance utilisation appear to be high-income replacement combined with designated father targeted or reserved schemes rates. Evidence shows that blocks of time which are labelled 'daddy days' or 'father's quota' are attractive to men and their partners (Eydal et al., 2015). Designs with low income replacement or based on maternal transfer, both features of UK's Additional paternity leave and its successor Shared Parental Leave, are known not to encourage paternal uptake.

In the United Kingdom, governments have shown caution in reforming parental leave architecture, despite policy statements by successive governments to activate fathers' use of leave (Baird & O'Brien, 2015). Nonetheless there has been a gradual enhancement of British fathers' rights in the workplace. Since April 2003, for the first time, British fathers acquired a legal right to take a 2-week paid paternity leave, building on a 3-month unpaid parental leave entitlement available since 1999 through the European Parental Leave Directive. Evidence shows that by the end of the decade over 90 per cent of fathers did take some time off work at childbirth (Chanfreau et al., 2011) but only 3 per cent were estimated to use the shared form of parental leave transferred from mothers (Gordon & Szram, 2013). By 2016 British mothers have one of the longest periods of maternity leave in Europe, 52 weeks, but only decompensated at a high level for the first 6 weeks and at a low flat rate for the subsequent 33 weeks.

Impact

Despite early research (e.g. Haas, 1992) empirical enquiry into the specific personal and family experiences and impact of maternal, paternal and paternity leave is still relatively undeveloped. There is still surprisingly little empirical research on what parents 'do' during parental leave and even less on what fathers 'do' (Haas & Hwang, 2008; O'Brian, 2009) and as such, understanding the processes by which parental leave may operate to promote or hinder gender equity or child and family wellbeing are still unclear.

In addition, in attempting to understand the impact of parental leave policies there are important macro- and micro-level methodological considerations. At a macro level, parental leave is a black box of diverse arrangements which vary both within and between countries despite common nomenclatures. Eligibility criteria also vary; although in general tend to exclude insecure and informal workers. Also in attempting to understand the specific impact of parental leave it is important to contextualise parental leave as part of societal level public investment.

In most countries public investment in paid leave policies is often highly associated with more general public spending on family benefits as a proportion of GDP (Adema & Ali, 2015). As such, claims from macro-level studies of impact have been controversial, with pathways of influence difficult to disentangle, particularly as any gains can be linked to prior characteristics of fathers (gender egalitarian and child-oriented) rather than the policy itself. Methodological issues, for example about sample selectivity, are also relevant for micro-level analyses although qualitative research has the advantage of fine-tuned dimensional sampling not always available for large-scale administrative or survey data sets.

Where impact research does exist the focus has been mainly on the effects of maternity leave provision with several studies showing child health benefits for instance in immunisation uptake and employment retention (Tanaka, 2005; Han, Ruhm & Waldfogel, 2009). Positive health gains for children are maximised when the maternity leave is: paid, provided in a job secure context and with a duration of at least 10 weeks.

In terms of fathers and leave, the logic has been that giving fathers the opportunity to spend more time at home through leave after childbirth should result in greater involvement in domestic life and childcare. More studies on fathers taking leave have been published over the last decade spanning both comparative and within country policy analysis, particularly concerning implementation and impact at a macro level (e.g. Nepomnyaschy & Waldfogel, 2007; Huerta et al., 2010; Kotsadam & Finseraas, 2011; Rege & Solli, 2012; Buenning, 2015).

The Nordic countries and Germany have provided fertile ground for 'before and after' studies of impact at a country level (Ekberg Eriksson & Friebel, 2005; Duvander & Johansson, 2012; Schober, 2014; Buenning, 2015). The natural experiment paradigm, which has framed many of these studies, has produced evidence for greater engagement of fathers in the care of children after policy reforms, in comparison with father who do not take leave. For instance, Kotsadam and Finseraas (2011) found that men whose last child was born in the year after Norway's father quota introduction in 1993 reported 11 per cent lower levels of conflict over household division of labour and were 50 per cent more likely to share clothes washing than men whose last child was born just before the reform. However, there has been some concern that greater engagement by fathers who have taken leave may be short lived rather than long term. Indeed, German longitudinal analysis by Schober (2014) suggested that fathers increased their participation in childcare only temporarily during the first year after taking parental leave but subsequent research has suggested sustained longer term effects up until the third year of the child's life (Buenning, 2015; Reimer, Warnholtz & Pfau-Effinger, 2015).

Notably, Reimer et al.'s (2015) study found a large effect of paid parental leave taken alone by the father. In particular, an observed relationship between fathers' use of leave and their time for childcare persisted when at least one leave month was taken alone by the fathers. Both Buenning (2015) and Reimer et al.'s (2015) studies were able to use nationally representative German panel data sets (German

Socio-economic panel and Families in Germany) which include items on duration and whether leave is taken alone or with a partner. Also the datasets allow the same fathers to be tracked before and after they take parental leave which enables exploration of selection effects.

Other country level natural experiments have assessed 'duration' effects of fathers' leave on a wide range of outcomes. In a further Norwegian case, it has been found that 4 weeks' exposure to the leave quota during a child's first year was associated with a 1–3 per cent drop in fathers' earnings over the next 5 years (Rege & Solli, 2012). In an another study of duration and fathers' engagement in childcare, research in Australia has found that taking some leave (2 or 4 weeks) increased the likelihood of fathers engaging in sole care at weekends when the child was older 4–19 months (Hosking et al., 2010). Notably, studies are emerging about child outcomes of non-normative fathers with respect to parental leave in particular countries; for instance, Flacking et al., (2010) found that Swedish infants whose fathers did not take paternity leave in the first year were significantly less likely to be breast fed at 2 and 6 months.

Although the body of macro-level research is still emergent it does suggest that fathers' as well as mothers' leave taking has direct as well as indirect influences on infants, family and work life. Moreover, there are indications that leave taking alone by fathers may be especially salient in priming subsequent greater engagement in the care of infants. Earlier and more recent qualitative studies have suggested that being home alone sensitises or enhances fathers' awareness of infant life 'slow time' (Brandth & Kvande, 2002; O'Brian & Wall, 2017).

Parental leave policies and a good quality of infant life

Specification of the dimensions of a good quality of life for an infant is fraught with political dilemmas, economic considerations and, of course, relates to the models of optimal infant development dominant in any one culture at a particular historical juncture. As Waldfogel (2006: 180) states: 'The tensions between respecting choice, promoting quality and supporting employment are higher in the first few years of life than at any other period.'

Infant life has not traditionally been considered the province of social policy, possibly because of an historic gendered assumption that only mothers can provide the permitting circumstances. An explicit review of the infancy period is important, however, as its elements make up any hypothetical benefits of parental leave or leave from employment to care. In the field of parental leave policies, the focus has not so much been on the state of infancy per se but on the parenting or carer processes perceived as necessary for infant life.

Contemporary hallmarks of 'a good enough' infancy depend to some extent on cultural factors and the theoretical models of psychologists or sociologists. Psychologists tend to research the personal characteristics of the parents in providing the care environment such as their parenting style, whereas sociologists pay more attention to resource and community influences on child development. An ecological-parental capital approach (Pleck, 2007) requires a multilayered and multidimensional framework, attempting to incorporate governmental, community, family and individual levels for understanding infancy.

In the ecological context of early childhood and parental employment, the quality of life infants experience is made up of a complex set of processes and resources. The daily life of the infant is organised around regular feeding on six to eight (or more) occasions in a 24-hour cycle, holding, soothing, nappy changing, bathing, dressing as well as sociable interaction, in between regular phases of infant sleeping. In this highly dependent phase of childhood the infant needs at least one carer (not necessarily the same person, although cultural norms vary) to be in close physical proximity. A century of psychological research evidence shows that the nature of adult care (in particular its sensitivity, stability and attentiveness) fosters infant sociability although there is not a linear association between parental time availability and the quality of emergent human relationships (Pleck & Masciadrelli, 2004). At a more distal level, the infant needs economic care for material resources. In essence an adequate quality of infant life requires both economic and emotional investment.

For instance, Galtry's (2003) international comparison demonstrates a positive association between postbirth leave polices and duration of breast feeding. She shows how the Swedish model encourages both high female employment participation rates over a mother's working life and high breast-feeding rates through a parental leave and flexible working policy, which enables many mothers to be more home based for the first 6 months of a child's life and extends men's access to paid parental leave beyond the first year of a child's life. The issue of breast feeding highlights how specific national leave policies can simultaneously invest in children's health while also addressing gender equity and father involvement. As such economic investment in time for breast feeding can be seen as a 'societal good', for instance, in support of WHO health norms which currently advise a 6 month breast feeding period for optimal health benefits to infants (WHO, 2001).

More research needs to be carried out to understand maternal and paternal policies and practices in unison. In particular, the interaction of maternity and paternity leave arrangements and experiences requires further scrutiny. Similarly, more mixed methods research programmes, combining qualitative and quantitative designs, are required in order to explore underlying familial and workplace processes.

Concluding reflections

In the current economic context the future of men's behaviour as fathers, partners and workers is uncertain. There are countervailing value positions and the preference for father as economic provider-in-chief remains a strong cultural force in many countries. Nevertheless governments and civil societal actors across the world are attempting to fit fathers into work-family polices and continuing these efforts despite global economic turbulence.

Expanding national policies and programmes to promote a stronger engagement of men in family care activities through the life course will help modernise work-family policies to catch up with the changing role of women. In the twentieth century many postwar public polices created systems and services which assumed a full-time home female carer, supporting a full-time male breadwinner, a work-family model which no longer fits the circumstances of infants in twenty-first-century families.

References

Adema, W., & Ali, N. (2015). Recent changes in family outcomes and policies in OECD countries: the impact of the economic crisis. *Community, Work and Family, 18*(2), 145–166.

Baird, M. & O'Brien, M. (2015). Dynamics of parental leave in Anglophone countries: The paradox of state expansion in the liberal welfare regime. *Community, Work and Family,* 18(2), 198–217.

Brandth, B., & Kvande, E. (2002). Reflexive fathers: Negotiating parental leave and working life. *Gender, Work and Organization, 9*(2), 186–203.

Buenning, M. (2015). What happens after the 'daddy months'? Fathers' involvement in paid work, childcare, and housework after taking parental leave in Germany. *European Sociological Review,* 1–11. doi:10.1093/esr/jcv072

Chanfreau, J. Gowland, S., Lancaster, Z., Poole, E., Tipping L., & Toomse, M. (2011). *Maternity and Paternity Rights and Women Returners Survey* 2009/10, Department for Work and Pensions, Research Report No 777.Duvander, A.-Z., & Johansson, M. (2012). What are the effects of reforms promoting fathers' parental leave use? *Journal of European Social Policy, 22*(3), 319–330.

Eydal, G.B., Gislason, I., Rostgaard, T., Brandth, B., Duvander, A.-Z., & Lammi-Taskula, J. (2015). Trends in parental leave in the Nordic countries: has the forward march of gender equality halted? *Community, Work and Family, 18*(2), 167–181.

Flacking, R., Dykes F., & Ewald, U. (2010). The influence of fathers' socioeconomic status and paternity leave on breastfeeding duration: a population-based cohort study. *Scand J Public Health.* 2010 Jun; 38(4):337-43

Galtry, J. (2003). The impact on breastfeeding of labour market policy and practice in Ireland, Sweden, and Soc Sci Med. Jul; 57(1), 167-77.

Geisler, E., & Kreyenfeld, M. (2011). Against all odds. Fathers' use of parental leave in Germany. *Journal of European Social Policy, 21,* 88–99.

Gislason, I.V. (2007). *Parental leave in Iceland: Bringing the fathers in. Development in the wake of new legislation in 2000.* Akureyri: Jafnerettisstofa.

Gordon H. and Szram, J. (2013). 'Paternity leave experiences of NHS doctors', *Clinical Medicine,* Vol.13, No.5:426-30.

Haas, L. (1992). *Equal parenthood and social policy: A study of parental leave in Sweden.* Albany: State University of New York Press.

Haas, L., & Hwang, C.P. (2008). The impact of taking parental leave on fathers' participation in childcare and relationships with children: Lessons from Sweden. *Community, Work and Family, 11*(1), 85–104.

Han, W.-J., Ruhm, C., & Waldfogel, J. (2009). Parental leave policies and parents' employment and leave-taking. *Journal of Policy Analysis and Management, 23*(1), 29–54.

Hosking, A. Whitehouse, G. & Baxter, J. (2010). Duration of Leave and Resident Fathers' Involvement in Infant Care in Australia. *Journal of Marriage and the Family,* 72, 5, 1301–1316.

Huerta, M., Adema, W., Baxter, J., Han, W., Lausten, M., Lee, R., Waldfogel, J. (2013). 'Fathers' leave, fathers' involvement and child development: are they related? Evidence from four OECD countries',OECD Social, Employment and Migration Working Papers No 140.Available at: www.oecd.org/els/workingpapers

ILO (International Labor Organization) (2014). *Maternity and paternityat work: law and practice across the world*, Geneva: ILO.

Kolbeinn, A. Eydal, G., & Gíslason, I. (2008). Conclusion. In Eydal, G. and Gislason, I. (Eds) *Equal rights to earn and care: parental leave in Iceland*. Reykjavik: Félagsvīsindastofnun.

Kotsadam, A. & Finseraas, H. (2011). The state intervenes in the battle of the sexes: causal effects of paternity leave. *Social Science Research*, 40, 1611-1622.

Moss, P. (2016). International Review of Leave Policies and Related Research 2016. Retrieved from website: http://leavenetwork.org/fileadmin/Leavenetwork/Annual _reviews/2016 annual_review_october.pdf

Nepomnyaschy, L., & Waldfogel, J. (2007). Paternity leave and fathers' involvement with their young children. *Community, Work and Family*, 10(4), 427–453

O'Brien, M. (2009). Fathers, parental leave policies and infant quality of life: International perspectives and policy impact. *The Annals of the American Academy of Political and Social Science*, *624*, 190–213.

O'Brien, M., & Wall, K, (Eds.) (2017). *Comparative Perspectives on Work-Life Balance and Gender Equality: Fathers on Leave Alone*. New York: Springer.

Reimer,T., Warnholtz, L., & Pfau-Effinger, B. (2015). Daddy Months' as a sustainable policy? Discerning the long-term influence of a new parental leave legislation in Germany on fathers' engagement in childcare. Presentation at Workshop Fathers' Involvement in the Life Course Berlin, September 3 and 4.

Schober, P.S. (2014). Parental leave and domestic work of mothers and fathers. A longitudinal study of two reforms inWest Germany. *Journal of Social Policy*, 43, 351–372.

Tanaka, S. (2005). Parental Leaves and child health across OECD countries, *Economic Journal*, *115*(501), F. 7–28.

Waldfogel, J. (2006). *What children need*. Cambridge, MA: Harvard University Press.

17

TOWARDS AN EVIDENCE-BASED POPULATION APPROACH TO SUPPORTING PARENTING IN THE EARLY YEARS

Matthew R. Sanders and Alina Morawska

Parenting and children's development

The crucial importance of the parent–child relationship in the early years of life is well established. Parenting influences children's development through the day-to-day interactions between parents and children. The quality of these interactions lays the foundations for optimal development by promoting healthy brain development, secure attachment, growth of early language, emotional regulation capacity, prosociality and school readiness. Supporting parents in their role can help to create knowledgeable, skilled and confident parents, who can in turn promote healthy, happy and capable children who are less likely to experience adverse childhood experiences.

Historically parenting interventions have focused on high-risk or vulnerable groups or populations. In this chapter we make the case for a more inclusive whole of population framework to promote the wellbeing of all children and concurrently reduce the prevalence rates of child and family problems. Parental self-regulation is discussed as a primary goal of parenting support and we discuss the criteria that need to be met for a population approach to work.

Theoretical basis for positive parenting of very young children

Positive parenting of infants and toddlers includes five core principles (Spry, Morawska & Sanders, 2011). i) *A safe, engaging and nurturing environment*. Key to early childhood development is the establishment of strong infant-carer bonds, and the quality of this relationship is important to the developing brain (Schore, 2004). Sensitive, responsive parenting, characterised by a warm approach, combined with effective strategies for helping infants soothe and settle, underpin the development of this bond and contribute to strong attachment relationships. This strong bond continues to be important as the infant grows into a toddler and preschooler, and provides the foundation for exploration, development of self-regulatory capacities and prosocial skills. A nurturing environment provides access to age appropriate activities that engage children, appropriate supervision and is relatively free from environmental hazards or risks. In such an environment children initiate inter-actions frequently with parents and carers who provide a secure base for exploratory behaviour. ii) *A positive learning environment* is one that is responsive to children and attuned to their behaviour, emotions and needs. Responsivity means that parents are observant and provide care, attention, approval and encouragement to children when needed. iii) *A predictable environment.* In infancy, a consistent, predictable environment helps babies to learn that their world is safe and they can trust those around them. It assists with the development of routines and healthy habits from a young age. Discipline encounters inevitably arise as children become mobile and enter toddlerhood. Early socialisation of children to follow reasonable directions and instructions is facilitated by parents providing positive attention when children behave appropriately and consistent, contingent consequences when children are disobedi-ent or behave inappropriately. iv) *Having realistic expectations.* Parents who are realistic about what children are capable of at various stages of their development are better able to respond to their children's needs. This includes knowing at what age and stage of development children are typically ready to learn new skills and accepting that sometimes change in their child's behaviour is neither possible nor desirable. Having reasonable expectations also includes expectations of oneself as a parent. Parents need to avoid being too self-critical of themselves and others in the parenting role. All parents make mistakes from time to time. v) *Taking care of oneself as a parent and as a couple.* Positive parenting involves taking care of oneself physically, emotionally, socially and financially so that parents have the necessary personal and physical resources (knowledge, skills, energy and interpersonal and practical support in place) to undertake their parenting role. Parents who monitor and keep their emotions in check, particularly in discipline situations, are more likely to respond calmly, consistently, firmly and decisively. When parents are lonely, isolated, and live in conflictual or violent relationships or in extreme poverty, parenting is more difficult, stressful and overwhelming. Involvement with others who are also in the parenting role in their community reduces isolation and can lead parents to form peer support and friendship networks that fosters parental self-care.

Parenting support for every parent

Understanding the broader ecological context for parenting

Ecological models of human development have had a major impact on the study of child development (Bronfenbrenner, 1979). Such a model reminds us that parent-ing takes place in a wider environmental context that includes the laws of the land, family and child friendly policies, access to affordable child care, funding available for early intervention, rates of employment, affordable housing, violent crime, effectiveness of policing and so on. The favourability of the broader socio–political context in supporting early intervention has significant implications for population-based approaches to parenting support. In more favourable circumstances early intervention and parenting will be considered a priority and funds made available for both implementation and evaluation. This broader context in turn interacts with a set of factors to promote change that are more immediately under the control of programme developers and implementers of parenting programmes. These enabling factors can be directly influenced by programmers to change and programme outcomes such as participation rates, programme completion and programme outcomes.

A population approach to parenting support may be particularly useful during the first 3 years of life when parents are new to the role and infants have greater developmental plasticity (Centre on the Developing Child, 2007). This approach offers parenting support to all parents to enhance the capacity of communities to more effectively engage more parents in an evidence-based parenting intervention than would otherwise occur (Prinz & Sanders, 2007). It achieves this by de-stigmatising preparation for parenthood so it becomes a socially normative experience to participate (Sanders, 2012). This increased reach improves capacity to reduce the prevalence rates of significant childhood problems. The adoption of a population-based approach contrasts with the typical way parenting programmes have been used as a treatment for children with conduct problems (Herschell & McNeil, 2007; Patterson, Mockford & Stewart-Brown, 2005). The term 'population-based approach to parenting support' represents a paradigm shift in how we tackle the task of supporting good parenting in the community.

There are numerous examples of early intervention services, particularly in the health and early care domains, that are delivered universally to all parents. For example, child health and welfare services in both Australia and the United Kingdom offer early support to all parents in areas such as supporting breastfeeding, early infancy care and basic parenting skills. Likewise, universal home–visiting programmes also provide early support to all families regardless of risk. Similarly, parental leave policies, government supported early childhood care and education are all examples of population approaches to supporting parents.

A widely studied and disseminated example of a population approach to parenting support is the Triple P-Positive Parenting Program (Sanders, 2012). The multilevel system incorporates five levels of intervention, on a tiered range of interventions of increasing strength and narrowing population reach, for parents of children aged 0–16 (see Figure 17.1 for a graphical representation of the Triple P system, and Table 17.1 for programme variants). It involves a mix of universal and targeted programmes, and is consistent with the public health principle of 'progressive or proportionate universalism'. This concept refers to the fact that focusing exclusively on delivering interventions to the most disadvantaged will not sufficiently reduce health inequalities. To reduce the steepness of the social gradient

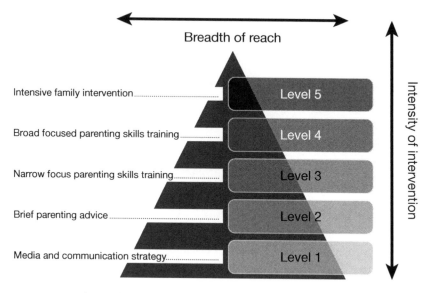

FIGURE 17.1 The Triple P System of parenting and family support

in health, actions must be universal, but with a scale and intensity that is proportionate to the level of disadvantage (Marmot, 2010). Although many existing rollouts of the Triple P system have included parents of very young children there have been no specific evaluations of differential effects in children under the age of three.

One unique feature of the Triple P system is the adoption of a self-regulation framework. This framework encourages parents to view parenting support as supportive and helpful, rather than intrusive, prescriptive or dependency promoting. The five key elements to parental self-regulation include: use of self-management tools (goal setting relating to desired changes in one's own behaviour, cognition or emotion, self-monitoring, self-evaluation, feedback), self-efficacy (belief in one's capacity to complete parenting tasks), personal agency (attributing change to one's own efforts rather than luck or uncontrollable factors), self-sufficiency and problem solving. Parental goals are informed by culture, history, tradition and personal priorities.

Criteria that need to be met for a population approach to work

Having evidenced-based interventions readily available. A population-based parenting programme targeting the first three years of life should deploy interventions that have been shown to be effective through careful evaluation of outcomes including randomised controlled trials (RCTs). To date the evidence supporting Triple P with this age group focuses primarily on parents of toddlers. Several RCTs have

TABLE 17.1 The triple P system of parenting and family support

Level of intervention	Target population	Intervention methods	Facilitators
Level 1 Communications strategy • *Universal Triple P* • *Stay Positive*	All parents interested in information about parenting and promoting their child's development.	Coordinated communications strategy raising awareness of parent issues and encouraging participation in parenting programs. May involve electronic and print media (e.g. brochures, posters, websites, television, talk-back radio, newspaper and magazine editorials).	Typically coordinated by communications, health or welfare staff.
Level 2 Health promotion strategy/ brief selective intervention • *Selected Triple P* • *Selected Teen Triple P*	Parents interested in parenting education or with specific concerns about their child's development or behaviour.	Health promotion information or specific advice for a discrete developmental issue or minor child-behaviour problem. May involve a group seminar format or brief (up to 20 minutes) telephone or face-to-face clinician contact.	Practitioners who provide parent support during routine well-child healthcare (e.g. health, education, allied health and childcare staff).
Level 3 Narrow focus parent training • *Primary Care Triple P* • *Triple P Discussion Groups* • *Primary Care Teen Triple P* • *Teen Triple P Discussion Groups* • *Primary Care*	Parents with specific concerns as above who require consultations or active skills training.	Brief program (about 80 minutes over four sessions, or 2-hour discussion groups) combining advice, rehearsal and self-evaluation to teach parents to manage a discrete child problem behaviour. May involve telephone contact.	Same as for Level 2.
• *Stepping Stones Triple P*	Parents of children with disabilities, with concerns as above.	A parallel program with a focus on disabilities.	Same as above.

continued

TABLE 17.1 *continued*

Level of intervention	Target population	Intervention methods	Facilitators
Level 4 Broad focus parent training • *Standard Triple P* • *Group Triple P* • *Self-Directed Triple P* • *Triple P Online* • *Standard Teen Triple P* • *Group Teen Triple P* • *Self-Directed Teen Triple P*	Parents wanting intensive training in positive parenting skills. Typically parents of children with behaviour problems such as aggressive or oppositional behaviour.	Broad focus program (about 10 hours over 8–10 sessions) focusing on parent-child interaction and the application of parenting skills to a broad range of target behaviours. Includes general-ization-enhancement strategies. May be self-directed, involve telephone or face-to-face clinician contact, or group sessions.	Intensive parenting intervention workers (e.g. mental health and welfare staff, and other allied health and education professionals who regularly consult with parents about child behaviour).
• *Standard Stepping Stones Triple P* • *Group Stepping Stones Triple P* • *Self-Directed Stepping Stones Triple*	Parents of children with disabilities who have or are at risk of developing behavioural or emotional disorders.	A parallel series of tailored programs with a focus on disabilities.	Same as above.
Level 5 Intensive family intervention modules • *Enhanced Triple P*	Parents of children with behaviour problems and concurrent family dysfunction such as parental depression or stress, or conflict between partners.	Intensive individually tailored program with modules (60–90 minute sessions) including practice sessions to enhance parenting skills, mood management and stress coping skills, and partner support skills.	Intensive family intervention workers (e.g. mental health and welfare staff).
• *Pathways Triple*	Parents at risk of child maltreatment. Targets anger-management problems and other factors associated with abuse.	Intensive individually-tailored or group program with modules (60–120 minute sessions depending on delivery model) including attribution retraining and anger management.	Same as above.

continued

Level of intervention	Target population	Intervention methods	Facilitators
• *Group Lifestyle Triple P*	Parents of overweight or obese children. Targets healthy eating and increasing activity levels as well as general child behaviour.	Intensive 14-session group program (including telephone consultations) focusing on nutrition, healthy lifestyle and general parenting strategies. Includes generalization-enhancement strategies.	As above plus dieticians / nutritionists with experience in delivering parenting interventions.
• *Family Transitions Triple P*	Parents going through separation or divorce.	Intensive 12-session group program (including telephone consultations) focusing on coping skills, conflict management, general parenting strategies and developing a healthy co-parenting relationship.	Intensive family intervention workers (e.g., counsellors, mental health and welfare staff).

shown positive effects on child behaviour and parenting practices of brief 2-hour topic specific discussion groups (low intensity interventions). Positive effects have been shown for discussion groups focusing on disobedience, hassle free shopping, mealtimes and toddler aggression (Dittman, Farruggia, Keown & Sanders 2016; Joachim, Sanders & Turner, 2010; Morawska, Adamson, Hinchliffe & Adams, 2014; Morawska, Haslam, Milne & Sanders, 2011). More intensive group and individual interventions (e.g. Adamson, Morawska & Sanders, 2013; Bor, Sanders & Markie-Dadds, 2002; Morawska & Sanders, 2006a, 2006b; Sanders, Markie-Dadds, Tully & Bor, 2000) have reported moderate to large effects in children's behaviour, parenting and parental self-efficacy.

A new version of Triple P (Baby Triple P) developed by Spry et al. (2011) targets parents of infants and aims to prepare new parents for a positive transition to parenthood by teaching them skills in the domains of parenting their baby and looking after their own wellbeing, as well as maintaining a positive relationship with their partner. The outcome evaluations of Baby Triple P are ongoing. An initial feasibility RCT conducted by Spry (2013) investigated Baby Triple P in a universal population. While the 129 couples who participated in Baby Triple P were satisfied with the help they received, none of the outcomes differed between the intervention and care as usual groups. However, the sample was older, more educated, better off financially and better adjusted than the general population, thus leaving little room for improvement on any of the outcome measures. Other studies of Baby Triple P have reported high acceptability and feasibility among families with premature babies (Ferrari, Whittingham, Boyd, Sanders & Colditz, 2011), mothers in a psychiatric unit (Butler, Hare, Walker, Wieck & Wittkowski, 2014), and mothers suffering postnatal depression (Tsivos, Calam, Sanders & Wittkowski, 2015). Several large scale studies are ongoing with more high risk and vulnerable families. These studies will provide more definitive evidence pertaining to longer term effects of Baby Triple P.

Using effective engagement strategies. Just because a programme works, is free and has high consumer satisfaction ratings, there is no guarantee parents will 'flock' to it. However, lack of awareness that a programme exists is a major barrier to engaging large numbers of families. In promoting awareness and engagement, it is useful to consider ecological models of human development (Bronfenbrenner, 1979). Such models remind us that parenting occurs in a wider social context that creates opportunities and restrictions. There is a range of variables that can be targeted to facilitate engagement by particular parent groups. Variables include *programme variables* (programme features that can be adapted or tailored to ensure that programmes are accessible, low or no cost, culturally and personally relevant), *social influence factors* (whether participation is supported by a parent's social network, activation of social contagion through parent to parent social conversations), *cognitive variables* (positive expectations of a favourable outcome of participation), *motivational factors* (offering preferred delivery formats, free food or snacks, child care or other financial incentives to counter the competing demands and stress that may prevent parents attendance). The goal is to create 'pull demand' from parents for good quality parenting programmes so that parents will view participation in a parenting programmes as advantaging their families.

Using an effective implementation framework. The successful implementation of population-based programmes requires careful programme implementation, working with key stakeholders and partner organisations to ensure the implementation process is smooth, timely and responsive to the contextual needs and constraints of the community (McWilliam, Brown, Sanders & Jones, 2016). A key consideration is determining the appropriate model of implementation that will best fit the needs and desired outcomes of the community. This involves exploring multiple parameters including the size and characteristics of the target population, the known effectiveness of the proposed intervention and the level of practitioner activity in delivering the intervention. As these parameters are interdependent, a change in one parameter can produce change in the others. Dirscherl, Dirscherl, McWilliam and Sanders (2016) described a planning tool CAPCAL that linked all relevant parameters that could be varied (e.g. size of population) with the associated consequences on other parameters (e.g. required workforce).

Deployment of interventions of varying intensity. Successful implementations of population-level interventions have typically used a substantial amount of programme delivery (at least 25 per cent) through low intensity 'light touch' interventions. Apart from seeking to normalise and destigmatise participation, parents can be encouraged to share their learnings and insights and therefore 'spread the word' to friends, neighbours and relatives in their social network through peer advocacy, thus encouraging programme attendance. The most intensive multisession programmes should be used sparingly for the most vulnerable families. Our experience in delivering both low and high intensity interventions to vulnerable families is that light touch interventions can be surprisingly helpful to parents of young children. For example, a parent may present in a depressed state, complaining about night time waking problems with a 20-month old child and marital conflict. Rather than viewing the depression and the marital conflict as major complicating factors that potentially disqualify the parent from being offered a brief sleep intervention, further exploration may reveal that the depressed mood of the parents began after months of chronic sleep deprivation and marital arguments related to neither parent knowing how to best manage the child's sleep. In such circumstances the sleep management plan may address all three problems concurrently. In other instances, the mother's depression may be so severe that she has difficulty coping with the implementation of a new bedtime routine. In that instance the parent may need more intensive therapeutic support than could be provided by a brief primary care sleep intervention.

Consumer and end-user engagement. Sanders and Kirby (2012) argued that parenting programmes are more likely to be adopted and implemented if the planning process is supported by strong local partnerships and knowledge of the needs and preferences of parents. However, it is important to note that just because a group of parents from a defined target population identifies a programme as being relevant, useful and culturally appropriate does not guarantee that when the programme is trialled it produces positive outcomes for children.

Using multiple access points. A range of professionals and nonprofessionals are involved in the delivery of parenting advice to parents of young children. This includes family doctors, specialist paediatricians, nurses, health visitors, psychologists, social workers, child care providers and early childhood teachers. Training primary care professionals who have a legitimate and accepted part of their role to provide parenting advice and support has considerable advantages. We have successfully trained many health visitors, GPs, specialist paediatricians and community child health nurses to deliver evidence-based parenting advice. Such training is consistent with policy advocacy on the importance of parent education in paediatric care (AAP Council on Community Pediatrics, 2016). However, whether a trained practitioner goes on to deliver programmes directly with parents is influenced by the level of organisational support the practitioner receives for delivering parenting programmes (Hodge, Turner, Sanders & Filus, 2016; Shapiro, Prinz & Sanders, 2010). It is essential that practitioners are selected who have the capacity, interest and organisational support to deliver the interventions.

Ensuring adequate organisational support for sustained implementation. The field of prevention science has shown that the successful implementation of the population level approach involves ensuring that agencies and practitioners are well supported by purveyor organisations, or in some cases by intermediary organisations who specialise in assisting organisations to adopt and implement evidence-based practices. See McWilliam et al. (2016) for a discussion on the implementation framework used to support agencies in adopting the Triple P system.

Ensuring interventions are culturally appropriate. Due to the diverse number of nationalities and languages spoken in many countries, it is crucial that parenting programmes can be delivered in multiple community languages and in a culturally informed manner. There is growing evidence that positive parenting programmes can be effective in both individualistic cultures in the West and more collectivistic cultures in Asia and the Middle East (e.g. Guo, Morawska & Sanders, 2016; Leung, Sanders, Leung, Mak & Lau, 2003). A major challenge is identifying and training practitioners who can deliver programmes to minority groups, refugees and migrants in their first language.

Using a sustainable system of dissemination and training to ensure programmes can be scaled. Evidence-based parenting programmes are more likely to be scaled if all the resources needed by an agency to implement the programme are available. This includes professionally produced training programmes, parent resources (e.g. workbooks, tip sheets) and promotional tools to engage parents (local websites, posters, brochures, bill boards, and advertising).

Ongoing mixed method evaluation of outcomes. A major challenge is to ensure that suitable measures are available for assessing both outcomes with participating families and population-level outcomes. This approach was employed in the Sanders et al. (2008) study and the Fives, Purcell, Heary, NicGabhainn and Canavan (2014) study in Ireland. Sanders et al. employed a household telephone survey using Random Digit dialling, whereas Fives et al. employed an in person household survey to assess child problems and parenting practices. In both instances participating families completed standardised assessment measures such as the Strengths and Difficulties Questionnaire (SDQ), Parenting Scale and consumer satisfaction measures. Fives et al. used exclusively aggregate population level data on the number of founded cases of child maltreatment, hospitalisation and emergency room visits and out of home placements using a state data repository. An even more powerful method of evaluation involves linked administrative data at the individual case level. In addition to ensuring consumers views are taken into account with any rollout surveys, focus group methods can be used to identify common themes in parents' feedback concerning the programmes implementation.

Conclusions and implications

Children have greater developmental plasticity during the early phases of development and changes in their environment can have major effects on their development in the long term. A population-based approach to parenting support has shown promise in reducing child maltreatment and behavioural problems in children, however the approach needs to be trialled specifically with parents of children in the first 1000 days of life.

References

AAP Council on Community Pediatrics (2016). Policy statement: Poverty and child health in the United States. *Pediatrics, 137*(4). doi:10.1542/peds.2016–0339

Adamson, M., Morawska, A., & Sanders, M.R. (2013). Childhood feeding difficulties: A randomised controlled trial of a group-based parenting interaction. *Journal of Developmental and Behavioral Pediatrics, 34*, 293–302. doi:10.1097/DBP.0b013e3182961a38

Bor, W., Sanders, M.R., & Markie-Dadds, C. (2002). The effects of the Triple P-Positive Parenting Program on preschool children with co-occurring disruptive behavior and attentional/hyperactive difficulties. *Journal of Abnormal Child Psychology, 30*(6), 571–587. doi:10.1023/a:1020807613155

Bronfenbrenner, U. (1979). *The ecology of human development: Experiments by nature and design.* Cambridge, MA: Harvard University Press.

Butler, H., Hare, D., Walker, S., Wieck, A., & Wittkowski, A. (2014). The acceptability and feasibility of the Baby Triple P Positive Parenting Programme on a mother and baby unit: Q-methodology with mothers with severe mental illness. *Arch Womens Ment Health, 17*, 455–463. doi:10.1007/s00737–014–0429–4

Centre on the Developing Child (2007). The science of early childhood development (InBrief).

Dirscherl, T., Dirscherl, R., McWilliam, J., & Sanders, M.R. (2016). CAPCAL: A planning tool for scaling up evidence-based public health interventions. *Manuscript in preparation.*

Dittman, C., Farruggia, S., Keown, L., & Sanders, M.R. (2016). Dealing with disobedience: An evaluation of a brief parenting intervention for young children showing noncompliant behavior problems. *Child Psychiatry & Human Development, 47*(1), 102–112. doi:10.1007/s10578–015–0548–9

Ferrari, A., Whittingham, K., Boyd, R., Sanders, M.R., & Colditz, P. (2011). Prem baby triple P a new parenting intervention for parents of infants born very preterm: Acceptability and barriers. *Infant Behavior & Development, 34*(4), 602–609. doi:10.1016/j.infbeh.2011.06.004

Fives, A., Purcell, L., Heary, C., NicGabhainn, S., & Canavan, J. (2014). Parenting support for every parent: A population-level evaluation of Triple P in Longford Westmeath. Final Report. Athlone: Longford Westmeath Parenting Partnership.

Guo, M., Morawska, A., & Sanders, M.R. (2016). A randomized-controlled trial of Group Triple P with Chinese parents in Mainland China. *Behaviour Modification*, 1–27. doi:10.1177/0145445516644221

Herschell, A.D., & McNeil, C.B. (2007). Parent-child interaction therapy with physically abusive families. In J.M. Briesmeister & C.E. Schaefer (Eds.), *Handbook of Parent Training,* 3rd ed., 234–267. New Jersey, US: John Wiley & Sons, Inc.

Hodge, L., Turner, K.M.T., Sanders, M.R., & Filus, A. (2016). Sustained Implementation Support Scale: Validation of a measure of program characteristics and workplace functioning for sustained program implementation. *Journal of Behavioral Health Services and Research.*

Joachim, S., Sanders, M. R., & Turner, K.M.T. (2010). Reducing preschoolers' disruptive behavior in public with a brief parent discussion group. *Child Psychiatry and Human Development, 41*, 47–60. doi:10.1007/s10578–009–0151-z

Leung, C., Sanders, M.R., Leung, S., Mak, R., & Lau, J. (2003). An outcome evaluation of the implementation of the Triple P-Positive Parenting Program in Hong Kong. *Family Process, 42*(4), 531–544. doi:10.1111/j.1545–5300.2003.00531.x

Marmot, M. (2010). *Fair society, healthy lives: The Marmot Review; Strategic review of health inequalities in England post-2010.* London, England: The Marmot Review.

McWilliam, J., Brown, J., Sanders, M.R., & Jones, L. (2016). The Triple P implementation framework: The role of purveyors in the implementation and sustainability of evidence-based programs. *Prevention Science, 17*(5), 636–645. doi:10.1007/s11121–016–0661–4

Morawska, A., & Sanders, M.R. (2006a). Self-administered behavioral family intervention for parents of toddlers: Part I. Efficacy. *Journal of Consulting and Clinical Psychology, 74*(1), 10–19. doi:10.1037/0022–006x.74.1.10

Morawska, A., & Sanders, M.R. (2006b). Self-administered behavioural family intervention for parents of toddlers: Effectiveness and dissemination. *Behaviour Research and Therapy, 44*(12), 1839–1848. doi:10.1016/j.brat.2005.11.015

Morawska, A., Adamson, M., Hinchliffe, K., & Adams, T. (2014). Hassle Free Mealtimes Triple P: A randomised controlled trial of a brief parenting group for childhood mealtime difficulties. *Behaviour Research and Therapy, 53*, 1–9. doi:10.1016/j.brat.2013.11.007

Morawska, A., Haslam, D., Milne, D., & Sanders, M.R. (2011). Evaluation of a brief parenting discussion group for parents of young children. *Journal of Developmental and Behavioral Pediatrics, 32*(2), 136–145. doi:10.1097/DBP.0b013e3181f17a28

Patterson, J., Mockford, C., & Stewart-Brown, S. (2005). Parent's perceptions of the value of the Webster-Stratton Parenting Programme: A qualitative study of a general practice based initiative. *Child: Care, Health and Development, 31*, 53–64.

Prinz, R.J., & Sanders, M.R. (2007). Adopting a population-level approach to parenting and family support interventions. *Clinical Psychology Review, 27*(6), 739–749. doi:10.1016/j.cpr.2007.01.005

Sanders, M.R. (2012). Development, evaluation, and multinational dissemination of the Triple P-Positive Parenting Program. *Annual Review of Clinical Psychology, 8*, 1–35. doi:10.1146/annurev-clinpsy-032511–143104

Sanders, M.R., & Kirby, J.N. (2012). Consumer engagement and the development, evaluation and dissemination of evidence-based parenting programs. *Behavior Therapy, 43*, 236–250. doi:10.1016/j.beth.2011.01.005

Sanders, M.R., Markie-Dadds, C., Tully, L.A., & Bor, W. (2000). The Triple P-Positive Parenting Program: A comparison of enhanced, standard, and self-directed behavioral family intervention for parents of children with early onset conduct problems. *Journal of Consulting and Clinical Psychology, 68*(4), 624–640. doi:10.1037/0022–006x.68.4.624

Sanders, M.R., Ralph, A., Sofronoff, K., Gardiner, P., Thompson, R., Dwyer, S.B., & Bidwell, K. (2008). Every family: A population approach to reducing behavioral and emotional problems in children making the transition to school. *Journal of Primary Prevention, 29*(3), 197–222. doi:10.1007/s10935–008–0139–7

Schore, A.N. (2004). *Affect regulation and the origin of self: The neurobiology of emotional development.* Hillsdale, NJ: Erlbaum.

Shapiro, C.J., Prinz, R.J., & Sanders, M.R. (2010). Population-based provider engagement in delivery of evidence-based parenting interventions: Challenges and solutions. *Journal of Primary Prevention, 31*(4), 223–234. doi:10.1007/s10935–010–0210–z

Spry, C. (2013). *The baby triple P project: Effects of a parenting intervention to promote a successful transition to parenthood.* (Doctor of Philosophy), The University of Queensland.

Spry, C., Morawska, A., & Sanders, M.R. (2011). *Baby Triple P group workbook.* Milton, Australia: Triple P International Pty. Ltd.

Tsivos, Z.L., Calam, R., Sanders, M.R., & Wittkowski, A. (2015). A pilot randomised controlled trial to evaluate the feasibility and acceptability of the Baby Triple P Positive Parenting Programme in mothers with postnatal depression. *Clin Child Psychol Psychiatry, 20*(4), 532–554. doi:10.1177/1359104514531589

D: Specific programmes demonstrating improved outcomes

18

RELATIONSHIP-BASED INTERVENTIONS IN THE EARLY YEARS

Robin Balbernie

Therapeutic interventions covering the first 1001 critical days can be roughly categorised either as group or individual work, both using relationships to change relationships. The examples in this chapter are not exhaustive, but are backed up by practice-based evidence. These interventions are best delivered from a children's centre offering universal services as that, coupled with an attitude of being available for all vulnerable families, lowers the reluctance of parents to become involved as far as is possible. Away from projects powered by research, it is unlikely that relying on a *single* mechanism of change will produce positive results, perhaps because fidelity to process gets placed above the therapeutic relationship. As Daniel Stern emphasises, in clinical work different 'ports of entry' are needed to help a family, and whichever part of the system is worked with the rest will change as well (Stern, 1995).

Therapeutic interventions

To begin with therapeutic groups: the Mellow approach is designed for families where there are extreme difficulties in the attachment relationship. It has been successful in helping improve the quality of caregiving, with maternal mood improvement and positive feedback from parents (Puckering, 2004; Puckering et al., 2010). The aim is to engage with high-risk families struggling with multiple difficulties such as child protection, domestic violence and a parental history of maltreatment. Also based on attachment theory, the Circle of Security group has shown a positive impact on the attachment-caregiving patterns of high-risk toddlers, preschoolers and their primary caregivers (Hoffman, et al., 2006). A clinical trial, in this case with an age range of 1 to 7 years, demonstrated improvements for parent ratings of child protective factors, internalising and externalising symptoms with a consistent finding that those children who began with the most severe problems showed the best improvement (Huber et al., 2015a). The same intervention also produced an improvement in parental reflective function, caregiving representation and attachment security in the child (Huber et al., 2015b).

Both Mellow and Circle of Security use video feedback to help caregivers see themselves from the outside in, and this is the basis of Interaction Guidance. Here the aim is to encourage positive aspects of caregiver-infant interaction.

> 'This nonintrusive method of family treatment has proven to be especially successful for infants with failure to thrive, regulation disorders, and organic problems. Parents who are either resistant to participating in other forms of psychotherapy, or young, inexperienced, or cognitively limited, respond positively to this treatment approach'
>
> (McDonough, 1993: 414)

Interaction Guidance has been used to improve sensitivity and decrease the amount of disrupted communication between mothers and babies with feeding problems (Benoit et al., 2001); and a modified version has helped mothers with postnatal depression reconnect with their babies (Vik & Braten, 2009).

A meta-analysis of early, attachment-based, interventions suggests that disorganised attachment is most successfully addressed by using sensitivity-focussed video feedback (Bakermans-Kranenburg et al., 2005). Clinical and research work from Leiden University has led to a programme to enhance parental sensitivity called 'Video-feedback Intervention to Promote Positive Parenting' (Juffer et al., 2007) or VIPP. This focussed and relatively short-term intervention has prevented externalising problems in preschool children from high-risk families (Velderman et al., 2006) and has been shown to be helpful with multiply disadvantaged families where it improved maternal nonintrusiveness, child responsiveness and involvement (Negrao et al., 2014), and has enhanced sensitivity and infant attachment in first time mothers who had insecure attachment themselves (Cassibba et al., 2015). However, although VIPP generally promotes an increase in maternal sensitivity this can sometimes have no effect at all on infant security (Kalinauskiene et al., 2009).

The technique of video feedback is well suited to be used in conjunction with more psychodynamic methods of treatment as it

> 'serves to activate powerful feelings, based on early attachment representations, in the therapeutic sessions where the parent can be helped to become aware of these thoughts and feelings that underlie their behaviour with their children, thereby opening up new ways of being with their children'
>
> (Steele, et al., 2014: 407)

Such a combination has been used to treat mothers suffering from PTSD following a history of violence-related trauma (Schechter, et al., 2006).

This intervention, over three visits, was able to reduce the degree of negativity and distortion of maternal attributions. Another short-term attachment-based intervention using video feedback set out to target maltreating families with children between the ages of 1 and 5 years old. They also used focussed discussion around attachment and emotional regulation. Comparisons between pre- and post-test scores revealed significant improvements in the intervention group in parental sensitivity and child attachment security, along with a reduction in children's disorganised attachment. The older children showed lower levels of both externalising and internalising behaviour (Moss et al., 2011, 2014). To be effective both mechanics and clinicians need a full toolbox. This is exemplified by a pilot study with vulnerable teenage mothers that combined three intervention strategies: video feedback, developmental guidance and parent-infant counselling. This immediately improved the quality of interaction and play between mother and infant, with the former becoming less controlling. Both the mothers and the babies showed a better capacity for mutual regulation, with an increase in maternal sensitivity and infant cooperation (Crugnola et al., 2016).

A research project in Geneva compared brief infant-parent psychotherapy with Interaction Guidance. Both interventions brought about positive changes in the mother-infant relationship. 'Marked symptom relief was observed in several areas, with the greatest improvements in sleeping, feeding and digestion (i.e. symptoms affecting physiological functions)' (Robert-Tissot et al., 1996: 105). In general, mothers became less intrusive and infants more cooperative, with maternal sensitivity to the baby's signals increasing after treatment. 'The results of the study indicate that brief mother-infant psychotherapies were effective in treating cases consulting for early functional disorders' (p. 108). They found that Interaction Guidance brought about more change in mothers' sensitivity, while psychodynamic therapy had a greater impact on maternal self-esteem.

In infant-parent psychotherapy the 'patient' is the relationship between baby and caregiver, not parental mental ill-health as with perinatal services. This has been shown to be effective in high-risk family situations involving maternal depression, poverty, domestic violence, mothers with a traumatic childhood and children already known to have suffered maltreatment. A psychodynamic approach does not see caregiving difficulties as stemming just from a lack of knowledge; rather the parent's problems in relating to their infant are caused by unconscious conflicts stemming from their own experiences in childhood and what is projected onto the infant. In a study designed to evaluate the effectiveness of infant-parent psychotherapy it was found that those mothers who became most engaged in the therapeutic process became more actively attuned to their children, who in turn 'showed less anger and avoidance, more security of attachment, and more reciprocal partnership in the negotiation of mother-child conflict' (Lieberman & Pawl, 1993: 441). This intervention evolved into one for 3- to 5-year olds traumatised by domestic abuse; and in a randomised clinical trial these children 'improved significantly more than children receiving case management plus treatment as usual in the community, both in decreased total behavioural problems and decreased PTSD symptoms' (Lieberman et al., 2005: 1246). The gains in the treatment group were 'evident 6 months after the termination of treatment when compared to the control group' (Lieberman et al., 2006: 916). A variation has also been successfully applied to situations of domestic violence in the perinatal period (Lieberman et al., 2009).

A comparison of the effect of toddler-parent psychotherapy between two, randomly assigned, groups of mothers with a major depressive disorder found that child attachment was improved by the end of treatment. 'Toddlers of depressed mothers who received TPP evidenced rates of secure attachment that were no different from those of the nondepressed control group' (Cicchetti et al., 1999: 58). Using a variant of parent infant psychotherapy, which focuses on the analyst's ability to 'contain' the infant's distress by interacting and communicating with the infant, a randomised controlled trial in Stockholm showed that this improved mother infant relationships, as well as maternal sensitivity and depression (Salomonsson & Sandell, 2011). When these children were followed up at age four and a half, and compared to the control group, they were found to show better results on global functioning and to be less troubled (Salomonsson et al., 2015a). Their mothers appeared to have been helped with a sense of personal wellbeing, to become more sensitive to their baby's suffering and to better support and appreciate their children throughout infancy and toddlerhood (Salomonsson et al., 2015b).

Infant-parent psychotherapy was the main therapeutic modality applied to improve the relationship between mother and child in vulnerable and high-risk families in the Florida Infant Mental Health Pilot Programme. This is an intervention for families with infants who were likely to be removed from their parents because of abuse. The results are significant because of the wide range of family arrangements that fell within the scheme, which was thus less 'choosy' and far more clinically realistic than any research project. At the end of this study

> 'there were no further reports of abuse or neglect during the treatment period and up to postassessment for participants. There was a major reduction in reports of child abuse and neglect . . . from 97 per cent of children prior to treatment to none of the children completing treatment during the first 3 years of the pilot project . . . (Also), the health and developmental status of children improved'
>
> (Osofsky et al. 2007: 273)

In addition there was a reduction of depressive symptoms in the caregivers along with a measured and reported improvement in the parent-child relationships. But a lot of time went into these achievements, as would be expected for high-risk situations, with 10 hours spent on efforts to engage the family for every one of treatment.

It could be argued that the two different approaches of Interaction Guidance and infant-parent psychotherapy overlap in task while being different in method, since each may improve 'reflective function', a parental capacity that promotes and fuses with secure attachment. Both infant-parent psychotherapy and all the brands of video feedback are different ports of entry into the parents' internal representations of their infant as well as their interactions, providing the opportunity to free up and improve the observational skills, understanding and empathy that are usually so taken for granted as to go unnoticed. A gain in reflective function may lie behind many successful interventions that aim to improve the sensitive and appropriate responsiveness that contributes to secure attachment. A programme based on this aspect of attachment theory, aiming to help substance abusing mothers, found that at post-treatment the mothers demonstrated improvements in reflective functioning, sensitivity and parenting behaviour (Suchman et al., 2010). And a meta-analysis of 10 interventions targeting maternal reflective function and sensitivity with the aim of improving the quality of infant attachment concluded that 'compared to infants who did not receive the attachment intervention, infants who received the intervention were nearly three times as likely to be securely attached' (Letourneau et al., 2015: 383). Treatments that focussed on both reflective function and sensitivity produced the most beneficial effect; and programmes targeting high-risk populations showed the most benefit – 'effects were greatest for maltreated and highly irritable children' (ibid.).

A weekly home-visiting intervention called the Minding the Baby Program is grounded in enhancing reflective functioning, focussing on the mother-infant relationship with the relationship the mother forms with the workers being the vehicle of change. A preliminary evaluation (Slade et al., 2005) indicated a marked gain in maternal reflective function in relation to the spectrum of their child's developmental domains, and no children with disorganised attachment. For the mothers, the trend was towards lower levels of depression and post-traumatic stress symptoms along with higher levels of self-efficacy. A later RCT showed 'a move towards less-disrupted interactions at 4 months, higher rates of secure attachment and lower rates of disorganised attachment at 12 months, and a strong trend towards lower rates of child protection service referrals at 24 months' (Sadler et al., 2013: 401).

A final example is the technique of Watch, Wait and Wonder, again aiming for changes in both behaviour and perception. In this approach the parent is encouraged to be more directly involved with their child by engaging in play that follows the latter's lead. This mode of treatment has good outcomes for mothers struggling with borderline personality disorder (Newman & Stevenson, 2008). A team in Toronto compared the effects of infant-parent psychotherapy (PPT) with Wait, Watch and Wonder. It was found that the latter produced a more pronounced move towards secure attachment. The infants in this group also 'exhibited a greater capacity to regulate their emotions with a concomitant increase in cognitive ability' (Cohen et al., 1999: 445). Their mothers 'reported more satisfaction with parenting than mothers in the PPT group and lower levels of depression at the end of treatment' (ibid.). Both techniques showed similar positive gains. 'They were associated with a reduction of presenting problems, improvement in the quality of the mother-child relationship, and reduction in parenting stress' (ibid.). However, at the 6-month follow up the two groups were similar on all measures. The Wait, Watch and Wonder group had retained its positive gains while the group receiving parent-infant psychotherapy had 'caught up'.

The infant mental health specialist needs to call upon a wide range of skills that 'contribute to the parent's understanding of the infant, the awakening or repair of the early developing attachment relationship, and the parent's capacity to nurture and protect a young child' (Weatherston, 2000: 6). Starting from the premise that all parents want to do the best they can for their babies, an infant mental health team engages with families, rather than instructing them, to build on strengths in order to remove obstacles. Parents, unsurprisingly, may not appreciate others thinking they need 'training'; indeed, such an attitude 'may send a message of presumed incompetence, which might undermine a mother's or father's self-confidence and contribute inadvertently to less effective performance' (Shonkoff & Phillips, 2000: 371), reducing service take-up. Infant mental health specialists may be experts, but they relate to parents on the basis of partnership, modelling the relationships they wish to promote.

Conclusion

There is a growing body of evidence demonstrating how early, targeted and strength-based interventions focussing on relationships can bring about positive changes in the emotional environment of vulnerable babies. An ecological perspective makes clear that what may work brilliantly in one place might have no impact somewhere else, since 'evidence-based practices in prevention science which may have been tried and shown to be effective in one location under one set of historical and contextual conditions cannot be assumed to be effective in another' (Schensul, 2009: 243). One size does not fit all. 'Lists of evidence-based practices are based on studies of unrepresentative samples that do not represent the diversity of the individuals that most practitioners encounter in the field' (Shean, 2014: 503). In early intervention relationships have a more significant effect than techniques, a nightmare for those who commission since the person will be more important than the procedure and those who are good at making therapeutic relationships will be refractory to policies.

- Early intervention teams have a limited range of therapeutically proven techniques to call upon.
- An availability of mixed modalities, a flexible approach delivered by properly trained practitioners, is likely to be the most effective.
- More research is needed, but this will never be conclusive as the gap between an academic exercise and sitting in the home of a distressed, vulnerable and multiply burdened family may be unbridgeable.
- Inconclusive research does not justify inaction.

References

Bakermans-Kranenburg, M.J., van Ijzendoorn, M.H., & Juffer, F. (2005). Disorganized infant attachment and preventative interventions: A review and meta-analysis. *Infant Mental Health Journal, 26*(3), 191–216.

Benoit, D., Madigan, S., Lecce, S., Shea, B., & Goldberg, S. (2001). Atypical maternal behaviour toward feeding-disordered infants before and after intervention. *Infant Mental Health Journal*, 22(6), 611–626.

Cassiba, R., Castoro, G., Constantino, E., Sette, G., & Van Ijzendoorn, M. (2015). Enhancing maternal sensitivity and infant attachment security with video feedback: An exploratory study in Italy. *Infant Mental Health Journal*, 36(1), 53–61.

Cicchetti, D., Toth, S.L., & Rogosch, F.A. (1999). The efficacy of toddler-parent psychotherapy to increase attachment security in offspring of depressed mothers. *Attachment & Human Development*, 1(1), 34–66.

Cicchetti, D., Rogosch, F.A., & Toth, S.L. (2000). The efficacy of toddler-parent psychotherapy for fostering cognitive development in offspring of depressed mothers. *Journal of Abnormal Child Psychology*, 28, 135–148.

Cicchetti, D., Rogosch, F.A. & Toth, S.L. (2006). Fostering secure attachment in infants in maltreating families through preventative intervention. *Developmental Psychopathology*, 18, 623–649.

Cohen, N.J., Muir, E., Parker, C.J., Brown, M., Lojkasek, M., Muir, R., & Barwick, M. (1999). Watch, Wait and Wonder: Testing the effectiveness of a new approach to mother-infant psychotherapy. *Infant Mental Health Journal*, 20(4), 429–451.

Crugnola, C.R., Lierdi, E., Albizzati, A., & Downing, G. (2016). Effectiveness of an attachment-based intervention program in promoting emotion regulation and attachment in adolescent mothers and their infants: A pilot study. *Frontiers in Psychology*, February, 7, article195. Downloaded on 05/05/2015 from: http://journal.frontiersin.org/article/10.3389/fpsyg.2016.00195/full

Hoffman, K.T., Marvin, R.S., Cooper, G., & Powell, B. (2006). Changing toddlers' and preschoolers' attachment classifications: The Circle of Security intervention. *Journal of Consulting and Clinical Psychology*, 74, 1017–1026.

Huber, H., McMahon, C., & Sweller, N. (2015a). Improved child behavioural and emotional functioning after Circle of Security 20-week intervention. *Attachment & Human Development*, 17(6), 547–569.

Huber, H., McMahon, C., & Sweller, N. (2015b). Efficacy of the 20-week Circle of Security intervention: Changes in caregiver reflective functioning, representations, and child attachment in an Australian clinical sample. *Infant Mental Health Journal*, 36(6), 556–574.

Juffer, F., Bakermans-Kranenburg, M. J., & van IJzendoorn, M.H. (Eds). (2007). *Promoting Positive Parenting: An Attachment-Based Intervention*. London: Lawrence Erlbaum Associates.

Kalinauskiene, L., Cekuoliene, D., Van IJzendoorn, M.H., Bakermans-Kranenburg, M.J., Juffer, F., & Kusakovskaja, I. (2009). Supporting insensitive mothers: The Vilnius randomized control trial of video-feedback intervention to promote maternal sensitivity and infant attachment security. *Child: Care, Health and Development*, 35(5), 613–623.

Letourneau, N., Tryphonopoulos, P., Giesbrecht, G., Dennis, C.L., Bhogal, S., & Watson, B. (2015). Narrative and meta-analytic review of interventions aiming to improve maternal-child attachment. *Infant Mental Health Journal*, 36(4), 366–387.

Lieberman, A.F., Diaz, M.A., & Van Horn, P. (2009). Safer beginnings: Perinatal child-parent psychotherapy for newborns and mothers exposed to domestic violence. *Zero to Three*, 29(5), 17–22.

Lieberman, A.F., Ippen, C.G., & Van Horn, P. (2006). Child-parent psychotherapy: 6-month follow-up of a randomised controlled trial. *Journal of the American Academy of Child and Adolescent Psychiatry*, 45(8), 913–918.

Lieberman, A.F., & Pawl, J.H. (1993). Infant-parent psychotherapy. In C.H. Zeanah (Eds.), *Handbook of Infant Mental Health*, 427–442. New York: The Guilford Press.

Lieberman, A. F., Van Horn, P., & Ippen, C.G. (2005). Towards evidence-based treatment: Child-parent psychotherapy with preschoolers exposed to marital violence. *Journal of the American Academy of Child and Adolescent Psychiatry*, *44*(12), 1241–1248.

McDonough, S. (1993). Interaction guidance: Understanding and treating early infant-caregiver relationship disturbances. In C.H. Zeanah (Eds.), *Handbook of Infant Mental Health*, 414–426. New York: The Guilford Press.

Moss, E., Dubois-Comtois, K., Cyr, C., Tarabulsy, G.M., St-Laurent, D., & Bernier, A. (2011). Efficacy of a home-visiting intervention aimed at improving maternal sensitivity, child attachment, and behavioural outcomes for maltreated children: A randomised control trial. *Development and Psychopathology*, *23*, 195–210.

Moss, E., Tarabulsy, G.M., St-Georges, R., Dubois-Comtois, K., Cyr, C., Bernier, A., St-Laurent, D., Pascuzzo, K., & Lecompte, V. (2014). Video-feedback intervention with maltreating parents and their children: program implementation and case study. *Attachment and Human Development*, *16*(4), 329–342.

Negrao, M., Pereira, M., Soares, I., & Mesman, J. (2014). Enhancing positive parent-child interactions and family functioning in a poverty sample: A randomised control trial. *Attachment & Human Development*, *16*(4), 315–328.

Newman, L., & Stevenson, C. (2008). Issues in infant-parent psychotherapy for mothers with borderline personality disorder. *Clinical Child Psychology and Psychiatry*, *13*(4), 505–514.

Osofsky, J.D., Kronenberg, M., Hammer, J.H., Lederman, C., Katz, L., Adams, S., Graham, M., & Hogan, A. (2007). The development and evaluation of the intervention model for the Florida Infant Mental Health Pilot Program. *Infant Mental Health Journal*, *28*(3), 258–280.

Puckering, C. (2004). Mellow Parenting: An intensive intervention to change relationships. *The Signal*, *12*(1), 1–5.

Puckering, C., McIntosh, E., Hickey, A., & Longford, J. (2010). Mellow Babies: A group intervention for infants and mothers experiencing postnatal depression. *Counselling Psychology Review*, *25*(1), 28–40.

Robert-Tissot, C., Cramer, B., Stern, D.S., Serpa, S.R., Bachmann, J.P., Palacio-Espasa, F., Knauer, D., De Muralt, M., Bernay, C., & Mendiguren, G. (1996). Outcome evaluation in brief mother-infant psychotherapies: Report on 75 cases. *Infant Mental Health Journal*, *17*(2), 97–114.

Sadler, L.S., Slade, A., Close, N., Webb, D.L., Simpson, T., Fennie, K., & Mayes, L.C. (2013). Minding the baby: Enhancing reflectiveness to improve early health and relationship outcomes in an interdisciplinary home-visiting program. *Infant Mental Health Journal*, *34*(5), 391–405.

Salomonsson, B., & Sandell, R. (2011). A randomizes controlled trial of mother-infant psychoanalytic treatment: 1. Outcomes on self-report questionnaires and external ratings. *Infant Mental Health Journal*, *32*(2), 207–231.

Salomonsson, M.W., Sorjonen, K., & Salomonsson, B. (2015a). A long-term follow up of a randomised controlled trial of mother-infant psychoanalytic treatment: Outcomes on the children. *Infant Mental Health Journal*, *36*(1), 12–29.

Salomonsson, M.W., Sorjonen, K., & Salomonsson, B. (2015b). A long-term follow-up study of a randomized controlled trial of mother-infant psychoanalytic treatment: Outcomes on mothers and interactions. *Infant Mental Health Journal*, *36*(6), 542–555.

Schechter, D.S., Myers, M.M., Brunelli, S.A., Coates, S.W., Zeanah, C.H., Davies, M., Grienenberger, J.F., Marshall, R.D., McCaw, J.E., Trabka, K.A., & Liebowitz, M.R. (2006). Traumatized mothers can change their minds about their toddlers: Understanding how a novel use of videofeedback supports positive change of maternal attributions. *Infant Mental Health Journal*, *27*(5), 429–447.

Schensul, J.J. (2009). Community, culture and sustainability in multilevel dynamic systems intervention science (published online: 22 April 2009). *American Journal of Community Psychology, 43*, 214–256.

Shean, G.D. (2014). Some methodological and epistemic limitations of evidence-based therapies. *Psychoanalytic Psychology, 32*(3), 500–516.

Shonkoff, J.P., & Phillips, D.A. (Eds). (2000). *From Neurons to Neighbourhoods: The Science of Early Childhood Development.* Washington D.C: National Academy Press.

Slade, A., Sandler, L.S., & Mayes, L.C. (2005). Minding the baby: Enhancing parental reflective functioning in a nursing/mental health home visiting program. In L.J. Berlin, Y. Ziv, L. Amaya-Jackson, & M.T. Greenberg (Eds), *Enhancing Early Attachments*, 152–177. New York: The Guilford Press.

Slade, A., & Sadler, L. (2013). Minding the baby: Complex trauma and home visiting. *International Journal of Birth and Parent Education, 1*(1), 32–35.

Steele, M., Steele, H., Bate, J., Knafo, H., Kinsey, M., Bonuck, K., Mísner, P., & Murphy, A. (2014). Looking from the outside in: The use of video in attachment-based interventions. *Attachment & Human Development, 16*(4), 402–415.

Stern, D. (1995). *The Motherhood Constellation.* New York: Basic Books.

Suchman, N.E., DeCoste, C., Castiglioni, N., McMahon, T.J., Rounsaville, B., & Mayes, L. (2010). The Mother and Toddler programme, an attachment-based parenting intervention for substance using women: Post-treatment results from a randomized clinical pilot. *Attachment & Human Development, 12*(5), 433–504.

Velderman, M.K., Bakermans-Kranenburg, M.J., Juffer, F., & Van Ijzendoorn, M.H. (2006). Preventing preschool externalizing behavior problems through video-feedback intervention in infancy. *Infant Mental Health Journal, 27*(5), 466–493.

Vik, K., & Braten, S. (2009). Video interaction guidance inviting transcendence of post-partum depressed mothers' self-centred state and holding behavior. *Infant Mental Health Journal, 30*(3), 287–300.

Weatherston, D.J. (2000). The infant mental health specialist. *Zero to Three, 21*(2), 3–10.

19

CHILD PROTECTION IN THE COMMUNITY

Recognising and responding to signs of child neglect

Ruth Gardner and Camilla Rosan

Drawing on international research and practice development, this chapter will address the following questions:

- Why is child neglect of particular concern in the first 3 years of an infant's life?
- How can early signs of incipient neglect best be picked up?
- What are some of the current models of best practice in the field of intervention?
- How can we effectively engage parents in family-focused work?

Why such concern with child neglect?

Suboptimal parenting short of neglect is very often transient and reversible. Child neglect, however, refers to children lacking the care necessary for them to achieve a level of development commensurate with their personal potential (WHO, 1999). Neglect is defined in English guidance (with similar definitions in other jurisdictions) as:

> the persistent failure to meet a child's basic physical and/or psychological needs, likely to result in the serious impairment of the child's health or development. Neglect may occur during pregnancy as a result of maternal substance abuse. Once a child is born, neglect may involve a parent or carer failing to:
>
> - provide adequate food, clothing and shelter (including exclusion from home or abandonment);
> - protect a child from physical and emotional harm or danger;

- ensure adequate supervision (including the use of inadequate caregivers) or ensure access to appropriate medical care or treatment.

It may also include neglect of, or unresponsiveness to, a child's basic emotional needs.

(DfE, 2015 (a) 93)

Young children may also be exposed to acts of commission (i.e. emotional abuse rather than neglect), in which the parent responds in highly inappropriate ways, for example by frightening a child who is seeking comfort. While a failure of parental responsibility is identified, some commentators see other levels of failure as implicated – for instance the failure of support systems or 'societal neglect' (Horwath, 2014).

The high prevalence and incidence of neglect

According to the most recent general population study in the UK, neglect is the most prevalent form of maltreatment children experience within the family (Radford et al., 2013). Child neglect is also the most common reason for a child to be on a child protection plan in England (Department for Education, 2015 (a)), and the same is true in Scotland and Wales, as well as in the United States and many other developed societies. Neglect recurs more frequently than other forms of maltreatment (Fluke, 1999) and unlike other forms of harm it has not markedly reduced over recent decades (Finkelhor et al., 2014). Those working with children and families often find parental neglect particularly challenging (Gardner, 2008). Despite or perhaps because of these challenges, there is currently a growing focus on neglect, with the development of national strategies to tackle neglect in Wales and Scotland, and in England, inspections of multi agency practice in this area (Ofsted, 2014).

Why is neglect of particular concern in the first 1000 days of a child's life?

The timing of child neglect

The first 1001 critical days represent a sensitive period in infant development involving enormous cognitive and socio-emotional developments, when the infant may be more susceptible to adversity including neglect (Michel & Tyler, 2005).

Longitudinal prospective research now indicates specific profound and far-reaching impacts of early child neglect on a range of child development domains.

- As long ago as 1983, Egeland et al. showed early neglect to be associated with a wide range of problematic behaviours later in childhood such as noncompliance; negativistic and impulsive behaviour; high dependence on teachers; nervous signs; and self-abusive behaviour. On follow-up over 20 years, the majority of children who had experienced early neglect were found to have later received at least one diagnosis of mental illness and 73 per cent were comorbid for two or more disorders (Egeland, 2009).

- Kotch et al. (2008), investigating child neglect experienced from birth to age 2 years and childhood aggression at ages 4, 6, and 8 years, concluded that 'only early neglect significantly predicted aggression scores' (p. 725).

- Child maltreatment has been shown to hinder language development, because language is initially acquired in the context of the infant's relationship with the primary caregivers. Studies suggest that this is particularly true of neglect. Early language delays are linked to social and behavioural difficulties for many children (Merritt & Klein, 2015).

- Recent research on population data indicates that childhood neglect does indeed have greater adverse effects on cognition, as measured at 16 years and at 50 years, than any other form of maltreatment (Geoffroy et al., 2016).

These developmental consequences mean that child neglect is acknowledged as a huge drain on the public purse, both internationally and nationally (Gilbert, 2009); and this is a powerful rationale for early, sensitive detection and intervention.

How can early signs of incipient neglect best be picked up?

To increase the effectiveness of interventions we need to understand more about the risk factors and mechanisms linking child neglect to adverse child outcomes. None of these factors is predictive of neglect. The challenge for those involved in policy, research and practice is to find nonstigmatising yet accurate means to first identify and support vulnerable children and families, and second to engage them with services that are subject to evaluation and research, SafeCare® and Video Interaction Guidance are two such services (see chapters by Rostad, Lutcker & Guastaferro, and Kennedy, Macdonald & Whalley, in Gardner, 2016).

Neglect is present across all socio-economic groups, including affluent and educated families where it may be least expected (Action for Children, 2010) but research on individual parent or child factors has indicated the following risks: parental mental health difficulties; parents who experienced abuse or neglect in their own childhoods; poor social support; being a single parent; parental substance misuse; young parenthood; domestic abuse; and a premature or low birth weight baby (Sidebotham et al., 2006). Stalker and McArthur (2012) also found having a child with a disability to be an additional individual risk factor. Where several risk factors apply, there may be a 'multiplier effect' of accumulated damage to children's outcomes (Davidson et al., 2012). Some of these adversities are discussed later in the chapter.

The parent-child relationship

One established theory of how the effects of parental factors might be mediated is through an impaired parent-infant relationship, which is likely to be both a risk factor, mediator and consequence of child neglect (Stith et al., 2009). Research has highlighted the importance of early bonding from pregnancy. The richness of mothers' mental representations during pregnancy, of themselves as a parent and their growing fetus as a baby, have been significantly linked with the security of the infant's attachment to the parents at 1 year of age (De Woolf & van Ijzendoorn, 1997; Huth-Bocks et al., 2004). Among mothers who find it difficult to develop such representations may be some at risk of neglecting their child, if they cannot adjust quickly from their 'imagined' baby to the 'real' baby, and as a result retain unrealistic or idealised representations of the child (Raphael-Leff, 2010).

After babies are born, they need their caregivers to recognise and respond in a timely and consistent way to their feelings and needs (Wolff & van Ijzendoorn, 1997). However, mothers at risk of neglecting their infant display interactions that are marked by less sensitive and responsive interactions, higher rates of negative emotional expression, and an increased likelihood of implementing unpredictable and inconsistent parenting techniques (Barlow, 2016).

Current models of best practice in approaches to child neglect

Well-designed, evidence-based assessment tools that have been tested with practitioners, can assist them in early detection of incipient neglect and in signposting families to timely, accurately targeted support. Two approaches to the assessment of potential or actual child neglect have been tested by the NSPCC in a 5-year programme of work (NSPCC, 2015).

The graded care profile

The Graded Care Profile (GCP) is a paper and online tool designed to help practitioners to identify when a child is at risk of neglect and assess the quality of care being given to a child over time as well as any changes. A revised GCP2 has now been tested for reliability and validity and is being piloted with training across the United Kingdom (Johnson et al., 2015). The assessment is completed with families during home visits. It identifies strengths and difficulties with parental care in the domains of physical care, safety, love and the child's development. In a recent evaluation, use of this approach was found to improve practitioners' skills and practice in recording and reporting neglect across a range of case types. It helped to clarify the effects of neglect on the child as well as the parents' strengths, the changes they needed to make and the support that they needed (Johnson & Cotmore, 2015).

North Carolina family assessment scale

Because of their anxiety about complex child neglect, practitioners often take a passive 'wait and see' stance which allows neglect to persist or recur (Farmer & Lutman, 2013). Supporting professional judgement and decision making is thus a central issue. The North Carolina Family Assessment Scale (NCFAS-G) is a tested assessment tool that can be used across the spectrum of need, from early intervention through to complex cases of child neglect and adoption cases. Using NCFAS-G in a series of meetings with the family, the assessor has to provide evidence for a score of strength or difficulty across seven domains: parental capabilities; family interaction; family safety; child wellbeing; social and community life; family health – including alcohol and drug use, and mental health; and the environment. The assessor then makes a judgement as to whether support or intervention is needed in any of these areas. Family members can be fully involved in the family review, as can a joint assessor; people scoring differently can open up valuable discussion. A qualitative evaluation by the NSPCC (Williams, 2015) tells us that this process can clarify issues that have not been unearthed, and prompt better-informed decision making as well as helping to structure reports and risk assessments.

Research on interventions

A recent systematic review of all the intervention research designed to address the adverse consequences of maltreatment of children age 0 to 14 (Fraser et al., 2013), identified 25 studies. Only two had even a medium strength of evidence, reflecting the extreme dearth of evidence in this under-resourced area of child protection. A subsequent meta-analysis with a similar focus, identified 20 randomised controlled trials of intervention programmes aimed at preventing the occurrence of child maltreatment, or reducing its incidence in maltreating families (Euser et al., 2015). The authors found limited evidence for prevention programmes, but they found that programmes with families already identified were most effective when they provided parent training instead of only support and were of a moderate length (6–12 months) or included a moderate number of sessions (16–30). Two such evidence-based change services have been tested by the NSPCC in the United Kingdom specifically with families where concerns existed about child neglect (Churchill, 2015 (a); Whalley, 2015) with findings sufficiently encouraging to justify further research. They are detailed in other chapters (p. 224 Kennedy).

More broadly, community-based, early-years programmes can successfully focus in on specific outcomes that we know to be crucial for very vulnerable children and specifically those at risk of neglect. In a population sample of 5,872 children, Merritt and Klein (2015) found that among vulnerable children already involved with child welfare services (CWS), those who were involved in the community programme Head Start had modestly improved language development outcomes. This impact was significant for the third of the study sample who had been referred to CWS for supervisory neglect. The authors were concerned that, in comparison with low-income children in the general population, relatively few vulnerable children actually attended these programmes, which had the potential to 'mitigate negative outcomes and promote their school readiness' (p. 194). This underscores the challenge of reaching families who find it difficult to access services.

Engaging parents more effectively in family-focused work

Service developers and providers need to be aware of the real-life delivery context, both within the family itself and the wider community setting. A study of local interagency child protection practice across England (Barton & Welbourne, 2005) concluded that 'a major weakness with the "what works" culture . . . is that an explicit consideration of the impact of the *context* for joint working is not built in to the evaluation of its performance' (p. 191).

Gascoigne (2015) says that interventions should all sit within a 'Balanced System' of local service commissioning, that is, be jointly planned to complement one another across all levels and sectors. Developers also need to specify as far as possible what aspects of the intervention have been found to comprise the essential ingredients for efficacy and where it is possible for service providers to be flexible to meet each family's circumstances.

Adjustments that do not compromise the core of a model can still increase its reach. Research now tells us more about possible influences and mechanisms of risk transmission beyond the mother–child dyad and these findings should influence service design and delivery. For example, Malmberg et al. (2015) found that while both parents' sensitivity and responsiveness, as rated in play interactions with children aged 10 to 12 months, was associated with improved cognitive outcomes at 18 and 36 months, it was *paternal* sensitivity that had a significantly greater impact on later infant cognitive development at 18 months and language capabilities at 36 months. There was also evidence that one parent's greater sensitivity could compensate for the other's lower sensitivity. In the light of this, an essential ingredient might be the inclusion of fathers in sensitivity training and support.

Challenges to parental engagement: family adversities

Evaluations can tell us about implementation issues that are crucial to successful service delivery. In the evaluation of SafeCare in the United Kingdom (Churchill, 2015 (b)), the importance of contextual features in its implementation were emphasised; with parents reporting that its *delivery in the safety of their home and from a trusted professional* were critical factors in their engagement and retention in the programme. Other work has demonstrated the importance of building local networks of support (Gardner, 2005; Westhorp, 2012).

These elements of service delivery have already been identified as key to engaging vulnerable families suffering hardship (e.g. Hooper et al., 2007). However they are not always easy to achieve, precisely because of the stress and disruption that such families face. For example, families facing housing insecurity and frequent moves have added difficulty in engaging with local help. Hogg et al. (2015) report that in 2014 there were just under 70,000 households in temporary accommodation in England, containing 87,420 children of whom 15,700 were aged 0 to 2 years.

Relationship stress and domestic abuse are other factors that, if not addressed early and preventively, can adversely affect children's emotional and physical health. Analysis of data collected from over 800 children and young people indicated that those exposed to more severe domestic violence were more likely to experience neglect or physical harm, and that harm was also likely to be more severe (Coordinated Action Against Domestic Abuse, 2014). International research suggests that 4 to 8 per cent of all pregnant women are victims of domestic abuse (Gazmararian et al., 1996). The transition to parenthood is a major life change and can place considerable stress on the couple relationship; possibly intensifying existing sources of conflict (DWP, 2015). In this context, one study suggested that rates of domestic abuse (severe to moderate violence) increase after birth compared to the antenatal period (Geilen et al., 1994). This translates to 39,000 babies under 1 year old living in a house with domestic violence occurring (Manning, 2011).

Understanding the full pattern of adversities within any particular family is central to prevention of child neglect. Unless these are identified and addressed sensitively and early in problem development, with a multiagency lens, they may compromise delivery of even the best-evidenced programmes. This chapter has offered some examples of promising evidence-based approaches to this work.

To conclude, while the causes of child neglect are multifaceted and complex, there is a clear relationship between risk factors and the intergenerational transmission of related adversities. Research has exposed the profound and far-reaching (but far from inevitable) effects of neglect on a range of child-developmental domains. We now have good quality evidence not only about how this damage occurs but also about what can help prevent it (Gardner, 2016). We now need political commitment to make child neglect a thing of the past.

We recommend:

- more research into family and service contexts that best support the advancement of specific developmental outcomes in children, for example on the role of fathers and coparenting in children's language development
- creative ways of communicating to the general public, policy makers and professionals, the latest encouraging evidence on ways of helping vulnerable parents to meet the developmental needs of their children
- fostering an inclusive approach to intervention development that includes parents (including fathers and male carers) and young people in co-design and delivery, so that they are fully engaged in improving the care of current and future generations.

References

Action for Children (2010). *Neglecting the issue: Impact, causes and responses to child neglect in the UK*. London: Action for Children.

Barlow, J. (2016). The effects of emotional neglect during the first two years of life'. In R. Gardner (ed.), *Tackling child neglect: Research, policy and practice*. London: Jessica Kingsley Publishers.

Barton, A., & Welbourne, P. (2005). Context and its significance in identifying 'What Works' in child protection. *Child Abuse Review, 14*, 179–194.

Churchill, G. (2015a). *SafeCare: Evidence from a home based parenting program for neglect*. London: NSPCC.

Churchill, G. (2015b). *SafeCare—parents' perspectives on a home-based parenting program for neglect*. London: NSPCC. https://nspcc.org.uk/services-and-resources/research-and-resources/2015/safecare-evidence-evaluation-report/ (accessed 24 June 2015).

Community Care (2013). Social workers unlikely to act quickly on neglect cases. www.communitycare.co.uk/2012/09/26/social-workers-unlikely-to-act-quickly-on-neglect cases-2, (accessed 11 September 2015).

Co-ordinated Action Against Domestic Abuse (2014). *In plain sight: Effective help for children exposed to domestic abuse*. Bristol: CAADA.

Davidson, G., Bunting, L., & Webb, M.A. (2012). Families experiencing multiple adversities: A review of the international literature, Barnardo's, NSPCC and Queen's University Belfast.

De Wolff, M.S., and van Ijzendoorn, M.H. (1997). Sensitivity and attachment: A meta-analysis on parental antecedents of infant attachment security. *Child Development, 68*, 604–609.

Department for Education (DfE). (2015a). *Working together to safeguard children: A guide to inter-agency working to safeguard and promote the welfare of children*. London: Department for Education.

Department for Work and Pensions (DWP). (2015). *Social Justice Outcomes Framework: Family Stability Indicator*. London: DWP. (accessed 8th April 2015) at https://gov.uk/government/uploads/system/uploads/attachment_data/file/409336/social-justice-family-stability-indicator-2012–2013.pdf

Egeland, B., Sroufe, L., & Erickson, M. (1983). The developmental consequence of different patterns of maltreatment. *Child Abuse & Neglect, 7*(4), 459–469.

Egeland, B. (2009). Taking stock: Childhood emotional maltreatment and developmental psychopathology. *Child Abuse & Neglect, 33*, 22–36.

Euser, S., Alink, L.R., Stoltenborgh, M., Bakermans-Kranenburg, M.J., & van IJzendoorn, M.H. (2015). A gloomy picture: a meta-analysis of randomized controlled trials reveals disappointing effectiveness of programs aiming at preventing child maltreatment. *BMC public health, 15*(1), 1.

Farmer, E. & Lutman, E. (2010). *Case management and outcomes for neglected children returned to their parents: A five year follow-up study*. Bristol: School for Policy Studies, University of Bristol.

Finkelhor, D., Vanderminden, J., Turner, H., Hamby, S., & Shattuck, A. (2014). Child maltreatment rates assessed in a national household survey of caregivers and youth. *Child Abuse & Neglect, 38*(9), 1421–1435.

Fluke, J., Yuan, Y-Y.T., & Edwards, M. (1999). Recurrence of maltreatment: An application of the National Child Abuse and Neglect Data System (NCANDS). *Child Abuse & Neglect, 23*(7), 633–650.

Fraser, J.G., Lloyd, S.W., Murphy, R.A., Crowson, M.M., Casanueva, C., Zolotor, A., & Crotty, K. (2013). *Child exposure to trauma: Comparative effectiveness of interventions addressing maltreatment. Comparative Effectiveness Reviews, No. 89*. Rockville (MD): Agency for Healthcare Research and Quality.

Gardner, R. (2005). *Family support: Child protection in the community*. Wiley.

Gardner, R. (2008). *Developing an effective approach to neglect and emotional harm to children*. London: UEA and NSPCC.

Gardner, R. (ed.). (2016). *Tackling child neglect: Research, policy and evidence-based practice*. London: Jessica Kingsley Publishers.

Gascoigne, M.T. (2015). Commissioning for speech, language and communication needs (SLCN): Using the evidence from the better communication research programme. Better Communication.

Gazmararian, J.A., Lazorick, S., Spitz, A.M., Ballard, T.J., Saltzman, L.E., & Marks, J.S. (1996). Prevalence of violence against pregnant women. *JAMA, 275,* 1915–1920.

Geoffroy, M.-C., Pereira, S.P., Li, L., & Power, C. (2016). Child neglect and maltreatment and childhood-to-adulthood cognition and mental health in a prospective birth cohort. *Journal of the American Academy of Child and Adolescent Psychiatry, 55,* 33–40.

Gielen, A.C., O'Campo, P.J., Faden, R.R., Kass, N.E., & Xue, X. (1994). Interpersonal conflict and physical violence during the childbearing year. *Social Science & Medicine, 39,* 781–787.

Gilbert, R., Widom, C.S., Brown, K., Fergusson, D., Webb, F., & Johnson, S. (2009). Burden and consequences of maltreatment in high income countries. *Lancet, 373*(9657), 68–81.

Hogg, S., Haynes, A., Cuthbert, C., & Baradon, T. (2015). *An unstable start – All Babies Count: Spotlight on homelessness.* London: NSPCC.

Hooper, C.-A., Gorin, S., Cabral, C., & Dyson, C. (2007). Living with hardship 24/7: The diverse experiences of families in poverty in England. The Frank Buttle Trust.

Horwath, J. (2013). *Child neglect: Planning and intervention.* Basingstoke: Palgrave Macmillan.

Huth-Bocks, A.C., Levendosky, A.A., Bogat, G.A., & von Eye, A. (2004). The impact of maternal characteristics and contextual variables on infant-mother attachment. *Child Development, 75,* 480–496.

Johnson, R., & Cotmore, R. (2015). *National evaluation of the Graded Care Profile.* London: NSPCC.

Johnson, R., Smith, E., & Fisher, H. (2015). Testing the reliability and validity of the Graded Care Profile version 2. NSPCC. https://nspcc.org.uk/services-and-resources/research-and-resources/2015/graded-care-profile-evaluation-report/ (accessed 24 June 2016).

Kennedy, H., Macdonald, M. and Whalley, P. *Video Interaction Guidance: Providing an effective response for neglected children.* In Gardner, R. (2016).

Kotch, J.B., Lewis, T., Hussey, J.M., English, D., Thompson, R., Litrownik, A. J., Runyan, D.K., Bangdiwala, S.I., Margolis, B. & Dubowitz, H. (2008). Importance of early neglect for childhood aggression. *Pediatrics, 121*(4), 725–729.

Malmberg, L.E., Lewis, S., West, E., Sylva, K., & Stein, A. (2015). 'The influence of mothers' and fathers' sensitivity in the first year of life on children's cognitive outcomes at 18 and 36 months'. *Child: Care, health and development, 42*(3), 1–7.

Manning, V. (2011). *Estimate of the numbers of infants (under the age of one year) living with substance misusing parents.* London: NSPCC.

Merritt, D.H., & Klein, S. (2015). Do early care and education services improve language development for maltreated children? Evidence from a national child welfare sample. *Child Abuse and Neglect, 39* 185–196.

Michel, G.F., & Tyler, A.N. (2005). Critical period: A history of the transition from questions of when, to what, to how. *Developmental psychobiology, 46*(3), 156–162.

NSPCC (2015). Spotlight on preventing child neglect; an overview of NSPCC services and research. https://nspcc.org.uk/globalassets/documents/research-reports/spotlight-preventing-child-neglect-report.pdf (accessed 24 June 2016).

Office of Standards in Education, Children's Services and Skills (Ofsted). (2014). *In the child's time: Professional responses to neglect.* Manchester: Ofsted.

Radford, L., Corral, S., Bradley, C., & Fisher, H. (2013). The prevalence and impact of child maltreatment and other types of victimization in the UK: Findings from a population survey of caregivers, children and young people and young adults. *Child Abuse & Neglect, 37*(10), 801–813.

Raphael-Leff, J. (2010). Mothers' and fathers' orientations: Patterns of pregnancy, parenting and the bonding process. In S. Tyano, M. Keren, H. Herman, & J. Cox (Eds.), *Parenthood and mental health: A bridge between infant and adult psychiatry,* 9–30. Oxford: Wiley-Blackwell.

Rostad, W.L., Lutzker, J.R. and Guastaferro, K.M. *Practices targeting child neglect: The use of Safe Care[R] to enhance parenting skills to reduce neglect*. In Gardner, R. (2016).

Sroufe, L.A. (2005) Attachment and development: A prospective, longitudinal study from birth to adulthood. *Attachment & Human Development, 7*(4), 349–367.

Sidebotham, P., Heron, J., & ALSPAC Study Team. (2006). Child maltreatment in the 'children of the nineties': A cohort study of risk factors. *Child Abuse & Neglect, 30*(5), 497–522.

Stalker, K., & McArthur, K. (2012). Child abuse, child protection and disabled children; A review of recent research. *Child Abuse Review, 21*(1), 24–40.

Stith, S.M., Liu, T.L., Davies, C., Boykin, E.L., Alder, M.C., Harris, J.M., Som, A., McPherson, M., & Dees, J. (2009). Risk factors in child maltreatment: A meta-analytic review of the literature. *Aggression and Violent Behavior, 14*, 13–29.

Westhorp, G. (2012) *Family by Family Evaluation Report (2011–12)*. Mt Torens, SA: Community Matters.

Whalley, P., & Williams, M. (2015) Child neglect and Video Interaction Guidance: An evaluation of an NSPCC service offered to parents where initial concerns of neglect have been noted. London: NSPCC. https://nspcc.org.uk/services-and-resources/research-and-resources/2015/video-interaction-guidance-vig-evaluation-report/ (accessed 24 June 2016).

WHO (World Health Organization) (1999). *Report of the Consultation on Child Abuse Prevention, Geneva, 29–31March 1999*. Available at www.yesican.org/definitions/WHO.html (accessed 27 June 2016).

Williams, M. (2015). *Evidence-based decisions in child neglect: An evaluation of an exploratory approach to assessment using the North Carolina Family Assessment Scale*. London: NSPCC.

Wolff, M.S., & Ijzendoorn, M.H. (1997). Sensitivity and attachment: A meta-analysis on parental antecedents of infant attachment. *Child development, 68*(4), 571–591.

20

MELLOW PROGRAMMES FOR ESPECIALLY VULNERABLE PARENTS AND PARENTS-TO-BE

Christine Puckering

Mellow Parenting has developed a family of group programmes to support parents-to-be and parents with additional health and social needs to make the best possible relationships with their babies right from the start. This chapter will describe the methods and contents of Mellow Bumps and Dad Matters, antenatal programmes for mums and dads-to-be, Mellow Babies for mums and dads of babies up to around 15 months, and Mellow Futures for parents with learning difficulties (LDs) or disabilities, illustrated with case studies.

'Mellow Bumps' and 'Mellow Dads-to-be' (Dad Matters)

There are strong reasons to begin interventions to support good parent-child relationships in pregnancy. Depression in mothers during pregnancy is more common than postnatal depression (Ferguson, Horwood & Thorpe, 1996). There is growing evidence that children of women with antenatal depression and anxiety have a high risk of anxiety and depressive disorders at 18 years old (Capron et al., 2015).

The Avon Longitudinal Study of Parents and Children (ALSPAC) study also demonstrates that paternal depression in pregnancy increases the risk of later antisocial behaviour problems particularly in boys and especially when compounded by postnatal depression (Ramchandani et al., 2008).

In the light of this evidence of effects on children of stress in mothers and fathers during pregnancy (Glover TBC), two programmes were devised to engage parents-to-be. It is Mellow Parenting practice to offer single gender groups, partly on empirical evidence (Bakermans-Kranenberg et al., 2003) and partly because of participant feedback that sensitive issues, such as historic sexual abuse and intimate partner violence, are more easily discussed in single gender groups.

The two parallel programmes each last 6 weeks, with sessions of about 2 hours. To ensure that the most vulnerable families, who are least likely to access the very services they need (Maybelis & Maryatt, 2011), are recruited and engaged, transport assistance and light refreshments are provided, to make parents-to-be feel welcome. All materials and activities make low literacy demands, with a focus on discussion, quizzes and psychoeducational videos such as those prepared by the Harvard Center on the Developing Child (http://developingchild.harvard.edu). Each session comprises activities to promote parental wellbeing and stress management, including relaxation and mindfulness exercises, and activities to reveal the growing capacity of the foetus and new-born infant to respond to intimate interaction. The effects of early interaction on the developing brain were a revelation to most parents-to-be, even those who had previously borne children.

Following Mellow Bumps, the average baby is born at 38 weeks +/- 5 days and weighs 3.27 kg/7 lb 3.5 oz, close to national norms in a group who are at high risk of premature delivery and low birth weight. A randomised controlled study has shown that Mellow Bumps leads to promising results in terms of maternal mental health (Patterson & Ibrahim, 2015) and increased confidence and later service engagement but larger studies, including outcomes for the babies, are needed (White et al., 2015).

The likelihood of a man becoming depressed doubles as he approaches parenthood (Paulson & Bazemore, 2010). Men can feel excluded from the whole process of pregnancy and birth and mothers in the Mellow Bumps groups identified a lack of support for fathers-to-be. The Mellow Dads-to-be programme follows the same model as Mellow Bumps, with some adaptation to make the activities and language 'dad friendly'. Outcomes for Dads-to-be are promising but still at the preliminary stage (Macolm & Ibrahim, 2016).

Case study[1]

Maria, aged 40 had a history of drug and alcohol abuse. She had two teenage children from a previous relationship who were already in trouble with the police for minor misdemeanours. She also had a 2-year-old with her current partner and was 32 weeks pregnant when she was referred to the group by a local alcohol counselling service. Her partner, Keith, also had a history of substance problems, but both parents were clean by the start of the group. Keith joined a dads-to-be group and Maria attended every session of Mellow Bumps. She remarked in astonishment at the video of neonatal imitation and the representation of baby brain development saying, 'Why did no one ever tell me this before?' Maria's Total Adult Wellbeing Scale Scores fell from 18 to 11, and her baby was born at term weighing 3.1 kg. Despite a difficult labour with an unsupportive midwife who remembered Maria from her previous deliveries and treated her with disdain and contempt, Maria remained up-beat and reported 'When I first saw my baby, I felt like I already knew her'. She volunteered to return to a subsequent group as a helper and spoke at a conference, to report as an expert-by-experience.

Mellow Babies for mums or dads

Mellow Babies is a group programme for parents of children under 15 months. The impetus to develop Mellow Babies groups emerged from the evidence of the importance of the early months and the role of interaction with parents in babies' brain development. More recent evidence has shown that good postnatal relationships can go some way to offsetting the damaging effects of stress during the pregnancy (Bergman, Sarkar, Glover & O'Connor, 2008; p. 98 Glover). The group lasts 14 weeks, one full day each week. The programme addresses the lives of the parents as people, using reflection on their own story, self-esteem, assertiveness and some simple cognitive behavioural interventions for low mood and anxiety. More didactic, behavioural programmes, lacking support for the parents, can fail to engage the most troubled families and may have high attrition rates (28 per cent attrition, Bor, Sanders & Markie-Dadds, 2002; 44–46 per cent attrition, Marryatt et al., 2014). Parents attend a personal group while the children are in a children's group. At its best, the children's group becomes a therapeutic group, with carefully planned child activities picking up the same themes as the parents' group. At lunchtime, parents and children join in a shared meal, some nursery rhymes and songs and a joint activity designed to bring parent and child into close interaction. All the activities are free or use inexpensive materials so that the family can continue to use them outside the group. Parents, who have never experienced play in their own lives and never played with their child, can find out how much fun messy play or simple craft activities can be. Outings to the local children's library or the park also open the doors to all the local facilities, of which the parents may have been unaware or too lacking in confidence to try out. After the activity session, the parents return to their own groups for a parenting workshop based around personalised video feedback from each parent's interaction with their baby, recorded at their home during a caretaking activity such as feeding, nappy changing or dressing. The use of personalised, strengths-based video feedback has been identified as one of the characteristics of effective programmes to improve parental sensitivity. While it can seem challenging for parents and practitioners to use, it pays very great rewards (Bakermans-Kranenberg, van Ijzendoorn & Juffer, 2003; p. 224 Kennedy).

A small waiting list randomised controlled trial has been shown to reduce symptoms of maternal depressed mood and enhance the mother–child relationship (Puckering, Macintosh & Hickey, 2010). As yet, there is no separate data for Mellow Dads with babies.

Case study

Nicola was referred by her health visitor because of an extremely high Edinburgh Post Natal Depression Scale (EPDS) score. She was on sick leave because of the effects of her depression following the birth of her second child. Jodi, now aged 10 months, had thrived while breast fed but had become very ill upon the introduction of solid food. After two hospitalisations, this was traced to a severe cow's milk allergy which had left her dangerously dehydrated. She was therefore on a very strict exclusion diet to eliminate all milk protein, with very stringent demands to ensure she still received enough to eat.

This left Nicola stressed and anxious and also unable to give up breast feeding though she felt the time was right. Jodi did not sleep through the night and Nicola was exhausted. She knew she should be preparing her older daughter, aged four, for the new adventure of starting school but could raise no enthusiasm for this and dreaded the separation.

In the group, Nicola also discussed the premature death of her disabled sibling in childhood and how this gave her the sense that 'Children can die'. Two other mothers had lost siblings in childhood. The dead siblings were a present force for each of the families.

The interaction between Nicola and Jodi was warm and loving during play, with close, mutually responsive interaction and creative play with a puppet. However, mealtimes were very different. Jodi had developed a learned aversion to solid food. She demonstrated both eager hunger, opening her mouth and leaning forward, and avoidance, raising her arms to shield herself from the spoon and shaking her head. Meanwhile, Nicola struggled with her fears, making mealtimes fraught with anxiety. Her presentation was of a tense, false brightness, meeting Jodi's fear with her own, barely disguised, anxiety.

Nicola attended the group regularly. Separating from Jodi was difficult, with Nicola sitting poised on the edge of her chair, ready to respond if she heard the slightest squeak from Jodi in the children's group. Over the weeks, she began to be able to trust for the first time that Jodi would survive if separated. Nicola weaned her and Jodi began to sleep through the night. By the end of the group Nicola's EPDS had fallen to a subclinical level and she was preparing to return to work part time on a phased basis.

Mellow futures for parents with LDs or disabilities

Parents with LDs are a particularly vulnerable group. McGaw (1997) estimates there are 250,000 parents with LDs who may or may not have a diagnosis. About 50 per cent of these parents have their children removed largely on the presumption of incompetence, a deficiency perspective focussing on what the parent *cannot* do and a discriminatory practice which undermines rather than supports coping (Booth, Booth & McConnel, 2005). Around 16 per cent of children in child protection hearings have at least one parent with a learning disability. Services for adults with learning disabilities do not routinely address the topic of parenting, often seeing their own skills to be in supporting the adult, not infant mental health. In 2012, Mellow Parenting and Mencap developed and field tested a programme to support parents with LD from pregnancy to age 1. We had the support of the parent's reference group from the Elfrida Society, an advocacy service for people with learning disabilities and difficulties, which vetted our materials for their appropriate use of language and accessibility. To support generalisation of learning from the group, volunteer mentors were added to reinforce the group activities at home and integrate parents into the local community.

The first difficulty lay in recruiting families. Despite much liaison with maternity services, few women with LDs were referred in pregnancy. Mothers-to-be were understandably reluctant to reveal a vulnerability they knew was associated with a high risk of children being removed. Busy midwives were perhaps unaware of the woman's difficulties or reluctant to probe for fear of stigmatising. Referrals from health visiting were much more common, as the challenges of parenting a new baby became evident. The lives of the families were exceptionally complex, with partners and extended family taking an unusually active role, for protective or less noble reasons. Struggles with social services, child protection, housing and legal services were also commonplace.

The programme was evaluated by Beth Tarleton of the Norah Fry Institute, at the University of Bristol. Interviews with participants, referrers and group practitioners were complemented by quantitative measures at the start and end of the postbirth group. Eighteen of the 24 mothers who completed the pilot programmes consented to take part in the evaluation. The mothers had very complicated life circumstances: two of the mothers grew up in local authority care themselves, six of the mothers had had previous children removed from their care and ten of the unborn children or babies were subject to child protection plans and/or their grandparents had parental responsibility. Only three mothers were not involved with children's services, while four of the babies were initially regarded as 'child in need'. Three of the mothers had older children in their own care. There were a range of current issues in the mothers' lives such as use of alcohol, depression and self-harm (Tarleton & Turner, 2015).

The mentors involved in the programme were mostly mothers who wanted to share their skills and support other mothers. A number were undertaking voluntary work to support a change in career.

Case study[2]

Cheryl lived with a mother and father who had a history of alcohol abuse. She had an undiagnosed LD with an impaired memory, for which she compensated by writing everything down.

Her relationships with men were troubled. She would become fixated on failed relationships and would become very hostile and angry when she spoke about them. She had two children both of whom had been removed into the care of her ex-partner, who was the father of one of the boys. The reason for the children's removal was reported as neglect, due to Cheryl's history of alcohol abuse, volatile relationships and the condition of the home that she shared with her parents.

Cheryl found the loss of the two children extremely difficult and had a hostile relationship with her ex-partner which spilled into her contact sessions with the children, when she would allege in very explicit language that they were being neglected by him.

Cheryl was told by social services that if she was to keep her baby she must attend the Mellow Futures group, and have a strand test for alcohol use each week. She was to move out of her parents' house and stop having contact with them. All this she did.

When she first attended the Bumps module of Mellow Futures she was quiet and totally disconnected from her baby, of whom she never spoke. She never touched the bump, only becoming animated when talking about her anger towards her ex-partner and all he had done and was doing. She despised social services and had a negative and hostile relationship with her social worker. Case conferences were always bad experiences for her and she would usually get angry and leave.

Though her LD was obvious, it was undiagnosed. She had no advocacy services or source of additional support and understanding.

The group began to see how scared, hurt, helpless and traumatised she was. Strengths-based support from the group helped her to recognise how her behaviour was going to result in her losing a third child. Acknowledging the pain and anger she felt, she also realised that her aggression was compounding that possibility. She began to talk about her baby and had already chosen a name for him. She also started to let her bump show, having previously kept it hidden and she began to caress the bump during the groups.

She was set up with an advocate and mentor and developed extremely good relationships with them. Her mentor was honest with her, but kind and attended appointments with her to visit housing and other services.

The group also helped Cheryl to prepare for her case conference, helping her to think about her strengths and how to manage difficult and angry feelings in the meeting. The chair of the case conference contacted the group facilitators to say the change in her was enormous and they had begun to see how it was possible that she might keep her child although her social worker was very against this.

Cheryl's baby was born prematurely and was thought to have foetal alcohol syndrome even though she had negative strand tests all through her pregnancy. An undefined congenital problem was diagnosed. Parents with additional needs parenting children with additional needs is a complex issue that was not uncommon in the group.

The Mellow Practitioners wrote a supportive report for court, based on observations in the group and video recordings. This was at odds with the report of another highly regarded agency and the social work agency. However, on the basis of the report, Cheryl kept her baby. She continued to have volatile relationships with men, however she had a strong attachment to the baby which was highly protective.

Cheryl flourished in her relationships within the group where she formed one very reliable friendship. Video work on her interaction with the baby led to her handling him extremely sensitively, but she could still become dysregulated when discussing her former partner. Cheryl will always need support, however she has a strong relationship with her baby and they are still together. He is a thriving, sociable baby.

Discussion

Mellow programmes deliver some very subtle messages in apparently simple and concrete ways, to parents who find routine services hard to use, for fear of stigma and suspicion of service providers. A commitment to work with the most vulnerable groups in society and reduce social and health inequalities drives all the programmes. Through hands-on work and video feedback parents are nurtured to help them nurture their children, while difficult issues like safeguarding are never neglected. No group ever proceeds without both tears and laughter.

All the programmes have well-structured manuals, but the strength of the intervention lies with the practitioners, who must build a trusting relationship with parents who have little experience of trust in their lives, starting from childhood through to current partners and services. The first contact is by a letter, quickly followed by a telephone call, as literacy can be a hurdle. The first meeting is always in the parent's home, or in a place the parent nominates. The programme is presented as an offer, for them to accept or decline. Even if there is an external mandate, the wishes of the parent are given precedence, with the Mellow Parenting practitioner taking responsibility for reporting back to the referrer that the group is not the right intervention for this parent at this time. Under careful negotiation, parents who previously felt they had few choices may choose to join the group. Given that all the parents who attend do so because they see some hope for themselves and their children in the group, attendance is high and attrition low.

Mellow Parenting groups use strengths-based video feedback. The method has some similarities to other video feedback methods but differs both from Video Interaction Guidance (VIG) (sometimes called Video Home Training) and from Video-feedback Intervention to Promote Positive Parenting and Sensitive Discipline (VIPP-SD) (Fukkink, 2008: Kennedy, Landor & Todd, 2011). Mellow Parenting gives greater control of the process to the parent, who is seen to 'own' the whole recorded interaction and to choose what to share with the group, rather than seeing a recording edited by the guider or trainer. The opportunity to help parents see strengths they did not know they possessed and the immediate, intimate responses of the babies is a revelation to most parents. While the emphasis is strongly on the positives, the opportunity to see things they might want to change, and get group support to do that is also valuable. Seeing other parents negotiating the same issues gives immediate confirmation that they are not the only parents who are struggling.

In summary, Mellow Parenting programmes are designed to help families with complex needs and to address health and social inequalities. High rates of engagement and low rates of attrition confirm that parents find the programmes acceptable. Our hope is that no parent will need to say in the future 'Why did no one ever tell me this before?' as we strive to meet their needs and give their babies the best chance from pregnancy through the first 1001 critical days.

- Previous adverse experiences, for example of poor parenting, domestic violence and lack of trust can overwhelm the parent's capacity to respond to the baby.

To be able to make a sensitive relationship with a baby, parents need to be free of the shadows of previous and current difficulties.

- To enable positive change, parents need support to address their own challenges in a nurturing environment, alongside active work on parenting.
- Strengths-based video feedback is a powerful agent for change and empowers parents to respond accurately to the baby's cues.

Notes

1 Names in this and later case studies have been changed to protect anonymity.
2 My thanks are due to Rachel Stephen for sharing this case from the Mellow Futures group in Islington.

References

Bakermans-Kranenburg, M.J., Van Ijzendoorn, M.H., & Juffer, F. (2003). Less is more: Meta-analyses of sensitivity and attachment interventions in early childhood. *Psychological Bulletin, 129*(2), 195–215.

Bergman, K., Sarkar, P., Glover, V., & O'Connor T.G. (2008). Quality of child–parent attachment moderates the impact of antenatal stress on child fearfulness. *Journal of Child Psychology & Psychiatry & Allied Disciplines, 49*(10), 1089–1098.

Booth, T., Booth, W., & McConnell, D. (2005). The prevalence and outcomes of care proceedings involving parents with learning difficulties in the family courts. *Journal of Applied Research in Intellectual Disabilities, 18*(1), 7–17.

Bor, W., Sanders, M.R., & Markie-Dadds, C. (2002). The effects of the triple P–Positive parenting program on preschool children with co-occurring disruptive behavior and attentional/hyperactive difficulties. *Journal of Abnormal Child Psychology, 30*(6), 571–587.

Capron, L.E., Glover, V., Pearson, R.M., Evans, J., O'Connor, T.G., Stein, A., Murphy, S.E., & Ramchandani, P.G. (2015). Associations of maternal and paternal antenatal mood with offspring anxiety disorder at age 18 years. *Journal of Affective Disorders*, 187, 20–26.

Fergusson, D.M., Horwood, L.J., & Thorpe, K. (1996). Changes in depression during and following pregnancy. *Paediatric and Perinatal Epidemiology, 10*(3), 279–93.

Fukkink, R. (2008) Video feedback in widescreen: A meta-analysis of family programs. *Clinical Psychology Review, 28*, 904–916.

Kennedy, H., Landor, M., & Todd, L. (eds). (2011). Video Interaction Guidance: A relationship-based Intervention to promote attunement, empathy and wellbeing. London. Jessica Kingsley

Mabelis, J., & Marryat, L. (2011). *Growing Up in Scotland: Parental service use of formal and informal networks in the early years.* Edinburgh: Scottish Government. ISBN 978–1–78045–199–2 (Web only publication) DPPAS11600

Malcolm, R., & Ibrahim, R. (2016). Mellow Dads-to-be: An antenatal attachment-based parenting programme for expectant fathers. Poste presented at the 15th World Association for Infant Mental Health Conference, Prague.

Marryat, L., Thompson, L., McGranachan, M., Barry, S., Sim, F., Jane White, J., & Wilson, P. (2014). Parenting Support Framework Evaluation. August 2009 to December 2013. Final Report.

McGaw, S. (1997). Practical support for parents with learning disabilities. In J.O'Hara & A. Sperlinger (Eds.), *Adults with Learning Disabilities: A Practical Approach for Health Professionals* (pp. 123–138). Chichester: John Wiley and Sons.

O'Connor, T.G., Heron, J., Golding, J., & Glover, V. ALSPAC Study Team. (2003). Maternal antenatal anxiety and behavioural/emotional problems in children: A test of a programming hypothesis. *Journal of Child Psychology & Psychiatry & Allied Disciplines, 44*(7), 1025–1036.

Paterson, K., & Ibrahim, R. (2015). Mellow Bumps; outcomes of an antenatal programme focussing on attachment. Poster presented at the Young People and Families conference, British Psychological Society Children, Annual conference, Birmingham.

Paulson, J.F., & Bazemore, S.D. (2010). Prenatal and postpartum depression in fathers and its association with maternal depression: A meta-analysis. *Jama, 303*(19), 1961–1969. experiencing postnatal depression. *Counselling Psychology Review, 25*(1), 28–40.

Puckering, C., McIntosh, E., & Hickey, A. (2010). Mellow babies: A group intervention for infants and mothers experiencing postnatal depression. *Counselling Psychology Review, 25*(1), 28–40.

Ramchandani, P.G., O'Connor, T.G., Evans, J., Heron, J., Murray, L., Stein, A. (2008). The effects of pre- and postnatal depression in fathers: A natural experiment comparing the effects of exposure to depression on offspring. *Journal of Child Psychology & Psychiatry & Allied Disciplines, 49*(10), 1069–1078.

Tarleton, B., & Turner, W. (2015). *Mellow Futures: Parent Pioneers Pilot programme evaluation.* University of Bristol.

White, J., Thompson, L., Puckering, C., Waugh, H., Henderson, M., MacBeth, A., & Wilson, P. (2015). Antenatal parenting support for vulnerable women. *British Journal of Midwifery, 23*(10), 724–732.

21

FATHERS IN THE PERINATAL PERIOD

Taking their mental health into account

Jill Domoney, Jane Iles, Paul Ramchandani

The perinatal period (pregnancy and the first postnatal year) is important in a number of ways. Not only is new life developing and entering into the world, but parents experience a significant transition into parenthood, frequently requiring them to meet a number of new demands and adaptations to life with a newborn. While this can be a rewarding experience for many, it can also be a time of high stress and worry, with the potential for early difficulties to have long-lasting consequences for the wellbeing of the family.

While difficulties related to mothers' experience of parenthood have received a significant amount of attention in both research and policy, leading to improvements in screening and treatment programmes, the impact of this transition on fathers has only more recently become a focus of attention. Issues of how to engage fathers in services, research into the impact of paternal behaviour on child outcomes, and the understanding of paternal mental health are growing areas but policy often lags behind. The inclusion of fathers in parenting programmes and perinatal interventions remains patchy (Panter-Brick et al., 2013).

This chapter will discuss the challenges and benefits of including fathers in intervention programmes during the perinatal period, as well as exploring the impact of paternal mental illness at this time.

Engagement of fathers in intervention

Fathers have a unique and important role in caring for their children, including using different types of play and encouraging different social experiences (e.g. using 'rough play' more frequently than mothers). Prosocial father behaviour (such as taking children on outings and to visit friends/family) has been linked with positive socialisation in later childhood (Flouri & Buchanan, 2004), including improved peer relationships (Martin et al., 2010), and a warm consistent father-child relationship can protect or buffer children from potential adverse effects of maternal depression (Goodman & Gotlib, 1999). Indeed, a wealth of research now highlights the potential beneficial impact of fathers on children's long-term outcomes. In addition, a meta-analysis of early childhood interventions focused on enhancing parental sensitivity and infant attachment indicated that those interventions involving fathers appeared to be significantly more effective than mother-only interventions (Bakermans-Kranenburg et al., 2003). Therefore it is surprising and disappointing that fathers are so infrequently included either in general perinatal care or in parenting interventions (Panter-Brick et al., 2014), and that their mental health needs at this time are rarely assessed.

Failure to include fathers may sometimes be due to their reluctance to engage with services, or even reluctance on the part of mothers to have their partners involved. However, it seems likely that a key factor is the failure of healthcare and mental health providers to adapt practices to encourage the inclusion of fathers. This issue was highlighted in a recent study looking at why health visitors rarely screen fathers for postnatal depression (Whitelock, 2016). The findings indicated that the health visitors in the study believed their role to be mother and child-focused and they often did not feel confident or safe engaging with fathers. The NSPCC's 'Dad Project', published as part of the All Babies Count campaign, included surveys and focus groups with a wide range of fathers. This research indicated that many fathers feel isolated during the perinatal period because attention is focused on the mother and baby, and that many dads do not therefore get the support they need (NSPCC, 2014).

All these findings suggest that shifts within services are needed to overcome barriers to father engagement. A recent review by Panter-Brick and colleagues (2014) highlighted the issue of father engagement in parenting interventions. The review identified some of the important potential barriers to consider in the design, implementation and evaluation of co-parenting interventions in order to engage men. These included a number of biases in programme design, such as cultural and institutional biases relating to how father-friendly the organisation is, and professional biases around staff capability and attitudes. In terms of delivery, issues around staff training, communication to parents and basics such as the time and location of sessions were highlighted. Finally, when considering evaluation, the types of data collected as well as thinking about reach and sustainability of outcomes were identified as important areas. One of the barriers to this being implemented is the fact that fathers are generally less frequently involved in child mental health, healthcare and welfare services (Cameron et al., 2014). Therefore, a challenge to services is to actively engage both parents from the earliest point of contact. Examples of this include: addressing letters to both parents; maintaining active engagement throughout the intervention by continuing to acknowledge the father's role as important; and actively seeking to understand what may encourage individual parents' ongoing participation. There is also a more substantial change needed to ensure that perinatal and early years' services are focused on families rather than mother-infant dyads and thus ensure optimal outcomes for children (Ramchandani & Iles, 2014).

Paternal mental health

Being left out of antenatal and postnatal healthcare services may lead to suboptimal outcomes for fathers' mental health since fathers who are experiencing depressive symptoms may suffer alone and without support. Early involvement of fathers in perinatal services is therefore not only a means to improve infant outcomes but also an opportunity to pick up on paternal mental health difficulties. Mothers, infants and fathers typically access healthcare services more frequently during pregnancy and the postnatal period than at almost any other stage of adult life. Although national guidance, such as National Institute for Health and Care Excellence (2007) and the Joint Commissioning Panel for Mental Health (2012), recommend routine screening for maternal perinatal depression and anxiety, as well as timely access to treatment, there are no recommendations regarding fathers' mental health. This is surprising as we know that men also suffer from mental health difficulties during the perinatal period. This may be a potential avenue through which to increase paternal access to services and screening for perinatal difficulties. Indeed, Fletcher et al. (2015, 2016) describe a father-inclusive model of perinatal care in which fathers are included and screened from the very first contacts with maternity services. It is to this topic of paternal mental health that we now turn.

Perinatal mental health difficulties can have significant implications for parents' day-to-day functioning, as well as impacting on the wider family. This highlights the need for timely and effective perinatal interventions to alleviate and reduce the effects on families (NICE, 2015). We focus here on paternal perinatal depression as this is the most widely studied mental health difficulty, although there is a growing evidence base for the impacts of other disorders (Ramchandani & Psychogiou, 2009). Recent research indicates that around 5–10 per cent of fathers are affected by postnatal depression (Paulson & Bazemore, 2010), and the figures grow substantially where a partner is also experiencing postnatal depression (Goodman, 2004). We consider two key questions relating to perinatal depression: first, why do men get depressed during this period? Second, what are the effects of this depression on family functioning and children's development?

Why do fathers get depressed?

It is increasingly understood that becoming a parent is a significant time of adjustment and change for men as well as women (Goodman, 2004). Men can be exposed to a number of key changes at this time including changes in sleep patterns, new roles and responsibilities, changes in social support networks and changes to the relationship with their partner, as well as potentially feeling excluded from the process of mother-infant bonding (Goodman, 2005). Men can have similar worries and fears to women around the health of their infant and their adequacy as a parent (Ferketich & Mercer, 1995) and may also receive mixed messages from society about their role and responsibilities. Over recent decades society has come to expect significant increases in levels of paternal involvement. These changes mean that many men lack a good role model and can be left unsure about what is expected of them. The father-infant bond may develop more gradually than the mother-infant relationship, in part because fathers typically spend less overall time with their infants, compared to mothers. This may contribute to a sense of anxiety and lower self-confidence in relating and caring for the infant and may mean that the father receives less-positive reinforcement in the form of smiles from their baby (Anderson, 1996) and may perceive themselves to have lower levels of parenting efficacy (de Montigny et al., 2012).

Other key risk factors for paternal perinatal depression, identified in research studies, include having a history of depression prior to the partner's pregnancy and experiencing symptoms of depression or anxiety in the prenatal period, each of which can increase the chances of perinatal depression by between 2 and 4 times (Ramchandani et al., 2008). In some cases this is because the transition to becoming a father acts as a stressor or trigger for men with an existing vulnerability to depression, but there can also be a strong continuity of depression from the prenatal period on through the postnatal period (Paulson et al., 2016). This pattern is also seen in mothers' perinatal depression, although it has been suggested that fathers may experience the onset of persistent depressed mood later in the postnatal period than mothers (Matthey et al., 2000).

Depression in the partner is also a strong predictor of paternal depression (Goodman, 2004) and maternal depression has been shown to impact detrimentally on the couple relationship (Howard et al., 2013). Relationship dissatisfaction and couple conflict has been found to increase during this time, and couples may not be able to support each other in the ways they had hoped or expected to during this period (Cowan et al., 1985). Couple disharmony can subsequently increase risk of depression, and the couple relationship may be impacted by presence of postnatal depression, indicating a reciprocal relationship. Conversely, social support, including partner support, is a highly protective factor for depression in the postnatal period for both men and women (Matthey et al., 2000; Milgrom et al., 2008).

Paternal perinatal depression and familial outcomes

Paternal depression not only has a significant impact on the health and functioning of the affected father, but can also affect the wellbeing of the family, including impacting on the mother's psychological health, the couple relationship, and the health of the developing baby. The associations between maternal postnatal depression and child outcomes are well documented in a large body of literature (Stein et al., 2014) but it is only in recent years that researchers and practitioners have considered whether paternal depression might similarly effect children's development.

Paternal depression has been found to have adverse impacts on similar childhood outcomes to those affected by maternal symptoms, including infant temperament, emotional and behavioural problems, and peer relationships (Davé et al., 2008; Hanington et al., 2010; Ramchandani et al., 2005; Ramchandani et al., 2008).

Children's risk of behavioural problems in childhood is approximately doubled if their fathers had depression in the perinatal period. This increased risk has been shown in studies across the world, including Norway, Australia and the Netherlands, as well as the United Kingdom. In addition the findings of some, though not all, studies have suggested that male infants may be at greater risk for later behavioural, emotional and temperamental difficulties than female infants (Hanington et al., 2010; Ramchandani et al., 2005).

The mechanisms for the transmission of risk from fathers' depression to their children are not yet fully understood, but include the effect of depression on the parental relationship, the partner's mood, and an effect on the developing father-child relationship (Guttierez Galve et al, 2015). Parental psychopathology can also impact directly on the couple relationship. Studies often find a concordance of postnatal depressive symptoms between parents (Iles et al., 2011), and the co-occurrence of depression in both mother and father is often associated with deterioration in the couples' relationship. Reduced cooperation at such a crucial time can leave both partners feeling isolated, unsupported and unable to fulfil the parental role they may have hoped for (Matthey et al., 2000). Increased parental conflict and reduced cooperation have an impact on the emotional environment in which a child is growing and developing. It is particularly pertinent when thinking about the early months of an infant's life, when important aspects of brain development are taking place, as well as the development of key attachment relationships with caregivers. If the environment does not foster positive growth in either of these areas the infant may be at greater risk for later developmental and relational difficulties. Indeed, a recent review of the effects of paternal depression on child outcomes found that couple conflict partly mediates the relationship between depression and offspring development. That is, at least some of the effect of paternal depression on child outcomes is because depression can lead to increased couple conflict, and this in turn is associated with an increased risk of adverse outcomes for children (Sweeney et al., 2016).

Paternal depression may also impact more directly on the child through its effect on parenting behaviour. An example of this is seen in early father–infant interaction. Fathers with depression tend to be more withdrawn in their interactions with infants (Field, 2010; Sethna et al., 2015) and withdrawn and disengaged interactions between fathers and their infants from as young as 3 months of age are associated with a significantly increased risk of later behavioural problems (Ramchandani et al., 2013). Early father–infant interaction thus represents a direct way in which paternal depression may affect children's emotional and behavioural development.

Implications for policy and clinical practice

A growing body of evidence points to a need to increase the engagement of fathers in early years' services, both to optimise positive child outcomes, and to maximise the opportunity for screening and treating paternal mental health disorders.

One practical step is for healthcare providers to engage fathers in wider-ranging perinatal screening and detection programmes (Gawlik et al., 2014). The potential costs and benefits of universal screening need to be carefully assessed, and it may be necessary to consider screening only fathers known to be at increased risk, such as those fathers with a depressed partner, younger fathers and those with a history of depression. Once depression is detected, it is important that affected fathers are offered appropriate and effective interventions, such as psychological therapy. Despite its immediate costs, improved screening and intervention could have a positive financial impact in the longer-term as paternal perinatal depression is associated with increased healthcare costs (Edoka et al., 2011).

There is debate about the best method of screening for depression in men, a range of different screening measures, cut-off thresholds and measurement time-points have been suggested. The Edinburgh Postnatal Depression Scale (EPDS; Cox et al., 1987) is perhaps the most widely used measure, and has been validated for use with fathers with a suggested cut-off score of 10 indicating likely depression (Edmondson et al., 2010, Matthey et al., 2001). It has been suggested that it may be possible to validly screen for paternal depression using mothers' reports (Fisher et al., 2012) although fathers own views and responses are likely to capture their experiences more accurately.

This debate also raises the question of whether the models and pathways that have been developed to care for mothers in the perinatal period can be used as a template to build father-inclusive practices, or whether there are important differences in the way fathers express distress and seek support that would necessitate different types of service. For example some researchers have suggested that men may express distress by becoming aggressive or using alcohol (Cochran & Rabinowitz, 2003) and that screening instruments for perinatal disorders may therefore need to be adapted or used differently (Massoudi et al., 2013). Some practitioners are looking to new communication technologies, such as text messaging, to overcome some of the barriers to engagement and offer support to new fathers (Fletcher et al., 2016).

In terms of prevention, a wider social understanding of the risk factors for paternal depression and subsequent changes in practice may be necessary. Both mothers' and fathers' attitudes towards parenting, their mental health and their readiness to ask for support will impact on adjustment to having a baby. Increased information about the possible difficulties of becoming a father can help to normalise men's experiences and encourage disclosure of problems early on. In addition, encouraging men to attend antenatal clinics and classes with their partners can help to build a social network of parents who are experiencing similar changes, thus increasing social support for both mothers and fathers while interventions targeted at the couple as parents can increase mutual partner support (e.g. Parents as Partners, Cowan et al., 2009). It is not yet clear whether changes in paternity leave which allow men to take a more active role in their children's early life will have an impact on depressive symptoms and family relationships.

Conclusions

There are a number of challenges to engaging fathers in early interventions to optimise outcomes for children and families. However, the benefits of father engagement are now well established and therefore it is incumbent on policy makers, commissioners and practitioners to design and implement father-inclusive services to promote whole-family wellbeing. This includes services which can screen for and treat perinatal mental health disorders in men as well as women. Knowledge and understanding regarding the risk factors and implications of paternal depression has increased significantly in recent years, providing substantial evidence for the potential impact of paternal depression on family functioning and child development. While there is much still to learn about the specific mechanisms whereby paternal depression leads to adverse child outcomes, the overall shift in understanding of the important role that fathers play in family life is a positive step forward. Research into maternal depression has led to improvements in screening and intervention which have had a significant impact on maternal and child healthcare. Parallel changes in practice related to fathers have a similar potential to improve family outcomes.

References

Anderson, A.M. (1996). Factors influencing the father-infant relationship. *Journal of Family Nursing, 2*, 306–324.

Cameron, G., Coady, N., & Hoy, S. (2014). Perspectives on being a father from men involved with child welfare services. *Child & Family Social Work, 19*, 14–23.

Cochran, S.V., & Rabinowitz, F.E. (2003). Gender-sensitive recommendations for assessment and treatment of depression in men. *Professional Psychology: Research and Practice, 34*, 132.

Cowan, C.P., Cowan, P.A., & Heming, G. (1985). Transitions to parenthood: his, hers and theirs. *Journal of Family Issues*, 6(4), 451–481.

Cowan, P.A., Cowan, C.P., Pruett, M.K., Pruett, K., & Wong, J.J. (2009). Promoting fathers' engagement with children: Preventive interventions for low-income families. *Journal of Marriage and Family, 71*, 663–679.

Cox, J.L., Holden, J.M., & Sagovsky, R. (1987). Detection of postnatal depression. Development of the 10-item Edinburgh Postnatal Depression Scale. *The British journal of psychiatry, 150*, 782–786.

Davé, S., Sherr, L., Senior, R., & Nazareth, I. (2008). Associations between paternal depression and behaviour problems in children of 4–6 years. *European child & adolescent psychiatry, 17*, 306–315.

Dawson, G., Ashman, S.B., Panagiotides, H., Hessl, D., Self, J., Yamada, E., & Embry, L. (2003). Preschool outcomes of children of depressed mothers: Role of maternal behavior, contextual risk, and children's brain activity. *Child Development, 74*, 1158–1175.

De Montigny, F., Lacharité, C., & Devault, A. (2012). Transition to fatherhood: Modeling the experience of fathers of breastfed infants. *Advances in Nursing Science, 35*, E11–E22.

Edmondson, O.J., Psychogiou, L., Vlachos, H., Netsi, E., & Ramchandani, P.G. (2010). Depression in fathers in the postnatal period: Assessment of the Edinburgh Postnatal Depression Scale as a screening measure. *Journal of affective disorders, 125*, 365–368.

Edoka, I.P., Petrou, S., & Ramchandani, P.G. (2011). Healthcare costs of paternal depression in the postnatal period. *Journal of affective disorders, 133*, 356–360.

Essex, M.J., Klein, M.H., Miech, R., & Smider, N.A. (2001). Timing of initial exposure to maternal major depression and children's mental health symptoms in kindergarten. *The British Journal of Psychiatry, 179*, 151–156.

Ferketich, S.L., & Mercer, R.T. (1995). Predictors of role competence for experienced and inexperienced fathers. *Nursing research, 44*, 89–95.

Field, T. (2010). Postpartum depression effects on early interactions, parenting, and safety practices: A review. *Infant Behavior and Development, 33*, 1–6.

Fisher, S.D., Kopelman, R., & O'Hara, M.W. (2012). Partner report of paternal depression using the Edinburgh Postnatal Depression Scale-Partner. *Archives of women's mental health, 15*, 283–288.

Fletcher, R., Garfield, C., Matthey S. (2015). Fathers' Perinatal Mental Health. In *Identifying perinatal depression and anxiety: Evidence-base practice in screening, psychosocial assessment and management.* Edited by Milgrom and Gemmill.

Fletcher, R., May, C., Wroe, J., Hall, P., Cooke, D., Rawlinson, C., Redfern, J., & Kelly, B. (2016). Development of a set of mobile phone text messages designed for new fathers. *Journal of Reproductive and Infant Psychology*, 10.1080/02646838.2016.1214250

Flouri, E., & Buchanan, A. (2004). Early father's and mother's involvement and child's later educational outcomes. *British Journal of Educational Psychology, 74*, 141–153.

Gawlik, S., Müller, M., Hoffmann, L., Dienes, A., Wallwiener, M., Sohn, C., Schlehe, B., & Reck, C. (2014). Prevalence of paternal perinatal depressiveness and its link to partnership satisfaction and birth concerns. *Archives of Women's Mental Health, 17*, 49–56.

Goodman, S.H., & Gotlib, I.H. (1999). Risk for psychopathology in the children of depressed mothers: A developmental model for understanding mechanisms of transmission. *Psychological Review, 106*, 458.

Goodman, J.H. (2004). Paternal postpartum depression, its relationship to maternal postpartum depression, and implications for family health. *Journal of Advanced Nursing, 45*, 26–35.

Goodman, J.H. (2005). Becoming an involved father of an infant. *Journal of Obstetric, Gynecologic, & Neonatal Nursing, 34*, 190–200.

Hanington, L., Ramchandani, P., & Stein, A. (2010). Parental depression and child temperament: Assessing child to parent effects in a longitudinal population study. *Infant Behavior and Development, 33*, 88–95.

Health, N.C.C.F.M. (2007). Antenatal and postnatal mental health: Clinical management and service guidance. NICE Clinical Guideline CG45. London: National Institute for Health & Clinical Excellence.

Health, J.C.P.F.M. (2012). Guidance for Commissioners of Perinatal Mental Health Services. Joint Commissioning Panel for Mental Health.

Hogg, S. (2014). All babies count: The dad project. NSPCC, London.

Iles, J., Slade, P., & Spiby, H. (2011). Posttraumatic stress symptoms and postpartum depression in couples after childbirth: The role of partner support and attachment. *Journal of anxiety disorders, 25*, 520–530.

Kim, P., & Swain, J.E. (2007). Sad dads: Paternal postpartum depression. *Psychiatry (Edgmont), 4*, 35.

Martin, A., Ryan, R., & Brooks-gunn, J. (2010). When fathers' supportiveness matters most: Maternal and paternal parenting and children's school readiness. *Journal of Family Psychology, 24*, 145–155.

Massoudi, P., Hwang, C.P., & Wickberg, B. (2013). How well does the EPDS identify depression and anxiety in fathers: A validation study in a population based Sedish sample. *Journal of Affective Disorders, 149*(1), 67–74.

Matthey, S., Barnett, B., Kavanagh, D.J., & Howie, P. (2001). Validation of the Edinburgh Postnatal Depression Scale for men, and comparison of item endorsement with their partners. *Journal of Affective Disorders, 64*, 175–184.

Matthey, S., Barnett, B., Ungerer, J., & Waters, B. (2000). Paternal and maternal depressed mood during the transition to parenthood. *Journal of Affective Disorders, 60*, 75–85.

Milgrom, J., Gemmill, A.W., Bilszta, J.L., Hayes, B., Barnett, B., Brooks, J., Ericksen, J., Ellwood, D., & Buist, A. (2008). Antenatal risk factors for postnatal depression: A large prospective study. *Journal of Affective Disorders, 108*, 147–157.

Murray, L. (1992). The impact of postnatal depression on infant development. *Journal of Child Psychology and Psychiatry, 33*, 543–561.

Murray, L., & Cooper, P. (2003). Intergenerational transmission of affective and cognitive processes associated with depression: Infancy and the pre-school years. *Unipolar Depression: A Lifespan Perspective*, 17–46.

Murray, L., Hipwell, A., Hooper, R., Stein, A., & Cooper, P. (1996). The cognitive development of 5-year-old children of postnatally depressed mothers. *Journal of Child Psychology and Psychiatry, 37*, 927–935.

Panter-Brick, C., Burgess, A., Eggerman, M., Mcallister, F., Pruett, K., & Leckman, J.F. (2014). Practitioner review: Engaging fathers – recommendations for a game change in parenting interventions based on a systematic review of the global evidence. *Journal of Child Psychology and Psychiatry, 55*, 11.

Paulson, J.F., & Bazemore, S.D. (2010). Prenatal and postpartum depression in fathers and its association with maternal depression: A meta-analysis. *Jama, 303*, 1961–1969.

Paulson, J.F., Bazemore, S.D., Goodman, J.H., & Leiferman, J.A. (2016). The course and interrelationship of maternal and paternal perinatal depression. *Archives of Women's Mental Health, 19*, 655–663.

Ramchandani, P., Stein, A., Evans, J., & O'Connor, T. (2005). Paternal depression in the postnatal period and child development: A prospective population study. *The Lancet, 365*, 2201–2205.

Ramchandani, P., Stein, A., O'Connor, T., Heron, J., Murray, L., & Evans, J. (2008). Depression in men in the postnatal period and later child psychopathology: A population cohort study. *Journal of the American Academy of Child and Adolescent Psychiatry, 47*, 390–398.

Ramchandani, P., & Psychogiou, L. (2009). Paternal psychiatric disorders and child development. *The Lancet, 374*(9690), 646–653.

Ramchandani, P.G., Domoney, J., Sethna, V., Psychogiou, L., Vlachos, H., & Murray, L. (2013). Do early father-infant interactions predict the onset of externalising behaviours in young children? Findings from a longitudinal cohort study. *Journal of Child Psychology and Psychiatry, 54*(1).

Ramchandani, P., & Iles, J. (2014). Commentary: Getting fathers into parenting programmes – a reflection on Panter-Brick et al. (2014). *Journal of Child Psychology and Psychiatry, 55*, 11.

Sethna, V., Murray, L., Netsi, E., Psychogiou, L., Ramchandani, P.G. (2015). Paternal depression in the postnatal period and early father-infant interactions. *Parent Sci Pract.* 2;15(1), 1–8.

Stein, A., Pearson, R.M., Goodman, S.H., Rapa, E., Rahman, A., McCallum, M., Howard, L.M., & Pariante, C.M. (2014). Effects of perinatal mental disorders on the fetus and child. *Lancet, 384*(9956), 1800–19.

Sweeney, S., & Macbeth, A. (2016). The effects of paternal depression on child and adolescent outcomes: A systematic review. *Journal of Affective Disorders*, 205, 44–59.

Whitelock, A. (2016). Why do health visitors screen mothers and not fathers for depression in the postnatal period? *Journal of Health Visiting*, 4(6).

Acknowledgement

An earlier version of part of this paper was published in the International Journal of Birth and Parenting Education. We are grateful to the Editor and publisher, Mary Nolan, for permission to produce a revised version for this collection. The original can be accessed and cited as: *Paternal depression in the postnatal period: reflections on current knowledge and practice. Jill Domoney, Jane Iles, Paul Ramchandani. Int. J. Birth and Parenting Education, 2015, 1 (3), pp. 17–20.*

22

'SAFECARE', THE CASE FOR PARENT–INFANT LANGUAGE TRAINING

Angie S. Guinn, John R. Lutzker, Mark Chaffin

In 1995, Hart and Risley published a book, *Meaningful Differences in the Everyday Experience of Young American Children* (1995), which was nominated for a Pulitzer Prize for Nonfiction. The book described years of intensive research with over 40 families in a Midwestern U.S. state tracking the use of language directed at their babies and young children and vocabulary growth by mothers. Low socio-economic status (SES) families were compared to middle- and upper-middle class families and over years, the gap in vocabulary and language use between the low SES and the other families became alarmingly wide.

As children develop, vocabulary is a major predictor of academic and social success. Further, over 50 years of research has increasingly demonstrated that brain development is negatively affected by any form of neglect, including low exposure to language (Shonkoff, 2011). The 'good news', however, is that the malleability of a young child's brain is such that if parents can increase their attention, stimulation and language use with their infants, brain development can be enhanced and accelerated (Kuhl, 2011). Thus, teaching parents to speak to their babies as often as possible is a necessary element of any parent training programme for families at risk for child maltreatment and other sequela of poverty.

This chapter will describe the Hart and Risley research, applications of their work, and its role with SafeCare, an evidence-based parent training programme that has a footprint in 25 US states, the United Kingdom, Israel, Canada, Australia, Spain and Belarus. It will briefly describe the historical development of the SafeCare model, review its evidence base and describe the Parent-Infant Interaction training module (PII).

Meaningful differences: A prophecy

The work of Hart and Risley (1995) was prophetic and revealing. By the time they summarised their work, research in child development had continued to describe the importance of early stimulation of young children in fostering desirable academic and social outcomes. However, Hart and Risley's work was among the first to highlight how large the gap across SES of families became over time in the critical elements of vocabulary and language use.

Basic methods and results

Forty-two children ranging in age from 9 to 36 months old and their caregivers were observed every day in their natural settings where trained observers recorded all language and utterances of the caretakers and the children. Initially, there were large differences in parental utterances to their children aged 11 months to 18 months old, between professional and managerial parents, working class parents, and parents receiving welfare. By 36 months old, the children of the professional and managerial parents heard around 642 utterances per hour; children of middle SES parents heard 535 parental utterances per hour, and children of welfare parents heard 321 utterances per hour. At 36 months old, this translated into children's vocabularies averaging 1,100 words in the high SES group, around 700 words in the middle SES group, and under 500 words in the low SES group. Nine years later, when the children were 12 years old, there were vast differences in academic achievement running in the same directions as the utterance and vocabulary data.

Lessons learned

More words heard by children lead to larger and faster vocabulary growth. The first 3 years of life are critical for brain development and essential for social and academic skills as many child development professionals have noted for many years. There was no 'catching up' on the vocabulary curve for the low SES children. Low SES parents spoke less language and what they did speak was perfunctory, that is to say, disciplinary or practical language, but not educational or developmental language.

The rate of vocabulary growth correlates with IQ. Positive affect by parents bolsters child exploration, inquisitiveness, relationships and listening skills. Language practice causes children to use new and different forms of language. Using language with children is cost free. Nothing needs to be purchased, not expensive toys or software programmes. Language use makes for more fun for parents and children. Thus, the bottom line of this very important research is for parents to *talk, talk, talk, and talk some more to their children.*

Applications of the Hart and Risley research

Most child development programmes and evidence-based models aimed at the prevention of child maltreatment include some form of caretaker or teacher training that involves using language with children. What ensues here is the platform for 'Word Gap' research, the Providence Talks programme, SafeCare, and its predecessor, Project 12-Ways, the latter two being models addressing prevention and intervention in child maltreatment.

'Word gap' research

Since the publication of Hart and Risley's findings, extensive research has increased to understand the importance of language and vocabulary development at the earliest stages of life. Parenting programmes have begun to focus on language development for parents and children, and increase school readiness in language skills and communication (Gridley, Hutchings & Baker-Henningham, 2015). Variations in parenting programmes to target specific groups of parents, such as fathers and parents with limited English proficiency, have also been implemented, resulting in a consistent increase in language development and effectively implementing skills that promote child social interactions (Cooke et al., 2009; Elder et al., 2011). Interventions to encourage parent child communicative interactions have consistently shown an increase in maternal responses and the rate of child communications, highlighting the importance of socio-emotional and cognitive development (DiCarlo, Onwujuba & Baumgartner, 2014). In a recent meta-analysis of 67 studies, researchers found that language interventions had a significant positive impact on children's ability to listen and understand and their ability to talk effectively (Marulis & Neuman, 2010).

Providence talks

With the discovery and understanding of the 'word gap' identified by Hart and Risley's research, the city of Providence, Rhode Island, US found that two-thirds of their prospective kindergarteners arrived at school with below national academic reading levels. In an effort to address this problem, the City of Providence launched 'Providence Talks', the first municipality-driven intervention programme aiming to close the 'word gap' and increase childhood literacy. The programme provides participating families with a free 'word pedometer', developed by LENA Research Foundation, that filters out television and background noise to record a daily summary of adult word count and the child's conversational interactions. Families learn about their language use during bi-weekly coaching visits by trained home visitors and are given information on community resources to ultimately prepare children for academic success in kindergarten. The quantity of language spoken by families who completed at least four coaching sessions was improved by 9.4 per cent. For families whose baseline adult word counts were below 50th percentile at ~8,000 words per day, the number increased up to ~12,500 adult words (Providence Talks, 2015). This model has the potential to be generalised to cities bent on improving the language environments of children.

Evidence-based practices

Home visiting has been a strategy for delivering public health and early education services since the 1960s, providing support to families with pregnant women and young children. A growing number of programme models have been evaluated. The Patient Protection and Affordable Care Act signed into law by President Barrack Obama expanded the availability of home visiting creating the federal Maternal, Infant, and Early Childhood Home Visiting (MIECHV) programme. Since then, MIECHV has supported funding of over $1.5 billion to states, territories and tribal entities for home visiting services. Over 75 per cent of these funds are allocated to home visiting services that have been evaluated as having effective strategies and being cost effective with successful outcomes. Currently, 16 home visiting models have been identified as meeting the criteria of rigorous evaluation by the MIECHV programme, including the SafeCare model.

Project 12-Ways

In the late 1970s, few interventions in the United States aimed at preventing child maltreatment. There was, however, a growing literature on parent and child risk factors for child maltreatment. To address these factors, Project 12-Ways was developed based on the social-ecological model outlined by Bronfenbrenner (1979) on the principles of applied behaviour analysis (Lutzker, Martin & Rice, 1981). From examinations of the risk factor literature, Project 12-Ways provided up to 12 discrete services to families in their homes in rural southern Illinois (Lutzker, 1984). Delivered by graduate students and supervised by master-level supervisors, the services were: parent-child training, stress reduction and assertiveness training, self-control training, basic skills training for children, leisure time counselling, marital counselling, alcoholism treatment or referral, social support groups, job-finding training, money management training, health maintenance and nutrition training, and home safety training. A number of published articles documented individual behaviour change in the families' homes, such as removal of home safety hazards (Tertinger, Greene & Lutzker, 1984), changes in positive parenting (Lutzker et al., 1985), child behaviour (Dachman et al., 1984), healthcare skills (Delgado & Lutzker, 1988), headaches (Campbell et al., 1983), and mothers' use of language with their children (Lutzker et al., 1987). Three different outcome evaluations showed that families who received Project 12-Ways services had lowered risks of recidivism (repeated child maltreatment reports) even 4 years after the services, compared with families in a matched comparison group who did not receive those services but received other family preservation services in the same region (Lutzker & Rice, 1984; Lutzker & Rice, 1987). Also, families referred to Project 12-Ways had significantly more child maltreatment reports to child protective services prior to any intervention than the comparison families did, suggesting that the Project 12-Ways families were more 'difficult' to begin with. Because it has always been delivered from an academic setting, its ability to be replicated is limited. That is, the use of highly supervised graduate students as home visitors is far less costly than full or part-time agency-based home visitors. Thus, SafeCare was created (Lutzker & Chaffin, 2012).

SafeCare model

Utilising the most frequently used components from Project 12-Ways, SafeCare includes three modules: parent–child/parent–infant interaction, home safety and health (Guastaferro et al., 2012). Through a series of single-case research design studies with one family, individuals or group of families, each module was developed to focus on behavioural parenting skills to improve parent and child interactions. SafeCare is for children birth to age 5 whose caretakers have been involved with child protective services or referred by community-based organisations for being at risk. SafeCare has shown positive results in reducing child maltreatment and increasing positive parent and child interactions. The National SafeCare Training and Research Center (NSTRC) engages in research efforts and implementation of the SafeCare model on a local, national, and international scale to prevent child maltreatment.

At the beginning of any module, parents receive an assessment followed by explanation and modelling by the home visitor. Each module is commonly implemented in five training sessions and parents must meet the criteria for the skill sets. The health module, for example, teaches parents how to determine when their children are sick or injured and helps identify child symptoms and illnesses to reduce the risk of medical neglect. Parents learn to keep health records, know when to take care of a sick child at home, when to call the pediatrician, or seek emergency care. Nutrition and proper hygiene information is included. To prevent unintentional injury in the home, the home safety module provides skills to identify and eliminate health and safety hazards. A checklist is used for parents to remove hazards within their home or make them inaccessible to their children. The parent–child/parent–infant interactions module consists of training according to the child's age to address differences in developmental needs of infants and young children. It teaches parents how to engage with their children to increase positive interactions and prevent difficult child behaviour.

Results

There are a number of examples of SafeCare's efficacy and effectiveness. Studies have shown behaviour change both within and among individual families. These have included parent–child interactions (Cordon et al., 1998), parent–infant interactions (Guastaferro et al., 2013), use of the model with Spanish-speaking families (Cordon et al., 1998), teaching developmental milestones within the model (Guastaferro, Lutzker & Graham, 2016), using video to teach parent–child interactions (Bigelow & Lutzker, 1998), using smartphones to help families remove accessible hazards in their homes (Jabaley et al., 2011), and improving parents use of child healthcare skills including in a residential facility for mothers with drug addictions (Strong et al., 2014).

The first SafeCare outcome study compared 41 families in Los Angeles, CA who received SafeCare to 41 families who had the same demographic characteristics as the SafeCare families, but received other services. Three years after the end of services, the SafeCare families' recidivism rate was 14 per cent whereas the recidivism rate of the matched families was 44 per cent, a very significant difference. Chaffin and his colleagues (2012) in Oklahoma conducted the largest and longest study in the history of child welfare in the United States with 2,175 families who were referred for child maltreatment across two urban and four rural areas in the state of Oklahoma. Half of the families received enhanced services provided by home visiting agencies and the other half received SafeCare. Randomisation determined which of the areas would receive SafeCare and which would not. Home visitors were trained to deliver SafeCare services in areas randomised to them. Four and a half years after the services ended, large differences in recidivism favoured SafeCare (Chaffin et al. 2012).

SafeCare has been increasingly disseminated in the United Kingdom (Gardner et al., 2014), reducing child neglect. It is cost effective, and well received by mothers. Two quotes from a recent report (Churchill, 2015) exemplify mothers' feelings: 'I saw my health visitor the other day and she said "would you advise SafeCare to other families?" and I said "yeah totally" it's definitely life changing if you stick to it and if you listen it will definitely change your kids' life and your own.' From a health worker: 'Mum has developed a greater understanding of her children's behaviour related to their age and been helped to develop positive parenting strategies. Mum very much valued the SafeCare programme.'

Parent–infant interactions

Language and nurturing are the keys to successful child development. Thus, there is a dedicated SafeCare module on PII for infants from birth to walking. The focus of this module is to teach parents to engage and stimulate their babies, and to learn the critical importance of talking to them as much as possible. All SafeCare training involves *explaining* the target skills and their importance to the parents. For example, the parent would be told how important talking to her baby is even if the baby does not yet understand the words. The sounds of their parents' voices are soothing, and the more language they hear the better their vocabularies will be. Each parenting skill is *modelled* by the home visitor. Thus, for example, the home visitor would show the parent how to play a stretching game with the baby. After observing the home visitor the parent is asked to *show* the home visitor the skill and the mother would also play a stretching game with the baby. *Feedback* from the home visitor on how well the parent is doing in mastering the skills training might include telling the mother that she stretched the baby's arms and legs well, but that she should smile when doing so and tell the baby what she is doing. Feedback continues until the parent has mastered the skills and needs only praise for doing them. Each PII module begins with a review of developmental milestones for infants 0–2-year-old, making sure that parents know what to expect from their babies and to ensure they are alert to delays in developmental milestones. Studies have shown that SafeCare home visitors can successfully teach these milestones developed by the US Centers for Disease Control and Prevention (e.g. Morales, Lutzker, Shanley & Guastaferro, 2015).

Skills are divided into physical (touching, holding and rocking) and nonphysical (smiling, looking, talking and imitating), and their importance is documented. Early research (Lutzker et al., 1987) showed that very high-risk mothers could be taught to improve the quality and quantity of the use of words with their infants. Other SafeCare studies on the PII module showed that it can be used with Spanish speaking mothers (Morales, Lutzker, Shanley & Guastaferro, 2015), and by using technological enhancements (a digital game with pictures of the mothers engaging in the requisite skills running on a continuous loop to view), mothers with intellectual disabilities could learn the skills as well as typically developing mothers (Guastaferro, Lutzker & Graham, 2016).

The SafeCare PII module can be taught to high-risk mothers in six sessions. It equips mothers with essential skills for cognitive, social, and vocabulary development of their infants. This is the most preventive aspect of SafeCare and the module fulfils Hart and Risley's (1985) call to teach young at risk parents these critically important skills.

Key recommendations

- There are a number of evidence-based parenting practices, each serving different age groups and parents with differing levels of risk. There needs to be more collaboration among researchers and workers using different parenting programmes to develop an evidence base for finding the best practices for every individual family.
- Need to develop a system for rating not just the quality of programmes but, importantly, their implementation practices.
- All of these programmes promote talking with babies and children, but none look as closely and systematically at word counts as Hart and Risley or Providence Talks, and thus more research on word counts should take place.
- More long-term data should be collected on vocabulary, academic and social outcomes for children over time.
- Bottom line: All parents need to talk and talk and talk to their babies.

References

Bigelow, K., & Lutzker, J. (1998). Using video to teach planned activities to parents reported for child abuse. *Child & Family Behavior Therapy, 20*(4), 1–14.
Bronfenbrenner, U. (1979). *The ecology of human development*. Cambridge, MA: Harvard University Press.

Campbell, R., O'Brien, S., Bickett, A., & Lutzker, J. (1983). In-home parent training, treatment of migraine headaches, and marital counseling as an ecobehavioral approach to prevent child abuse. *Journal of Behavior Therapy and Experimental Psychiatry, 14*(2), 147–154.

Chaffin, M., Hecht, D., Bard, D., Silovsky, J., & Beasley, W. (2012). A statewide trial of the SafeCare home-based services model with parents in child protective services. *Pediatrics, 129*(3), 509–515.

Churchill, G. (2015). *SafeCare: Evidence from a home based parenting programme for neglect.* London, NSPCC.

Cooke, N., Mackiewicz, S., Wood, C., & Helf, S. (2009). The use of audio prompting to assist mothers with limited English proficiency in tutoring their Pre-Kindergarten children on english vocabulary. *Education and Treatment of Children, 32*(2), 213–229.

Cordon, I., Lutzker, J., Bigelow, K., & Doctor, R. (1998). Evaluating Spanish protocols for teaching bonding, home safety, and health care skills to a mother reported for child abuse. *Journal of Behavior Therapy And Experimental Psychiatry, 29*(1), 41–54.

Dachman, R., Halasz, M., Bickett, A., & Lutzker, J. (1984). A home-based ecobehavioral parent-training and generalization package with a neglectful mother. *Education and Treatment of Children, 7*, 183–202.

Delgado, L., & Lutzker, J. (1988). Training young parents to identify and report their children's illnesses. *Journal of Applied Behavioral Analysis, 21*(3), 311–319.

DiCarlo, C., Onwujuba, C., & Baumgartner, J. (2014). Infant communicative behaviors and maternal responsiveness. *Child & Youth Care Forum, 43*(2), 195–209.

Elder, J., Donaldson, S., Kairalla, J., Valcante, G., Bendixen, R., Ferdig, R., Self, E., Walker, J., Palau, C., & Serrano, M. (2011). In-home training for fathers of children with autism: A follow up study and evaluation of four individual training components. *Journal Of Child & Family Studies,* 20(3), 263–271.

Gardner, R., Hodson, D., Churchill, G., & Cotmore, R. (2014). Transporting and implementing the safeCare(r) home-based programme for parents, designed to reduce and mitigate the effects of child neglect: An initial progress report. *Child Abuse Review, 23*(4), 297.

Gridley, N., Hutchings, J., & Baker-Henningham, H. (2015). The incredible years parent-toddler programme and parental language: A randomised controlled trial. *Child: Care, Health & Development, 41*(1), 103–111.

Guastaferro, K., Lutzker, J., Graham, M., Shanley, J., & Whitaker, D. (2012). SafeCare: Historical perspective and dynamic development of an evidence-based scaled-up model for the prevention of child maltreatment. *Psychosocial Intervention, 21*, 171–180.

Guastaferro, K., Lutzker, J., Jabaley, J., Shanley, J., & Crimmins, D. (2013). Teaching young mothers to identify developmental milestones. *International Journal of Child Health and Human Development, 6*(2), 223–233.

Guastaferro, K., Lutzker, J., & Graham, M. (2016). Using a technological augmentation to enhance parent-infant interactions with parents at risk. *Child & Family Behavior Therapy, 38*(1), 15–31.

Hart, B, & Risley, T. (1995). *Meaningful differences in the everyday experience of young American children.* Baltimore: P.H. Brookes.

Jabaley, J., Lutzker, J., Whitaker, D., & Self-Brown, S. (2011). Using iPhones(tm) to enhance and reduce face-to-face home safety sessions within safeCare(r): An evidence-based child maltreatment prevention program. *Journal of Family Violence, 26*(5), 377–385.

Kuhl, P.K. (2011). Early language learning and literacy: Neuroscience implications for education. *Mind, Brain, and Education, 5*(3), 128–142.

Lutzker, J., Martin, J., & Rice, J. (1981). Behavior therapy in rehabilitation. *Progress in Behavior Modification, 7*, 171–225.

Lutzker, J. (1984). Project 12-Ways: Treating child abuse and neglect from an ecobehavioral perspective. *Parent training: Foundations of research and practice.* 260–291.

Lutzker, J., & Rice, J. (1984). Project 12-ways: Measuring outcome of a large in-home service for treatment and prevention of child abuse and neglect. *Child Abuse & Neglect, 8*(4), 519–524.

Lutzker, J., Megson, D., Webb, M., & Dachman, R. (1985). Validating and training adult-child interaction skills to professionals and to parents indicated for child abuse and neglect. *Journal of Child and Adolescent Psychotherapy, 2,* 91–104.

Lutzker, J., & Rice, J. (1987). Using recidivism data to evaluate Project 12-Ways: An ecobehavioral approach to the treatment and prevention of child abuse and neglect. *Journal of Family Violence, 2*(4), 283–290.

Lutzker, S., Lutzker, J., Braunling-McMorrow, D., & Eddleman, J. (1987). Prompting to increase mother–baby stimulation with single mothers. *Journal of Child and Adolescent Psychotherapy, 4,* 3–10.

Lutzker, J., Bigelow, K., Doctor, R., Gershater, R., & Greene, B. (1998). An ecobehavioral model for the prevention and treatment of child abuse and neglect: History and applications. *A Handbook Of Child Abuse Research And Treatment.* 239–266.

Marulis, L., & Neuman, S. (2010). The effects of vocabulary intervention on young children's word learning: A meta-analysis. *Review of Educational Research, 3,* 300.

Providence Talks (2015). *Providence Talks Pilot Findings & Next Steps.* [online] Available at: http://providencetalks.org/wp-content/uploads/2015/10/providence-talks-pilot-findings-next-steps.pdf (Accessed June 15, 2016).

Self-Brown, S., Cowart-Osborne., M, Baker, E., Thomas, A., et al. (2015). Dad2K: An adaptation of safecare to enhance positive parenting skills with at-risk fathers. *Child & Family Behavior Therapy, 37*(2), 138–155.

Shonkoff, J.P. (2011). Protecting brains, not simply stimulating minds. *Science, 333*(6045), 982–983.

Strong, L., Lutzker, J., Jabaley, J., Shanley, J., et al. (2014). Training mothers recovering from substance abuse to identify and treat their children's illnesses. *International Journal Of Child Health & Human Development, 7*(2), 156–166.

Sumner, S., Mercy, A., Saul, J., Motsa-Nzuza, N., Kwesigabo, G., Buluma, R., Marcelin, L.H., Lina, H., Shawa, M., Moloney-Kitts, M. & Kilbane, T. (2015). Prevalence of sexual violence against children and use of social services—seven countries, 2007–2013. *MMWR. Morbidity And Mortality Weekly Report, 64*(21), 565–569.

Tertinger, D., Greene, B., & Lutzker, J. (1984). Home safety: Development and validation of one component of an ecobehavioral treatment program for abused and neglected children. *Journal of Applied Behavioral Analysis, 17*(2), 159–174.

23

VIDEO INTERACTION GUIDANCE

Promoting secure attachment and optimal development for children, parents and professionals

Hilary Kennedy and Angela Underdown

Video Interaction Guidance (VIG) is an intervention that promotes secure attachment and optimal development for children, parents and professionals through embodiment of its theoretical framework, values and beliefs and the Principles of Attuned Interaction and Guidance (PAIG) (see Figure 23.1 and Table 23.1).

VIG aims to promote enhanced sensitivity and capacity to mentalise in both client and practitioner. VIG has a strong ethical and theoretical base (attachment, cooperative intersubjectivity and mediated learning). It is based on the parent and VIG practitioner reflecting together on strengths-based micro-moments of video, and is client-centred which means moving at the client's pace with their goals in mind. It is an adaptable method that can be applied to any client group, any helping professional and to the system around the client. VIG has an established UK training and accreditation programme through AVIGuk (www.videointeractionguidance. net) which includes ongoing video-reflective supervision and rigorous accreditation criteria. This provides the fidelity of the method.

There are other effective video feedback interventions based on the same aims of enhancing parental sensitivity while helping parents guide their children's development and behaviour, e.g. Video Feedback Intervention to promote Positive Parenting – sensitive discipline, VIPP-SD (Bakermans-Kranenburg et al., 1998), Marte Meo method (Osterman et al., 2010) and Filming Interactions to Further Development, FIND, (Fisher et al., (in press)). It is beyond the scope of the chapter to provide an indepth comparison of VIG but the similarities between the methods are great, all using video of strengths-based moments where parents follow their children's lead to provide the focus of a reflective discussion. The main differences are on the educative-therapeutic continuum with VIG sitting in the middle with a balanced approach where the VIG practitioner judges from moment to moment when to be more educative or therapeutic and when people need information. One unique feature of VIG is that it was developed by putting theory (intersubjectivity) into practice and not as a research method in a university. This means that the fidelity is not in a manual but in the way VIG is delivered. The VIG process is an art, aiming to activate parents into learning to believe in themselves (rather than teaching them what works) while providing support and information as required. The science of VIG is connected to the neurophysiological effect of the intervention. It has been proposed that mirror neurons could be the 'biological correlate' (Wolf et al., 2001) of intersubjectivity.

'The emerging model of mirror neuron functioning corresponds to the second feature of the intersubjective core experience: that as others are encountered they are simultaneously taken as similar and different from oneself' (Seligman, 2009: 504).

The VIG training process, after a short introduction, starts in practice with VIG trainees learning VIG with their first families under close supervision. The VIG supervision process mirrors the core attuned principles and beliefs, in which the supervisor scaffolds each trainee's learning, building on their unique strengths. The trainee practitioner engages in high levels of reflective practice by micro-analysing themselves delivering VIG on video, thus maximising their professional develop-ment while ensuring that the VIG principles are put into practice.

This chapter starts with the strong theoretical core of VIG based on observations of attuned parent-infant interactions, followed by a description of VIG in practice. Strong evidence for the effectiveness of video feedback interventions (and VIG in particular) are presented followed by two innovative UK developments in the perinatal period developed and delivered by the second author. The future for VIG in the 1001 critical days is then considered.

Theoretical core of VIG

The concept of cooperative intersubjectivity (inter-related connectedness) is at the heart of VIG. This means there are two equally important subjects in every con-versation whether adult-adult or adult-child.

Infants thrive when they have loving attention from at least one adult who has the capacity to focus on the infant's needs. Parents and infants both thrive when they are able to enjoy getting to know each other, to read each other's signals, and to develop together. If support is required, parents can be helped to make this emotional connection with their infant through a respectful relationship with a helping professional, working together towards a better future.

In the VIG theoretical model, intersubjectivity (Trevarthan, 1979; Stern, 1995) which is about companionship and collaboration sits as the core, straddled by attach-ment (Bowlby 1969, 1982) which is about nurturing and being nurtured, safety and protection (Cortina & Liotti, 2010) and mediated learning (Vygotsky, 1962) above which is development and the learning from more experienced adults.

Figure 23.1 shows how the theoretical constructs relate to the main categories of the VIG Principles of Attuned Interaction and Guidance (PAIG). This shows that a firm foundation for optimal development within a secure attachment (loving relationship) is built by the adult being attentive to the child, while 'making space'

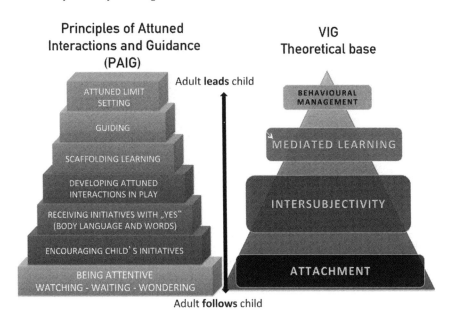

FIGURE 23.1 VIG PAIG and theoretical base

and watching carefully for the child's initiatives. The child feels loved, recognised and important when their parents are interested in their activities and wishes. Once parents notice and respond to their children's initiatives in an attuned way, the relationship can move beyond attachment (the need for safety and protection) to intersubjectivity (play) (sharing and social understanding). This is reached when parents follow their children and children follow the parents in a balanced joyful exchange that makes those involved and onlookers smile. Children and parents thrive and develop at a natural pace enjoying each other's company. Mediated learning (work) provides the theory underpinning 'attuned guidance' when the adult is required to lead the child. For the guidance to be attuned, it has to be in the 'zone of proximal development' (Vygotsky, 1962) of the learner. If the adult's contribution is either too advanced or complex for the child or delivered in such a way that the child does not grasp it, then the interaction ceases to be attuned. This process was first described as 'scaffolding' by Wood et al. (1976) in the context of caregiver–child interaction and the term is now firmly established in early education literature. With babies, interaction frequently moves from attuned to misattuned and VIG supports parents to recognise babies' need for a break ('rupture') and gentle re-attunement to their new emotional state (repair) as described by Tronick (1989) in infant mental health literature.

There are times when adults have to take a stronger lead to repair ruptures and manage their child's problematic behaviour. The theory behind VIG proposes that children are much more likely to follow adults' instructions when they themselves have been understood and followed. When parents are encouraged to provide a firm foundation of love, play and work they find *managing problematic behaviour* much easier.

The Principles (PAIG) in Table 23.1 were derived from the observations of Colwyn Trevarthen, a psychologist and psychobiologist, using ethnological methods. He observed how the tiniest infants are active in developing cooperative activities with their parents. His observations demonstrated the way in which the mother's responsiveness to her baby's initiatives support and develop 'intersubjectivity' (Trevarthen, 1979). Trevarthen viewed this shared understanding as the basis of all effective communication, interaction and learning. Emese Nagy (2014) demonstrates that babies are born ready to take part in an interaction with a partner who is receptive and understands them. She demonstrates that newborn infants can imitate tongue and complex finger gestures. They can take part in a *communicative dialogue* where they also initiate previously imitated gestures. She demonstrated that neonates show distress with an unresponsive interaction partner, make attempts to initiate contact and show joy when the interaction is restored (Nagy et al., 2014).

The 'encouraging initiatives' step of PAIG (Figure 23.1 and Table 23.1) is an important building block in VIG. Here the parent is supported to 'make space' (i.e. become less intrusive) and to 'name' their own and their child's behaviour, thoughts and feelings (termed 'mind-mindedness' by Elizabeth Meins). Encouraging parents to 'use their voice' to let their child know that they are attentive and thinking about the child is crucial for their optimal emotional and language development. The use of parental mind-minded talk by parents has been shown to predict secure attachment, increased play abilities at 2 years, and decreased behaviour problems during the preschool years (Meins et al., 2013).

The central importance in VIG of the *'reception'* of the child's initiative by another is shown in Table 23.1 and Figure 23.2. The important point is that the parent must receive the child, and the child must receive the parent to achieve an attuned interaction. VIG starts with the child's initiative, then looks at the parent's response, which is only deemed 'attuned' if the child receives the response and continues the interaction with another 'turn'. This extended turn-taking and equal contribution to the interaction is core to VIG.

The values and belief system underpinning VIG plays a crucial role in the effectiveness of VIG practitioners. Cooperative intersubjectivity is key to the intervention process (see Figure 23.3), emphasising the importance of a compassionate approach, when hope is maintained and trust is formed through building respectful attuned relationships. VIG practitioners demonstrate these values from the first meeting with parents, through their own attuned interaction. The practitioner conveys that change, even in adverse situations, is always a possibility, and that the key to supporting change is an affirmation and appreciation of *strengths* alongside an empathic regard for what people are already managing in difficult circumstances.

Professionals thrive when they are able to empower parents to make the positive changes; this professional capacity is enhanced if supervision focuses on the practitioner's strengths and how they themselves make attuned connections with

TABLE 23.1 Principles of attuned interactions and guidance (PAIG)

Being attentive	• Looking interested with friendly posture • Giving time and **space** for other • Turning towards • Wondering about what they are doing, thinking or feeling • Enjoying watching the other
Encouraging initiatives	• **Waiting** • Listening actively • Showing emotional warmth through intonation • **Naming** what the child is doing, might be thinking or feeling • Naming what you are doing, thinking or feeling • Using friendly and/or playful intonation as appropriate • **Looking for initiatives**
Receiving initiatives	• Showing you have heard, noticed the other's initiative • Receiving with body language • Being friendly and/or playful as appropriate • Returning eye-contact, smiling, nodding in response • Receiving what the other is saying or doing with words • Repeating/using the other's words or phrases
Developing attuned interactions	• **Receiving and then responding** • Checking the other is understanding you • Waiting attentively for your turn • Having fun • Giving a second (and further) turn on same topic • Giving and taking short turns • Contributing to interaction / activity equally • Co-operating - helping each other
Guiding	• Scaffolding • **Saying 'no' in the 'yes' cycle** (attuned limit setting) • Extending, building on the other's response • Judging the amount of support required and adjusting • Giving information when needed • Providing help when needed • Offering choices that the other can understand • Making suggestions that the other can follow
Deepening discussion	• Supporting goal-setting • Sharing viewpoints • Collaborative discussion and problem-solving • Naming difference of opinion • Investigating the intentions behind words • Naming contradictions/conflicts (real or potential) • Reaching new shared understandings • Managing conflict (back to being attentive and receiving initiatives with the aim of restoring attuned interactions)

DOES PARENT RECEIVE CHILD'S INITIATIVE?

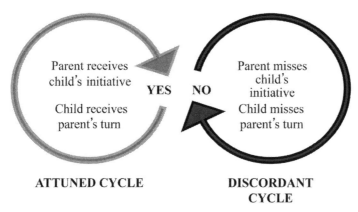

FIGURE 23.2 Yes and no cycle

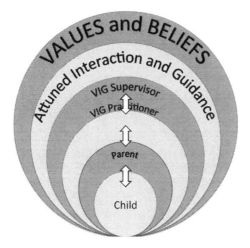

FIGURE 23.3 Nested intersubjectivity

a parent. An understanding of this reflective process, and the development of the VIG practitioner's capacity for attunement and creating an interpersonal yes-cycle is key to the satisfaction and enjoyment discovered by VIG trainees.

VIG in Practice

VIG practitioners take a client-centred approach. At all times they are attentive to the client and receive their concerns. They support the client to be actively engaged in their own change journey. The VIG practitioner takes a short video (5–10 minutes) of parent–child interaction. This video can be coached and is often 'better

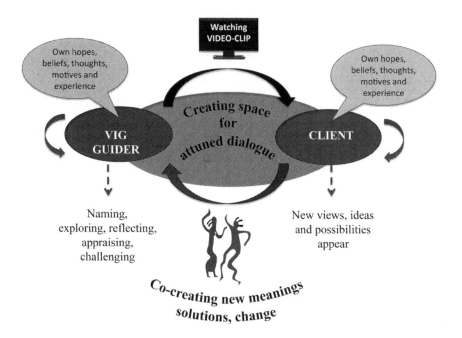

FIGURE 23.4 The VIG shared review

than usual'. The VIG practitioner selects clips to highlight moments of attuned interactions which also relate to the client's goals. These are very likely to be exceptions to the usual pattern and exemplify various principles of attuned contact (Figure 23.1), especially the parent's reception of their child's initiatives (Figure 23.2).

The VIG practitioner shares these video clips with the client in a 'shared review' (Figure 23.4), exploring the video carefully together with the aim of supporting the client to see what they are doing that is making a positive difference to their relationship. Through seeing their own attuned responses, parents can start to observe and to understand how important these experiences are for their child, themselves and for their relationship. Figure 23.4 illustrates the systemic nature of VIG in which space created for attuned dialogue is key to the co-creation of new ideas and narratives. This process is repeated usually for 3–4 'cycles' where a cycle is a video of the client followed by a shared review.

Each VIG cycle is crafted through the skilful use of the PAIG enabling the VIG practitioner to activate the parents in their own learning process, first describing what they see themselves and their child doing, and then exploring their thoughts, feelings and their child's developmental needs. At the same time as viewing an attuned image, the parent is experiencing an attuned interaction with the VIG practitioner who follows their initiatives and values their expertise as a parent.

Research

There is strong evidence for the effectiveness of VIG. Summaries of research are provided in Kennedy et al. (2011), including a chapter by Klein Velderman specifically on promoting parent-infant interaction. Studies since 2011 have found evidence of the effectiveness of video feedback in terms of enhanced sensitivity and improvements in attachment patterns when measured, in the following contexts: parents of preterm babies (Barlow, et al., 2016), Hoffencamp et al., 2015); parents with low-sensitivity (Kalinauskiene et al., 2009); fathers (Lawrence et al., 2013); parents in the child protection system (Moss et al., 2011); postnatal eating disorder (Woolley et al., 2008); infant-parent interaction problems (Høivik et al., 2015); mothers with insecure attachment representations (Cassibba et al., 2015); and adopted infants (Stams et al., 2001). Video feedback methods used with standard paediatric care also show significant impact on child development and maternal depression (Berluke et al., 2014).

As a result of this research video feedback, including VIG, is now recommended as an evidence-based intervention in the National Institute for Clinical Excellence (NICE) guidelines: *Children's Attachment: attachment in children and young people who are adopted from care, in care, or at high risk of going into care* (NICE, 2015), and *Social and Emotional Wellbeing – Early Years* (NICE, 2012).

Looking specifically at VIG, a meta-analysis of 29 studies showed that video feedback produced statistically significant improvement in parenting sensitivity (effect size 0.49); parenting behaviour and attitudes (effect size 0.37); and child development (effect size 0.33) for children aged 0–8 years (Fukkink, 2008). Many of these studies involved 'high risk' dyads (e.g. low SES 63 per cent; parent clinical problems 17 per cent; child clinical problems 52 per cent). Furthermore, a subgroup of studies that examined the effects of VIG using Video Home Training [VHT] interventions) found even larger improvements (e.g. parental behaviour 0.76; parenting skills 0.56 and child development 0.42), although it should be noted that these were mostly pre- to poststudies rather than randomised controlled trials (RCTs).

VIG trained parent-infant psychotherapists are impressed by the speed with which some parents with significant mental health problems can change their representations of themselves as parents and their perception of their child. They document VIG's power to enable parents to move from a negative representation of their relationship with their child to a more positive and hopeful narrative (Pardoe, 2016) while decreasing anxiety in the parents (Celebi, 2013). Celebi proposes that effective VIG intervention changes neural pathways and internal representations by creating moments of connectedness which impact on internal chemicals.

Innovative perinatal VIG in the United Kingdom

Over the last quarter of a century in the Netherlands video has been used to support early relationships, and pioneering programmes developed offering the intervention in maternity units. The next sections describe the development of recent innovative

UK work, focusing on early primary prevention. First a research study is outlined where VIG was offered to parents whose babies were born preterm. The second example illustrates a case study using VIG antenatally to support a mother with a history of babies removed because of neglect.

Supporting families where babies were born preterm

Babies born preterm face a range of adverse outcomes and although the evidence suggests that many of the difficulties result from compromised neurological functioning, recent research suggests that other factors, such as parental sensitivity also play a role (Milgrom et al., 2010). Babies born preterm who experience sensitive responsive interaction have better socio-emotional and cognitive developmental outcomes (Landry et al., 2006). However, studies show that parents and preterm babies are likely to experience less sensitive responsive interaction. This is due to a whole range of factors such as high levels of parental anxiety and babies who are less mature interactional partners.

A pilot randomised control trial (RCT) (Barlow et al., 2016) examined whether VIG was effective support for early interaction between babies born preterm and their parents. Thirty-one parents were recruited from a neonatal intensive care unit (NICU) and were randomised into two groups. Following discharge from the NICU all families were offered usual healthcare and, additionally, the intervention group received three visits where VIG was offered. Semistructured interviews were conducted following the intervention and the analysis indicated that all parents found the intervention acceptable and many found it extremely beneficial:

> I really like the baby cues that we learnt from the additional visits . . . Just being able to get some idea of what he wants, that's magical that, that's really really good . . . I think it was incredible to watch and to see from such a small baby, that already they are giving you some communication . . . to think that there's some communication from babies, is really wow. It's really good.

> I worried about the time that we missed when I wasn't able to kind of hold him all the time or be with him. Um. And worried about the kind of bond if you like then. So having those visits and looking at that and seeing that it was already there was really helpful for me.

The quantitative results showed large but nonsignificant differences favouring the intervention group for parental sensitivity ($d = 0.86$; $p = 0.069$) and infant cooperativeness ($d = 0.78$; $p = 0.10$). There were medium to large nonsignificant differences favouring the intervention group for depression ($d = 0.33$; $p = 0.41$), anxiety ($d = 0.38$; $p = 0.30$), and parenting stress ($d = 0.87$; $p = 0.14$). The study concluded that VIG appears to be a promising early intervention while more research is needed to strengthen the evidence base.

Supporting parents in the ante natal period with VIG

The next example illustrates how VIG has been used to support relationships between mothers and their unborn babies in the 'Family Drug and Alcohol (FDAC)' project. FDAC is a court-based programme aiming to improve children's care by early intervention and helping parents tackle entrenched problems. FDAC successfully uses VIG to enable parents to focus on the interactional relationship between themselves and their child. As the project developed more mothers were referred in the antenatal period. This posed challenges regarding whether VIG could be effective in building the relationship between mothers and their unborn children. The following case study records this work.

Case study

Mia, who had been in care from the age of 15 years, experienced childhood trauma including sexual abuse. She had a history of homelessness, drug addiction and being in violent relationships. Mia had two previous babies removed because of neglect, despite being in rehabilitation and a mother-baby placement. She described how she felt 'emotionally detached' and 'not really there at all'. Now in her thirties and pregnant for the third time, Mia was motivated to try VIG with her worker, Fay. Mia met with Fay three times prenatally and again postnatally and the sessions were video taped and brought to supervision. Fay used the attunement principles skilfully to build a trusting relationship with Mia who gained confidence in reflecting on her unborn child. For example, Mia brought her baby's scan picture to one session and Fay gave Mia space and time-to-talk by receiving each comment meaningfully. Mia's confidence visibly grew and she became animated imagining what her baby was like, touching her 'bump' and talking to her unborn baby. By taking short conversational turns, Fay validated Mia's growing enthusiasm and sense of wonder about her baby. Mia reported enjoying the space and time to think about the connection she had with her baby.

Postnatally Fay shared the videos she made of early interaction between Mia and her new baby. Mia identified where she and the baby held one another's gaze and mirrored each other's expressions and she talked enthusiastically about her baby's likes and dislikes. Mia said she felt very connected to her baby this time.

Theory-practice links

The prenatal sessions validated Mia's perceptions about her baby and enabled her rich representations to be heard and affirmed. Watching the film in supervision, Fay identified how she attuned with Mia and scaffolded her growing sense of wonder about her developing baby. For Mia the VIG sessions offered opportunities to build new representations of herself as a mother alongside imagining what this baby might be like. A mother's mental representation of herself as a parent and her growing fetus as a baby has been significantly linked with the security of the infant's attachment to the parents at 1 year of age (Benoit et al., 1997). Mother's bonding is associated with making healthier choices, and with later caregiving (Goecke et al., 2012).

Being reflective about the unborn baby can be challenging when mothers have experienced previous perinatal loss, particularly if grieving is unresolved (Slade et al., 2009). Using the film within an attuned validating relationship enabled Mia to rethink her representations of herself as a mother and to engage with her baby as an individual with his own feelings and personality. Evidence indicates that parental capacity to reflect on infants as individuals with their own temperament and feelings has significant consequences for baby's developing sense of self, capacity for regulation and engagement with the environment (Fonagy et al ., 2004).

Conclusion

The use of VIG at the very start of life (even in the perinatal period) shows extremely promising results for the development of an attuned parent-child relationship and secure attachment. Beyond this, parents develop the capacity to mentalise, understanding what they are doing when things work and why they have found it difficult in the past. Very few interventions focus so equally and clearly on increasing sensitivity *and* mentalisation. It is this that makes VIG such an efficient intervention.

VIG practitioners (e.g. psychiatrists, psychologists, social workers, health visitors, nursery nurses) all experience the power of VIG to promote positive change. To many it is surprising that such entrenched and complex presenting problems can start shifting after the first session and that these changes trigger further improvement in many areas of the parent's life. Each success makes it easier for them to engage a new family on a VIG journey and they meet them with authentic hope that things will change. It is a nourishing way for professionals and parents to work and the changes for the parents and children are heart-warming and of central importance for all involved.

Take away points

- Training in VIG should be core for all professionals providing support to parents during the first 1001 critical days.
- Innovative VIG training methods should be developed to enhance and shorten the training process.
- Further development of VIG is needed in specialist centres (e.g. Family Drug and Alcohol Court, Specialist Perinatal Mental Health Teams (in and out-patient) domestic violence programmes).
- Research is required to test the effectiveness and cost-effectiveness of VIG intervention compared to 'care as usual' and other video feedback methods.

The authors would like to thank Monica Celebi, Angela Latham and Rachel Pardoe for their reflections on this chapter, which has shaped the final version.

References

Bakermans-Kranenburg, M.J., Juffer F., & Van Ijzendoorn M.H. (1998). Interventions with video feedback and attachment discussions: Does type of maternal insecurity make a difference? *Infant Mental Health Journal, 19*(2), 202–219.

Barlow, J., Sembi, S., & Underdown, A. (2016). Pilot RCT of the use of Video Interaction Guidance with preterm babies. *Journal of Reproductive and Infant Psychology, 34*(5), 511–524.

Benoit, D., Parker, K., & Zeanah, C. (1997). Mothers' representations of their infants assessed prenatally: Stability and association with infants' attachment classifications. *Journal of Child Psychology and Psychiatry, 38*(3), 307–313.

Berluke, S.B., Cates, C.B., Dreyer, B.P., Huberman, H.S., Arevalo, J., Burtchen, N., Weisleder, A., & Mendelsohn, A.L. (2014). Reducing maternal depressive symptoms through promotion of parenting in pediatric primary care. *Clinical Pediatrics, 53*(5), 460–469.

Bowlby, J. (1969/1982). *Attachment*. Vol. I. New York: Basic Books.

Cassibba, R., Castoro, G., Costantino, E., Sette, G., & Van Ijzendoorn, M.H. (2015). Enhancing maternal sensitivity and infant attachment security with video feedback: An exploratory study in Italy. *Infant Mental Health Journal, 36*, 53–61.

Celebi, M. (2013). Helping to reduce parental anxiety in the perinatal period. *Journal of Health Visiting, 1*(8), 438–442.

Cortina M., & Liotti, G. (2010). Attachment is about safety and protection, Intersubjectivity is about sharing and social understanding: The relationships between Attachment and Intersubjectivity. *Psychoanalytic Psychology, 27*(4), 410–441.

Fisher, P.A., Frenkel, T.I., Noll, L.K., Berry, M., & Yockelson, M. (in press). Promoting healthy child development via a two-generation translational neuroscience framework: The FIND video coaching program. *Child Development Perspectives, 10*(4), 251–256.

Fonagy, P., Gergely, G., Jurist, E., & Target, M. (2004). *Affect Regulation, Mentalization and the Development of the Self.* London: Karnac.

Fukkink, R.G. (2008). Video feedback in widescreen: A meta-analysis of family programs. *Clinical Psychology Review, 28*(6), 904–16.

Goecke, T., Voight, F., Faschingbauer, F., Spangler, G., Beckman, M., Beckman, M., & Beetz, A. (2012). The association of prenatal attachment and perinatal factors with pre and postpartum depression in first time mothers. *Archives of Gynecology and Obstetrics, 286*(2), 309–316.

Hoffenkamp H.N., Tooten, A., Hall, R.A.S., Braeken, J., Eliëns, M.P.J., Vingerhoets, A.J.J.M., & van Bakel, H.J.A. (2015). Effectiveness of hospital-based video interaction guidance on parental interactive behavior, bonding, and stress after preterm birth: A randomized controlled trial. *Journal of Consulting and Clinical Psychology, 83*(2), 416–429.

Hoivik M.S., Lydersen S., Drugli M.B., Onsoien R., Hansen M.B., & Berg-Nielsen, T.S. (2015). Video feedback compared to treatment as usual in families with parent–child interactions problems: A randomized controlled trial. *Child and Adolescent Psychiatry and Mental Health, 9*(1), 3.

Kalinauskiene, L., Cekuoliene, D., VanIJzendoorn, M.H., Bakermans-Kranenburg, M.J., Juffer, F., & Kusakovskaja, I. (2009). Supporting insensitive mothers: The Vilnius randomized control trial of video-feedback intervention to promote maternal sensitivity and infant attachment security. *Child: Care, Health and Development, 35*(5), 613–623.

Kennedy, H., Landor, M., and Todd, L. (eds). (2011). *Video Interaction Guidance: A Relationship-based Intervention to Promote Attunement, Empathy and Wellbeing.* London: Jessica Kingsley Publishers.

Landry, S.H., Smith, K.E., Swank, P.R. (2006) Responsive parenting; establishing early foundations for social, communication, and independent problem-solving skills. *Developmental Psychology, 42*(4), 627–42.

Lawrence, P.J., Davies, B., & Ramchandani, P.G. (2013). Using video feedback to improve early father-infant interaction: A pilot study. *Clinical Child Psychology and Psychiatry, 18*(1), 61–71.

Meins, E., Muñoz-Centifanti, L.C., Fernyhough, C., & Fishburn, S. (2013). Maternal mind mindedness and children's behavioral difficulties: Mitigating the impact of low socioeconomic status. *Journal of Abnormal Child Psychology, 41,* 543–553

Milgrom, J., Newnham, C., Anderson, P.J., Doyle, L.W., Gemmill, A.W., Lee, K., Hunt, R.W., Bear, M., & Inder, T. (2010) Early sensitivity training for parents of preterm infants: impact on the developing brain. *Pediatric Research, 67,* 330–335.

Moss, E., Dubois-Comtois, K., Cyr, C., Tarabulsy, G.M., St-Laurent, D., & Bernier, A. (2011). Efficacy of a home-visiting intervention aimed at improving maternal sensitivity, child attachment, and behavioral outcomes for maltreated children: A randomized control trial. *Development and Psychopathology, 23,* 195–210.

Nagy, E.,Pal, A., & Orvos, H. (2014). Learning to imitate individual finger movements by the human neonate. *Developmental Science, 17*(6), 841–857.

NICE (2012). *NICE Guidelines: Social and Emotional Wellbeing,* online at: http://nice.org.uk/guidance/PH40 (accessed 03/07/16).

NICE (2015). NICE Guidelines: *Children's attachment: attachment in children and young people who are adopted from care, in care or at high risk of going into care,* online at: http://nice.org.uk/guidance/ng26 (accessed 03/07/16).

Osterman, G., Möller, A., & Wirtberg, I. (2010). The Marte Meo method as a means of supporting new adoptive parents. *Adoption & Fostering, 34,* 49–57.

Pardoe, R. (2016). Integrating Video Interaction Guidance (VIG) and Psychoanalytic Psychotherapy in Work with Parents and Infants. *Bulletin of the Association of Child Psychotherapists,* May 2016.

Seligman, S. (2009) Anchoring intersubjective models in recent advances in developmental psychology, cognitive neuroscience and parenting studies: Introduction to Papers by Trevarthen, Gallese, and Ammaniti and Trentini *Psychoanalytic Dialogues, 19,* 503–506, 2009.

Slade, A., Cohen, L., Sadler, L., Miller, M. (2009). The psychology and psychopathology of pregnancy. Reorganization and transformation. In *Handbook of infant mental health,* 22–39. 3rd ed. New York: The Guilford Press.:

Stams G-J.J.M., Juffer F., van IJzendoorn M.H., Hoksbergen R.C. (2001). Attachment-based intervention in adoptive families in infancy and children's development at age 7: Two follow-up studies. *British Journal of Developmental Psychology, 19,* 159–80.

Trevarthen, C. (1979). Communication and cooperation in early infancy: A description of primary intersubjectivity. In M. Bullowa (Ed.), *Before speech: The beginning of human communication,* 321–346. London: Cambridge University Press.

Tronick, E.Z. (1989). Emotions and emotional communication in infants. *American Psychologist, 44,* 112–119.

Vygotsky, L.S. (1962). *Thought and language.* Cambridge, MA: MIT Press (Original work published 1934).

Wolf, N., Gales, M., Shane, E., & Shane, M. (2001) The developmental trajectory from amodal perception to empathy and communication: The role of mirror neurons in this process. *Psychoanalytic Inquiry, 21*(1), 94 –112.

Wood, D., Bruner, J.S., & Ross, G. (1976), The role of tutoring in problem-solving. *Journal of Child Psychology and Psychiatry*, 17, 89–100.

Wooley, H., Hertzman, L., & Stein, A. (2008). Video feedback intervention with mothers with postnatal eating disorders and their infants. In F. Juffer, M. Bakermans-Kranenburg, & M. van IJzendoorn (Eds.), *Promoting positive parenting: An attachment based intervention*. New York, NY: Taylor & Francis.

24

LIFE 'IS LIKE A BOX OF CHOCOLATES'

Interventions with special-needs babies

Stella Acquarone

Cognitive potential is essential for everyday life. But a baby's cognitive potential can be impaired by destructive emotions, insecure attachments and fragile relationships brought on by surprise complications. For special-needs babies, early interventions use the power of early interactions to recover cognitive potential. So, how can the early interventionist divert special-needs babies' development away from parents' increasing concern, worry, distress and despair towards better outcomes, even to joy and happiness?

Such recoveries are possible for three reasons:

- *re-Wiring* and the neuroscience of early development (**recovery from the inside-out**) . . . from conception to around 3 years old, the baby's brain undergoes tremendous growth and displays enormous plasticity;
- *re-Discovering* the unique personality of the infant (**recovery from discovery**) . . . the desire to develop intimacy, keeping in mind family history, the accumulation of trauma and prior personal experience; and
- *re-Developing* and the psychoanalytic tools for intervening early (**recovery from the outside-in**) . . . the therapist uses family relationships, feelings and emotions and the psychological functioning of the mind to re-direct family dynamics and the baby's development.

In parent-infant psychotherapy and early intervention, the baby, the parents and the therapist each have a role to play in re-wiring, re-discovering and re-developing their relationships.

Boxful of (costly) complications

Some parents of the 699,000 babies born in the United Kingdom each year face a boxful of assorted complications. Around 6 per cent of their babies will be disabled children. And the parents themselves may struggle: 16 per cent of working age adults and 45 per cent of adults over State Pensions age are in some way disabled. These are big numbers. And costly. Over a lifetime, for example, 7,690 of the babies born this year are headed to a life with autism, one in every 91 births. Each one will require an estimated £2.5 million in additional services, so the total cost to society for preautistic babies born just this year is *£242.8 million* (699,000/ 91 × £2,500,000/79.1 years, the average life expectancy of males in the UK in 2012). And this doesn't include:

- the social costs . . . more specialised institutions and a greater use of social services,
- the family costs . . . stretching of family resources . . . more divorce, and misery, and
- the costs to the special-needs children . . . who find it difficult to develop their potential beyond their label and to relate to the family.

(Acquarone, 2007)

These very real risks and costs are why having a child is a bit like opening a box of chocolates . . . you can be surprised *and* disappointed. Paraphrasing Forrest Gump, you never know what you're going to get (hence the surprise) and, paraphrasing Japanese novelist Haruki Murakami, even the chocolates you left in the box (to avoid disappointment) can help get you through painful and difficult circumstances.

When parents receive news of complications, birth defects or chromosomal problems or when their infant shows difficulties in attachment very early on, some of them will need a kind of specialised and focused help to offset destructive emotions and re-establish the family on a healthy line of development. This help is called parent–infant psychotherapy and it comes in the form of an early intervention, sometimes an *intensive* early intervention. Consider the following case landscape:

- *Abigail*, 9 months old, had been diagnosed with cerebral palsy 2 months before. The mother told me that even though she had yet to hurt her baby, she feared her impulse to leave Abigail alone in a room when she started screaming, or to shake her until she stopped.

  [Cerebral palsy is a group of permanent movement disorders and occurs in about 2.1 in 1,000 births (Oskoui et al., 2013).]
- *Peter*, 3 weeks old, was abandoned in the maternity ward, left for adoption because he has Downs syndrome.

  [Downs syndrome is a genetic disorder occurring in about 1 in 1000 births (Weijerman & de Winter, 2010).]

- *Christian*, 2 years old, would lie on the floor looking in the air, moving his open hands in front of him. If in the nursery he would lie under a table, never interacting with anyone.

    [Autism is a neurodevelopmental disorder characterised by impaired social interaction, verbal and nonverbal communication, and restricted and repetitive behaviour and occurs in 1.1 per cent of the general population (Baird, 2003) and in 25 per cent of the children born premature (Limperopoulos et al., 2008, Samra et al., 2008).]

Psychotherapy and early (usually preverbal) interventions like the ones detailed below for Abigail, Peter and Christian have been shown to prevent secondary developments of psychosis (Massie & Rosenthal, 1984) and relieve children of an extra burden on their overall development potential (Acquarone, 2004).

Hypothesis

Early interventions are necessary when the destructive emotional factors underlying family dynamics interfere with relationships and development. Destructive emotions can smother constructive development. Unless we deal with the underlying emotional dynamics, special-needs babies can't reach their cognitive potential . . . and might even die. One of the strengths of this hypothesis is that it recognises secondary disability, that whatever a child's specific difficulty may be, the parent's sorrow, anger and guilt can be just as damaging to a healthy relationship as the disability itself.

We have to be careful. The disability at birth 'evokes primitive fears and fantasies, including damage, guilt and loss' (Hollins, 2000). To deal with destructive emotions, she says, 'experience and skill are required to put into words what someone cannot say for themselves [particularly about their past trauma] . . . and help them understand more than they can communicate in words'.

The hypothesis at work

So, how can we use our hypothesis, experience and skill to recover at-risk parent–infant relationships? Keep in mind that in dealing with the underlying emotional dynamics there are powerful hidden components at play:

- *ghosts* from their own past which parents have to face or suppress,
- *excitement* or *sorrow* that the newcomer incites,
- *impact* and *effect* of bad news, genetic disorders and syndromes,
- *continuous search* that parents make for the unique personality of their infant(s),
- *desire for intimacy* with them.

The push and pull of these dynamics can make any early intervention tricky, particularly when they are unspoken (as with parents) or preverbal (as with babies). Take, for example, dealing with parents' 'ghosts'. *Ghosts* are the intergenerational transmission of conflict when children are not seen as themselves but as others. These *ghosts* can be reactivated by the parents' fear of having damaged their own child, or as they face the real challenges of their special-needs children. Any hate, anger, or other negative feeling needs to be integrated with the positive rather than left detached and dissociated, creating secondary disabilities. In putting our hypothesis to work and free from destructive emotions, the child and the family are also free to believe that they *can* do rather than they *cannot*.

Points to consider

The power of the early intervention is its ability to produce better outcomes (Massie & Rosenthal, 1984). Our findings confirm this. Early interventions work for three reasons:

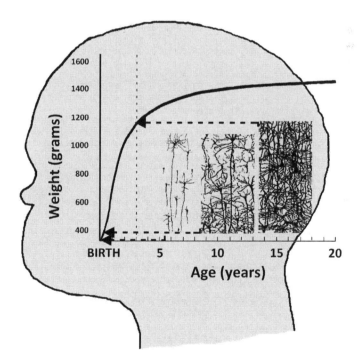

FIGURE 24.1 Baby brains wire-up fastest

Reprinted by permission of the publisher from *The Postnatal Development of the Human Cerebral Cortex, Vols. I–VIII* by Jesse LeRoy Conel, Cambridge, Mass.: Harvard University Press. Copyright ©1939, 1975 by the President and Fellows of Harvard College.

After a baby is born, new synapses form at the rate of one million connections per second, making baby brains more active than adult brains. At birth there are few connections. As a result babies are more open to learning from their environment (Levine & Munsch, 2013). The experiences actually shape the development of synaptic connections and the formation of their brains (Rosenzweig, Breedlove & Watson, 2005).

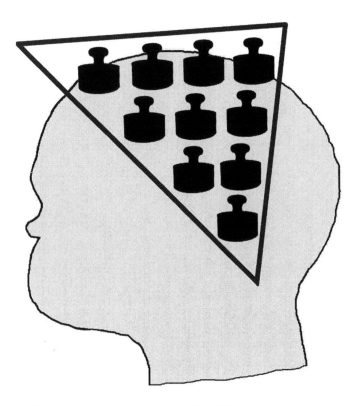

FIGURE 24.2 Accumulated trauma can impact later life

Before the first encounter with special-needs children, family history and experiences must be considered:

1) circumstances around conception and pregnancy (deaths, trauma, IVF, *etc.*)
2) birth experience (more or less trauma)
3) vulnerability of the child, brain damage or deficiency, either congenital or acquired, birth defect, multiple early operations, a syndrome, prematurity, or emotional disability, and sometimes
4) autistic behaviours, here considered as a child being overwhelmed by their circumstances because of their physical disability and/or emotional inability to regulate and cope.

FIGURE 24.3 Eternal triangle relationships can change neural connections

The 'eternal triangle' is the basic premise on which we build relationships. It helps us:

- visualise the psychodynamics of our emotional aspects,
- see the individual child beyond the label,
- perceive potential and development as a challenge, not a disgrace,
- internalise a different life, but not less, and
- offset the destructive behaviours and emotions that interfere with good neural connectivity of the baby's frontal cortex.

Our approach

Because of the tricky emotional landscape, treating parents with special-needs children is challenging. The landscape opened up when Ferenczi (1929) first described the vulnerability of the unwelcome child. Other professionals have since observed:

- parents fear their murderous wishes, which sometimes go back to prenatal experiences (Mannoni, 1973),
- what *is* the bonding attachment at birth between parent and their special-needs child? (Blacher & Meyers, 1983),
- a high proportion of psychosis before 4 years of age is found in children born with or developing an early physical disability (Massie and Rosenthal, 1984),

- children defending themselves against trauma are also defending themselves against psychosis (Sinason, 1986), and
- parents find it difficult to speak about their child as a separate person, as if they have never mourned an expected healthy one (Sinason, 1988).

Whatever the special-needs disability of the newcomer, the box-of-chocolates dynamic places an extra burden on emotions and thinking. In front of bad news, parents can be shocked and hurt. Without the availability of a relationship, the baby may or may not find the resources for self-preservation. It's no wonder that both parents and babies need the services of an outside professional to hold their avalanche of feelings – reactivated as well as experienced – and talk about them openly.

How to identify special needs infants

Broadly speaking, we can identify the special-needs child by looking for the early signs of alarm and believing mothers when they express their feelings and their perceptions about their babies. They are mostly right when they say that their babies don't feel close to them, or interested in them, or do not mould to them when picked up, or prefer to be alone, or mostly look blank and not engaged with who-ever speaks or feeds them.

Based on the work of Massie and Rosenthal (1984), we developed a scale to guide us through the relationship recovery process. Our scale is a succinct and stra-tegic arrangement of standard components of an infant and mother in interaction. In addition to looking for any past psychiatric illness or traumas, we look for the capacity and quality of the:

- **interpersonal relationship**: do they look at each other? Babble? Imitate each other? Take turns? Does the baby provoke the mother into interaction? Play? Expressing emotions directly?
- **sensorial perception**: hyper/hypo sensibility of hearing, seeing, touching, tasting and smelling.
- **motor area**: hyper/hypo tonicity of the muscles, postural aspects, head stance and language of the body as areas that need help to respond appropriately.
- **affects**: the capacity to express the right emotion at the right moment as a right response to satisfying physical or psychological needs or expressed as a result of being aware of what is happening around them.
- **parents' concerns about their child's emotional wellbeing**: lack or too much response to their interactions.

What we are looking for is what babies need most: interaction with caregivers. Without this interaction, special-needs babies can get stuck in fighting or avoiding the persons around them and become scared. Interactions are the normal way babies develop – or alter – their fundamental feelings about themselves and their link with the world. Without interaction and with their cognition impaired, these babies-at-risk are unable to link emotions. And if their babies do not relate to them, the mothers become more anxious or depressed (St Clair, Danon-Boileau & Trevarthen, 2007) and find it difficult to experience joy and fun. Most regrettably, they are not believed by the primary system of care.

How to treat

Basically, there are consultations, interventions, early interventions and intensive early interventions. The goal of these forms of treatment is to help parents find other ways to relate, to interest, and to stimulate their special-needs child without being intrusive:

- *Consultations*: of 1 hour to help parents gain insight to what is going on in their baby's mind, their sensitivities (to noise or light or to tension and anger), what causes them upsets, or people around who trigger emotional dys-regulation.
- *Interventions*: in many cases, interventions can be handled by child-centric cognitive, behavioural, speech and language, occupational, physio, music and play therapists.
- *Early interventions*: with non- and preverbal children will probably require specialist parent-infant psychotherapists, or psychologists and occupational therapists specialised in the understanding of nonverbal communications and their unconscious meanings.
- *Intensive early interventions*: a multidisciplinary treatment with all of the above, plus child, couple, sibling and adult psychotherapists *at the same time*. The intensive early intervention is particularly effective with toddlers already showing autistic-like behaviours. This all-inclusive intervention includes working with nurseries and schools staff that with training can do much to ameliorate a great deal of the severity of autistic behaviours.

The good interventionist works with the parents as well as with the baby. This is important. Parents must know first-hand what affects attachment . . . is it the child's inability to relate, a physical or psychological impediment, and what effect does it trigger in themselves? Keep in mind that parents are 24/7 with their child and once they discover something new and helpful, they can continue think-ing and discussing it further at home, and inform the grandparents and other caregivers.

The results

We've developed a unique way of graphing concerns over time – before and after treatment, and later – so that we can see and track improvement (or regression).

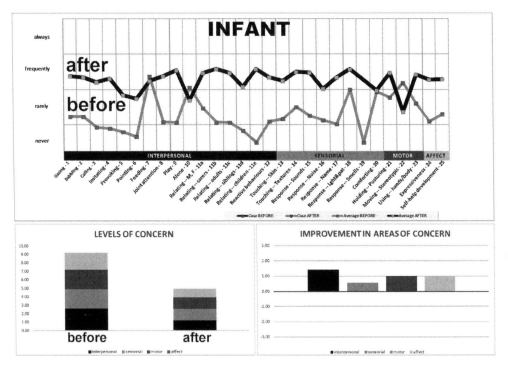

FIGURE 24.4 Graphs of infant and mother before and after treatment

The horizontal lines in the top charts show the before and after treatment averages of 30 cases (Figure 24.4). The bar graphs show improvements (or not) in the primary areas of concern: interpersonal, sensorial, motor and affect areas.

The table of ratios show the average outcomes in different age ranges and in each area of concern (Figure 24.5). Overall, babies show far more change than their mothers, by a ratio of 1.67 to 1. And the effect of intervening early is clear: the younger the baby, the more the baby changes relative to the changes in the mother. You can see, for example, that an intensive intervention in the baby's first year will result in twice as much change in the infant as in the mother – almost 2 to 1 (see Figure 24.5 circle A, or 1.99 to 1). The table shows that as babies get older and mothers 'accommodate' or adapt to them, for the baby to change, the mother must change too. For example, following an intensive intervention, infants in the 0–1 age group saw the biggest change in their 'sensorial' area, but mothers changed most in 'affect', suggesting when babies responded better physically, the mothers responded better emotionally. In the more 'accommodated' 2–3 age range, the intervention caused a bigger change in the babies' 'interpersonal' behaviour, but in the mothers – as in the mothers in all age groups – the intensive intervention caused them to feel better emotionally towards their babies.

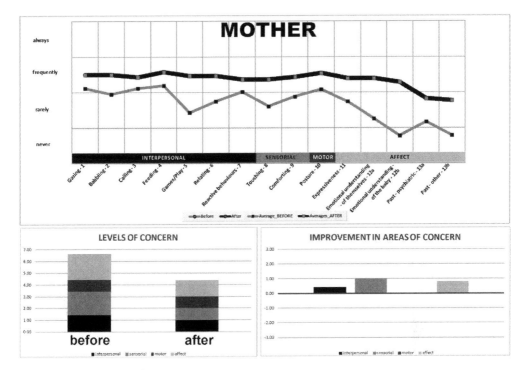

FIGURE 24.4 *continued*

Changes BY AGE	Ratio of Changes BABY:MOTHER		BABIES				MOTHERS			
All Babies	**1.67 : 1** = 0.97 / 0.58		1.17	0.93	0.74	1.02	0.46	0.50	0.38	0.97
AGE 0-1	Ⓐ **1.99 : 1** = 1.02 / 0.51		0.98	1.52	0.43	1.15	0.40	0.20	0.40	1.05
AGE 1-2	Ⓑ **1.71 : 1** = 1.31 / 0.77		1.42	0.67	1.17	2.00	0.78	0.83	0.33	1.33
AGE 2-3	Ⓒ **1.61 : 1** = 1.08 / 0.67		1.23	1.06	0.96	1.09	0.83	0.63	0.38	0.85

average BABIES average MOTHERS INTERPERSONAL SENSORIAL MOTOR AFFECT INTERPERSONAL SENSORIAL MOTOR AFFECT

FIGURE 24.5 Table of ratios before and after treatment

Cases explained

Abigail

Abigail was 9 months old, diagnosed with cerebral palsy. She was not thriving. I observed her hanging from her mother's arm. They didn't look at each other.

The mother transmitted unspoken anger and frustration. Because she had an elder daughter, she said she knew early on something was terribly wrong with Abigail. She had had a bad pregnancy, she explained, with near-death experiences. Abigail's reaction to her way of being held and her mother's murderous feelings was of complete panic, screaming as if she was going to die. The two of them seemed caught by life and unable to move on.

I formulated an approach based on:

- Bick's (1968) concept of the skin and its function in the formation of relation-ships,
- Spitz's (1948) studies on the somatic consequences of emotional starvations in connection with mother's grief and
- Ferenczi's (1929) insights of the unwelcomed baby's wish to die.

Then, I devised the following strategy: I would 'listen' for the baby's needs and state of mind, and decode them for the mother. At the same time, I encouraged the mother to touch her baby while maintaining a secure empathetic relationship with me. By continuing to interpret and translate her baby's reactions to new needs over 18 fortnightly sessions, Abigail's inner world developed, and their ideas of each other changed. And once positive interaction became established, other pro-fessionals could get involved to further secure the attachment.

Ten and 15 years later the follow ups from the school and interviews with the mother and child showed a severely physically disabled child who was thriving acade-mically and socially and was loved and admired by everybody (Acquarone, 1995).

Peter

Peter, 3 weeks old, Down's syndrome, was left in the hospital. The mother was very troubled about having had such a disabled child so soon after her mother and mother-in-law died. She was told a lot of negatives: that Peter was not going to go to university, may develop heart trouble, followed by even more troubles, etc. But what did she feel about Peter? . . . look at him and describe him to me, I asked. She just cried a lot saying that in her culture she had to allow the father-in-law to come to the house to live and it was too much for her.

Both parents had five sessions in total where they learned to find the positives in their baby. They also learned to speak about feelings and cultural issues. Follow ups showed a good relationship with Peter's parents and siblings (who had come to the later sessions). He was integrated in mainstream education, and finished university in film studies.

Christian

Christian, 2 years old, with severe autistic behaviours, was diagnosed in the United States but the family had moved permanently to the United Kingdom. He was brought up in a bilingual household, the youngest of three boys, but he didn't speak, didn't imitate, preferred isolation, kept stiff open hands in front of his eyes, made flapping movements and strange breathing noises each time he felt under pressure to move or go out. Both parents worked and Christian was in a nursery for very young children. He lived happily in his own world composed of his hands and almost constant lethargy.

Christian was a good candidate for the Re:Start Infant-Family Programme, our intensive treatment programme for preautism. We saw him, his parents and siblings for 6 hours every day for 3 weeks. Christian was accustomed to being treated like a teddy bear, being tossed about without feelings because he never showed any. He was hypersensitive to noises and any emotional upsets. But in our programme, Christian learned about feelings and himself as a person. He became motivated to speak, slowly at first, verbalising his fears, anger, and expectations. Using scaffolding techniques, his parents and nanny taught him to use his hands differently for each activity and stay with the activity, paying attention and concentrating. In the process they discovered much about Christian and as much or more about themselves. Emotionally, the family changed, accepting different members at their own pace. We trained the one-to-one at the nursery and continued seeing the family once a week for a year. Follow ups showed steady social and academic progress and he married at 28 years old.

Conclusion

'Box-of-chocolates' is a suggestive metaphor for parents' expectations and their baby's 'assortment' of special needs. It is a way of explaining the complex matrix of primitive emotions which can disrupt development. We've seen how these complications and emotions can prevent parents from establishing a good attachment with their special-needs child. I have described four types of interventions we've developed to help parents better understand their newcomer. Without that understanding, parents may find it difficult to accommodate, adapt to and love their child.

Our experience has shown that unless professionals help parents deal with the underlying emotional dynamics, their special-needs children will find it difficult to recover enough cognitive potential to deal in the everyday world. Parent–infant psychotherapists are trained to deal with the emotions in a child's preverbal world and it takes experience and skill to intervene early, particularly in cases of preautism when a multidiscipline, intensive, family, early intervention is needed.

But while the early intervention is not easy, the results are well worth the effort. In order to help the 'needle in a haystack' we have to:

- look for the early signs of alarm,
- take advantage of *re-wiring* brain growth and plasticity in the first years,
- *re-discover* the baby and offset the accumulative effects of trauma, and

- use psychoanalytic tools and family dynamics to *re-develop* the secure attachments necessary for forming a coherent, fun, enjoyable relationship with clear boundaries instead of aggression, anger, guilt and pity.

Imagine if all parents could know what kind of child they will have and how to have a good relationship with them, even if their child is not what they expected. Imagine that life is indeed a lot like a box of chocolates? Indeed, imagine that!

Recommendations for action to recover cognitive potential:

- Recovery from the inside-out . . . because your baby's mind is wiring up, it is amazingly plastic. Use this window and The Eternal Triangle to re-wire development. Be proactive and persistent!
- Recovery from the outside-in . . . because your emotions can disrupt development – especially if problems emerge or the baby in front of you doesn't match your ideal – engage with professionals to help you deal with the underlying emotional dynamics and use family relationships to re-direct development. Professionals can help deal with the 'ghosts' from your own past!
- Recovery from discovery . . . cognitive potential grows from intimacy and interaction. How is your child unique? Touch, look, listen, verbalise, scaffold. Be aware of the effect of accumulated trauma and personal experience . . . even your own!

References

Acquarone, S. (1995). Mens sana in corpore sano: Psychotherapy with a cerebral palsy child aged nine months. *Psychoanalytic Psychotherapy*, *9*(1), 41–57.

Acquarone, S. (2004). *Infant-parent psychotherapy*. London: Karnac.

Acquarone, S. (2007). *Signs of autism in infants*. London: Karnac.

Baird, G. (2003). Diagnosis of autism. *BMJ*, *327*(7413), 488–493.

Bick, E. (1968). The experience of the skin in early object relations. *Psychoanalytic Journal*, *49*, 484.

Blacher, J., & Meyers, C. (1983). A review of attachment formation and disorder of handicapped children. *American Journal of Mental Deficiencies*, *87*, 359–371.

Ferenczi, S. (1929). The unwelcome child and the death instincts. *International Journal of Psycho-Analysis*, *10*, 125–129.

Forrest Gump. (1994). [film] Paramount Pictures: Dir. Robert Zemeckis. By Eric Roth. Perf. Tom Hanks, Robin Wright, Gary Sinise, Sally Field, and Mykelti Williamson.

Hollins, S. (2000). Psychotherapy, learning disabilities and trauma: New perspectives. *The British Journal of Psychiatry*, *176*(1), 32–36.

Limperopoulos, C., Bassan, H., Sullivan, N., Soul, J., Robertson, R., Moore, M., Ringer, S., Volpe, J., & du Plessis, A. (2008). Positive screening for autism in ex-preterm infants: Prevalence and risk factors. *Pediatrics*, *121*(4), 758–765.

Levine, L., & Munsch, J. (2013). *Child Development*, 180. Thousand Oaks: SAGE Publications.

Mannoni, M. (1973). *The retarded child and the mother*. London: Tavistock Publications.

Massie, H., & Rosenthal, J. (1984). *Childhood psychosis in the first four years of life*. New York: McGraw-Hill.

Murakami, H., & Rubin, J. (2000). *Norwegian wood*. New York: Vintage International.

Oskoui, M., Coutinho, F., Dykeman, J., Jetté, N., & Pringsheim, T. (2013). An update on the prevalence of cerebral palsy: A systematic review and meta-analysis. *Dev Med Child Neurol, 55*(6), 509–519.

Rosenzweig, M., Breedlove, S., & Watson, N. (2005). *Biological psychology*. Sunderland, MA: Sinauer Associates.

Samara, M., Marlow, N., & Wolke, D. (2008). Pervasive behavior problems at 6 years of age in a total-population sample of children born at <= 25 weeks of gestation. *Pediatrics, 122*(3), 562–573.

Schore, A.N. (1994). *Affect regulation and the origin of the self: The neurobiology of emotional development*. Hillsdale, NJ. Lawrence Erlbaum.

Sinason, V. (1986). Secondary mental handicap and its relationship to trauma. *Psychoanalytic Psychotherapy, 2*(2), 131–154.

Sinason, V. (1988). Richard III, Hephaestus and Echo: Sexuality and mental/multiple handicap. *Journal of Child Psychotherapy, 14*(2), 93–105.

Spitz, R. (1948). *Emotional starvation in infants: Somatic consequences*. Video.

St Clair, C., Danon-Boileau, L., & Trevarthen, C. (2007). Signs of Autism in infancy: Sensitivity for rhythms of expression in communications. In S. Acquarone (ed.), *Signs of Autism in Infants: Recognition and Early Intervention*, 1st ed, pp.21–45. London-New York: Karnac.

Weijerman, M., & de Winter, J. (2010). Clinical practice. *European Journal of Pediatrics, 169*(12), 1445–1452.

PART III

Action

25

THEMES ARISING

Penelope Leach

Research findings reported and discussed in Part II greatly contribute to our knowledge of many aspects of pre-and perinatal development and their outcomes. However this book is not only about research but also about policy and practice. While each of the 40 contributing scientists was concerned to spread knowledge arising from research in his or her particular area, all were also determined to show how that knowledge could and should be acted upon and what differences such actions would make. Many would support the message with which Aynsley-Green ends his paper and Part 1: 'My challenge to each and every reader of every paper in this book is this: Here is evidence. What are you going to do about it?'

Although there are wide differences between the topics, methods and findings of the studies reported in the 25 research papers that are the book's core, there are important agreements between the authors. All acknowledge, explicitly or implicitly, the long-term impact of experiences in the first 1001 days on individuals' development. And where papers end with action points, whether especially addressed to parents, policy makers, politicians or other professionals, shared themes recur, running through those take-away messages.

Theme one: importance to infant wellbeing of events and experiences during pregnancy and birth

Pregnancy: the significance of the uterine environment to infants' long-term development: physical, mental and emotional

The relationship between mother and infant begins prenatally and is significantly associated with their postnatal interaction and attachment. This first relationship has a significant effect on the neurochemical foundations of the mind. Positive or negative experiences programme the developing brain's future biases accordingly.

The unborn baby's physical health and brain development and the developing relationship between infant and mother can be affected by the mother's emotional state and mental health as well as by her physical health and lifestyle. Furthermore it is not only the extremes of 'toxic stress or diagnosed mental illness that require attention but also antenatal depression, pregnancy-related or other anxiety, and a wide range of types of stress, including the relationship with the partner, and a history of trauma.

What is needed

- General understanding of the importance to children's optimal brain development of healthy unstressful pregnancies, and the importance of optimal early brain development for all to the wellbeing and competence of whole populations.
- Timely psychological and parenting support for all pregnant women.
- Increased training of midwives to listen to pregnant womens' previous experiences and to detect and respond to the needs of those who may require extra support as well as to women experiencing mental illness during pregnancy.
- Universally available specialist perinatal mental health services with the resources to support women experiencing mental health difficulties in pregnancy

Birth

The social expectation is that however difficult the labour, birth is a joyous event. However more births are traumatic to some degree than is widely recognised because the symptoms of birth trauma are often confused with postnatal depression, leaving traumatised parents misdiagnosed and untreated.

Birth trauma, especially if combined with insecure adult attachment patterns and support that is perceived as inadequate, can result in postnatal PTSD (Post Traumatic Stress Disorder) causing intergenerational bonding and attachment problems. The causes of birth trauma are multifaceted, involving some or all of the following: a high degree of obstetric interventions and/or complications; deficient and unsympathetic care during labour and delivery that women perceive as unsafe, dehumanised, disrespectful and uncaring; a perceived lack or loss of control and feelings of being powerless over events; intolerable pain; absence or perceived lack of support of partner during labour and at birth; and actions or inactions of maternity staff that leave women feeling unsupported and unheard.

Maternal PTSD has negative effects on infant cognitive development and infant emotional regulation. In addition to comorbidity within couples, PTSD has negative effects on the relationship of father and mother, interfering with intimacy, and often reducing the size of the intended family.

- Obstetric training and practice must acknowledge and act on the importance of women perceiving their care in labour and during delivery, as safe and sympathetic
- During labour and delivery women should be helped to retain a sense of being in control of themselves and of events.

- Good pain management is crucial.
- The presence and support of a birth partner should be encouraged.
- The training of all maternity staff should stress the importance of women feeling heard and cared for.

After delivery

PND (postnatal depression) is common, and has negative effects on the mother-infant relationship and on child development:

- Health professionals should be alert to maternal moods and partners, grand-parents employers and friends, encouraged to help support the emotional wellbeing of pregnant women and new mothers.
- Socio-economic adversity is an important contributor to PND. Actions to reduce the risk, stress and impacts of poverty in households with, or expecting children is critical.
- An increase in the availability of specialist help is urgently needed.

Theme two: early child development

Healthy brain development is not only of crucial importance to individual children and their families but also to whole populations' competence and well-being. It is not widely enough understood that brain development, beginning before birth, depends on interaction with the mother and that the early phases of development are characterised by developmental plasticity. Changes in children's environment and relationships in the first year of life can have major and lasting effects, for good or ill, on their development in the long term. The science of early child development should therefore be incorporated into public health models and ECD should be promoted in national decision making as a first step in poverty reduction and human capital formation. ECD research capacity should be strengthened and practitioners helped to understand what makes for quality ECD and to target their services to children in greatest need.

Innovative research in infant wellbeing should include evaluation studies that measure the impact of particular parenting or professional interventions on specific developmental outcomes in children, such as the role of fathers and co-parenting in children's language development.

Assessment of early childhood outcomes should be linked to program and policy data, promote a trans-disciplinary science of human development, and translate this science into ECD programs and policies that foster healthy development.

Action should include

- Developing a comprehensive, population-based, multinational database of children's outcomes (with and without ECD interventions).
- Wider-spread use of existing methods of measuring child outcomes during early periods of development, such as coded observations of child behaviours and longitudinal follow-up studies.

- Collection of more long-term data on academic and social outcomes for children over time.
- Development of new methods enabling attachment studies to be carried out in routine practice: such as a scientifically robust but straightforward instrument measuring parental sensitivity and parent–infant relationships.
- More studies of attachment interventions, increasing the range of family circumstances and difficulties addressed and making such interventions manageable and widely available within routine health and social care systems,

Theme three: service provision

Increasing scientific knowledge – especially in the fields of neurobiology, developmental psychopathology and epidemiological outcomes studies – makes it clear that social disadvantage and adversity have direct negative impacts on child development. Poverty during the prenatal period is associated with an increased risk of low birthweight; with a lesser likelihood of breastfeeding; with insecure attachment and with postnatal depression. Reducing these and other risks and impacts of social adversity in households where there is a pregnancy or a young baby is therefore critical and perinatal mental health interventions should be a public health priority. Since health systems necessarily have finite resources, money spent on health programmes must be demonstrably well spent. Investment in the earliest possible interventions produces the highest possible rates of return.

National policies should prioritise maternal mental health, especially within public health, maternity care and mental health care.

The UK needs an explicit national commitment to maternal mental health from the very top and an overall policy, with defined objectives and desired outcomes. Social policies should be redirected to focus on the early years and responsibility for *all* aspects of policy affecting children should be integrated across Government and the best possible resources made available. Both policy and resource allocation needs to think a generation ahead.

Local areas should prioritise strategic commissioning of services to ensure that high-standard services are consistent across the country. Data on family vulnerabilities should be collected routinely during pregnancy and early childhood, and this information used to promote access to services.

Families do not only consist of mothers and children but of fathers also

Fathers' inclusion in services and their engagement in early interventions is known to promote family wellbeing, while there is substantial evidence for the potential impact of paternal depression on family functioning and child development.

- Services to families must be designed and redesigned to include fathers framework for the delivery of services should be built on the multidisciplinary training of staff.
- Discussion of pregnant women's own experiences of childhood care and abuse is an essential aid to identifying those who may need extra antenatal support.

- High-quality childcare provision, responsive and mental-health aware GPs, nurses and health visitors are crucial to helping families with young children to access services on their behalf.
- Specialist perinatal mental health services in which professionals are able to recognise family need and services can be accessed in a non-stigmatising way must be universally available.

Theme four: service planning

Plans should include

- Aggregation of anonymised data on vulnerabilities during pregnancy and early childhood, factored into the local JSNA and service planning.
- Fostering of interagency cooperation and integration in training and delivery of perinatal services.
- Seamless and simple access to integrated care for all parents and infants, those at low as well as high risk.
- Adopting the concept of proportionate universality would help to control the costs of universal services. Defined as 'programs, services, and policies that are universal, but with a scale and intensity that is proportionate to the level of disadvantage' proportionate universality can provide the social advantages of universal services with the economic advantages of selection.
- Governments should regularly report to Parliament on progress in improving pregnancy and ECD outcomes, including in reducing socio-economic and geographical inequalities.

Theme five: parent education and support

The crucial importance of parent-child relationships in the early years of life, including the antenatal months, deserves to be universally accepted. Ongoing research in this millennium has shown that relationships with parents are prime influences on infants' longterm development. Close relationships with parents who are sensitive and responsive to their infant's attachment cues tend to promote security of attachment, reducing the likelihood of later emotional or behavioural difficulties; optimal brain development; the ability to self-regulate, cognitive ability and the development of language.

Babies arrive without an instruction manual and child-rearing is widely considered to be the most difficult and demanding task of adult life. Since every parent and child is unique, parent education programmes cannot teach all parents how best to parent their baby or child: there can be no one-size-fits-all. However supporting parents in their self-perceived roles can help to create knowledgeable, skilled and confident mothers and fathers, who can in turn promote the development of healthy, happy and capable children.

- Historically, parenting research and interventions have focused on mother-child dyads, however there is now ample evidence of the important role that fathers play in family life and child rearing. There are a number of challenges to engaging fathers in early interventions so as to optimise outcomes for children and families. These include designing and providing services which can screen for and treat perinatal mental health disorders in men as well as women. While there is much still to learn about the specific mechanisms whereby paternal mental health issues impact on infants and young children, knowledge and understanding regarding the risk factors and implications of paternal depression now provides substantial evidence for its likely impact on family functioning and child development.

As well as focusing exclusively on mother-child dyads, parenting interventions have mostly concentrated on high-risk or vulnerable groups or populations. There are now strong arguments for greater inclusion: for a whole-population approach. Families must be supported and where interventions are needed on behalf of a child they must be provided via families. What is needed now are mentalising educational, health and social care systems that can reach out to parents, and which parents are able to reach without shame, obstruction or undue delay

- Encouraging evidence of ways in which vulnerable parents can be helped to meet the developmental needs of their children, such as recent research concerning video-interaction guidance, should be communicated to the general public and policy makers, as well as to professionals.
- In order to develop an evidence base within which best practices for every individual family may be found, more collaboration is needed among researchers and service providers.

Currently many and various evidence-based parenting programmes are used to serve different age groups of childen and parents with differing levels of risk.

- Evaluation studies are urgently needed to measure the impact of parenting interventions on specific child outcomes.
- Systems for rating the implementation practices as well as the quality of programs are urgently needed.
- It is incumbent on policy makers, commissioners and practitioners to design and implement father-inclusive services.

Since leading experts in different aspects of perinatal research have contributed to these themes and recommendations they surely demand everyone's attention. But are the actions called for professionally achievable? Politically acceptable? Economically affordable? If they are, current inaction cannot be justified.

I believe that altough the needs of, and recommendations for, one speciality are different from another as the range of contributors' bullet points makes clear, the general agreement on important themes arising shows that successful outcomes in particular professional areas can put down markers for others. One such project is the *Norfolk Parent Infant Mental Health Project (PIMHAP)* – a specific program whose success suggests that it could be generalised to other geographical and professional areas.

26

NORFOLK PARENT-INFANT MENTAL HEALTH ATTACHMENT PROJECT (PIMHAP)

Working towards integration in attachment, mental health and social care

Verity Smith, Richard Pratt, Catherine Thomas, Danny Taggart

Introduction

The Norfolk Parent-Infant Mental Health Attachment Project (PIMHAP) was developed to address the needs of 'at risk' families in keeping with previous innovations within the area of parent-infant mental health both in the United Kingdom and internationally (Galbriath, Balbernie &White, 2015; Hosman, van Doesum & van Santvoort, 2009). This account highlights the need for 'transformational change' at individual, family and structural levels. Of particular importance to the successes of this project has been the shared negotiation of risk and effort to integrate safeguarding and therapeutic tasks. Broadly PIMHAP can be seen as a localised response to the imperative to provide early intervention to 'high-risk' families (Leadsom et al., 2013) with recognition that such work needs to be multidimensional (Galbriath, Balbernie & White, 2015) and in many cases intensive (Sadler et al., 2013).

PIMHAP was commissioned to reduce the number of babies removed from their families, as part of a wider Looked After and Adopted Children (LAAC) reduction scheme. This need within the county was translated into the development of a therapeutic service that would be of direct benefit to families. PIMHAP was made possible by Transformational Challenge funding provided by The Department of Communities and Local Government.

The aim of offering intensive support in the first 1001 days to 'at risk' families was informed by evidence that outcomes are poor for Looked After Children (Dozier et al., 2008); that within the United Kingdom and specifically within

Norfolk there were higher than average rates of children, including infants, taken into care (United Nations, 2009; HM Government: Department for Education, 2015). In addition, a high proportion of families working with the project come from significant disadvantage in communities of heightened inequality (Wilkinson & Pickett, 2010; Rowlingson, 2011). It was proposed that if PIMHAP could increase number of infants safely held within their families there would be measurable benefits in terms of wellbeing and economics.

PIMHAP was commissioned to offer psychiatric, psychotherapeutic and systemic interventions for 45 high-risk families across Norfolk, in addition to providing consultation with their professional network. PIMHAP's inclusion criteria specify significant concerns regarding attachment relationships, parental mental health and safeguarding. PIMHAP operates on the basis that developmental trauma underpins many adult mental health problems in this population. The origins of such trauma in past neglect and abuse, including sexual abuse, are confirmed by the experiences of the parents with whom PIMHAP worked. It was recognised that the majority of parents have significant mental health difficulties but due to the nature of their difficulties many were unable to access adult mental health services.

Of central importance to the success of PIMHAP was the shared vision between children's services and the mental health trust. Senior members of both organisations were involved at inception and throughout implementation. In this respect the transformational element was breaking down some of the barriers between organisations and cultures. Contextually the County Council and the Trust were under scrutiny and used this to change practice (in this respect perhaps mirroring the experience of the families with whom PIMHAP was working). Senior members of the team were asked to join the county council panel that made decisions about packages of 'edge of care' provision and thus had a closer part in decision making and an influence on the way families were discussed by bringing in a more psychologically minded perspective.

Typically, the local authority would commission independent assessments of 'edge of care' families. This sometimes led to decontextualised recommendations that could not reflect knowledge of local services. One advantage of a local therapeutic service is that the assessments PIMHAP completed could better take into account such factors and follow through the interventions. By regularly meeting in local groups the professional network is able to review and develop this understanding which is also informed by the active involvement of families. Further, meeting at specific children's centres in high risk areas enabled families to link in with local groups and provide a step down to known universal services following intervention. Working closely with children's services, some reciprocal understanding occurred through dialogue and use of some procedures implemented by children's services such as 'Signs of Safety' (Turnell, 1998). The method of Signs of Safety, if successfully employed, allows for transparency in managing risk with families, ensuring all views are heard (including the parents) and identifying strengths as well as risks.

The PIMHAP team includes clinical psychologists, assistant psychologists, child and adult psychiatrists, psychotherapists and community mental health practitioners and is underpinned by attachment, psychodynamic and systemic approaches. PIMHAP work is carried on from three bases across the county in wider networks that include link social workers, children's centre leads, specialist midwives and health visitors. From the initial point of referral PIMHAP works to achieve integration across agencies through formulating an appropriate package of support with input from psychotherapy, psychiatry, social care and local children's centres. This multidisciplinary cooperation allows a key feature of the project: the offer of assessment and treatment of both adult mental health difficulties and parent-infant attachment. A referral pathway is shown below.

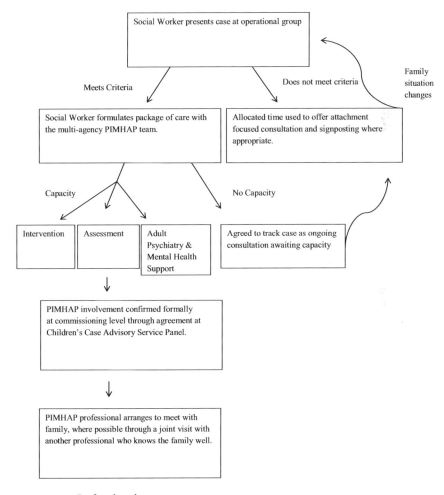

FIGURE 26.1 Referral pathway

Assessment

The use of nuanced assessment approaches that seek to engage the parents enabled the service to formulate a clear understanding of need. Assessments routinely included CARE Index (Crittenden, 2007), a video-based measure of the parent-infant relationship pattern and risk in terms of later difficulties for the infant, and the Meaning of the Child Interview (Grey, 2014) that provided an indication of parental reflective functioning and the way parents represented their infant and their relationships. Alongside the assessment of parental mental health this enabled PIMHAP to gain an understanding of the areas of resource and need to focus upon. For some parents the service was able to ensure a review with a psychiatrist (who would see parents in their homes or community setting) and the allocated worker. Together they were able to provide a developmental context for current difficulties. Appropriate diagnosis and medication at this stage made a significant difference to some parents quite quickly. The very wide range of interventions offered is summarised below.

Intervention	Description
Perinatal Psychiatry Support, including Community Mental Health Support	• Regular appointments with a mental health practitioner and perinatal psychiatrist. • Time given to think about experiences. • Care Co-ordination. • A helpful way to come alongside families who are not ready to engage in a more intensive therapy.
Video Interaction Guidance (VIG)	• A strength based video intervention. • The practitioner edits film for moments that fit a developed 'helping question' and explores it with the parent in the shared review. • VIG specific supervision.
Attachment Focused Therapy	• An individualised combination of play sessions and talking about relationships. • All interventions place a focus on parents' early experiences as a starting point to think about attachment strategies. • Making links between different relationships is intense and long term work. • Aim to promote increased attunement and consistency in the care of infants and to promote parents ability to think reflectively about their experiences.

FIGURE 26.2 Offered interventions

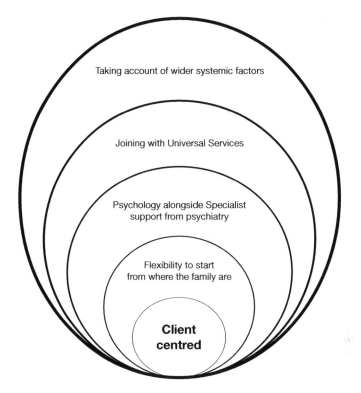

FIGURE 26.3 PIMHAP team's conceptualisation of 'What is distinct'

Relationships

PIMHAP emphasises an outreach working model, aiming to come alongside the families in their homes and in local resources. The relationships established with the families by key professionals are seen as the main vehicle of change. This enables shared understanding and also provides a way in which differences can be recognised and tolerated. There are many instances, particularly in the early phases of engagement, where team members' response to the immediate needs of families helped to establish trust. For people who have no experience of secure attachment or felt safety, an emphasis on forming a relationship is not only the first step but, when working well, is also the safe base to return to after periods of uncertainty, fear and crisis. The threat of removal of their infant into care will often trigger parents' dysfunctional attachment strategies regularly and unpredictably. Maintenance of the therapeutic relationship in these circumstances is an ongoing challenge.

Coming alongside individuals in a way that is neither intrusive nor procedurally 'done to' is a delicate balance. Through team formulation, PIMHAP decide how to intervene at a level the family can tolerate, and review the family's progress regularly. Through engagement, reflection and review, the intervention extends further than treating a series of traumas, to include the meaning they hold for the parent and their relationship with their infant. As the therapeutic relationship becomes richer there are opportunities to work at more deep-seated levels, working symbolically with more mundane everyday issues, and thus for example opening up the meaning behind household conditions, as opposed to organising support to help clean up.

There is recognition of the importance of self-awareness across professionals' disciplines and a need for reflective supervision which explores the roles of unconscious processes. A weekly reflection group provides an additional space for sharing video work, making links and reflecting on what is evoked in members of the team.

Outcomes

£623,395 was invested in the project. It was hypothesised that PIMHAP would recoup that investment if 33.3 per cent of infants remained safely in the care of their parents. It was calculated that the annual average cost of a Looked After child in Norfolk is £51,000 and on these figures, the annual savings minus the cost of project operation would be £309,605. Data collected in June 2016, show 75 per cent of infants remaining safely in parental care, more than doubling the hypothesised figure for cost saving. Assuming these infants would otherwise have been taken into care, the savings would be considerably higher. However, this calculation fails to acknowledge that while there was a likelihood of infants being taken into care this was not a certainty. Furthermore it must be recognised that while PIMHAP was a central intervention it was most often in combination with other services, notably children's centres.

PIMHAP has achieved a reduction of risk for families, as measured by level of safeguarding through social care structures. The level of safeguarding has reduced for 46 per cent of our families, increased for 26 per cent and remained the same for 27 per cent (one piece of data missing). It is important to hold in mind when interpreting these numbers that interventions sometimes highlight risk thus ensuring infants do not remain in unsafe homes (Barlow et al., 2007).

Infant Outcomes	Frequency	Percentage
Remained with Parents	41	74.5%
With Extended Family	6	10.9%
Foster Placement	5	9.1%
Adoption Plan	2	3.6%
Reunification Plan	1	1.8%

FIGURE 26.4 Infant outcomes

Nature of Removal	Frequency	Percentage
Remained with parents	41	74.5%
Removed before project involved	2	3.6%
Removed during project	9	16.4%
Removed after disengagement	3	5.5%

FIGURE 26.5 Nature of removal

	Referral		Discharge	
Level of Safeguarding	**Frequency**	**Percentage**	**Frequency**	**Percentage**
Section 17	16	29.1	11	20.4
Section 47	35	63.6	10	18.5
Interim Care Order	2	3.6	6	11.1
LAC	1	1.8	2	3.7
Closed to Children's Services	0	0	16	29.5
Foster Care	1	1.8	2	3.6
Kinship Care	0	0	3	5.4
Family Support Plan	0	0	1	1.8
Supported Accommodation	0	0	1	1.8

FIGURE 26.6 Change in safeguarding status

These robust findings indicate the effectiveness of the service and suggest that therapeutic services that closely link in to safeguarding processes and provide interventions that match need can promote infant safety.

The findings using relational and psychological measures are less clear largely due to the difficulties of gathering full sets of pre and postfindings in the context of safeguarding where levels of parental trust are low. In order to build up a therapeutic alliance there was in some cases delay in complete initial assessment meaning that change had already started with some families. In other cases there may have been with self-report questionnaires a degree of 'false positive' responses as either parents were wary of being open within a safeguarding context or due to their own defensive strategies lacking, into the level of difficulties.

Challenges

While PIMHAP is relationally focused, the child protection mandate is focused upon the child. At times social work colleagues have experienced the service as advocating for the parent and underestimating the risks for the infant. This is recognised as important although the service maintains that the needs of the infant are dependent upon the needs of the parent. Often the team is able, through close dialogue with social workers and parents, to have enough shared understanding to safely manage these differences but there have been occasions where differences are not reconciled. Observations suggest that the further cases are down the 'legal route', with associated truncated time scales, the less possible it is to work therapeutically.

Conversely because PIMHAP provides thorough assessments there have been occasions where PIMHAP has identified a higher level of risk (in attachment terms) than social work colleagues. For the infant this can potentially be helpful particularly where there are indications of compulsivity (inhibited need) that aren't evident. However it has meant that at times the role in amplifying concern has prevented PIMHAP from engaging with families therapeutically.

PIMHAP conceptualises intervention through an ongoing commitment to integration at individual, parent–infant and structural levels. That is, to respond to the lack of psychic integration in people who have experienced developmental trauma, to the lack of integration within relationships and lack of integration in terms of service delivery and the wider community. It is through an acknowledgement of the fragmentation at all levels that there is an opportunity to move away from a procedural-based care and towards a process of need based upon some degree of shared understanding. Linked to this is the role of 'epistemic trust' (Fonagy et al., 2014) in the process of change within a safeguarding context.

It is not possible to identify a case that is fully representative of the work since families and needs are complex and varied. However the case outlined below illustrates some key features.

Sara, Henry, Summer age 5 and Mia 18 months, were referred into PIMHAP by their local children's centre. Summer and Mia were made subject to a child protection plan. Sara and Henry had difficulty in being available for their children or each other, being preoccupied with their own unmet mental health needs.

Combined with initial reluctance towards professional help, this resulted in concerns around neglect and a hypothesis that the family were often 'alone together'. There were also concerns about Summer's low school attendance and her aggression towards staff and other children, and about Mia's attempts to meet her attachment needs through indiscriminate affection towards less known adults.

Sara and Henry met with PIMHAP's consultant adult psychiatrist. For Henry, a diagnosis was given of complex post-traumatic stress disorder, through a combination of developmental trauma, including a period of time spent in the military. Sara spoke about her experiences of low mood, and times of irritability alongside periods of feeling disconnected and 'spaced out'. Both parents were prescribed medication for their mental health, under regular review.

The parents' individual needs were also understood through developmental history taking. Both Sara and Henry engaged with The Meaning of The Child Interview (Grey, 2014) and spoke about difficult childhood experiences, characterised by a combination of punitive and unresponsive caregiving. Themes for Sara and Henry were fathers who were punishing and controlling and mothers who were often unable to be protective. Sara spoke about past relationships characterised by domestic violence. Henry discussed struggling with what he had witnessed in the army as well a difficult separation from his ex-wife and from his son. The PIMHAP team developed a formulation using the Dynamic Maturational Model of Attachment (Crittenden, 2005) that both Sara and Henry had developed high 'A type' attachment strategies, where cognition held dominance over affect. These strategies had been important in promoting safety historically; however difficulties integrating cognition and affect were impacting on their current relationships. The intervention began here for Sara and Henry on the basis that once parent(s) have capacity for more reflective functioning and safe integration of the self they are better able to understand the needs of their child. Therefore offering responsive adult psychiatry time is an essential step in recognising and supporting parental need, so that ultimately PIMHAP support the needs of parent-infant relationships.

PIMHAP addressed relational integration through attachment therapy. While there were challenges facilitating moments of connection at home, the sensory room at the family's local children's centre offered containment and opportunities for playful states to emerge. The team shared moments of sensitivity using the language of The Circle of Security (Powell et al., 2013). Providing Sara and Henry with time in sessions to talk about their feelings enabled them to provide more opportunities for connection with Summer and Mia. In time more integrated parental roles developed, whereas historically Sara would have provided more comfort and gentle play and Henry provided boundaries. Mia and Summer showed us that they could move flexibly between their parents for their comfort and exploratory needs. Over time the team observed that the parents' ability to regulate themselves enabled them to watch over the girls in a way which supported Summer's regulation in play and enabled Mia to emerge as expressive and appropriately demanding. A strength for Sara and Henry was their creative and humorous use of language. This emerged as an opportunity to develop a joint 'playfulness in thought' in order to make sense of different issues, and allowing feelings to have an increased awareness in sessions.

PIMHAP observed fragmentation in the professional system, characterised by contrasting interpretations of safety, need and progress. There have been opportunities for celebrating successes and communicating about concerns in sensitive ways, although it has felt difficult to join these up. Firm position-holding impacted on the ability for the group to think about issues in nuanced ways. Sara and Henry's role with the professional system seems at times to be defined around defending and rationalising pre-existing points of discussion. During periods of increased anxiety or uncertainty opportunities for collaboration and the group meeting in open adult states were diminished, as Sara and Henry respond in child-like ways, to excuse themselves or to make promises which they often cannot achieve, as if in relation to a powerful or parental other. As work progressed, however, there have been times where the parents have been able to advocate. They have raised concerns about the professional system, for example the impact of the child protection process on their sense of intimacy as a family and their freedom to express feelings. Henry has spoken about times when he has felt disempowered by the system as well as times when he has felt pressurised and 'cornered'. Recently Sara and Henry have expressed a wish for further collaborative thinking, suggesting that responsibilities for decisions should be shared.

Structural intervention represents further integration through facilitating capacity to think more flexibly about the complexity of the system. This in turn allows a more relational understanding, the beginning of making sense of roles as professionals and individuals in relation to a case. Integration is key at this level because it is in part through jointly holding a worry and thinking together about the ranging implications of a specific constellation of risk, that there is opportunity for openness and curiosity. This can be understood as a series of dialogues, enabling opportunity to share different perspectives across individuals, theoretical perspectives, organisations and professional accountability. From a psychological perspective, this can be understood as a decrease in vigilance and an increase in mentalising and trust across systems brought about through the therapeutic relationship (Fomagy et al., 2014).

Conclusion

PIMHAP attempted to address the needs of 'high-risk' families. The outcomes of PIMHAP were positive enough for the County Council to commit to ongoing funding.

Key features of its success are the intensity of the work influenced by the specific needs of families within particular communities, and the attempt to integrate the needs of parents and infants. Perhaps most distinctive is the collaborative nature of the project as outcomes for infants are not just due to the resources and difficulties 'within' individuals and families but also influenced by the services available and the way systems communicate with one another. The challenge of providing effective services and maintaining dialogues at all levels is ongoing and PIMHAP remain hopeful to continue with them in order to better serve parents and infants.

This project highlights the need for further development in the following areas:

- seamless access to integrated, accessible care for a wider range of parents and infants,
- perinatal services aspiring to interagency integration in service delivery for parents and infants,
- long-term follow-up comparison studies of high-risk infants who remain with their parents or are removed,
- emphasis on outreach approaches with higly vulnerable families.

References

Barlow, J., Davis, H., McIntosh, E., Jarrett, P., Mockford, C., & Stewart-Brown, S. (2007). Role of home visiting in improving parenting and health in families at risk of abuse and neglect: Results of a multicentre randomised controlled trial and economic evaluation. *Archives of disease in childhood, 92*(3), 229–233.

Crittenden, P.M. (2007). Infant/Toddler Care-Index Coding Manuals, Miami Florida: Family Relations Institute (unpublished).

Crittenden, P. (2005). Attachment theory, psychopathology and psychotherapy: The dynamic-maturational approach. *Psicoterapia, 30,* 171–182.

HM Government: Department for Education (2015). National Statistics Children looked after in England including adoption: 2014 to 2015. [pdf] Department for Education Available at: https://gov.uk/government/statistics/children-looked-after-in-england-including-adoption-2014-to-2015 (Accessed 28.08.2016).

Dozier, M., Peloso, E., Lewis, E., Laurenceau, J.P., & Levine, S. (2008). Effects of an attachment-based intervention on the cortisol production of infants and toddlers in foster care. *Development and psychopathology, 20*(3), 845–859.

Fonagy, P., & Allison, E. (2014). The role of mentalising and epistemic trust in the therapeutic relationship. *Psychotherapy, 10,* 1037/a0036505

Galbriath, M., Balbernie, R., & White, C. (2015). Delivering psychological services for children and families in early years mental health and emotional wellbeing settings. *Child and Family Clinical Psychology Review.* The British Psychological Society.

Grey, B. (2014). The Meaning of the Child to the Parent: The Development and Validation of a New Method of Classifying Parenting Interviews for the Nature of the Parent-Child Relationship, PhD thesis, London: University of Roehampton.

Hosman, C.M., van Doesum, K.T., & van Santvoort, F. (2009). Prevention of emotional problems and psychiatric risks in children of parents with a mental illness in the Netherlands: I. The scientific basis to a comprehensive approach. *Australian e-Journal for the Advancement of Mental Health, 8*(3), 250–263.

Leadsom, A., Field, F., Burstow, P., & Lucas, C. (2013). *The 1001 Critical Days: The importance of the conception to age two period.* London: A Cross Party Manifesto.

Sadler, L.S., Slade, A., Close, N., Webb, D.L., Simpson, T., Fennie, K., & Mayes, L.C. (2013). Minding the baby: Enhancing reflectiveness to improve early health and relationship outcomes in an interdisciplinary home-visiting program. *Infant mental health journal, 34*(5), 391–405.

Powell, B., Cooper, G., Hoffman, K., & Marvin, B. (2013). *The circle of security intervention: Enhancing attachment in early parent-child relationships.* Guilford Publications.

Rowlingson, K. (2011). Does income inequality cause health and social problems? [pdf] Available at: https://jrf.org.uk/sites/default/files/jrf/migrated/files/inequality-income-social-problems-full.pdf (Accessed 28.08.2016).

Turnell, A. (1998). September. aspiring to partnership; the signs of safety approach to child protection or reflections on the road toward a comprehensive partnership practice for child protection casework. In *Twelfth International Congress on Child Abuse and Neglect in Auckland, September* (pp. 6–9).

United Nations (2009). Child Adoption: Trends and Policies. Department of economic and social affairs, population division, New York. [pdf] Available at: http://un.org/esa/population/publications/adoption2010/child-adoption.pdf (Accessed 28.08.2016).

Wilkinson, R., & Pickett, K. (2010). *The spirit level: Why equality is better for everyone.* Penguin Books, London.

27

BUILDING RESEARCH FINDINGS INTO POLICY AND POLICY INTO ACTION

Timothy Loughton

The most distinctive feature of the success of the Norfolk Parent-Infant Mental Health Attachment Project (PIMHAP) success was its collaborative nature. Good or poor outcomes for infants and their families were not just due to resources or difficulties within them but also to the services available and the way systems communicated with each other. On a countywide scale PIMHAP established 'Joined up government'. Can such a model be scaled up to be countrywide?

That phrase 'Joined-up government' is coined whenever an administration wants to explain how a new policy initiative, a new department or a new minister will be different and more effective than those that have gone before. But does such a thing actually exist in practice? Timothy Loughton MP had always doubted it and when he became the minster for children and young people in May 2010, he was soon sure that it did not. The UK's civil service and the structure of its government put ministers and their policies into 'silos, hermetically sealed within their departments'. The quick chats with colleagues over the policy implications of a new proposal for other departments don't just happen anymore. Any such meeting has to be diarised at some distant date in the future, often subject to post-ponement and always subject to a vast panoply of officials and minute takers. Even quick chats with officials within a minister's own department need to be diarised and formally marshalled. Attempts to 'play hooky' with the private office and seek out information via an informal 'quick chat, with a civil servant from another department meets with stern disapproval. 'That's not the way we do things in the Department Minister!'

Getting things done: the Early Intervention Grant

Timothy Loughton tells of working on the 'Early Intervention Grant' designed to shift the focus of government intervention from fire-fighting symptoms to tackling causes of everything from attachment dysfunction between babies and parents to teenagers from chaotic families going off the rails.

Inevitably the policy had implications for public health, local government, the police, the benefit system and social finance being worked up by the cabinet office. So difficult was it to overcome the protocols of dealing with officials in other departments that the principles behind the Early Intervention Grant were eventually agreed by using mobile-phones to issue personal invitations to the relevant ministers to meet for a ministerial pizza supper.

The grant came into operation from April 2011 but the important approach it established soon disappeared; victim of a greater (misguided) Government offensive to remove ring fencing from departmental funding. The Early Intervention Grants now fragmented, raided and inevitably downgraded by various departments. This has made it harder to protect and promote public health and other budgets so crucial to the practical applications of early intervention, early help, youth interventions and so on.

A further example of the apparent impossibility of genuine interdepartmental cooperation was the 'Youth Action Group', created in 2011. This group consisted of up to 10 government ministers and senior officials from departments who had an interest in youth policy. They sat round a table with the heads of six youth charities led by chief executives of The Prince's Trust and Barnardo's. The aim was to 'youth proof' all relevant government policy and to find solutions to problems affecting young people that crossed departmental responsibilities. For a while it seemed that ministers with a genuine interest in young people actually turned up and left officials from their departments in no doubt about the imperative of finding solutions, rather than shuffling the problem around the distinctly unjoined up governmental merry-go-round. But the YAT soon fizzled out and in recent years the responsibilities of the minister for children, families and young people in the DfE have been dissipated out of all recognition across government. Youth justice has gone to the ministry of justice; child sexual exploitation has gone to the home office; the 'problem families' (now 'troubled families') initiative went to the Department for Communities and Local Government (DCLG); child protection on the Internet to the Department for Culture, Media and Sport (DCMS); youth policy and National Citizen Service (NCS) to the Cabinet Office and now on to DCMS.

These examples illustrate just how unconventional (and therefore unexpected) attempts at real joined-up government actually are. And of course the struggle to get ministers and senior departmental civil servants working closely together becomes immeasurably more challenging when all the relevant government agencies, local authority organisations, professional bodies and NGO's are added in.

Indeed there is often a major disconnect between central government policy and local authority delivery level. As minister for child protection, Loughton spent a lot of time getting out of Westminster visiting local authorities with safeguarding problems. After the formal discussions at the Town Hall with chief executives and political leadership he always insisted on meeting up with social workers, unaccompanied by management, but he was alone in this and while his informal appearances were always welcomed they were also surprising. Few staff working in child protection even knew the name of the cabinet member for children.

There is hope, though. Against this rather depressing description of what doesn't easily happen in government must be set the growing and cheering profile of the 1001 critical days campaign and its cross-party manifesto. The substantial and weighty contributions to the series of parliamentary hearings organised by the All Party Parliamentary Group for The First 1001 Days, were Penelope Leach's inspiration for this book, and, as the chairman of the APPG I am immensely grateful to Penelope for the work she has done and to all the academics and practitioners who have so enthusiastically contributed to this volume. If only government were as 'joined up' and forthcoming.

The 1001 Critical Days Manifesto which complements the Group is endorsed by representatives of all the UK's major political parties, the chief medical officer, all the major medical colleges and a wide range of family and children's organisations from the NSPCC to the Tavistock Centre. It was also hugely significant that NHS England adopted perinatal mental health as one of its priorities a year ago and that it was specifically referenced by the current prime minister as part of her new year initiative of improving mental health services for children. With so much consensus, so much buy-in across the political divide, so much enthusiasm across practitioners and academics backed up by empirical evidence, and recently such a high profile, what is it going to take to translate policy into mainstream action?

The bottom line is probably leadership (continuous leadership), transparency, a sympathetic treasury and a political mindset which takes a genuinely long-term view even if it transgresses the electoral cycle. That is a long bottom line and not without political risk but there is no single silver bullet.

One of the high-profile priorities of the conservative part of the coalition government when it came into office in 2010 was to inject new life into adoption and improve conditions for children in care. It was personally championed by the then education secretary and prime minister. Loughton spent a lot of time putting together working groups of key people, personally rewriting much of the fostering and adoption regulations, and launching a recruitment campaign. Lots of evidence was produced to show how successful adoptions improved life chances and saved money. Indeed an adoption social impact bond made the financial case for the merits of using social investment to invest upfront. Yet initially not a lot happened. There was no joined-up follow through.

There were a lot of people in denial that there really was any great obstacle preventing more children from being adopted, yet the inexorable rise in children coming into care, post Baby P especially, and the stagnating number of adoptions, said otherwise. In the end what started things moving was the publication of 'Adoption score cards' and investment in adoption support. Every local authority had to lay bare its record on adoption, crucially not just on raw numbers but qualitative data on recruiting prospective adopters, adopting harder to place and British Medical Association (BMA) children and the speed of the process. All of a sudden there was nowhere to hide. There was little excuse for one London borough to be adopting at half the rate or at twice the pace of a neighbouring authority. Things started to improve, at least, frustratingly, until the Government failed to join up the initiative at the DfE with the fiercely guarded sensitivities of the judges in the courts run by the MoJ.

Another good early intervention initiative frustrated by a lack of a joined-up follow through has been the experience of recruiting health visitors, a crucial component in the 1001 Critical Days agenda. The former health secretary championed the recruitment of 4,300 new health visitors based on the successful model of the Dutch Kraamzorg system where postnatal care is provided to a new mother and her baby in the initial 8 to 10 days immediately after birth.

Impressively for a government target it was achieved in the lifetime of the last Parliament. Depressingly since then the numbers have started to drop dramatically. In June 2015 there were 10,042 full-time equivalent health visitors working in the United Kingdom but a year later that number had fallen to 9,491 and continues to slide.

More widely known, the number of children's centres across the country has also been falling, in places like Oxfordshire and even in the former prime minister's own constituency, quite dramatically. While numbers alone need not be the measure of success and some needed rationalising and were not reaching the right people in the right places, undoubtedly services are retrenching. At the same time public health budgets, now subject to extreme competing pressures within cash-strapped local authorities, are being scaled back. Despite additional money being poured into CAMHS very little of it is ringfenced and it is increasingly apparent that it is not ending up at the sharp end where it was intended. Even the minister ostensibly doling out the money cannot guarantee its destination nor his own continued seat in cabinet. Alistair Burt MP who gave the 1001 Days All Party Parliamenary Group a foot in the door to the department for health is no longer a minister and we have to start all over again 'educating' a new recruit.

So the United Kingdom now has a prime minister who has stated her commitment to putting mental health on a level playing field with physical health, which sounds forward looking except that that her predecessor endorsed a similar commitment in 'No Health without Mental Health' right back at the beginning of his administration. Her words about training teachers to identify mental health problems in the classroom (as if they did not have enough to do already) are welcome, but funds for individual schools are increasingly tight and the real challenge is the shortage of appropriate clinicians and support services to signpost them on to in a timely fashion. Better still would be to make sure that more children arrive at school well attached and well rounded in the first instance, and that as we know requires an holistic parent and baby solution. Unfortunately the minister who really bought into that proved unable to control funds going to the sharp end for which they were intended and very much needed and is no longer in place nor replaced. And when funds do get through there is a shortage of clinicians to deploy them, a shortage of health visitors to identify the clients and a dwindling number of children's centres from which to deliver support services.

Frustrating or what?

So having extended and proved the science behind the 1001 Critical Days strategy set out so eloquently in this book, and addressed the policy questions it raises, how can we deliver it in practice? Solutions go back to some of the dull but essential process and delivery mechanisms identified in the 'Building Great Britons' report from the All Party Group in February 2015.

- There needs to be leadership at the very top with the prime minister putting her name on the programme and using all the machinery of government to pull all the major departments and players together in a jointly owned strategy. That strategy needs to be directed by a senior minister attending cabinet who has the authority to coordinate (and command) all the relevant departmental ministers and those ministers need to attend themselves not delegate to officials.
- The policy needs to be sold to the treasury in terms of investment payback they understand. We invest in roads and infrastructure in order to facilitate economic growth so why would we not want to invest in the mental infrastructure of our children to ensure that our citizens flourish and become net contributors to society? That is why the social impact bond model is so popular because it is constructed on a clear return on capital (financially and socially) for an early managed intervention. Indeed there are opportunities within our sector for social finance on top of public funding too. Despite its unfairly bad press recently the Troubled Families Programme is a good model of investing up front through bringing together relevant professional support. But first and foremost we need a 'Pre-Troubled Families Programme' which genuinely addresses the causes of attachment dysfunction and perinatal mental illness before they manifest as symptoms.
- Policy implementation and take-up needs to be transparent, measurable qualitatively and properly monitored. However alien it may be to government thinking funds do have to be ring-fenced and an equivalent of the Adoption Scorecards put in place so local authorities reluctant to 'get with the programme' have nowhere to hide, and no way of diverting funding. And when we have achieved this we need to be much better at disseminating best practice around the whole system, something we have been remarkably bad at in our silos for too long.
- Above all there needs to be a change of mindset and buy-in at all levels from politicians and policy makers to practitioners and delivery agents. It has to be accepted that things have gone wrong and that someone else is needed to put them right. The mantra of 'This is the way we have always done things in Xshire' has been a large part of the problem. When £8.1 billion is being spent

by British taxpayers on the cost of not getting perinatal mental health right. And when the evidence shows that the increasing number of 15–16 years olds suffering from depression have a 90 per cent plus chance that their mothers suffered from depression around their pregnancies, then clearly we are not getting it right and we all need to buy in to another approach. PIP UK (the Parent and Infant Partnership charity) for instance matches funds for new PIP attachment projects proposed to it by enthusiastic local practitioners.

- None of this is going to be easy, and it will be a brave government that really embraces such a comprehensive programme at the heart of its approach to looking after the mental health of our future citizens at the very beginning. But surely in the light of everything we can now show about the value of an investment in getting it right, and the appalling financial and social cost of continuing to get it wrong, it is time to stop dreaming and take action.

INDEX

Printed in Great Britain
by Amazon

64192147R00174